Forty Years of Social and Literary Criticism
# A Krutch Omnibus

## By the same author

# A Krutch Omnibus

### Forty Years of Social and Literary Criticism

### by JOSEPH WOOD KRUTCH

MORROW QUILL PAPERBACKS
New York 1980

To Kenneth Bechtel and to Gerald Green
with gratitude

**Library of Congress Cataloging in Publication Data**

Krutch, Joseph Wood, 1893–1970.
   A Krutch omnibus.

   "Morrow quill paperbacks."

   I. Title.
AC8.K844      1980      081     80-14794
ISBN 0-688-01006-7
ISBN 0-688-06006-4 (pbk.)

Printed in the United States of America

First Morrow Quill Paperback Edition

1   2   3   4   5   6   7   8   9   10

# Contents

## I · The Modern Temper

## II · Life, Art and Peace

## III · Miscellanea

### Morals

### The Two Cultures

### The World We Live In

# IV ▪ On Some Men and Some Books

# ·I·

# The Modern Temper

I WAS BORN IN 1893. THIS MEANS THAT I CAN VERY DIMLY REMEMBER OUR preposterous fun war with Spain when Teddy Roosevelt charged up San Juan Hill and the returning hero Lieutenant Hobson kissed the ladies who attended his lectures. It means also that most of the mechanical inventions which now dominate our environment—the telephone, the phonograph, the automobile, the moving picture, the airplane, the radio and television— were all invented, or at least became an essential party of contemporary life, within my memory.

But these changes were ultimately less significant than another: The world in which I reached manhood was at the end of a golden age of optimism, confidence and security the like of which it seems unlikely any- one will enjoy again for a long long time.

Only those who can recall the atmosphere which prevailed just before the First World War can imagine how secure the future seemed, how firmly we believed in Progress—inevitable and almost automatic. We took it for granted that there would be no more major wars; that freedom, "broadening down" in Tennysonian fashion would presently prevail over all the world; that medical triumphs would conquer all mankind's most destructive plagues; that science would solve all mysteries; and that tech- nology would provide abundance for everyone. We were living in either a fool's paradise or what Charles Galton Darwin has called the end of one of the world's golden ages. If that was the Age of Confidence, the present is without question the Age of Anxiety. Every one of the assumptions so commonly made before 1914 has turned out to be false, and to those of us who can look back it seems as though each of the five decades just past found itself faced with some new problem without having solved that of its predecessors.

The twenties soon realized that the war to end war was not anything of the sort and that, far from making the world Safe for Democracy, it had spawned two dictatorships. At the very end of that decade the Wall Street debacle destroyed the myth of permanent and automatic prosperity and it created the problem with which the thirties was most aware; "What is wrong with our political and economic system? Are there any others which would work better?" The decade of the forties was dominated by the Second World War which we ourselves felt compelled to fight without believing, this time, either that it was a war to end war or that it would make the world safe for democracy. The fifties began to realize that the most fateful event of the war decade was not the war itself but the fact that, in the course of winning it, science had discovered the secret of atomic fission and thus presented mankind with an opportunity to destroy civilization and perhaps its own species but had not suggested any method by which we could prevent its being used against us by nations which, a generation earlier, had seemed so far away that they could constitute no threat.

The sixties, to which we have just said goodbye, inherited all these problems, including the realization that the threat of the atom bomb was only the most conspicuous example of a new phenomenon: technology as a threat which had, by now, begun to create more problems than it solved. Overpopulation, pollution, and a destruction of the environment were all consequences of medical advance, industrial expansion and a material abundance so lavish that it had found no way of disposing of either its by-products or even of the early indestructible accumulation of last year's possessions junked in favor of something newer. Yet there was at least one hopeful sign. Never before in our history had we begun to face up to the fact that all the problems are related and that we cannot afford simply to hope for the best, but must seek radical remedies.

Any writer who has been expressing himself in print from the very beginning of the twenties down to the present moment is pretty certain, when he looks back, to realize that his topics have tended to have some relation to the changing preoccupations of the five decades. This was certainly true in my own case, though being temperamentally a dissenter my emphasis was often not that of the majority.

As a graduate student of English literature during the years just before our involvement in the First World War, I chose for my thesis the comedies written in England during the carnival reign of Charles II. That means, I suppose, that despite the war in Europe, I felt secure enough in our civilization to concern myself with what many would now regard as a very remote subject. It meant also that by deliberately choosing to study a supposedly scandalous literature I was reflecting the conviction of many of our intellectuals that getting rid of puritanical scruples was what our civilization needed most.

My second book was a psychoanalytical study of Edgar Allan Poe—a chapter from which will be included in a later section of this book. And it, again, reflected a current interest in the recently discovered works of Dr. Freud. Both of these books might seem to indicate that I was going along with my contemporaries.

But on a deeper level I was not really satisfied by either the after-us-the-deluge gaiety of the twenties or the assumption that anti-puritanism was an adequate philosophy of life. These growing dissatisfactions came to a head when the editor of the *Atlantic Monthly* accepted a very pessimistic analysis of what I believed to be the fundamental assumptions of modern man concerning his relation to the universe in which he finds himself. A little more than a year later, just a few months before the Wall Street crash, this essay became the first chapter of a book called *The Modern Temper*. What I had come up with was essentially what is now called the existentialist's premise, namely, that the universe outside of man offers no support to his own desires for a meaningful life. I concluded that though this thesis might be a valid one, no civilization could be based upon it and that ours would certainly give way to that of some less sophisticated race that still cherished life-giving illusions.

It was not until a quarter of a century later that I felt that I had thought my way out of this despairing conviction with sufficient clarity to attempt to state my reasons for rejecting it in favor of a belief that man, having been created by nature, must owe his human characteristics to something inherent in what had created him.

The fact remains that the proper place to begin such a collection as this is three chapters from *The Modern Temper* (1929).

>=••=•=••=•=••=•=••=•=••=•=••=•=••=•=••=•=••=•=••=•=••=•=••=•=••=•=••=•=••=•=••=•=••=•=••=•

## The Genesis of a Mood

It is one of Freud's quaint conceits that the child in its mother's womb is the happiest of living creatures. Into his consciousness no conflict has yet entered, for he knows no limitations to his desires and the universe is exactly as he wishes it to be. All his needs are satisfied before even he becomes aware of them, and if his awareness is dim that is but the natural result of a complete harmony between the self and the environment, since, as Spenser pointed out in a remote age, to be omniscient and omnipotent would be to be without any consciousness whatsoever. The discomfort of being born is the first warning which he receives that any event can be thrust upon him; it is the first limitation of his omnipotence which he perceives, and he is cast upon the shores of the world wailing his protest against the indignity to which he has been subjected. Years pass before he learns to control the expression of enraged surprise which arises within him at every unpleasant fact with which he is confronted, and his parents conspire so to protect him that he will learn only by very slow stages how far is the world from his heart's desire.

The cradle is made to imitate as closely as may be the conditions, both physical and spiritual, of the womb. Of its occupant no effort is demanded, and every precaution is taken to anticipate each need before it can arise. If, as the result of any unforeseen circumstance, any unsatisfied desire is born, he need only raise his voice in protest to cause the entire world insofar as he knows it—his nurse or his parents—to rush to his aid. The whole of his physical universe is obedient to his will and he is justified by his experience in believing that his mere volition controls his destiny. Only as he grows older does he become aware that there are wills other than his own or that there are physical circumstances rebellious to any human will. And only after the passage of many years does he become aware of the full extent of his predicament in the midst of a world which is in very few respects what he would wish it to be.

As a child he is treated as a child, and such treatment implies much more than the physical coddling of which Freud speaks. Not only do those who surround him cooperate more completely than they ever will again to satisfy his wishes in material things, but they encourage him to live in a spiritual world far more satisfactory than their own. He is carefully protected from any knowledge of the cruelties and complexities of life; he is led to suppose that the moral order is simple and clear, that virtue triumphs, and that the world is, as the desires of whole generations of mankind have led them to try to pretend that it is, arranged according to a pattern which would seem reasonable and satisfactory to human sensibilities. He is prevented from realizing how inextricably what men call good and evil are intertwined, how careless is Nature of those values called mercy and justice and righteousness which men have come, in her despite, to value; and he is, besides, encouraged to believe in a vast mythology peopled with figments which range all the way from the Saints to Santa Claus and which represent projections of human wishes which the adult has come to recognize as no more than projections but which he is willing that the child, for the sake of his own happiness, should believe real. Aware how different is the world which experience reveals from the world which the spirit desires, the mature, as though afraid that reality could not be endured unless the mind had been gradually inured to it, allow the child to become aware of it only by slow stages, and little by little he learns, not only the limitations of his will, but the moral discord of the world. Thus it is, in a very important sense, true that the infant does come trailing clouds of glory from that heaven which his imagination creates, and that as his experience accumulates he sees it fade away into the light of common day.

Now races as well as individuals have their infancy, their adolescence, and their maturity. Experience accumulates not only from year to year but from generation to generation, and in the life of each person it plays a little larger part than it did in the life of his father. As civilization grows older it too has more and more facts thrust upon its consciousness and is compelled to abandon one after another, quite as the child does, certain illusions which have been dear to it. Like the child, it has instinctively assumed that what it would like to be true is true, and it never gives up any such belief until experience in some form compels it to do so. Being, for example, extremely important to itself, it assumes that it is extremely important to the universe also. The earth is the center of all existing things, man is the child and the protégé of those gods who transcend and who will ultimately enable him to transcend all the evils which he has been compelled to recognize. The world and all that it contains were designed for him, and even those things which seem noxious have their usefulness only temporarily hid. Since he knows but little he is free to imagine, and imagination is always the creature of desire.

The world which any consciousness inhabits is a world made up in part of experience and in part of fancy. No experience, and hence no knowledge, is complete, but the gaps which lie between the solid fragments are filled in with shadows. Connections, explanations, and reasons are supplied by the imagination, and thus the world gets its patterned completeness from material which is spun out of the desires. But as time goes on and experience accumulates there remains less and less scope for the fancy. The universe becomes more and more what experience has revealed, less and less what imagination has created, and hence, since it was not designed to suit man's needs, less and less what he would have it to be. With increasing knowledge his power to manipulate his physical environment increases, but in gaining the knowledge which enables him to do so he surrenders insensibly the power which in his ignorance he had to mold the universe. The forces of Nature obey him, but in learning to master them he has in another sense allowed them to master him. He has exchanged the universe which his desires created, the universe made for man, for the universe of Nature of which he is only a part. Like the child growing into manhood, he passes from a world which is fitted to him into a world for which he must fit himself.

If, then, the world of poetry, mythology, and religion represents the world as a man would like to have it, while science represents the world as he gradually comes to discover it, we need only compare the two to realize how irreconcilable they appear. For the cozy bowl of the sky arched in a protecting curve above him he must exchange the cold immensities of space and, for the spiritual order which he has designed, the chaos of Nature. God he had loved *because* God was anthropomorphic, because He was made in man's own image, with purposes and desires which were human and hence understandable. But Nature's purpose, if purpose she can be said to have, is no purpose of his and is not understandable in his terms. Her desire merely to live and to propagate in innumerable forms, her ruthless indifference to his values, and the blindness of her irresistible will strike terror to his soul, and he comes in the fullness of his experience to realize that the ends which he proposes to himself—happiness and order and reason—are ends which he must achieve, if he achieve them at all, in her despite. Formerly he had believed in even his darkest moments that the universe was rational if he could only grasp its rationality, but gradually he comes to suspect that rationality is an attribute of himself alone and that there is no reason to suppose that his own life has any more meaning than the life of the humblest insect that crawls from one annihilation to another. Nature, in her blind thirst for life, has filled every possible cranny of the rotting earth with some sort of fantastic creature, and among them man is but one—perhaps the most miserable of all, because he is the only one in whom the instinct of life falters long enough to enable it to ask the question "Why?" As long as life is regarded as having been created, creating may be held to imply a purpose, but merely to have come into being is, in all likelihood, merely to go out of it also.

Fortunately, perhaps, man, like the individual child, was spared in his cradle the knowledge which he could not bear. Illusions have been lost one by one. God, instead of disappearing in an instant, has retreated step by step and surrendered gradually his control of the universe. Once he decreed the fall of every sparrow and counted the hairs upon every head; a little later he became merely the original source of the laws of Nature, and even today there are thousands who, unable to bear the thought of losing him completely, still fancy that they can distinguish the uncertain outlines of a misty figure. But the rôle which he plays grows less and less, and man is left more and more alone in a universe to which he is completely alien. His world was once, like the child's world, three-quarters myth and poetry. His teleological concepts molded it into a form which he could appreciate and he gave to it moral laws which would make it meaningful, but step by step the outlines of nature have thrust themselves upon him, and for the dream which he made is substituted a reality devoid of any pattern which he can understand.

In the course of this process innumerable readjustments have been made, and always with the effort to disturb as little as possible the myth which is so much more full of human values than the fact which comes in some measure to replace it. Thus, for example, the Copernican theory of astronomy, removing the earth from the center of the universe and assigning it a very insignificant place among an infinitude of whirling motes, was not merely resisted as a fact but was, when finally accepted, accepted as far as possible without its implications. Even if taken entirely by itself and without the whole system of facts of which it is a part, it renders extremely improbable the assumption, fundamental in most human thought, that the universe has man as its center and is hence understandable in his terms, but this implication was disregarded just as, a little later, the implications of the theory of evolution were similarly disregarded. It is not likely that if man had been aware from the very beginning that his world was a mere detail in the universe, and himself merely one of the innumerable species of living things, he would ever have come to think of himself, as he even now tends to do, as a being whose desires must be somehow satisfiable and whose reason must be matched by some similar reason in Nature. But the myth, having been once established, persists long after the assumptions upon which it was made have been destroyed, because, being born of desire, it is far more satisfactory than any fact.

Unfortunately, perhaps, experience does not grow at a constant, but at an accelerated, rate. The Greeks, who sought knowledge not through the study of Nature but through the examination of their own minds, developed a philosophy which was really analogous to myth, because the laws which determined its growth were dictated by human desires and they discovered few facts capable of disturbing the pattern which they devised. The Middle Ages retreated still further into themselves, but with the Renaissance man began to surrender himself to Nature; and the sciences, each nourishing the other, began their iconoclastic march. Three centuries lay between the promulgation of the Copernican theory and the publication of the *Origin of Species,* but in sixty-odd years which have elapsed since that latter event the blows have fallen with a rapidity which left no interval for recovery. The structures which are variously known as mythology, religion, and philosophy, and which are alike in that each has as its function the interpretation of experience in terms which have human values, have collapsed under the force of successive attacks and shown themselves utterly incapable of assimilating the new stores of experience which have been dumped upon the world. With increasing completeness science maps out the pattern of Nature, but the latter has no relation to the pattern of human needs and feelings.

Consider, for example, the plight of ethics. Historical criticism having destroyed what used to be called by people of learning and intelligence "Christian Evidences," and biology having shown how unlikely it is that man is the recipient of any transcendental knowledge, there remains no foundation in authority for ideas of right and wrong; and if, on the other hand, we turn to the traditions of the human race, anthropology is ready to prove that no consistent human tradition has ever existed. Custom has furnished the only basis which ethics have ever had, and there is no conceivable human action which custom has not at one time justified and at another condemned. Standards are imaginary things, and yet it is extremely doubtful if man can live well, either spiritually or physically, without the belief that they are somehow real. Without them society lapses into anarchy and the individual becomes aware of an intolerable disharmony between himself and the universe. Instinctively and emotionally he is an ethical animal. No known race is so low in the scale of civilization that it has not attributed a moral order to the world, because no known race is so little human as not to suppose a moral order so innately desirable as to have an inevitable existence. It is man's most fundamental myth, and life seems meaningless to him without it. Yet, as that systematized and cumulative experience which is called science displaces one after another the myths which have been generated by need, it grows more and more likely that he must remain an ethical animal in a universe which contains no ethical element.

Mythical philosophers have sometimes said that they "accepted the universe." They have, that is to say, formed of it some conception which answered the emotional needs of their spirit and which brought them a sense of being in harmony with its aims and processes. They have been aware of no needs which Nature did not seem to supply and no ideals which she too did not seem to recognize. They have felt themselves one with her because they have had the strength of imagination to make her over in their own image, and it is doubtful if any man can live at peace who does not thus feel himself at home. But as the world assumes the shape which science gives it, it becomes more and more difficult to find such emotional correspondences. Whole realms of human feeling, like the realm of ethics, find no place for themselves in the pattern of Nature and generate needs for which no satisfaction is supplied. What man knows is everywhere at war with what he wants.

In the course of a few centuries his knowledge, and hence the universe of which he finds himself an inhabitant, has been completely revolutionized, but his instincts and his emotions have remained, relatively at least, unchanged. He is still, as he always was, adjusted to the orderly, purposeful, humanized world which all peoples unburdened by experience have figured to themselves, but that world no longer exists. He has the same sense of dignity to which the myth of his descent from the gods was designed to minister, and the same innate purposefulness which led him to attribute a purpose to nature, but he can no longer think in terms appropriate to either. The world which his reason and his investigation reveal is a world which his emotions cannot comprehend.

Casually he accepts the spiritual iconoclasm of science, and in the detachment of everyday life he learns to play with the cynical wisdom of biology and psychology, which explain away the awe of emotional experience just as earlier science explained away the awe of conventional piety. Yet, under the stress of emotional crises, knowledge is quite incapable of controlling his emotions or of justifying them to himself. In love, he calls upon the illusions of man's grandeur and dignity to help him accept his emotions, and faced with tragedy he calls upon illusion to dignify his suffering; but lyric flight is checked by the rationality which he has cultivated, and in the world of metabolism and hormones, repressions and complexes, he finds no answer for his needs. He is feeling about love, for example, much as the troubador felt, but he thinks about it in a very different way. Try as he may, the two halves of his soul can hardly be made to coalesce, and he cannot either feel as his intelligence tells him that he should feel or think as his emotions would have him think, and thus he is reduced to mocking his torn and divided soul. In the grip of passion he cannot, as some romanticist might have done, accept it with a religious trust in the mystery of love, nor yet can he regard it as a psychiatrist, himself quite free from emotion, might suggest—merely as an interesting specimen of psychical botany. Man *qua* thinker may delight in the intricacies of psychology, but man *qua* lover has not learned to feel in its terms; so that, though complexes and ductless glands may serve to explain the feelings of another, one's own still demand all those symbols of the ineffable in which one has long ceased to believe.

Time was when the scientist, the poet, and the philosopher walked hand in hand. In the universe which the one perceived the other found himself comfortably at home. But the world of modern science is one in which the intellect alone can rejoice. The mind leaps, and leaps perhaps with a sort of elation, through the immensities of space, but the spirit, frightened and cold, longs to have once more above its head the inverted bowl beyond which may lie whatever paradise its desires may create. The lover who surrendered himself to the Implacable Aphrodite or who fancied his foot upon the lowest rung of the Platonic ladder of love might retain his self-respect, but one can neither resist nor yield gracefully to a carefully catalogued psychosis. A happy life is a sort of poem, with a poem's elevation and dignity, but emotions cannot be dignified unless they are first respected. They must seem to correspond with, to be justified by, something in the structure of the universe itself; but though it was the function of religion and philosophy to hypostatize some such correspondence, to project a humanity upon Nature, or at least to conceive of a humane force above and beyond her, science finds no justification for such a process and is content instead to show how illusions were born.

The most ardent love of truth, the most resolute determination to follow Nature no matter to what black abyss she may lead, need not blind one to the fact that many of the lost illusions had, to speak the language of science, a survival value. Either individuals or societies whose life is imbued with a cheerful certitude, whose aims are clear, and whose sense of the essential rightness of life is strong, live and struggle with an energy unknown to the skeptical and the pessimistic. Whatever the limitations of their intellects as instruments of criticism, they possess the physical and emotional vigor which is, unlike critical intelligence, analogous to the processes of Nature. They found empires and conquer wildernesses, and they pour the excess of their energy into works of art which the intelligence of more sophisticated peoples continues to admire even though it has lost the faith in life which is requisite for the building of a Chartres or the carving of a Venus de Milo. The one was not erected to a law of

Nature or the other designed to celebrate the libido, for each presupposed a sense of human dignity which science nowhere supports.

Thus man seems caught in a dilemma which his intellect has devised. Any deliberately managed return to a state of relative ignorance, however desirable it might be argued to be, is obviously out of the question. We cannot, as the naïve proponents of the various religions, new and old, seem to assume, believe one thing and forget another merely because we happen to be convinced that it would be desirable to do so; and it is worth observing that the new psychology, with its penetrating analysis of the influence of desire upon belief, has so adequately warned the reason of the tricks which the will can play upon it that it has greatly decreased the possibility of beneficent delusion and serves to hold the mind in a steady contemplation of that from which it would fain escape. Weak and uninstructed intelligences take refuge in the monotonous repetition of once living creeds, or even reduced to the desperate expedient of going to sleep amid the formulae of the flabby pseudo-religions in which the modern world is so prolific. But neither of these classes affords any aid to the robust but serious mind which is searching for some terms upon which it may live.

And if we are, as by this time we should be, free from any teleological delusion, if we no longer make the unwarranted assumption that every human problem is somehow of necessity solvable, we must confess it may be that for the sort of being whom we have described no survival is possible in any form like that which his soul has now taken. He is a fantastic thing that has developed sensibilities and established values beyond the Nature which gave him birth. He is of all living creatures the one to whom the earth is the least satisfactory. He has arrived at a point where he can no longer delude himself as to the extent of his predicament, and should he either become modified or disappear, the earth would continue to spin and the grass to grow as it has always done. Of the thousands of living species the vast majority would be as unaware of his passing as they are unaware now of his presence, and he would go as a shadow goes. His arts, his religions, and his civilizations—these are fair and wonderful things, but they are fair and wonderful to him alone. With the extinction of his poetry would come also the extinction of the only sensibility for which it has any meaning, and there would remain nothing capable of feeling a loss. Nothing would be left to label the memory of his discontent "divine," and those creatures who find in Nature no lack would resume their undisputed possession of the earth.

Anthropoid in form some of them might continue to be, and possessed as well of all of the human brain that makes possible a cunning adaptation to the conditions of physical life. To them Nature might yield up subtler secrets than any yet penetrated; their machines might be more wonderful and their bodies more healthy than any yet known—even though there had passed away, not merely all myth and poetry, but the need for them as well. Cured of his transcendental cravings, content with things as they are, accepting the universe as experience had shown it to be, man would be freed of his soul and, like the other animals, either content or at least desirous of nothing which he might not hope ultimately to obtain.

*idolatry*

Nor can it be denied that certain adumbrations of this type have before now come into being. Among those of keener intellect there are scientists to whom the test tube and its contents are all-sufficient, and among those of coarser grain, captains of finance and builders of mills, there are those to whom the acquirement of wealth and power seems to constitute a life in which no lack can be perceived. Doubtless they are not new types; doubtless they have always existed; but may they not be the strain from which Nature will select the coming race? Is not their creed the creed of Nature, and are they not bound to triumph over those whose illusions are no longer potent because they are no longer really believed? Certain philosophers, clinging desperately to the ideal of a humanized world, have proposed a retreat into the imagination. Bertrand Russell in his popular essay, *A Free Man's Worship*, Unamuno and Santayana *passim* throughout their works, have argued that the way of salvation lay in a sort of ironic belief, in a determination to act as though one still believed the things which once were really held true. But is not this a desperate expedient, a last refuge likely to appeal only to the leaders of a lost cause? Does it not represent the last, least substantial, phase of fading faith, something which borrows what little substance it seems to have from a reality of the past? If it seems half real to the sons of those who lived in the spiritual world of which it is a shadow, will it not seem, a little further removed, only a faint futility? Surely it has but little to oppose to those who come armed with the certitudes of science and united with, not fleeing from, the Nature amid which they live.

And if the dilemma here described is itself a delusion, it is at least as vividly present and as terribly potent as those other delusions which have shaped or deformed the human spirit. There is no significant contemporary writer upon philosophy, ethics, or aesthetics whose speculations do not lead him to it in one form or another, and even the less reflective are aware of it in their own way. Both our practical morality and our emotional lives are adjusted to a world which no longer exists. Insofar as we adhere to a code of conduct, we do so largely because certain habits still persist, not because we can give any logical reason for preferring them, and insofar as we indulge ourselves in the primitive emotional satisfactions—romantic love, patriotism, zeal for justice, and so forth—our satisfaction is the result merely of the temporary suspension of our disbelief in the mythology upon which they are founded. Traditionalists in religion are fond of asserting that our moral codes are flimsy because they are rootless; but, true as this is, it is perhaps not so important as the fact that our emotional lives are rootless too.

If the gloomy vision of a dehumanized world which has just been evoked is not to become a reality, some complete readjustment must be made, and at least two generations have found themselves unequal to the task. The generation of Thomas Henry Huxley, so busy with destruction as never adequately to realize how much it was destroying, fought with such zeal against frightened conservatives that it never took time to do more than assert with some vehemence that all would be well, and the generation that followed either danced amid the ruins or sought by various compromises to save the remains of a few tottering structures. But neither patches nor evasions will serve. It is not a changed world but a new one in which man must henceforth live if he lives at all, for all his premises have been destroyed and he must proceed to new conclusions. The values which he thought established have been swept away along with the rules by which he thought they might be attained.

To this fact many are not yet awake, but our novels, our poems, and our pictures are enough to reveal that a generation aware of its predicament is at hand. It has awakened to the fact that both the ends which its fathers proposed to themselves and the emotions from which they drew their strength seem irrelevant and remote. With a smile, sad or mocking, according to individual temperament, it regards those works of the past in which were summed up the values of life. The romantic ideal of a world well lost for love and the classic ideal of austere dignity seem equally ridiculous, equally meaningless when referred, not to the temper of the past, but to the temper of the present. The passions which swept through the once major poets no longer awaken any profound response, and only in the bleak, tortuous complexities of a T. S. Eliot does it find its moods given adequate expression. Here disgust speaks with a robust voice and denunciation is confident, but ecstasy, flickering and uncertain, leaps fitfully up only to sink back among the cinders. And if the poet, with his gift of keen perceptions and his power of organization, can achieve only the most momentary and unstable adjustments, what hope can there be for those whose spirit is a less powerful instrument?

And yet it is with such as he, baffled, but content with nothing which plays only upon the surface, that the hope for a still humanized future must rest. No one can tell how many of the old values must go or how new the new will be. Thus, while under the influence of the old mythology the sexual instinct was transformed into romantic love, and tribal solidarity into the religion of patriotism, there is nothing in the modern consciousness capable of effecting these transmutations. Neither the one nor the other is capable of being, as it once was, the *raison d'être* of a life or the motif of a poem which is not, strictly speaking, derivative and anachronistic. Each is fading, each becoming as much a shadow as devotion to the cult of purification through self-torture. Either the instincts upon which they are founded will achieve new transformations or they will remain merely instincts, regarded as having no particular emotional significance in a spiritual world which, if it exists at all, will be as different from the spiritual world of, let us say, Robert Browning as that world is different from the world of Cato the Censor.

As for this present unhappy time, haunted by ghosts from a dead world and not yet at home in its own, its predicament is not, to return to the comparison with which we began, unlike the predicament of the adolescent who has not yet learned to orient himself without reference to the mythology amid which his childhood was passed. He still seeks in the world of his experience for the values which he had found there, and he is aware only of a vast disharmony. But boys—most of them, at least—grow up, and the world of adult consciousness has always held a relation to myth intimate enough to make readjustment possible. The finest spirits have bridged the gulf, have carried over with them something of a child's faith, and only the coarsest have grown into something which was no more than finished animality. Today the gulf is broader, the adjustment more difficult, than ever it was before, and even the possibility of an actual human maturity is problematic. There impends for the human spirit either extinction or a readjustment more stupendous than any made before.

## The Tragic Fallacy

Through the legacy of their art the great ages have transmitted to us a dim image of their glorious vitality. When we turn the pages of a Sophoclean or a Shakespearean tragedy we participate faintly in the experience which created it and we sometimes presumptuously say that we "understand" the spirit of these works. But the truth is that we see them, even at best and in the moments when our souls expand most nearly to their dimensions, through a glass darkly.

It is so much easier to appreciate than to create that an age too feeble to reach the heights achieved by the members of a preceding one can still see those heights towering above its impotence, and so it is that, when we perceive a Sophocles or a Shakespeare soaring in an air which we can never hope to breathe, we say that we can "appreciate" them. But what we mean is that we are just able to wonder, and we can never hope to participate in the glorious vision of human life out of which they were created—not even to the extent of those humbler persons for whom they were written; for while to us the triumphant voices come from far away and tell of a heroic world which no longer exists, to them they spoke of immediate realities and revealed the inner meaning of events amidst which they still lived.

When the life has entirely gone out of a work of art come down to us from the past, when we read it without any emotional comprehension —APPRECIATE whatsoever and can no longer even imagine why the people for whom it was intended found it absorbing and satisfying, then, of course, it has ceased to be a work of art at all and has dwindled into one of those deceptive "documents" from which we get a false sense of comprehending through the intellect things which cannot be comprehended at all except by means of a kinship of feeling. And though all works from a past age have begun in this way to fade there are some, like the great Greek or Elizabethan tragedies, which are still halfway between the work of art and the document. They no longer can have for us the immediacy which they had for those to whom they originally belonged, but they have not yet eluded us entirely. We no longer live in the world which they represent, but we can half imagine it and we can measure the distance which we have moved away. We write no tragedies today, but we can still talk about the tragic spirit of which we would, perhaps, have no conception were it not for the works in question.

An age which could really "appreciate" Shakespeare or Sophocles would have something comparable to put beside them—something like them, not necessarily in form, or spirit, but at least in magnitude—some vision of life which would be, however different, equally ample and passionate. But when we move to put a modern masterpiece beside them, when we seek to compare them with, let us say, a *Ghosts* or a *Weavers,* we shrink as from the impulse to commit some folly and we feel as though we were about to superimpose Bowling Green upon the Great Prairies in order to ascertain which is the larger. The question, we see, is not primarily one of art but of the two worlds which two minds inhabited. No increased powers of expression, no greater gifts for words, could have transformed Ibsen into Shakespeare. The materials out of which the latter created his works—his conception of human dignity, his sense of the importance of human passions, his vision of the amplitude of human life—simply did not and could not exist for Ibsen, as they did not and could not exist for his contemporaries. God and Man and Nature had all somehow dwindled in the course of the intervening centuries, not because the realistic creed of modern art led us to seek out mean people, but because this meanness of human life was somehow thrust upon us by the operation of that same process which led to the development of realistic theories of art by which our vision could be justified.

Hence, though we still apply, sometimes, the adjective "tragic" to one or another of those modern works of literature which describe human misery and which end more sadly even than they begin, the term is a misnomer since it is obvious that the works in question have nothing in common with the classical examples of the genre and produce in the reader a sense of depression which is the exact opposite of that elation generated when the spirit of a Shakespeare rises joyously superior to the outward calamities which he recounts and celebrates the greatness of the human spirit whose travail he describes. Tragedies, in that only sense of the word which has any distinctive meaning, are no longer written in either the dramatic or any other form, and the fact is not to be accounted for in any merely literary terms. It is not the result of any fashion in literature or of any deliberation to write about human nature or character under different aspects, any more than it is of either any greater sensitiveness of feeling which would make us shrink from the contemplation of the suffering of Medea or Othello or of any greater optimism which would make us more likely to see life in more cheerful terms. It is, on the contrary, the result of one of those enfeeblements of the human spirit not unlike that described in the previous chapter of this essay, and a further illustration of that gradual weakening of man's confidence in his ability to impose upon the phenomenon of life an interpretation acceptable to his desires which is the subject of the whole of the present discussion.

To explain that fact and to make clear how the creation of classical tragedy did consist in the successful effort to impose such a satisfactory interpretation will require, perhaps, the special section which follows, although the truth of the fact that it does impose such an interpretation must be evident to any one who has ever risen from the reading of *Oedipus* or *Lear* with that feeling of exultation which comes when we have been able, by rare good fortune, to enter into its spirit as completely as it is possible for us of a remoter and emotionally enfeebled age to enter it. Meanwhile one anticipatory remark may be ventured. If the plays and the novels of today deal with littler people and less mighty emotions, it is not because we have become interested in commonplace souls and their unglamorous adventures but because we have come, willy-nilly, to see the soul of man as commonplace and its emotions as mean.

Tragedy, said Aristotle, is the "imitation of noble actions," and though it is some twenty-five hundred years since the dictum was uttered there is only one respect in which we are inclined to modify it. To us "imitation" seems a rather naïve word to apply to that process by which observation is turned into art, and we seek one which would define or at least imply the nature of that interposition of the personality of the artist between the object and the beholder which constitutes his function and by means of which he transmits a modified version, rather than a mere imitation, of the things which he has contemplated.

In the search for this word the aestheticians of romanticism invented the term "expression" to describe the artistic purpose to which apparent imitation was subservient. Psychologists, on the other hand, feeling that the artistic process was primarily one by which reality is modified in such a way as to render it more acceptable to the desires of the artist, employed various terms in the effort to describe that distortion which the wish may produce in vision. And though many of the newer critics reject both romanticism and psychology, even they insist upon the fundamental fact that in art we are concerned, not with mere imitation but with the imposition of some form upon the material which it would not have if it were merely copied as a camera copies.

Tragedy is not, then, the *imitation* of noble actions, as Aristotle said, for, indeed, no one knows what a *noble* action is or whether or not such a thing as nobility exists in nature apart from the mind of man. Certainly the action of Achilles in dragging the dead body of Hector around the walls of Troy and under the eyes of Andromache, who had begged to be allowed to give it decent burial, is not to us a noble action, though it was such to Homer, who made it the subject of a noble passage in a noble poem. Certainly, too, the same action might conceivably be made the subject of a tragedy and the subject of a farce, depending upon the way in which it was treated; so that to say that tragedy is the *imitation* of a *noble* action is to be guilty of assuming, first, that art and photography are the same and, second, that there may be something inherently noble in an act as distinguished from the motives which prompted it or from the point of view from which it is regarded.

And yet, nevertheless, the idea of nobility is inseparable from the idea of tragedy, which cannot exist without it. If tragedy is not the imitation or even the modified representation of noble actions it is certainly a representation of actions *considered* as noble, and herein lies its essential nature, since no man can conceive it unless he is capable of believing in the greatness and importance of man. Its action is usually, if not always, calamitous, because it is only in calamity that the human spirit has the opportunity to reveal itself triumphant over the outward universe which fails to conquer it; but this calamity in tragedy is only a means to an end and the essential thing which distinguishes real tragedy from those distressing modern works sometimes called by its name is the fact that it is in the former alone that the artist has found himself capable of considering and of making us consider that his people and his actions have that amplitude and importance which make them noble. Tragedy arises then when, as in Periclean Greece or Elizabethan England, a people fully aware of the calamities of life is nevertheless serenely confident of the greatness of man, whose mighty passions and supreme fortitude are revealed when one of these calamities overtakes him.

To those who mistakenly think of it as something gloomy or depressing, who are incapable of recognizing the elation which its celebration of human greatness inspires, and who, therefore, confuse it with things merely miserable or pathetic, it must be a paradox that the happiest, most vigorous, and most confident ages which the world has ever known—the Periclean and the Elizabethan—should be exactly those which created and which most relished the mightiest tragedies; but the paradox is, of course, resolved by the fact that tragedy is essentially an expression, not of despair, but of the triumph over despair and of confidence in the value of human life. If Shakespeare himself ever had that "dark period" which his critics and biographers have imagined for him, it was at least no darkness like that bleak and arid despair which sometimes settles over modern spirits. In the midst of it he created both the elemental grandeur of Othello and the pensive majesty of Hamlet and, holding them up to his contemporaries, he said in the words of his own Miranda, "Oh, rare new world that hath *such* creatures in it."

All works of art which deserve their name have a happy end. This is indeed the thing which constitutes them art and through which they perform their function. Whatever the character of the events, fortunate or unfortunate, which they recount, they so mold or arrange or interpret them that we accept gladly the conclusion which they reach and would not have it otherwise. They may conduct us into the realm of pure fancy where wish and fact are identical and the world is re-made exactly after the fashion of the heart's desire or they may yield some greater or less allegiance to fact; but they must always reconcile us in one way or another to the representation which they make and the distinctions between the genres are simply the distinctions between the means by which this reconciliation is effected.

Comedy laughs the minor mishaps of its characters away; drama solves all the difficulties which it allows to arise; and melodrama, separating good from evil by simple lines, distributes its rewards and punishments in accordance with the principles of a naïve justice which satisfies the simple souls of its audience, which are neither philosophical enough to question its primitive ethics nor critical enough to object to the way in which its neat events violate the laws of probability. Tragedy, the greatest and the most difficult of the arts, can adopt none of these methods; and yet it must reach its own happy end in its own way. Though its conclusion must be, by its premise, outwardly calamitous, though it must speak to those who know that the good man is cut off and that the fairest things are the first to perish, yet it must leave them, as *Othello* does, content that this is so. We must be and we are glad that Juliet dies and glad that Lear is turned out into the storm.

Milton set out, he said, to justify the ways of God to man, and his phrase, if it be interpreted broadly enough, may be taken as describing the function of all art, which must, in some way or other, make the life which it seems to represent satisfactory to those who see its reflection in the magic mirror, and it must gratify or at least reconcile the desires of the beholder, not necessarily, as the naïver exponents of Freudian psychology maintain, by gratifying individual and often eccentric wishes, but at least by satisfying the universally human desire to find in the world some justice, some meaning, or, at the very least, some recognizable order. Hence it is that every real tragedy, however tremendous it may be, is an affirmation of faith in life, a declaration that even if God is not in his Heaven, then at least Man is in his world.

We accept gladly the outward defeats which it describes for the sake of the inward victories which it reveals. Juliet died, but not before she had shown how great and resplendent a thing love could be; Othello plunged the dagger into his own breast, but not before he had revealed that greatness of soul which makes his death seem unimportant. Had he died in the instant when he struck the blow, had he perished still believing that the world was as completely black as he saw it before the innocence of Desdemona was revealed to him, then, for him at least, the world would have been merely damnable, but Shakespeare kept him alive long enough to allow him to learn his error and hence to die, not in despair, but in the full acceptance of the tragic reconciliation to life. Perhaps it would be pleasanter if men could believe what the child is taught—that the good are happy and that things turn out as they should—but it is far more important to be able to believe, as Shakespeare did, that however much things in the outward world may go awry, man has, nevertheless, splendors of his own and that, in a word, Love and Honor and Glory are not words but realities.

Thus for the great ages tragedy is not an expression of despair but the means by which they saved themselves from it. It is a profession of faith, and a sort of religion; a way of looking at life by virtue of which it is robbed of its pain. The sturdy soul of the tragic author seizes upon suffering and uses it only as a means by which joy may be wrung out of existence, but it is not to be forgotten that he is enabled to do so only because of his belief in the greatness of human nature and because, though he has lost the child's faith in life, he has not lost his far more important faith in human nature. A tragic writer does not have to believe in God, but he must believe in man.

And if, then, the Tragic Spirit is in reality the product of a religious faith in which, sometimes at least, faith in the greatness of God is replaced by faith in the greatness of man, it serves, of course, to perform the function of religion, to make life tolerable for those who participate in its beneficent illusion. It purges the souls of those who might otherwise despair and it makes endurable the realization that the events of the outward world do not correspond with the desires of the heart, and thus, in its own particular way, it does what all religions do, for it gives a rationality, a meaning, and a justification to the universe. But if it has the strength, it has also the weakness of all faiths, since it may—nay, it must—be ultimately lost as reality, encroaching further and further into the realm of imagination, leaving less and less room in which that imagination can build its refuge.

It is, indeed, only at a certain stage in the development of the realistic intelligence of a people that the tragic faith can exist. A naïver people may have, as the ancient men of the north had, a body of legends which are essentially tragic, or it may have only (and need only) its happy and childlike mythology which arrives inevitably at its happy end, where the

*Naive*

only ones who suffer "deserve" to do so and in which, therefore, life is represented as directly and easily acceptable. A too sophisticated society ⟶ on the other hand—one which, like ours, has outgrown not merely the simple optimism of the child but also that vigorous, one might almost say adolescent, faith in the nobility of man which marks a Sophocles or a Shakespeare—has neither fairy tales to assure it that all is always right in the end nor tragedies to make it believe that it rises superior in soul to the outward calamities which befall it.

Distrusting its thought, despising its passions, realizing its impotent unimportance in the universe, it can tell itself no stories except those which make it still more acutely aware of its trivial miseries. When its heroes (sad misnomer for the pitiful creatures who people contemporary fiction) are struck down it is not, like Oedipus, by the gods that they are struck but only, like Oswald Alving, by syphilis, for they know that the gods, even if they existed, would not trouble with them, and they cannot attribute to themselves in art an importance in which they do not believe. Their so-called tragedies do not and cannot end with one of those splendid calamities which in Shakespeare seem to reverberate through the universe, because they cannot believe that the universe trembles when their love is, like Romeo's, cut off or when the place where they (small as they are) have gathered up their trivial treasure is, like Othello's sanctuary, defiled. Instead, mean misery piles on mean misery, petty misfortune follows petty misfortune, and despair becomes intolerable because it is no longer even significant or important.

Ibsen once made one of his characters say that he did not read much because he found reading "irrelevant," and the adjective was brilliantly chosen because it held implications even beyond those of which Ibsen was consciously aware. What is it that made the classics irrelevant to him and to us? Is it not just exactly those to him impossible premises which make tragedy what it is, those assumptions that the soul of man is great, that the universe (together with whatever gods may be) concerns itself with him and that he is, in a word, noble? Ibsen turned to village politics for exactly the same reason that his contemporaries and his successors have, each in his own way, sought out some aspect of the common man and his common life—because, that is to say, here was at least something small enough for him to be able to believe.

Bearing this fact in mind, let us compare a modern "tragedy" with one of the great works of a happy age, not in order to judge of their relative technical merits but in order to determine to what extent the former deserves its name by achieving a tragic solution capable of purging the soul or of reconciling the emotions to the life which it pictures. And in order to make the comparison as fruitful as possible let us choose *Hamlet* on the one hand and on the other a play like *Ghosts* which was not only written by perhaps the most powerful as well as the most typical of modern writers but which is, in addition, the one of his works which seems most nearly to escape that triviality which cannot be entirely escaped by anyone who feels, as all contemporary minds do, that man is relatively trivial.

In <u>*Hamlet*</u> a prince ("in understanding, how like a god!") has thrust upon him from the unseen world a duty to redress a wrong which concerns not merely him, his mother, and his uncle, but the moral order of the universe. Erasing all trivial fond records from his mind, abandoning at once both his studies and his romance because it has been his good fortune to be called upon to take part in an action of cosmic importance, he plunges (at first) not into action but into thought, weighing the claims which are made upon him and contemplating the grandiose complexities of the universe. And when the time comes at last for him to die he dies, not as a failure, but as a success. Not only has the universe regained the balance which had been upset by what *seemed* the monstrous crime of the guilty pair ("there is nothing either good nor ill but thinking makes it so"), but in the process by which that readjustment is made a mighty mind has been given the opportunity, first to contemplate the magnificent scheme of which it is a part and then to demonstrate the greatness of its spirit by playing a rôle in the grand style which it called for. We do not need to despair in *such* a world if it has *such* creatures in it.

Turn now to <u>*Ghosts*</u>—look upon this picture and upon that. A young man has inherited syphilis from his father. Struck by a to him mysterious malady he returns to his northern village, learns the hopeless truth about himself, and persuades his mother to poison him. The incidents prove, perhaps, that pastors should not endeavor to keep a husband and wife together unless they know what they are doing. But what a world is this in which a great writer can deduce nothing more than that from his greatest work and how are we to be purged or reconciled when we see it acted? Not only is the failure utter, but it is trivial and meaningless as well.

Yet the journey from Elsinore to Skien is precisely the journey which the human spirit has made, exchanging in the process princes for invalids and gods for disease. We say, as Ibsen would say, that the problems of Oswald Alving are more "relevant" to our life than the problems of Hamlet, that the play in which he appears is more "real" than the other glamorous one, but it is exactly because we find it so that we are condemned.

We can believe in Oswald but we cannot believe in Hamlet, and a light has gone out in the universe. Shakespeare justifies the ways of God to man, but in Ibsen there is no such happy end and with him tragedy, so called, has become merely an expression of our despair at finding that such justification is no longer possible.

Modern critics have sometimes been puzzled to account for the fact that the concern of ancient tragedy is almost exclusively with kings and courts. They have been tempted to accuse even Aristotle of a certain naïveté in assuming (as he seems to assume) that the "nobility" of which he speaks as necessary to a tragedy implies a nobility of rank as well as of soul, and they have sometimes regretted that Shakespeare did not devote himself more than he did to the serious consideration of those common woes of the common man which subsequent writers have exploited with increasing pertinacity. Yet the tendency to lay the scene of a tragedy at the court of a king is not the result of any arbitrary convention but of the fact that the tragic writers believed easily in greatness just as we believe easily in meanness. To Shakespeare, robes and crowns and jewels are the garments most appropriate to man because they are the fitting outward manifestation of his inward majesty, but to us they seem absurd because the man who bears them has, in our estimation, so pitifully shrunk. We do not write about kings because we do not believe that any man is worthy to be one and we do not write about courts because hovels seem to us to be dwellings more appropriate to the creatures who inhabit them. Any modern attempt to dress characters in robes ends only by making us aware of a comic incongruity and any modern attempt to furnish them with a language resplendent like Shakespeare's ends only in bombast.

True tragedy capable of performing its function and of purging the soul by reconciling man to his woes can exist only by virtue of a certain pathetic fallacy far more inclusive than that to which the name is commonly given. The romantics, feeble descendants of the tragic writers to whom they are linked by their effort to see life and nature in grandiose terms, loved to imagine that the sea or the sky had a way of according itself with their moods, of storming when they stormed and smiling when they smiled. But the tragic spirit sustains itself by an assumption much more far-reaching and no more justified. Man as it sees him lives in a world which he may not dominate but which is always aware of him. Occupying the exact center of a universe which would have no meaning except for him and being so little below the angels that, if he believes in God, he has no hesitation in imagining Him formed as he is formed and crowned with a crown like that which he or one of his fellows wears, he assumes that each of his acts reverberates through the universe. His passions are important to him because he believes them important throughout all time and all space; the very fact that he can sin (no modern can) means that this universe is watching his acts; and though he may perish, a God leans out from infinity to strike him down. And it is exactly because an Ibsen cannot think of man in any such terms as these that his persons have so shrunk and that his "tragedy" has lost that power which real tragedy always has of making that infinitely ambitious creature called man content to accept his misery if only he can be made to feel great enough and important enough. An Oswald is not a Hamlet chiefly because he has lost that tie with the natural and supernatural world which the latter had. No ghost will leave the other world to warn or encourage him, there is no virtue and no vice which he can possibly have which can be really important, and when he dies neither his death nor the manner of it will be, outside the circle of two or three people as unnecessary as himself, any more important than that of a rat behind the arras.

Perhaps we may dub the illusion upon which the tragic spirit is nourished the Tragic, as opposed to the Pathetic, Fallacy, but fallacy though it is, upon its existence depends not merely the writing of tragedy but the existence of that religious feeling of which tragedy is an expression and by means of which a people aware of the dissonances of life manages nevertheless to hear them as harmony. Without it neither man nor his passions can seem great enough or important enough to justify the sufferings which they entail, and literature, expressing the mood of a people, begins to despair where once it had exulted. Like the belief in love and like most of the other mighty illusions by means of which human life has been given a value, the Tragic Fallacy depends ultimately upon the assumption which man so readily makes that something outside his own being, some "spirit not himself"—be it God, Nature, or that still vaguer thing called a Moral Order—joins him in the emphasis which he places upon this or that and confirms him in his feeling that his passions and his opinions are important. When his instinctive faith in that correspondence between the outer and the inner world fades, his grasp upon the faith that sustained him fades also, and Love or Tragedy or what not ceases to be the reality which it was because he is never strong enough in his own insignificant self to stand alone in a universe which snubs him with its indifference.

In both the modern and the ancient worlds tragedy was dead long before writers were aware of the fact. Seneca wrote his frigid melodramas under the impression that he was following in the footsteps of Sophocles, and Dryden probably thought that his *All for Love* was an improvement upon Shakespeare, but in time we awoke to the fact that no amount of rhetorical bombast could conceal the fact that grandeur was not to be counterfeited when the belief in its possibility was dead, and turning from the hero to the common man we inaugurated the era of realism. For us no choice remains except that between mere rhetoric and the frank consideration of our fellow men, who may be the highest of the anthropoids but who are certainly too far below the angels to imagine either that these angels can concern themselves with them or that they can catch any glimpse of even the soles of angelic feet. We can no longer tell tales of the fall of noble men because we do not believe that noble men exist. The best that we can achieve is pathos and the most that we can do is to feel sorry for ourselves. Man has put off his royal robes and it is only in sceptered pomp that tragedy can come sweeping by.

IV

Nietzsche was the last of the great philosophers to attempt a tragic justification of life. His central and famous dogma—"Life is good *because* it is painful"—sums up in a few words the desperate and almost meaningless paradox to which he was driven in his effort to reduce to rational terms the far more imaginative conception which is everywhere present but everywhere unanalyzed in a Sophocles or a Shakespeare and by means of which they rise triumphant over the manifold miseries of life. But the very fact that Nietzsche could not even attempt to state in any except intellectual terms an attitude which is primarily unintellectual and to which, indeed, intellectual analysis is inevitably fatal is proof of the distance which he had been carried (by the rationalizing tendencies of the human mind) from the possibility of the tragic solution which he sought; and the confused, half-insane violence of his work will reveal, by the contrast which it affords with the serenity of the tragic writers whom he admired, how great was his failure.

Fundamentally this failure was, moreover, conditioned by exactly the same thing which has conditioned the failure of all modern attempts to achieve what he attempted—by the fact, that is to say, that tragedy must have a hero if it is not to be merely an accusation against, instead of a justification of, the world in which it occurs. Tragedy is, as Aristotle said, an imitation of noble actions, and Nietzsche, for all his enthusiasm for the Greek tragic writers, was palsied by the universally modern incapacity to conceive man as noble. Out of this dilemma, out of his need to find a hero who could give to life as he saw it the only possible justification, was born the idea of the Superman, but the Superman is, after all, only a hypothetical being, destined to become what man actually was in the eyes of the great tragic writers—a creature (as Hamlet said) "how infinite in capacities, in understanding how like a god." Thus Nietzsche lived half in the past through his literary enthusiasms and half in the future through his grandiose dreams, but for all his professed determination to justify existence he was no more able than the rest of us to find the present acceptable. Life, he said in effect, is not a Tragedy now but perhaps it will be when the Ape-man has been transformed into a hero (the *Übermensch*), and trying to find that sufficient, he went mad.

He failed, as all moderns must fail when they attempt, like him, to embrace the Tragic Spirit as a religious faith, because the resurgence of that faith is not an intellectual but a vital phenomenon, something not achieved by taking thought but born, on the contrary, out of an instinctive confidence in life which is nearer to the animal's unquestioning allegiance to the scheme of nature than it is to that critical intelligence characteristic of a fully developed humanism. And like other faiths it is not to be recaptured merely by reaching an intellectual conviction that it would be desirable to do so.

Modern psychology has discovered (or at least strongly emphasized) the fact that under certain conditions desire produces belief, and having discovered also that the more primitive a given mentality the more completely are its opinions determined by its wishes, modern psychology has concluded that the best mind is that which most resists the tendency to believe a thing simply because it would be pleasant or advantageous to do so. But justified as this conclusion may be from the intellectual point of view, it fails to take into account the fact that in a universe as badly adapted as this one to human as distinguished from animal needs, this ability to will a belief may bestow an enormous vital advantage as it did, for instance, in the case at present under discussion where it made possible for Shakespeare the compensations of a tragic faith completely inaccessible to Nietzsche. Pure intelligence, incapable of being influenced by desire and therefore also incapable of choosing one opinion rather than another simply because the one chosen is the more fruitful or beneficent, is doubtless a relatively perfect instrument for the pursuit of truth, but the question (likely, it would seem, to be answered in the negative) is simply whether or not the spirit of man can endure the literal and inhuman truth.

Certain ages and simple people have conceived of the action which passes upon the stage of the universe as of something in the nature of a Divine Comedy, as something, that is to say, which will reach its end with the words "and they lived happily ever after." Others, less naïve and therefore more aware of those maladjustments whose reality, at least so far as outward events are concerned, they could not escape, have imposed upon it another artistic form and called it a Divine Tragedy, accepting its catastrophe as we accept the catastrophe of an *Othello,* because of its grandeur. But a Tragedy, Divine or otherwise, must, it may again be repeated, have a hero, and from the universe as we see it both the Glory of God and the Glory of Man have departed. Our cosmos may be farcical or it may be pathetic but it has not the dignity of tragedy and we cannot accept it as such.

Yet our need for the consolations of tragedy has not passed with the passing of our ability to conceive it. Indeed, the dissonances which it was tragedy's function to resolve grow more insistent instead of diminishing. Our passions, our disappointments, and our sufferings remain important to us though important to nothing else and they thrust themselves upon us with an urgency which makes it impossible for us to dismiss them as the mere trivialities which, so our intellects tell us, they are. And yet, in the absence of tragic faith or the possibility of achieving it, we have no way in which we may succeed in giving them the dignity which would not only render them tolerable but transform them as they were transformed by the great ages into joys. The death of tragedy is, like the death of love, one of those emotional fatalities as the result of which the human as distinguished from the natural world grows more and more a desert.

Poetry, said Santayana in his famous phrase, is "religion which is no longer believed," but it depends, nevertheless, upon its power to revive in us a sort of temporary or provisional credence and the nearer it can come to producing an illusion of belief the greater is its power as poetry. Once the Tragic Spirit was a living faith and out of it tragedies were written. Today these great expressions of a great faith have declined, not merely into poetry, but into a kind of poetry whose premises are so far from any we can really accept that we can only partially and dimly grasp its meaning.

We read but we do not write tragedies. The tragic solution of the problem of existence, the reconciliation to life by means of the Tragic Spirit is, that is to say, now only a fiction surviving in art. When that art itself has become, as it probably will, completely meaningless, when we have ceased not only to write but to *read* tragic works, then it will be lost and in all real senses forgotten, since the devolution from Religion to Art to Document will be complete.

## Conclusion, The Modern Temper

It is not by thought that men live. Life begins in organisms so simple that one may reasonably doubt even their ability to feel, much less think, and animals cling to or fight for it with a determination which we might be inclined to call superhuman if we did not know that a will to live so thoughtless and so unconditional is the attribute of beings rather below than above the human level. All efforts to find a rational justification of life, to declare it worth the living for this reason or that, are, in themselves, a confession of weakness, since life at its strongest never feels the need of any such justification and since the most optimistic philosopher is less optimistic than that man or animal who, his belief that life is good being too immediate to require the interposition of thought, is no philosopher at all.

In view of this fact it is not surprising that the subtlest intellectual contortions of modern metaphysics should fail to establish the existence of satisfactory aims for life when, as a matter of fact, any effort to do so fails as soon as it begins and can only arise as the result of a weakening of that self-justifying vitality which is the source of all life and of all optimism. As soon as thought begins to seek the "ends" or "aims" to which life is subservient it has already confessed its inability to achieve that animal acceptance of life for life's sake which is responsible for the most determined efforts to live and, in one sense, we may say that even the firmest medieval belief in a perfectly concrete salvation after death marks already the beginning of the completest despair, since that belief could not arise before thought had rendered primitive vitality no longer all-sufficient.

The decadent civilizations of the past were not saved by their philosophers but by the influx of simpler peoples who had centuries yet to live before their minds should be ripe for despair. Neither Socrates nor Plato could teach his compatriots any wisdom from which they could draw the strength to compete with the crude energy of their Roman neighbors, and even their thought inevitably declined soon after it had exhausted their vital energy. Nor could these Romans, who flourished longer for the very reason, perhaps, that they had slower and less subtle intellects, live forever; they too were compelled to give way in their time to barbarians innocent alike both of philosophy and of any possible need to call upon it.

The subhuman will to live which is all-sufficient for the animal may be replaced by faith, faith may be replaced by philosophy, and philosophy may attenuate itself until it becomes, like modern metaphysics, a mere game; but each of these developments marks a stage in a progressive enfeeblement of that will to live for the gradual weakening of which it is the function of each to compensate. Vitality calls upon faith for aid, faith turns gradually to philosophy for support, and then philosophy, losing all confidence in its own conclusions, begins to babble of "beneficent fictions" instead of talking about Truth; but each is less confident than what went before and each is, by consequence, less easy to live by. Taken together, they represent the successive and increasingly desperate expedients by means of which man, the ambitious animal, endeavors to postpone the inevitable realization that living is merely a physiological process with only a physiological meaning and that it is most satisfactorily conducted by creatures who never feel the need to attempt to give it any other. But they are at best no more than expedients, and when the last has been exhausted there remains nothing except the possibility that the human species will be revitalized by some race or some class which is capable of beginning all over again.

Under the circumstances it is not strange that decadent civilizations are likely to think that the collapse of their culture is in reality the end of the human story. Perhaps some of the last of the old Roman intelligentsia realized that the future belonged to the barbarians from the north and that it belonged to them for the very reason that they were incapable of assimilating ancient thought, but even among the early Christian theologians there was a widespread belief that the end of Rome could mean nothing except the end of the world, and, for similar reasons, it is difficult for us to believe in the possibility of anything except either the continuation of modern culture or the extinction of human life. But a glance at history should make us hesitate before asserting that either one of these alternative possibilities is likely to become a reality. On the one hand all cultures have ultimately collapsed and human life has, on the other hand, always persisted—not because philosophers have arisen to solve its problems but because naïver creatures, incapable of understanding the problems and hence not feeling the need to solve them, have appeared somewhere upon the face of the globe.

If modern civilization is decadent then perhaps it will be rejuvenated, but not by the philosophers whose subtlest thoughts are only symptoms of the disease which they are endeavoring to combat. If the future belongs to anybody it belongs to those to whom it has always belonged, to those, that is to say, too absorbed in living to feel the need for thought, and they will come, as the barbarians have always come, absorbed in the processes of life for their own sake, eating without asking if it is worthwhile to eat, begetting children without asking why they should beget them, and conquering without asking for what purpose they conquer.

Doubtless even those among the last of the Romans who had some dim conception of the fact that the centuries immediately to follow would belong to the barbarians were not, for the most part, greatly interested in or cheered by the fact. Thoughtful people come inevitably to feel that if life has any value at all, then that value lies in thought, and to the Roman it probably seemed that it was hardly worthwhile to save the human animal if he could be saved only by the destruction of all that which his own ancestors had achieved, and by the forgetting of everything which he cared to remember. The annihilation of ancient culture was to him equivalent to the annihilation of humanity, and a modern who has come to think in a similar fashion can have only a languid interest in a possible animal rejuvenation which would inevitably involve a blunting of that delicate sensibility and that exquisite subtlety of intellect upon which he has come to set the very highest value.

But doubtless this ancient Roman speculated idly, and it is impossible for us not to do the same. Whence will the barbarians (and we may use that word, not as a term of contempt but merely as a way of identifying these people animated by vitally simple thoughts) come? We are not surrounded as the Romans were by childlike savages, and we can hardly imagine the black tribes of Africa pushing in upon us. Have we, within the confines of our own cities, populations quite as little affected by modern thought as the Greeks were affected by Greek philosophy, and hence quite capable either of carrying peaceably on as the aristocracy dies quietly off at the top or of arising sometime to overwhelm us? Has China, having died once, lain fallow long enough to have become once more primitive, or are the Russians indeed the new barbarians, even if they are such in a somewhat different sense than that implied in the sensational literature of anti-Communist propaganda?

These Russians are young in the only sense of the word which can have a meaning when applied to any part of the human family. If all men had a common ancestor, then all races are equally old in years, but those which have never passed through the successive and debilitating stages of culture retain that potentiality for doing so which constitutes them racially young, and the Russians, who have always lived upon the frontiers of Europe, are in this sense a primitive race, since European culture has never been for them more than the exotic diversion of a small class. For the first time in history the mass of the people is in a position to employ its constructive faculties, and it so happens that their domain is one which offers an enormous field for the employment of such faculties.

Young races like young individuals need toys to play with. Before the advent of the machine, the Romans amused themselves with military and social organization, pushing the boundaries of their empire farther and farther back into unknown territory until their energy was exhausted and they were compelled to begin a gradual retraction; today, the processes of industrial development are capable of absorbing much of the vitality which could formerly find an outlet only in conquest; but if modern people amuse themselves by building factories or digging mines they do so for exactly the same reason that the Romans annexed the British Isles—because, that is to say, there is little temptation to ask ultimate questions as long as there are many tangible things to do and plenty of energy to do them with. Russia has both, and for that very reason there is no other place in the world where one will find today an optimism so simple and so terrible.

We—particularly we in America—have done all that. We have dug our mines, piped our oil, built our factories, and, having done so, we have begun to settle down in our comfortable houses to ask what comes next. But the Russians are at least a century away from such a condition. They begin at a point at least as far back as we began a century ago and they are in the happy position of desiring certain things which they have good reason to believe ultimately achievable. Not only do they want to grow rich and to establish a form of society which will provide for an equitable distribution of their riches, but they find on every side some tangible task capable of being accomplished in such a way as to further their ambition. Perhaps when this ambition has been achieved, when all men are as materially comfortable as some few men are today, then the comfortable masses will discover what the comfortable few have discovered already, which is, of course, that comfort seems enough only when one happens not to have it. But that day is still long distant. Not only will the complete industrial development of the country occupy many years but the problems of the new society are themselves so complicated that they are not likely to be solved for generations and hence, in all probability, Russia will not grow ripe so rapidly as the United States did.

As a result of these conditions there has already developed in Russia a new philosophy of life which, in spite of the fact that it has taken a form influenced by modern industrial conditions, is easily recognizable as being essentially primitive in its simplicity. Sweeping aside the intellectual and emotional problems of Europe, refusing even in its art to concern itself with the psychology of the individual soul, communism assumes that nothing is really important except those things upon which the welfare of the race depends, and in assuming that it is assuming exactly what a primitive society always assumes. Its drama and its poetry celebrate the machine exactly as the literature of a primitive people celebrates the process of hunting or of agriculture, and they do so for exactly the same reason, for the reason, that is to say, that agriculture on the one hand and industry on the other are the two fundamental processes by which the life of the people is sustained.

Communistic Utopianism is based upon the assumption that the only maladjustments from which mankind suffers are social in character and hence it is sustained by the belief that in a perfect state all men would be perfectly happy. Fundamentally materialistic, it refuses to remember that physical well-being is no guarantee of felicity and that, as a matter of fact, as soon as the individual finds himself in a perfectly satisfactory physical environment he begins to be aware of those more fundamental maladjustments which subsist, not between man and society but between the human spirit and the natural universe. And though, for this reason, it must seem to the cultivated European essentially naïve, yet in that very naïveté lies its strength as a social philosophy. Thanks to the fact that the perfect Communist is not aware of the existence of any problems more subtle than those involved in the production and distribution of wealth, he can throw himself into the business of living with a firm faith in the value of what he is doing and he can display an energy in practical affairs not to be equaled by anyone incapable of a similar belief in their ultimate importance.

All societies which have passed the first vigor of their youth reveal their loss of faith in life itself by the fact that they no longer consider such fundamental processes as other than means toward an end. Food, clothes, and warmth are considered merely as instruments, and the most eager attention is directed, not toward attaining them but toward the activities which men are at liberty to pursue when such fundamental things are granted. Productive labor is regarded as an evil, and when anything is said concerning the possibility of improving the condition of the masses, such improvement is always thought of as consisting essentially in so shortening even their hours of labor as to make possible for them also certain hours of freedom. Primitive societies, on the other hand, have no desire to escape from such fundamental processes. They do not hunt in order to live but they live in order to hunt, because for them the value of life lies in the activities necessary to carry it on; and the Communist philosophy of labor is based upon a similarly primitive outlook. Factories are considered, not as means toward an end but as ends in themselves. A full life is to consist, not in one spent in the pursuit of those thoughts or the cultivation of those emotions which are possible only when productive labor has been reduced to a minimum, but in one completely absorbed by such labor.

Hence it is that to the good Communist, as to the good tribesman, any question concerning the meaning of life is in itself completely meaningless and he will live the complicated industrial life of today exactly as the tribesman lives the simple life of his tribe—not in thought but in action. He has a sort of god, but his god is in reality what anthropologists call a culture-god; merely, that is to say, the spirit which presides over and infuses itself with the germination of the seed, the ripening of the fruit, or the whirring of the machine.

Such a philosophy comes nearer than any other to that unformulated one by which an animal lives. It does not ask any of the questions which a weary people inevitably ask and it is, as a matter of fact, less a system of thought than a translation into simple words of the will to live and thrive. But it is, for all that, only the more impressive as an evidence of the vigorous youth of the Russian mind. The visitor to Moscow who sees how eagerly its inhabitants live under conditions which are still very difficult, how gladly they accept both labor and, when necessary, privation, cannot but realize that they are sustained by a fundamental optimism unknown anywhere else in the world. At the present moment the inhabitants of many European countries *have* much more but they *hope* much less, and they are incapable of any acceptance of life so vital and so complete.

If the Communistic experiment is economically a failure, then these hopes may be soon disappointed; if it becomes economically a success, then they will doubtless still be disappointed in that more distant day when, the perfect state having been achieved, its inhabitants come to realize that the natural universe is as imperfectly adapted as ever to human needs. But man-the-animal lives in Time. A hope is a hope up to the instant when it is dashed, and the Russia of today is filled with a confidence hardly less elementary than that of the animal which, under the influence of the vital urge, acts as though the litter which it has just brought into the world were so tremendously worth saving that nothing else which had occurred since the dawn of the first day were of equal importance.

Perhaps, then, Europe has good reason to speak of the "Bolshevik menace," but if so the events which she fears are not quite the ones most likely to occur. If Russia or the Russian spirit conquers Europe it will not be with the bomb of the anarchist but with the vitality of the young barbarian who may destroy many things but who destroys them only that he may begin over again. Such calamities are calamitous only from the point of view of a humanism which values the complexity of its feelings and the subtlety of its intellect far more than Nature does. To her they are merely the reassertion of her right to recapture her own world, merely the process by which she repeoples the earth with creatures simple enough to live joyously there.

To us, however, such speculations as these are doubly vain. In the first place the future may belong, not to the Russians but to some class of people not yet thought of in this connection, and in the second place, none of these possible futures is one which can have anything to do with us or our traditions. Though the new barbarians may forget, we will remember that the paradox of humanism and the tragic fallacy are not to be altered by the establishment of new societies and that the despair which was the fruit of both ancient and modern civilization must inevitably ripen again in the course of the development of any society which enters upon the pursuit of human values.

Some critics of communism have, to be sure, maintained that its tendencies were fundamentally antihuman and that, should it ever become established, it would so arrest the development of the humanistic spirit as to fix mankind forever in some changelessly efficient routine like that of an anthill. But even if this be true it does not alter the fact that its hopes are no hopes in which we can have any part, since we would be even more alien to such a society than to one which promised to recapitulate our own youth. The world may be rejuvenated in one way or another, but we will not. Skepticism has entered too deeply into our souls ever to be replaced by faith, and we can never forget the things which the new barbarians will never need to have known. This world in which an unresolvable discord is the fundamental fact is the world in which we must continue to live, and for us wisdom must consist, not in searching for a means of escape which does not exist but in making such peace with it as we may.

Nor is there any reason why we should fail to realize the fact that the acceptance of such despair as must inevitably be ours does not, after all, involve a misery so acute as that which many have been compelled to endure. Terror can be blacker than that and so can the extremes of physical want and pain. The most human human being has still more of the animal than of anything else and no love of rhetoric should betray one into seeming to deny that he who has escaped animal pain has escaped much. Despair of the sort which has here been described is a luxury in the sense that it is possible only to those who have much that many people do without, and philosophical pessimism, dry as it may leave the soul, is more easily endured than hunger or cold.

Leaving the future to those who have faith in it, we may survey our world and, if we bear in mind the facts just stated, we may permit ourselves to exclaim, a little rhetorically perhaps,

> Hail, horrors, hail,
> Infernal world! and thou profoundest hell,
> Receive thy new possessor.

If Humanism and Nature are fundamentally antithetical, if the human virtues have a definite limit set to their development, and if they may be cultivated only by a process which renders us progressively unfit to fulfill our biological duties, then we may at least permit ourselves a certain defiant satisfaction when we realize that we have made our choice and that we are resolved to abide by the consequences. Some small part of the tragic fallacy may be said indeed to be still valid for us, for if we cannot feel ourselves great as Shakespeare did, if we no longer believe in either our infinite capacities or our importance to the universe, we know at least that we have discovered the trick which has been played upon us and that whatever else we may be we are no longer dupes.

Rejuvenation may be offered to us at a certain price. Nature, issuing her last warning, may bid us embrace some new illusion before it is too late and accord ourselves once more with her. But we prefer rather to fail in our own way than to succeed in hers. Our human world may have no existence outside of our own desires, but those are more imperious than anything else we know, and we will cling to our own lost cause, choosing always rather to know than to be. Doubtless fresh people have still a long way to go with Nature before they are compelled to realize that they too have come to the parting of the ways, but though we may wish them well we do not envy them. If death for us and our kind is the inevitable result of our stubbornness then we can only say, "So be it." Ours is a lost cause and there is no place for us in the natural universe, but we are not, for all that, sorry to be human. We should rather die as men than live as animals.

[Above chapters, "The Genesis of a Mood," "The Tragic Fallacy," and "Conclusion," from *The Modern Temper*. Reprinted by permission of Harcourt Brace Jovanovich, Inc.]

>━0━0━0━0━0━0━0━0━0━0━0━0━0━0━0━0━0━0━0━0━0━0━0━0━0━0━0━0━0━0━0━0━0━0━0━<

ABOUT HALF OF "THE MODERN TEMPER" (INCLUDING THE FIRST OF THE CHAPTERS reprinted here) had been finished by the spring of 1928. At that time I was sent by the New York *Nation* on an assignment to Moscow, principally to observe the theater there, and I had promised myself a little holiday in Paris after escaping from the dreariness of Moscow. But a telegram came from Harcourt-Brace. They were anxious to publish the book the following spring. Could I deliver the manuscript by September—which was about the time I expected to reach New York again.

"Far from anticipating any such pressure I had only a very general idea how I was to go on from the point where I had broken off. But a publisher's request is a very stimulating thing to a young writer and I made a rapid calculation. Another thirty thousand words—approximately the same number as were already written—would be, I decided, about right, and there were just thirty days left until we were due to sail. A thousand words per day was the stint to which I had accustomed myself. If I could keep on schedule, I should be able to finish just in time to catch our boat. At the moment, we were staying with Marcelle's sister in her apartment on the Boulevard St. Jacques near the Boulevard Raspail and the concierge volunteered that there was an unused maid's room under the roof. That solved one problem by providing what was precisely the traditional garret.

"On the first morning I mounted to it, I plunged into the next chapter, the subject of which had somehow miraculously presented itself. Every morning thereafter, I climbed the stairs again and as I finished each section I found myself knowing what the next should be. As soon as a thousand words had been written I stopped where I was, descended to rejoin Marcelle, spent the afternoon either reading or walking the streets while thinking of entirely different things, and passed most of the evenings at the Dôme with the mixed company of Americans and Parisians gathered there. When I came to the end of the thirtieth session, the book was finished.

"Only once since, when writing the first of my 'nature' books, have I ever had the experience of going so regularly and steadily ahead with a discourse which I had not consciously thought through to the end and which, on the contrary, seemed merely to lead me on. No doubt the fact that I had a very definite deadline had something to do with the phenomenon in this first instance of it. But it was more important, I think, that in both cases I had been, without knowing it, long preparing what I had to say.

"Ideas, convictions, and attitudes, which had previously found no adequate expression and of the interconnection between which I was not fully aware, suddenly crystallized into a coherent discourse. I listened to what I had been saying to myself for several years, without being quite aware of the fact, and I simply wrote it down as I listened. Here were the conclusions I had come to as I digested or reacted against all I had read, heard, or discussed from the freshman days at college down to the latest book I had reviewed and the latest conversation I had heard in *The Nation* office. For the first time I was prepared to say what I, at that moment, believed; just what, in my opinion, the 'modern ideas' I had met came down to."

When I was asked in 1956 to supply a new preface for a paperback edition of this book, I wrote: "More than a quarter of a century later I find myself asking three questions: (1) Do educated people continue to believe that science has exposed as delusions those convictions and standards upon which Western civilization was founded? (2) Is the ultimate cause of the catastrophe with which that civilization is threatened this loss of faith in humanity itself? (3) Is it really true, as I once believed, that there is no escaping the scientific demonstration that religion, morality, and the human being's power to make free choices are all merely figments of the imagination?

"To the first two of these questions the answer still seems to me to be 'Yes.' Despite the so-called revival of popular religion which amounts to little more than the acceptance of the church as a social institution; despite also a perhaps increasingly strong undercurrent of psychological and sociological protest against determinism and relativism, the most prevalent educated opinion is still that men are animals and that animals are machines. One kind of intellectual may respond to this conviction by embracing the creed of atheistical Existentialism which is the tragic solution proposed in *The Modern Temper*. A larger group turns optimistically toward experimental psychology, the techniques for sociological conditioning, and the methods of indoctrination developed by the manipulators of the media of mass communication, and hopes from them for the creation of a Robot Utopia whose well-adjusted citizens will have comfortably forgotten that their forefathers believed themselves to be Men.

"But neither the one group nor the other rejects the assumption that Western man, traditionally endowed with reason, will, and a valid sense of value, is an exploded myth. And because this conviction still prevails among educated men I still believe it true that it poses the most serious of all threats to our civilization and is, indeed, the ultimate source of most of our specific dilemmas—as it is, for instance of our dilemma in the face of communism which embodies the really logical conclusion to be drawn from the premises which so many nominally anticommunists share with their formal opponents.

"The modern temper itself has developed somewhat, especially in the direction of that attempted 'adjustment' to dismal assumptions which makes Social Engineering rather than Existentialist resignation the dominant religion of today. But the description which I gave of the origins of this temper, and the consequences likely to follow from it, seem to me as valid as they ever were. It is only my own attitude toward it which is different. What I described and shared in I still describe but I no longer accept it. Hence the situation which *The Modern Temper* presents as hopeless does not now seem to me entirely so, though by the diagnosis I will still stand."

Just how I had arrived at this conclusion was the subject of *The Measure of Man* published in 1954 and given the National Book Award for nonfiction. Gradually I had come to feel that, intentionally or not, the three most influential thinkers of the century past—Marx, Darwin and Freud—had all tended to emphasize the helplessness of man in a universe which they assumed to be alien, and that they were responsible to a considerable extent for what I had called the modern temper.

[Quoted material in foregoing from *More Lives Than One,* 1962.]

## The Loss of Confidence

It so happens that H. G. Wells and Bernard Shaw died recently, and within a few years of each other. No two men writing in the English language—perhaps no two men writing in any language—had been so widely accepted by literate men as spokesmen for the last phase of the Age of Confidence. In curiously diverse but complementary ways, each had spent half a century telling the world that all was—or at least that all could be—well. Yet both died crying "Woe, woe" to the very people whom they had previously reassured. And the astonishing fact is that their complete reversal of opinion passed almost unnoticed. When each said, almost with his dying breath, "All is lost," the same public that had once accepted so trustingly their former assurances hardly noticed the about-face, because it had already been taken for granted that Shaw and Wells, like everybody else, had been compelled to make it.

In the case of Shaw it is easy to distinguish the successive phases of the transformation. Just after the turn of the century and at the time when he was still more orthodox Fabian than anything else, he wrote in *Major Barbara* a bouncing fable intended to demonstrate how inevitably and automatically an industrialized, capitalistic democracy would transform itself into a gentle, socialistic state, preserving all the virtues and abolishing all the defects of the England he knew. Scarcely more than a decade later, he admitted in *Heartbreak House* that the expected transformation was not taking place on schedule and urged on his fellow countrymen his new conviction that, instead of waiting for the dialectic process to work out its benevolent inevitabilities, they must either "learn navigation" or go on the rocks. Approximately a generation after that, *Back to Methuselah* took another step away from any optimism which could possibly be called easy. The contemporary human being, it told us, is not capable of "learning navigation." It would take any individual at least three hundred years to do so.

Thus Mr. Shaw informed us, successively and after the intervention of barely decent intervals: first, that all *would be* well; second, that all *might be made* well; and, third, that *nothing could possibly be* well unless man managed somehow to transcend all those human limitations which are symbolized by his unfortunate tendency to die not long after the expiration of the Biblical three score and ten. After this succession of retreats, it is not surprising to find him arriving finally at a position summed up in his reply to a visitor who had mentioned that one of Shaw's fellow playwrights in America was troubled about the state of the world. "Tell him not to worry. If, as I believe, man is about to destroy himself, he will be replaced by something better."

At every stage, the current conviction was represented as constituting some form of reasonable optimism. A good life for mankind will *begin* in perhaps a decade; it will be *achieved* in perhaps a generation; it cannot be *hoped for* until some age so distant that its place in time can be described only by the phrase "as far as thought can reach." This is "hope deferred" with a vengeance, hope deferred until hope itself becomes a grisly joke, offered in the inconceivably remote future and only to creatures who will not be men like ourselves, but "something better." In his early maturity Shaw ridiculed the Salvation Army and warned us to "Beware the man whose God is in the sky"; in his old age that is exactly where he placed the pie we were jokingly promised. For him, as for so many of his contemporaries, the vision of a "better world," which had once been so vivid, grew dimmer as the vision of the catastrophes which must precede it grew more and more clear.

The fact that the style and the mind of H. G. Wells were so much more prosaic and literal than Shaw's makes him, perhaps, an even better illustration of the typical course of the transformation by which early twentieth-century optimism was turned into mid-century despair. Both men began as more or less orthodox Fabian Socialists, but while Shaw always had mystical inclinations, Wells put his faith in technology, and the result was that their respective dreams of Utopia are comically unlike. Thus, while the Wellsian man of the future was happily engaged in pushing buttons and pulling levers, his Shavian counterpart in *Back to Methuselah* seemed to be inhabiting a country from which almost everything material had disappeared and which was thus returned to a sort of pastoral simplicity well suited to the tastes of the Ancients, who devoted themselves to contemplation rather than, like Wells's men, to the manipulation of super-gadgets. But even before Wells himself began to concern himself less and less with the mechanical wonders of the future as he imagined it, Aldous Huxley had transformed the Wellsian dream into that nightmare which, by the twenties, it was beginning to seem.

More significant is the fact that Wells and Shaw were more alike in their despairs than they had ever been in their hopes. The last of Wells's many prophecies was published by a newspaper syndicate very shortly before his death. He also cried "Woe, woe," predicting utter catastrophe as almost certain for the whole world and choosing phrases astonishingly like Shaw's when he spoke not only of the probability that man would "destroy himself," but also of the different creature which would replace him. Thus before they died, both the great popular educators of the English-speaking world did more than tell their pupils that unspeakable catastrophe lay just ahead: they also formally renounced the human race as a failure. What has been lost step by step is not only the conviction that we will manage to our own advantage the new world we have learned to create, but also the confidence in our ability to govern even ourselves. The fact that the same premises that attributed new potentialities to man soon began to deprive him of other supposed attributes and powers passed almost unnoticed, until at last we began to perceive how much less, as well as how much more, than he had formerly been the human being was now beginning to seem.

At least in many philosophies, as well as many theologies, he had been

endowed with both Free Will and the ability to recognize certain absolutes called Good and Evil. It made comparatively little difference whether
it was God or Nature, in the eighteenth-century use of the term, on whose
permanent, accessible criteria he could rely. In either case he could know
what he ought to choose or do, and it rested with himself to decide
whether or not he would do it. He was not, as the modern man has come
to believe, merely the product of the forces that have operated upon him.
He could make value judgments in the validity of which he truly believed, instead of telling himself that if one thing seems preferable to
another, it can be only because the interests or the traditions of our nation,
our society or our class make it seem so. And we can hardly be expected to
manage the machines that we have created when we no longer believe
that we have the power either of making ultimate decisions or of knowing
what ultimate decisions ought to be made.

Though many have tried, no one has ever yet explained away the decisive fact that science, which can do so much, cannot decide what it
ought to do, and that the power which it confers must be guided by
something outside it, if power is not to become—as it is already becoming
—an end as well as a means. Yet it is just at this moment, when choices
have become unprecedentedly fateful (because intentions can now be implemented as never before in the history of mankind), that scientific
theories have persuaded us to abandon the very premises which might have
made us feel capable of directing the power that science has put into our
hands. If in one sense man is now more like a god than he ever was before, he has in another sense become less godlike than he ever previously
imagined himself to be. The attributes of a god must include not merely
power itself, but also the knowledge of how power should be used. What
we have fallen victim to is thus not so much technology itself as the
philosophy that has grown with its growing.

It is true that neither Shaw nor Wells was a fanatical exponent of this
view which makes man not the captain of his soul, but the product of the
forces that operate upon him. Shaw, especially, was prone to indulge an
odd inconsistency when he alternately defended economic determinism
and the theory that the will and imagination of the individual are all-
important. Undoubtedly he was aware of the dangers inherent in too
absolute an affirmation of what his Marxism seemed to imply. But the
man whom he and Wells, each in his own way, were trying to educate
was a man already prone to accept that very restricted estimate of his
powers of self-direction that materialistic rationalism had encouraged.

Hence the man whom both finally pronounced a failure was the man who had himself come to believe what that rationalism described.

To entertain the possibility that the creature who has become "not good enough to survive" is not man himself but only that version of man that he has recently accepted, is not, necessarily, to assume that his thinking is either demonstrably or even actually false. Possibly, at least, his theories about his own nature are both correct and fatal. The atom bomb is no less a threat to the very people who made it because the revolutionary theory of matter in accordance with which it was designed is presumably true. Conceivably, we may be on the point of achieving spiritual as well as physical suicide because we have learned more than is good for us about both physical and human nature.

There remains, nevertheless, the cheerful possibility that we actually know less about the Science of Man than we do of the less difficult sciences of matter and that we may, just in time, learn more. Perhaps Hamlet was nearer right than Pavlov. Perhaps the exclamation "How like a god!" is actually more appropriate than "How like a dog! How like a rat! How like a machine!" Perhaps we have been deluded by the fact that the methods employed for the study of man have been for the most part those originally devised for the study of machines or the study of rats, and are capable, therefore, of detecting and measuring only those characteristics which the three do have in common. But we have already gone a long way on the contrary assumption, and we take it more completely for granted than we sometimes realize. The road back is not an easy one.

## Grand Strategy

Man has never seen very far ahead and perhaps he never will. He did not anticipate the real consequences of mechanical invention and he foresaw even less to what his intellectual processes would lead him. But when we look back from the vantage point of a later time we seem to perceive a sort of Grand Strategy. The steam engine seems to have been invented to make the Industrial Revolution possible; certain ideas seem to have been propagated to give social development a certain direction. And if we submit to this illusion it must seem that the Grand Strategy of nineteenth-century thought had as its aim the destruction of man's former belief in his own autonomy.

Long before that century began certain preliminary steps had already been taken. Some would put them as far back as the sixteenth when

Copernicus jolted us out of our simple assumption that the universe of which we were the center might reasonably be supposed to have in us its purpose and its explanation. Others, to whom the Copernican revolution seems less decisive than it must have seemed to many in its day, would credit the succeeding century with the first important phases of the slowly evolving Master Plan.

They would say that when Thomas Hobbes proposed to explain human conduct as a mere branch of animal behavior he took the first step; and that when Descartes undertook to describe the animal as a mere machine he took the second. In the synthesis which presently took place Descartes' refusal to include man among the animals was quickly forgotten and the lines of future development were laid down. Hobbes proves that man is an animal; Descartes proves that an animal is a machine. By a quasi-algebraical process one needs only to eliminate the term common to the two equations in order to get what by now most men seem to believe: Man is a machine.

Against this conclusion the eighteenth century struggled hard. For "God" it substituted "Nature," and its Deism, however shadowy it may now seem, forbade it to assume that either man or his fellow creatures were merely mechanical. It now saw Man as a creature "darkly wise and rudely great" and if God no longer clearly revealed his intentions, Man was nevertheless born with a brain which was not quite the blank slate of Hobbes because Nature had inscribed on it, before his birth, those outlines of her general principles which, as Pope has said, "touched but faintly, are drawn right."

Thus, if neither God's word nor the individual conscience was any longer a sure guide, the voice of Nature still was. Man was not a machine and he was not a creature to whom Good and Evil or Right and Wrong were merely the conventions, the mores, of his society. Nature afforded him "at least a glimmering light," something outside himself which he might stumblingly follow.

Yet before the nineteenth century was half over this compromise was already too old-fashioned to seem tenable, and the Strategy developed into its mature phase. During that century three inclusive new hypotheses— each in its own way as revolutionary as Copernicanism and each destined to affect as profoundly man's sense of his relation to the universe— achieved wide popular as well as professional acceptance. They were, of course, Evolution, Marxism, and Freudian psychology.

These three theories are not directly connected with one another. They cover somewhat different fields, they overlap considerably, and at points they are mutually exclusive. Any one of them may be accepted without implying an acceptance of the others and it would be difficult, if not impossible, to be an orthodox believer in all three. Yet they do have, nevertheless, certain important characteristics in common and each did in its own way contribute to the accomplishment of the Grand Strategy's purpose. Each emphasized the extent to which the human being is the product of forces outside his control.

From one point of view it makes very little difference whether we are told by Darwin that natural selection, operating with mechanical inevitability, has caused man to evolve from other forms of life; by Marx that we are the product of a society which is, in its turn, inevitably produced by the dialectic processes of matter; or by Freud that what we call our unique self is actually the result of the way in which the fixed "drives" of human nature have been modified by the things which have happened to us—especially by things which happened in an infancy now almost completely forgotten.

No matter to which of the three we listen with conviction, the result is to drift toward the assumption that we neither can nor need to do much of anything for ourselves. Throughout all time either natural selection has performed for us the function of what used to be called "aspiration," or the dialectic of matter has similarly performed the function of effort. Simultaneously the dominance of the unconscious motive has made it useless for us even to attempt to follow the ancient injunction: Know Thyself—at least without the aid of experts hired to know ourselves for us.

Disputes still rage concerning what each of the three great teachers "really meant." Freudians, for instance, sometimes assume that analysis releases freedom. But there can be no doubt about the fact that all three of the great teachers have been popularly interpreted in the fashion suggested. At worst each could be and has been made the excuse for a sort of secular Calvinism in the light of which man is seen as the victim of an absolute predestination.

At the very least and even when attempts have been made to explain away what seem the most obvious deductions, the effect has been to focus our attention on that part of ourselves over which we have least control. To science, especially when uninfluenced by Jung and Freud, the theories opened new fields of investigation into "the mechanical operations of the spirit" while they left everything not mechanical as mysterious as it was before. And scientists suffer from the effects of a human weakness from which science itself is theoretically exempt. Like ordinary men they tend unconsciously to assume that the phenomena with which they deal are more important and more real than those whose manifestations elude them; hence man himself began to seem more and more merely mechanical just because the mechanical aspects of his behavior were those most easily studied. Having begun with the legitimate purpose of discovering how much of human behavior could be accounted for in terms of physical law and animal psychology both literature and science now began, first, to answer "Nearly all" and then to disregard even the reservation implied in the "nearly."

Thus to accept the hypotheses of Darwin, of Marx and of Freud, to accept any one of them as even a partial account of the how and why of man's past development and future destiny, meant to emphasize strongly if not exclusively the extent to which he has played a passive role and to encourage him to see himself as essentially not merely a "product" but also a victim. To that extent all three encouraged what may be called "philosophies of exculpation." If Darwin seemed to deprive man of all credit for the upward evolution of himself as an organism, Marx and Freud seemed to relieve him of all blame for his sins and his crimes as well as for his follies.

Perhaps, indeed, we would not so readily have accepted the rôle of victim had it not been for the absolution which was offered in exchange for our surrender of importance and dignity. If there is a sense in which our teachers tell us that we cannot possibly succeed because, at best, we are only the lucky product of natural selection, fortunate infantile experiences, or a favored position in the social system, so, in the same sense, we cannot ourselves be failures. We may shift the blame for all that we have done or left undone upon the unfavorable environment, sociological or psychological, to which we were exposed. If there is some uneasy sense that our own shortcomings do really exist, we make even of them a sort of virtue when we permit them to function as the driving force behind a criticism of our social class, our nation, or the world at large upon which we thus unload any residual sense of personal responsibility.

Since dogmas do not have to be accepted in their full dogmatic rigidity in order to have a very powerful effect, the question of how clearly and how absolutely deterministic theories are held is of relatively little importance. What is important is the evident fact that educational, sociological, and even criminological principles and methods have come increasingly to focus attention and effort on that aspect of man and his behavior which seems most easily interpreted in accordance with such theories, so that even when man is not openly proclaimed to be no more than a "product" of "conditions" he is treated as though he were.

Educators, sociologists, and lawmakers have begun to act as though man were absolutely incapable of choice, of self-determination, or of any autonomous activity. The Man they have in mind when they describe their principles, plan their societies, or draw up their codes is something significantly, perhaps fatally, different from any creature who could possibly escape the catastrophe which many formerly confident "engineers" have now begun to predict.

Moreover and merely by being treated as though he could do nothing for himself Man is, perhaps, actually becoming less capable of doing so. Any society which not merely tells its members that they are automata but also treats them as though they were, runs the risk of becoming a society in which human capacities atrophy because they are less and less rewarded, or even tolerated, as well as less and less acknowledged.

As the individual becomes, either in theory or in fact, less capable of doing anything for himself the question what may be *done to him* inevitably comes to seem more and more interesting. If he is so much the product of his environment that neither spontaneously nor as the result of moral adjuration can his own will make effective decisions, then it seems to follow—not that he must be simply abandoned to evolution, the dialectic of matter, or the obscure workings of the unconscious mind—but that he may be reached indirectly through the manipulation of that total environment of which he is the product. Thus sociology begins to promise to achieve by scientific methods all that which religion and moral philosophy, proceeding on false assumptions, failed to accomplish.

In its mildest and most defensible form the result of this conviction is simply the whole broad, benevolent effort of social reformers to relieve poverty, provide opportunities for education, and remove as far as possible all obviously corrupting features from the environment in which the individual grows to maturity. Such merely pragmatic enterprises do not depend logically on anything more than a recognition of external influences as a factor in determining human fate and they do not demand for their justification any affirmation that human conduct or character is "nothing but" the product of the influences brought to bear upon the individual. Thus when Bernard Shaw declares that "the only trouble with the poor is poverty" his rhetoric may seem to imply an absolute determinism but, as his own writing makes clear, all he really meant to say was only that poverty is the factor which society can most easily control.

Unfortunately, however, working principles, especially when they seem actually to work, have a tendency to harden into exclusive dogmas. The fanatical contention that man is nothing but the product of his environment arises naturally in certain minds, and soon leads to the equally fanatical conviction that this same man is also limitlessly plastic. Though he cannot change himself at all, he may, nevertheless, be changed in any direction and to any extent. To the aspiring "human engineer" very heady possibilities seem then to open.

To him it seems that since man is a kind of machine there ought to be possible a Science of Man as exact and as effective as any other science which deals, as a Science of Man would deal, with the behavior of matter operating in accordance with known or knowable laws. Moreover, as the nineteenth century came so clearly to understand, such sciences reach their maturity when phenomena can demonstrably be both predicted and controlled.

These two last are, to be sure, not quite the same thing, and the second is subject to limits somewhat more narrow than the first: Astronomy can, for example, predict eclipses with great accuracy though it cannot at all control them. But the two are very often related and the aim of the Science of Man would be completely achieved when it became capable, first, of saying in advance what a human being would do and, second, within limits as wide as those within which the physical scientist works, of directing and manipulating the materials with which it deals.

Ultimately, of course, such a Science of Man would find itself faced, just as the sciences of matter already have been, with a corollary problem. It too would sometimes be compelled to ask not merely "how can this or that be done" but also whether, in some sense with which science itself seems unable to deal, we "ought" or "ought not" to do it. But this problem does not arise in the infancy of any science. The professor of the new Science of Man tends to think of himself as pure scientist rather than as educator or reformer. His only concern is to discover the methods by means of which prediction and control become possible.

In relatively crude and simple ways the social worker, the teacher, and the businessman are already using—often for simple and limited purposes —the methods, often crudely empiric, from the results of which the aspiring Science of Man begins to draw theoretical general conclusions in much the same way that the earliest theoretical physicists utilized the experience of mechanics and military engineers. The mental test, the aptitude test and the sampling technique are increasingly used to discover in advance what candidate will be elected, what radio program will prove popular, what advertising slogans effective, what course of instruction popular. And insofar as the methods are successful in achieving their immediate purposes they encourage, if they do not actually fully justify, the assumption that human behavior is predictable because, like the behavior of material particles, it follows inviolable laws.

In similar rough and ready ways the technician interested in results rather than in general theories has also been learning more and more how to control as well as merely to predict opinions and tastes, not only by advertising campaigns and other methods of propaganda but also by the stress put upon certain ideals or activities in the schools. Even in the realm of the popular arts commercial exploiters speak frankly of "making" a star or a song hit rather than of "discovering" him or it. They have their methods and the methods very frequently work. When the beginnings of popularity are detected, its full flowering can be directed and controlled.

Inevitably each success strengthens confidence in the soundness of the theory on which the enterprise was based. Human behavior must be predictable because it has been correctly predicted. Opinions, tastes, preferences, and actions must be controllable because they have been controlled. That being the case, there seems no reason why we should stop with random and piecemeal enterprises. Why should we not found all ethics and all aesthetics on what we know of man's predictable behavior, all education and government on what we know of the methods by which he may be conditioned? We have, it is said, found out at last both why so-called "human nature" is what it is and how it may be made into something else. We have now only to decide what people ought to be like and how we want them to behave. After that it is only a problem in engineering.

The more advanced theoreticians have already reached this point in the formulation of their ultimate aims. No longer concerned exclusively with the specific details of this or that specific evil or ill, they are already looking forward to the time when not only society but human nature itself will be completely remade. As the Dean of the Humanities at the Massachusetts Institute of Technology told the Convocation of 1949, we must now recognize our "approaching scientific ability to control men's thoughts with precision." It so happened that Mr. Winston Churchill was an honored guest on the occasion of the Dean's address and he remarked in reply that he would "be very content to be dead before that happens." But Mr. Churchill is a conservative who has been accused of finding "brave" an adjective more appropriate to the old world than the new, and, whether he likes it or not, he has lingered on into a society that is moving in the direction which seemed to him utterly horrible and which is also already pragmatically committed to theories the full implications of which it does not always face squarely.

In the course of this discussion we shall presently have occasion to undertake some analysis of the scientific and philosophical assumptions behind the new Science of Man as they are stated and defended by those who, up to the limit of their very considerable powers, do seriously attempt to face squarely all their implications. For the moment, however, we may return to the subject of things as they already are rather than things as they may some time be, and consider the significance of certain actual practices analogous on a somewhat higher level to the pragmatic use by politicians and merchants of the techniques already devised to predict and control public reaction.

Inevitably the opinions and attitudes of both the public and such of its leaders as operate on a level of critical awareness above that of those whom they lead, have been profoundly influenced by the practical success which predictors and controllers have achieved and by the general if vague assumption that all men are primarily either victims or at least products of the conditions to which they have been subject. An assumption of this sort is a commonplace in those popular psychological and sociological disquisitions which fill the magazines as well as the "feature" pages of the daily papers and which have completely taken the place of the sermonizings which were once equally ubiquitous. What is more important, both law and education have followed suit, and in the name of what are perversely called "humane" attitudes tend to treat the average man as though he were, indeed, the helpless creature implied by Marx or Freud and described in naturalistic fiction.

Thus the education which is offered Man comes more and more to be thought of in terms of "adjusting" or "conditioning" him to predetermined opinions or attitudes; and educational theory tends to be based more and more on the Pavlovian assumption that something should be done to him in much the same way that something is done to a monkey being taught tricks or a dog trained to bark and bite on the proper occasions. In a similar fashion "social legislation," which professes the intention to do him good, decides what he ought to have and then gives it to him, disregarding both the fact that he may want something else and that it might be more in accord with the best kind of human nature if he were permitted to get it for himself. Criminology—again in the name of a "humanity" which begins by depriving the criminal of all human attributes—proceeds on the assumption that those guilty of "antisocial conduct" have been in no way responsible for that conduct and that they are most likely to be redeemed if they are first told that they, like everybody else, are mere victims of their experiences, and then promised that they will be reconditioned. Thus—and again in the name of humanity—it assumes that to urge him to be a man and to choose Good rather than Evil would be both unscientific and inhumane.

Even in the nursery we begin the process of explaining to the man-to-be that any faults he may exhibit are not actually his—and therefore possibly corrigible by himself—but only the result of some defect in his training or his environment. On the radio one may hear preadolescent participants in the junior forums assuring one another that when other children are what used to be called "naughty" that is "only their way of showing that they need more love," and thus from their tenderest age the future citizens are taught the art of exculpation and conditioned to believe that nothing but conditioning is important.

The question is not whether deterministic theories are to some extent true. No doubt some "naughtiness" in adults as well as in children is partly attributable to what has been done to them. But the important question is whether or not it is always and entirely such and, whether, if it is not, a mistake is made when we fail to recognize and promote whatever autonomous powers a human being may have. Certainly in the case of adults and to some lesser extent in the case of children there is another side to the truth: "Human beings should be loved." It is: "Human beings should be lovable." Even in the nursery it might be just as well if both sides of this truth were acknowledged. Already eight-year-olds, having spilled the ink, broken the Ming vase and pulled the cat's tail are leaping up and down in an agony of self-righteousness as they scream, "I want to be loved." It is unnecessarily hard to love them.

In the adult world the parallel is the criminal who knows too well what the criminologists very properly admit: namely, that society is sometimes partly responsible for crimes. This truth is properly employed when it helps us to understand and perhaps to forgive someone else. It is not properly used to forgive ourselves either too much or too easily. Many a malefactor comes into court already convinced that he cannot justly be blamed for whatever he did. But sometimes, perhaps, the real culprit is not so much society as it is the conviction that society must be to blame. Those who are too thoroughly conditioned to assume that only conditioning counts are very badly conditioned indeed.

Moreover the implicit assumption that only "conditioning" counts is not always permitted to remain merely implicit and even on the level of popular discourse the bolder sociologists sometimes permit themselves to state it as an inflexible dogma. Thus Mr. Edwin J. Lukas, Executive Director of the Society for the Prevention of Crime, recently wrote as follows in an important national weekly magazine: "In today's thinking antisocial behavior is considered to be the product of unique economic, sociological, and psychological factors in each offender's past history."

From this beautifully clear and unqualified statement several startling facts emerge. In the first place, of course, it assumes that neither Wickedness nor (even) Crime is a reality, since both are redefined as "antisocial conduct." Moreover, as the result of this redefinition it becomes obvious that every individual, insofar as he remains an individual, exists in a moral vacuum so that Robinson Crusoe ceased to be either a good or bad man while on his island because he lived in no society and his conduct could not possibly be either social or antisocial. In the second place the redefinition not only gets rid of such theological concepts as Original Sin and the Reality of Evil but also of every vestige of any implied possibility that there is anything in man which is to any degree self-determining, or that he can possibly be anything more than the result of the forces which have impinged upon him. All men therefore are entirely innocent. Their exculpation is complete. But to accept pardon they must also admit that they are absolutely helpless.

Among psychologists, especially when they are concerned with the child, one may observe even more exalted states of fanatical exaltation. Thus Brock Chisholm, head of the World Health Organization, finds a publication as respectable as *Science* glad to publish his article on the causes of war, in the course of which he expresses the opinion that human aggressiveness is the result of a hatred of ourselves, arising out of the fact that we have sometimes been told that we were bad. "Babies need, not just want but need, uncritical love, love whose manifestations are quite independent of the babies' behavior." Given enough "uncritical love" they will grow up free from any "conviction of sin" and therefore free of aggressive tendencies.

It may seem strange that an age which has been on the whole rather too ready to explain human behavior by analogies with that of the lower animals and decidedly adverse to admitting any fundamental distinction between animal nature and human should be so ready, in a case like this, to overlook the suggestive fact that aggressiveness manifests itself at very low levels of animal life, even among creatures who have little or no parental care and so can hardly have had any conviction of sin instilled into them. In the light of that fact it might seem reasonable to suppose that aggressiveness, instead of being the artificial product of too little "uncritical love," arises out of impulses pretty deeply implanted in living creatures; that if, in the case of man, it is not the result of "Original Sin," then it must at least be a part of his animal heritage.

Nevertheless Mr. Chisholm is doing no more than making explicit and unqualified certain notions congenial to a whole school of influential psychologists and he is willing to abandon the whole, otherwise much favored, device of animal analogy if by so doing he can emphasize still more strongly the guiltlessness and the helplessness of the individual human being, who is now invited to imitate the too advanced child in the nursery and to excuse even his "antisocial behavior" as the result of the too little "uncritical love" which has fallen to his lot.

As in so many other instances, the most "advanced" view thus neatly reverses a previous conception. The "conviction of sin" which was once supposed to be a necessary preliminary to the first step in the direction of virtue becomes, instead, the source of evil. Men who say, "We have done those things which we ought not to have done and left undone those which we ought to have done," will hate themselves and, hating themselves, they will join others to launch wars of aggression, while those who have been taught to believe that they have no power over their own actions will live in peace with their neighbors. Stripped of its modern jargon Mr. Chisholm's position seems to be essentially that of what used to be called "philosophical anarchy." Men become criminals only because laws exist and wicked only because moral precepts have been taught. Confession, instead of being good for the soul, is poison.

Perhaps comparatively few people are ready yet to subscribe without reserve to this dogma when it is so nakedly stated but it is the ultimate logical conclusion from the less obviously absurd premises which they do accept and the only escape from it lies in some qualification imposed upon the premises at some lower stage of development.

Anyone who really accepts what the head of the Society for the Prevention of Crime calls "today's thinking" will find himself compelled to say to his children, or to any other young people whom he may be called on to advise, something like this:

"Some day the time may come when you will have an opportunity to murder your grandmother and to steal her purse. Do not, if that time comes, be foolish or unenlightened. In the first place murdering one's grandmother is now called 'antisocial conduct'—which doesn't sound so bad. But that is not the real point. The real point is that if you tried to resist temptation, even if you merely tried to summon prudence, you would only be calling on consciousness for aid which consciousness, being an epiphenomenon, is powerless to give. Be modern! Stand quietly by until the event informs you whether or not the 'unique economic, sociological, and psychological factors' in your past history have determined that you will or will not hit the old lady over the head with an ax."

Most people will agree that this will hardly do. Some, even among the sturdiest upholders of "conditioning" as the ultimate cause of everything, will probably admit that being taught to believe in the impossibility of choice is, itself, a conditioning factor. They may even admit that the concept of moral responsibility is a sometimes useful illusion.

No doubt our ancestors had too much faith in the sufficiency of moral injunctions. No doubt they were too much inclined to bid children be good and adults law-abiding. They needed a Burns to remind them how

> What's done we partly may compute,
> But know not what's resisted,

though even Burns, who lived too early to meet "today's thinking," seems to assume that some resistance is possible. When Bernard Shaw, as already quoted, asserts roundly that "the only trouble with the poor is poverty," or when Anatole France celebrates the impartiality of the law by remarking that rich and poor alike are forbidden to steal bread or to sleep under the bridges, each supplies a useful corrective to an exclusively moralistic approach. But what is genuinely an extenuating circumstance is not necessarily an all-sufficient and irresistible cause.

It seems quite obvious that the complete rejection of the concept of human responsibility and of all belief in the human being's ability to do anything for himself is pragmatically impossible. A society which consistently acted on the unqualified assumption that no one could be held in any sense responsible for himself or his acts is unthinkable, and if all contrary assumptions are really based on an illusion, then that illusion is indispensable both to the life of the individual and to the life of the social organism of which he is a part.

If the social and psychological sciences, which increasingly assert either that they are demonstrating the externally determined character of all acts, opinions, and tastes or at the least that we should assume for practical purposes that they are determined, are making claims supported by the facts, then the truth which they have discovered is, literally, a deadly truth. It is something which Man cannot afford to know because he can neither know nor even believe it without ceasing to be Man and making way for that something, either better or worse, which the more apocalyptically inclined occasionally predict.

## The Minimal Man

Our discussion of "today's thinking" has turned pretty persistently around a few brief quotations from three or four of "today's thinkers"—each of whom seems to assume that Man is either "nothing but" the product of external forces operating upon him or at least so largely such that psychology, education, and government should disregard whatever autonomous powers he may have.

Mr. Lukas of the Society for the Prevention of Crime has told us that "all antisocial behavior [and presumably all prosocial behavior as well] is considered to be the result of unique economic, sociological, and psychological factors in each offender's past history." The Dean of the Humanities at the Massachusetts Institute of Technology has assumed that we shall soon be able "to control men's thoughts with precision." Professor Skinner has joyfully imagined a utopian future in which we shall all be happy and "well adjusted" because the premises of Mr. Lukas and the Dean have been made the basis of a successful technique for conditioning all men to act in a certain way and to think certain things.

Inevitably the question how "representative" these thinkers are will be raised, and inevitably some readers will object that "most" psychologists and sociologists do not go so far in this direction. Obviously it is impossible to prove what "most people" think and for our purpose it is not necessary. For the moment our purpose is to define certain ideas to which we will ultimately oppose others. And for the moment therefore, our need is to define as sharply as possible the assumptions which we intend to repudiate. At least some distinguished persons do make them in the extreme form which the quotations illustrate.

To say this is not to say that these same assumptions are not sometimes repudiated by other contemporary thinkers or even that such repudiation is not usual among those who represent the best as opposed to the lagging thinkers of our time. Choosing almost at random from among books published within the last year one might cite Reinhold Niebuhr's *The Irony of American History* which includes an attack upon the whole school of sociological determinists; Eric Voegelin's *The New Science of Politics* which reaffirms the primary reality of absolute "values"; and Nicolai Hartmann's *The New Ways of Ontology,* written to defend a middle ground between an idealism which asserts that mind plays the only decisive role in the shaping of history and a materialism which sees the universe as affected by nothing except "things."

But up to the present, at least, only a very small public is so much as aware that the points of view represented by the books just cited have ever been defined. They certainly do not represent what most men would recognize as "today's thinking," which has, so far as the general public is aware, tended to assume more and more completely that Man is largely if not absolutely determined, predictable, and controllable. Perhaps this tendency represents the thinking of yesterday rather than of today; but it is still very widely accepted by those who are molding our institutions.

If the results of this tendency seem disastrous to those who do not want to see civilization ultimately become a Walden Two, then they must ask themselves on what basis they may oppose it; to what extent they may legitimately question the supposedly proved premises on which it rests. They must ask to what extent Man may hope to make free choices; to be responsible for his own conduct; to make, rather than to have imposed upon him, value judgments.

Those of us who do insist on asking these questions will ask them in terms far more modest than were once commonly employed when it was customary to state categorically that we are all "the captains of our souls." We will not expect, hope, or perhaps even want, to believe about ourselves what men at other times took for granted. Responsibility as full and as absolute as has sometimes been assumed is a terrible burden as well as a privilege. The important roles played by the mechanisms of heredity, by forgotten psychic traumas, and by the conditioning factors in the social environment will be—and perhaps gladly—accepted, just as the effectiveness of the techniques developed for predicting and controlling the beliefs as well as the behavior of large masses of men will be acknowledged. We will not expect to be able again to exclaim "What a piece of work is man; how infinite in capacity; in understanding how like a god," while believing that statement to be a full or complete account of the kind of creature Man is. Our protest will perhaps go no further than to ask whether the rival account offered by mechanistic social psychologists is itself as full and complete as we have been assured that it is.

Perhaps, indeed, before being so bold as to ask even that question, we will pose to ourselves another so purely hypothetical that those uninterested in merely hypothetical questions will not, for the moment, need even to attend: If men must now recognize that they are no more than machines, then at what point did they forfeit the right to talk about "Man" as though he were unique? What are the *minimal* powers and characteristics one would have to possess to be worthy of the designation Man? If these minimal specifications turn out to be modest enough, then perhaps we will be permitted the question we did not dare to ask before: Do these *minimum* specifications still include things which our real knowledge of the human animal positively forbids us to attribute to it?

The more closely we examine them the more modest the minimum specifications turn out to be. They certainly do not require us to affirm that the Minimal Man is completely autonomous, never predictable, and always beyond the reach of conditioning or manipulation. It is, we must remember, not we but the mechanists who deal in absolutes and are dogmatically inclined to "nothing but" generalizations. Their claims are not minimal but maximal. The forked stick in which they hold us will hold us only so long as their arguments admit of no qualifications and no exceptions.

If men are even sometimes and to some degree capable of independent choices, then men are not wholly or always the victims of their environment. And if those who deny that men are ever to that extent free go one step beyond what their evidence proves, they cannot logically compel us to accept their conclusions. If, for instance, they are ever guilty of using the negative argument which runs: "My methods enable me to prove that so and so often happens; my methods do not enable me to prove that the contrary ever does; therefore I assume that the 'often' means 'always,'" we can reply that the assumption is no more than an assumption and that if we have reasons for doubting that assumption our reasons may be given without our being to the slightest degree "unscientific." We shall, on the contrary, be more scientific than those who assert positively what they cannot prove.

These reasons, when we come to them, will not necessarily include any denial that "man is an animal" or even, perhaps, that he is "nothing but an animal." Our minimum specifications include only capacities in which the animal may also, to some lesser degree, have his share so that between us and him there need be no absolute discontinuity. The minimal beast—who is not quite a machine—could be a beast who has started on the road which leads ultimately to the minimal man and we still may be brothers because we both may be children of Nature rather than of God.

Grant us only that what we call "reasoning" is not always rationalization; that consciousness can sometimes be more than merely an epiphenomenon accompanying behavior; that "value judgments," even if never more than "tastes" or "preferences," are nevertheless not absolutely and "nothing but" what we have been conditioned to accept—grant us this, and those minimal concessions will free us from the dilemma in which the refusal to make them has placed us. They are levers with which, once more, we can move our world. They may possibly make us again "good enough to survive"; they are even more likely to make survival seem worth having. Perhaps they may also relieve us of that burden of anxiety and guilt which the sense that we had surrendered our humanity imposed on us.

Instead of saying to himself, "I am the product of my environment and will be compelled both to believe and to do what my infantile conditioning and my social environment have predetermined," the Minimal Man would say to himself something like this: "I am both an individual and part of an aggregate. The behavior of that aggregate, as statistically measured, may be something to some large extent determined by forces outside any individual, because most individuals do not exercise even to the degree of which they are capable the minimal freedom which, for them also, could exist. To some extent I no doubt move with that aggregate, doing what it does, thinking what it thinks, and I am perhaps destined to meet the fate it meets. But there is also some area of possibility within which I can move as an independent particle. I have some scope for choice and action. I have my realm of freedom as well as my realm of contingency. Henceforward, I shall cultivate an awareness of that realm of freedom, refuse to deny its existence just because it has, in my time, been less investigated and emphasized than the realm of bondage. I shall do at least part of my thinking on the premise that such a realm exists for others as well as for me. I shall live part of my inner as well as part of my outer life where I am aware of the extent to which I am free rather than of the extent to which I am not.

"Who knows how large that area of freedom is; how influential the example I set may be; or within what limits the behavior of the aggregate itself may be changed if some considerable number of the atoms which compose it realize that atoms, even the atoms of dead matter, do not, as individuals, obey the statistical laws of determinism? I shall act as though I were at least a Minimal Man and perhaps I will discover that this Minimal Man is 'good enough to survive.'"

*       *       *

After he had completed his visit to Walden Two, the narrator in Mr. Skinner's fantasy summarized some of the conclusions to which he had been led. For society as a whole to achieve what had been accomplished there: "Education would have to abandon the technical limitations it had imposed upon itself and step forth into the broader sphere of human engineering. Nothing short of the complete revision of a culture would suffice."

The words chosen are gentle and reassuring; very much indeed like that other gentle term "re-education," which we have recently seen given in other lands a new and terrifying definition. But what can the gentle terms used by Mr. Skinner really mean? What does it mean for "education to abandon the technical limitations which it has imposed upon itself" if it does not mean that it shall stop concerning itself with those processes of education which put their faith in the effectiveness of the cultivated powers of reasoning and go in for "conditioning" instead? What can "going forth into the broader sphere of human engineering" mean if it does not mean undertaking to do with men what the experimental psychologist has learned how to do with rats? What does "the complete revision of a culture" imply if it does not imply, as it always has ended by implying: those who will not accept re-education will have to be liquidated?

Considerations like those which have occupied the past few pages cannot, of course, have any real meaning unless the Minimal Man really exists. If it has been conclusively demonstrated that all animals, including Man, are merely machines, and that the behavior of a machine is fully determined; if what seems uncontrollable and unpredictable is only that which we have not yet learned enough about; then the assumption that some realm of freedom exists is an impossible assumption. Before we go any further with it we should examine a little more closely the proofs offered by those who assert that it is.

Have they or have they not proved as much as they sometimes say that they have? Do they themselves sometimes go beyond their own evidence? Are they guilty of claiming to have ruled out a possibility when they have actually done no more than say, "What we have been unable to measure or use by the methods we have chosen and for the purposes we have in mind, does not exist." Finally, and if their negative proofs turn out to be less than final, we should ask ourselves what positive reasons we ourselves may have for believing that what has not been proved impossible may in fact be both possible and actual.

❋    ❋    ❋

The more absolute and unqualified the contentions of any mechanist happen to be, the more likely he is to insist that "science proves" them true. Let us consider for a moment, not the persuasiveness of his theories, but the extent to which they have actually been demonstrated. How much of his creed do we have to accept simply because we cannot do otherwise?

To begin with, it is certainly not true that "today's thinking" is the inescapable result of what the laboratory has demonstrated. Merely to watch Pavlov's dogs or somebody else's rats would not, by itself, lead any sane man to say, "Obviously, free will is dead." The fact that the digestive juices begin to run in the canine stomach when the dinner bell rings does not, after all, demonstrate that all antisocial behavior is the result of individual conditioning! Neither, for that matter, is anything of the sort really demonstrated by the success of the advertiser in selling his wares or even the success—when he has it—of the sociologist in re-educating the delinquent youth.

By themselves such facts are perfectly compatible with the simultaneous existence of a realm of freedom. No one ever doubted that the Maximal, much less the Minimal, Man is sometimes and to some extent influenced by his circumstances. Even those who in the past have seen the human story as a drama of the individual soul freely choosing Good or Evil have recognized readily enough that this individual soul may be corrupted by the world. A Christian who prays, "Lead us not into temptation," thereby confesses that what we do may be in part dependent on the circumstances in which we find ourselves. But he does not conclude therefore that the conduct of all men depends on "nothing but" the temptations to which they are exposed.

The social scientist who has observed that gangsters often grow up in the slums and who leaps from that to the conclusion that nothing except the slum environment can have counted in determining the results is making a very large assumption indeed. So far as logical necessity goes he is not compelled to say—as he usually does—that "antisocial behavior" is always the result of individual conditioning. It would be at least as logical to say instead, "Since all men do not always do what my techniques are intended to make them do and the boy who grew up next door to the criminal sometimes turns out to be a reformer instead of a gangster, I therefore assume that certain factors are operative other than those on which my manipulative techniques are based."

When, on the contrary, he explains his failures by saying that they are due simply to a not yet perfected technique or to the presence of conditioning factors somehow overlooked, he may be advancing a tenable hypothesis but he has certainly left the realm of direct evidence for the realm of the hypothetical. He has conclusive evidence to prove only what even the most unqualified believer in free will is ready to grant—namely that men can be influenced. He has not presented evidence to *prove* that all human actions are determined. The possible reasons for believing that some realm of freedom does exist cannot be thus ruled out.

To proceed from the actual evidence accumulated in the laboratory, the sociological clinic and the advertising agency to the inclusive propositions often accepted by "today's thinking," one must accept, not merely the evidence itself, but a whole towering structure of assumptions, inferences, guesses and wild leaps across yawning lacunae.

All the real evidence in favor of mechanistic assumptions is partial. All the arguments against any other assumption are merely negative. They consist in saying only, "I have evidence that the body resembles, in certain respects, a machine; I have evidence also that the mind can, in certain ways and to a certain extent, be conditioned. Therefore I assume that nothing not explicable in mechanist terms exists."

Moreover, even this negative evidence is not so impressive as it is usually assumed to be. Once it has been admitted that human behavior has its mechanical aspects, then it ought to be obvious that these are the aspects which the methods appropriate to the study of a mechanism will most readily reveal. If you study Man by the method suited to chemistry, or even if you study him in the light of what you have learned about rats and dogs, it is certainly to be expected that what you discover will be what chemistry and animal behavior have to teach. But it is also not surprising or even significant if by such methods you fail to discover anything else.

When the behavior of lower animals is being investigated, the orthodox biologist constantly warns us that we must be on our guard against "anthropomorphic" interpretations. We are, he says, all too prone to assume that a given action means what it would mean if the animal were human and tend therefore to think of the birds and beasts as much more like human beings than they are. But at least one distinguished student of behavior, Dr. Konrad Lorenz, has called attention to an opposite, equally serious, source of error. And he has named it "mechanomorphism."

When we assume that animals are human we no doubt see human traits which are nonexistent. But when we assume that they are machines we make a mechanistic interpretation which may be equally wide of the mark. It is no easier to read *in* than it is to read *out*. And as really philosophical scientists are coming more and more to realize, the experimenter, the instruments he uses, and the hypotheses which he adopts, are all parts of the experiment and help determine its results. In the broadest possible sense, therefore, the kind of perfect detachment which science once hoped to achieve is impossible.

What many psychologists and social scientists seem to be doing is to denounce as a kind of "anthropomorphism" every attempt to interpret even human behavior on the assumption that men are men; to insist that we should proceed as though they were mere animals at most, even if not mere machines in the end. But how can Anthropos be understood except in anthropomorphic terms? Why should we assume that the mechanomorphic error is not really an error at all?

That nineteenth-century scientist who said that he refused to believe in the soul because "I cannot find it in my test tube" made a singularly foolish remark for the simple reason that a test tube is the last place in which a soul would be likely to be found even if, by chance, it did happen to exist. When the scientist replies to this objection by saying that every science must use the methods at its disposal, and that it cannot be expected to concern itself with anything with which it has no method of dealing, it is a legitimate reply—if no attempt is made to make it go beyond what it actually says. But scientists—who do not always share the infallibility and impartiality attributed to science itself—sometimes do, like the chemist who could not find the soul, go a long way beyond.

As a matter of fact they have developed what may be called a standard technique for going that long way without seeming too obviously to do so. The statement that something "does not exist for the purposes of my science" and the statement, "therefore I can never know anything about it" become, no less easily, "what we cannot know anything about does not exist." By that simple process the experimental psychologist can get rid of the whole possibility of a realm of freedom quite as easily as the orthodox Behaviorist got rid of consciousness.

Neither the strength nor the weakness of the modern determinist's position was ever more clearly revealed in a short statement than in a speech by Frazier, the benevolent manipulator of his subjects in Walden Two: "I deny that freedom exists at all. I must deny it—or my program is absurd. You cannot have a science about a subject matter which hops capriciously about. Perhaps we can never *prove* that man isn't free; it's an assumption. But the increasing success of a science of behavior makes it more and more plausible."

Mr. Skinner puts this speech into the mouth of a character and one cannot therefore assume that he takes full responsibility for it. But he must have thought that it at least represented a point of view with which he had a good deal of sympathy and it provides a manageable opportunity to examine the concrete claims and professions of faith which a typical exponent of "today's thinking" will make.

Let us suppose by way of parallel that a theologian should reply, "I affirm that God exists. I must affirm it or my whole program is absurd. You can't have a science of God unless God exists. Perhaps I can never *prove* that He does; it's an assumption. But the long-continued success of religion in dealing with men's souls makes it more and more plausible to say that He does."

Frazier would undoubtedly, and very justifiably, reply that this theologian was simply arguing in a circle. To say that God must exist because I would be talking nonsense if he did not, opens the way to the retort: "That is, my dear sir, precisely what you are doing. By admission you start with an unprovable assumption and you certainly have no right, in the name of either logic or yesterday's thinking, to insist that this assumption is inescapable. By your own admission it is 'plausible' at best and it can be plausible only if (1) you can really show me that you have had 'continuing success' and (2) that the success which you have had is not explicable on the basis of any other assumption."

Yet obviously Frazier's own position is precisely parallel to that of our theologian. Admittedly he is proceeding on an assumption, not on a demonstrated fact, and his argument could be restated something like this: "I desire a Science of Man. Without determinism, what I call a science cannot exist. Therefore determinism can be assumed." So far as pure logic goes that is no better than saying, "I desire a philosophical system of ethics; without assuming that man is free there can be no such philosophy of ethics; therefore man is free." But the necessity for a Science of Man in the sense implied by Frazier is no more self-evident than the necessity for a philosophy of ethics and any argument based on the assumption that it is, is again an argument based on *pure* assumption.

Mr. Frazier goes on to add: "I didn't say that behavior is always predictable, any more than weather is always predictable. There are often too many factors to be taken into account. We can't measure them all accurately, and we couldn't perform the mathematical operations needed to make the prediction if we had the measurements." But when he says this he is not only making another assumption—namely, that the unpredictable is nevertheless the determined—but making the very one which physics abandoned when it frankly acknowledged the opposite. The argument "I can't have a Science of Man without believing thus and so" is an argument completely without force unless one takes it for granted both that it is necessary to have such a science and that this science cannot exist if it recognizes something which physicists have been successfully recognizing for more than a generation.

If anything remains of Frazier's argument it is only the pragmatic boast "increasing success." But in what, one may ask, does that success really consist and by what standards is "success" to be judged? For the sake of argument one may grant that the Science of Man has successfully predicted and to some extent determined what the mass audience of the movies and the radio will like. Manufacturers of breakfast foods and lipsticks are enthusiastic about the results achieved. But the successes claimed in, say, education and criminology are not equally obvious. Its methods have been increasingly accepted and used but is it really beyond dispute that the graduate of a high school or a college is better educated than he used to be? On the other hand, it is universally admitted that both juvenile delinquency and adult crime are increasing. Is this in spite of improved scientific methods of combating them? Or is it, as a theologian might argue, *because* of them?

To what indubitable success in dealing with the most intelligent section of the public or with the highest activities of the mind can the Science of Man point? What genius or saint has ever become what he is by being "conditioned" as such? Has any Walden Two, even, been successfully established, and does either the successful conditioning of rats or the successful prediction that more people will listen to a jazz band than to a symphony orchestra give any very convincing proof that it could be?

The very word "success" is highly ambiguous unless somehow one makes it clear whether it is to be taken to mean "achieving limited ends without regard to their value" or "achieving something which we regard as desirable." Frazier uses it in the first sense when he is claiming that certain techniques can be made to work; in the second sense when he implies one of those value judgments which he claims never to make and asks us to surrender ourselves to his techniques because they are "successful" in the sense of promoting the Good Life. Yet the "success" on which his argument finally rests is dubious when dealing with any but the crudest manifestations of human nature; worse than dubious insofar as it implies that the Good Life has been promoted. "Psychology" has taught the merchant that he can charge more for "fat-free milk" than he could if he called it "skimmed," but it has not made it any easier to write a *Hamlet*. Advertising, not culture, is the most characteristic product of the scientific study of the mind on mechanistic principles.

When even a Frazier is compelled to admit that human conduct cannot always be predicted and that the unreality of individual freedom cannot be proved, it is obvious that a readiness to accept a purely mechanistic Science of Man does not rest on any ground more solid than the conviction that its premises are the most probable and the most useful. But if anyone doubts that the validity of such a purely mechanistic Science of Man is still being insisted upon by responsible persons, even outside the social sciences, he may consult a book recently addressed to the uninstructed by Dr. G. Gamow, Professor of Theoretical Physics at George Washington University, entitled *Mr. Tompkins Learns the Facts of Life,* and published by the Cambridge University Press. Defending mechanism, Dr. Gamow writes, "The mechanistic point of view is . . . that all phenomena observed in the living organism can be reduced in the end to regular physical laws governing the atoms of which that organism is constructed, and that the difference lies entirely in the relative complexity of living and non-living matter. According to this point of view, basic manifestations of life like *growth, motion, reproduction,* and even *thinking* . . . can be accounted for, at least in principle, by the same basic laws of physics which determine ordinary inorganic processes."

While the whole tendency of our generation has been toward a more and more general acceptance of the notion that a mechanism of some sort *must* be the explanation of every social or psychic phenomenon, the tendency has also been to acknowledge at the same time that the supposed mechanism is more complicated and subtle than the first mechanists supposed. Few would now be satisfied to say, as Descartes said in the seventeenth century, that animals "act naturally and by springs like a watch"; or, as the idea was elaborated by Malebranche, that all mere animals "eat without pleasure, they cry without pain, they grow without knowing it; they desire nothing, they fear nothing, they know nothing." Even fewer would accept as adequate the pronouncement of the eighteenth-century psychologist Cabanis that "the brain secretes thought as the liver secretes bile." Yet too many fail to perceive that the overwhelming arguments against any such absurd formulations are not actually removed simply by positing a more and more "subtle" machine whose methods of operation are never clearly explained. As a matter of fact, Professor Gamow's position, stripped of its hocus-pocus, is actually almost the same as that of Cabanis.

When, on the other hand, a Skinner brings himself to admit that the science of physics has itself abandoned the theory of absolute determinism, at least so far as the ultimate particles of matter are concerned, he can add only, "This question of microscopic indeterminacy is not awfully relevant here, because if we could do as much with human behavior as the physicist can do with physical nature (in spite of his admission that in the last analysis he isn't quite sure of a number of things), we could make decisions on some very important problems."

So indeed we could. So indeed, alas, we have done. And perhaps the most important of these decisions is the one which Mr. Skinner makes at the same moment that he declares it to be possible—the decision, that is, to regard all social and moral problems as problems of engineering and to treat the possible autonomy of the individual human being in exactly the same way that orthodox physicists treated the unpredictability of the atom —as long as they were able to do so. These physicists disregarded the "freedom of the atom" as a negligible annoyance of no importance so far as the control of the macroscopic aspects of physical nature is concerned; Mr. Skinner suggests that the possible freedom of the individual be disregarded in the same way. In the end, however, the physicist found that he could no longer disregard it, and as everyone now knows, the most concentrated source of power which science has ever released was made accessible, not by the old physics, but by the new, which accepted and studied the very phenomena that the old had dismissed as negligible. Perhaps it may someday turn out that in the microscopic freedom of the individual rather than in the macroscopic predictability and controllability of the mass resides a releasable force as much more powerful than any which the mechanistic psychology can manipulate as the energy within the atom is more powerful than that within the more predictable aggregate called a molecule.

To deny that the hypotheses of either the fictional Frazier or the very real Professor Gamow actually are the most useful for the promotion of a good life or a good society has been the purpose of much that has so far been said in the course of the present discussion. In this section of that discussion it has been suggested also that even the degree of probability claimed for the hypotheses may not be so great as is often assumed. Would any age before our own have been so readily convinced that man is nothing in himself, or would it, above all, have assumed so readily that to doubt his ability to do anything for himself is a useful or helpful doubt?

## The Old-Fashioned Science of Man

In the course of this discussion reference has been made more than once to the support given by recent science to those who find a paradoxical universe less difficult to believe in than the supposedly understandable one which mechanists undertake to picture. To us it seems that thought, consciousness and the power to choose are realities no matter how difficult they are to reconcile with those other realities which the mechanists stress, and we can say in our defense that both the physicist and the physiologist are now inclined to make the same choice we make when faced with the same difficulty. To them also it seems that they must either reject some of their data or admit that they cannot understand how some of it can be reconciled with the rest. And they also have decided to accept the data which they cannot wholly understand.

What this means is that the mysterious or the incomprehensible is again being recognized by the very sciences which were once supposed to be the implacable enemies of all unsolvable mysteries. And what this seems to mean in turn is that we are now on the point of entering upon a new phase of human thought at least as radically new as any we ever entered before. We had become accustomed to speak of ancient, of medieval, and of "modern" views of the universe and also to assume that the modern had now been established as somehow permanent. But if those physicists are right who remark quite casually that the revolution which the last few years has witnessed in their science is at least as fundamental as the revolution which took place in the sixteenth and seventeenth centuries when the "modern" view assumed definite shape, then the time may be approaching when "modern" will have to mean not the world view of the Newtonian but something quite different, and we shall have to find a new adjective to distinguish the first "scientific world view" from that which has taken its place.

Moreover, and what is perhaps not really surprising, the new "modern view" turns out to be, in at least one respect, more like the medieval than it is like that which immediately preceded it. It recognizes that the human mind is incapable of understanding the universe in quite the sense that nineteenth-century science believed it was on the point of understanding it.

Since the possibility that the revolution may be fully accomplished in time to save us from certain consequences of mechanistic hypotheses is one of the chief themes of this book, it may be worthwhile to examine more closely than we have so far done some of the things that the revolution implies and some of the ways in which the most modern view of the universe resembles—as well as some in which it differs from—that accepted by those who lived before the first great Age of Science opened. To do so will mean to think for a few minutes, first about what the contemporaries of Newton had to say to those who were still living in Dante's world, and then what the new physicist has to say to those of our contemporaries who are still living in Newton's.

Let us begin by remembering that at the center of Dante's conception of the visible world there was an accepted mystery. The stars in their courses moved in the paths which God had ordained, and this visible world was held together by something called "Love." But there was no attempt to understand the laws in accordance with which this Love operated except in the most general terms—no attempt, for example, to ask in accordance with what law love moved one celestial sphere at one speed and another at another. Perhaps just because Dante's contemporaries felt so sure that they knew the answer to the question "why" the universe existed, they never asked very persistently the question "how" or "in what fashion."

Newton substituted the technical word "gravity" for the frankly mysterious word "love," and he also went on to assure us that the farthest reaches of the universe operate in accordance with the same ascertainable laws that operate upon an apple or, as later philosophers preferred to put it, upon a billiard ball. Though Newton piously assumed that God does, nevertheless, still exist somewhere, he seemed to go a long way toward depriving Him of a continuing function.

What he told us was that in the whole vast extent of the visible universe there is nothing which is not essentially like our own backyard. Let us accept—as we all do—the simple fact that an apple falls. Let us then learn—as we can—the laws which govern the way in which it falls. Once we have done that, there is nothing within the range of our eyes, our telescopes, or even of our imagination that is not explicable by an extension of simple, pragmatic, common sense. There are no mysteries and no paradoxes, at least so far as the *way* in which the tangible universe behaves. So far as it is concerned we know perfectly well what to expect. The heavens are not going to fall unless and until God suddenly and willingly intervenes to blow a last trump. Until then we can say that $S = \frac{1}{2}gt^2$ and that $\frac{ds}{dt} = gt$. That is all there is to it.

This Newtonian universe may be a little bit dull, but at least there is nothing about it to provoke anxiety until the day of the last trump. Even now most people instinctively try to live in it. The general temper which it expresses is the one to which they try to cling, and it is only upon the periphery of their consciousnesses, upon that periphery where anxieties are generated, that they permit themselves to be somewhat vaguely aware of what the newer science in which they profess also to believe has done to this dully uniform and regular universe.

To take a single instance, we are being told by at least certain of Newton's successors that instead of living in an infinitely extended backyard, even the backyard is not at all what it seems; that so far as the universe as a whole is concerned we do not know how it is operating or where it is going; that common sense is wholly inadequate to comprehend it, and that, insofar as one can guess, we are actually somewhere in a sort of soap bubble which is expanding at an inconceivable but ever increasing rate and, for all we know, may burst. Obviously this universe seems a great deal less dependable, a great deal more an occasion for a certain amount of anxiety, than Newton's was. It is also a great deal more mysterious and a great deal more repugnant to common sense than even Dante's. We seem, in other words, to have come a full circle—out of what we used to call the darkness of ignorance into the light of common day, and then back again into the incomprehensible.

When what we still carelessly call the "modern" world view began to take shape in the seventeenth century, it was the result of a revolt of common sense against everything that was repugnant to it. It was a declaration of faith in the senses as opposed to the speculative mind and in the visible world as opposed to the unseen. Today, however, we are beginning to admit that common sense has been defeated again. Once more we live in a universe which is not at all what it seems, either to the senses or to common sense. Even the external world which we think we see does not exist in the form in which it is present to us. What we think we see with our eyes or touch with our hands seems to us to exist in that form only because our senses give us a false, or at least a grossly inaccurate, report of it; and hence even the world of matter as we think we perceive it is as illusory as it was ever said by the mystics to be.

To them the world was all Spirit. By us it is now said to be all Energy.

But to Animal Faith, to everyday experience, to that common sense to which the first modern scientists appealed, the one is as essentially meaningless as the other, and a Bacon, a Hobbes or, for that matter, a Lucretius would have seen little to choose between them. The doctrine of the Trinity was once thought to be hard to swallow. How, asked rationalists, can what is Three be also One? But how, for that matter, can time curve back upon itself or the finite universe be a sphere beyond whose boundaries there is not even nothingness—unless perhaps there are other finite universes. Can anyone maintain that the mysteries of the Trinity are any more mysterious than curving space? What can any modern physicist do except echo the phrase commonly attributed in garbled form to Tertullian and once regarded as the very ecstasy of unreason: "I believe because it is impossible"?

Moreover, the internal world as it is described by the "new psychology" is as contrary to our own conscious experience as is the external world described by the physicists. We are told, to begin with, that consciousness is only a small part, often a self-deceiving part, of our total selves. Both our thoughts and our actions are usually determined by mental processes of which we are unaware, and if it is at all possible for us to obey the classical injunction, "Know thyself," it is certainly not possible by any sort of mere self-examination.

When a medieval man committed a crime he might very well be in doubt why he did so. So far as what we should call his conscious mind was concerned, it may have seemed to him that he simply consented to wickedness. But he thought he knew, as many of us again think we know, that one is aware of only a very small part of what goes on in himself, that we are often under the domination of what the medieval man called "spiritual forces" and we call "the unconsciousness." In either case certain forces of which he or we can have no conscious knowledge were at work. To him there was always the possibility that a demon had tempted him; to us there is always the possibility—some would say the certainty—that some conditioning had made it inevitable that we should come to what appears to us as simply an evil decision.

It must be remembered moreover that the proofs offered by theologians on the one hand, and by social psychologists on the other, of the truths of their premises are essentially similar and come down in the end to pragmatic demonstrations addressed, as the theories are not, to common sense. Thus social psychologists offer to demonstrate that the criminal has been conditioned; that slums breed crime; and that bad boys become good boys when provided with a proper environment. In the Middle Ages, on the contrary, it seemed, and probably was equally evident, that conversion to Christianity often produced reform and that a man who was persuaded to repent often led a godly life henceforth. Certainly the saints were often genuinely saintly. It would be difficult to prove that modern education has ever produced superior prodigies of heroism and selflessness. But in either case only inference can assign a cause since in both cases the cause is said to lie outside the realm of direct self-knowledge.

The question at issue is not whether one theory is truer than the other. It is quite possible that the unconsciousness does exist and that demons do not. But the fact remains that the medieval mind accepted and the present-day mind again accepts a physical world which is not what it seems and a mental world which is dominated by forces of which it has no conscious awareness. These physical and mental worlds are more alike than the one is like the physical world of Newton or the other like the mental world of Hobbes, Locke, or even Hume. Willy-nilly we have become mystagogues again.

On the whole we are probably quite right to assume that the unconsciousness does exist. But it is a curious fact that Freud should remain in many of his attitudes so much a child of the Enlightenment despite that fact that he has based everything on a concept which would have seemed to the Enlightenment itself as dubious as, for instance, Conscience or the Voice of God. Freud himself, and even more conspicuously his more positivistic followers, dismiss with bluff contempt such concepts as "God," the "Soul," and the "Sense of Sin." In a manner strongly suggestive of the Enlightenment, they reinterpret all these as explicable divagations of the understandable processes of the mind. They will have nothing to do with the ineffable and the mysterious—or rather nothing to do with mysteries which are not new mysteries. Yet the truth is, of course, that the unconsciousness is as purely hypothetical as the Soul and that certain of Freud's other key concepts—notably that of the Censor—are obviously devoid of any objectively demonstrable correlatives and that they are sometimes admitted, even by those who employ them, to be no more than metaphors serving to recognize the existence of something whose nature and mode of operations are both uncomprehended. No anatomist can tell us in neurological terms how the Censor operates.

Once Freudianism was accepted, it put an end to the whole nineteenth-century dream of making the science of the mind a physical or physiological science. Freud himself stopped looking in the physical brain for the evidence or the cause of mental phenomena. To some extent he tried to conceal the real nature of what he was doing by calling the disorders "functional"; but that is largely a matter of vocabulary. What he really did was to reintroduce the concept of the Soul and that fact cannot be concealed by using only the Greek for it and calling it always the Psyche. To the old jibe of the materialist who said that he had never been able to find a soul in his test tube might be added a new one: "I have never been able to find a Censor there either."

Clerk-Maxwell's famous joke about his inability to explain what really happens during the interchange of two gases at different temperatures except on the assumption of a trap door operated by a demon who decides to exclude certain molecules while allowing others to pass, has turned out to be no joke. Demons of one kind or another have again become, as in the Middle Ages they were, indispensable in all kinds of sciences, from physics, which used to be no more than simple mechanics, to psychology which some of its earlier students tried to make no more than a matter of physiology. As William James was already insisting more than a generation ago, the Newtonian billiard-ball universe no longer affords a tenable description of even mechanical processes. Yet both the average man and the thinking man try desperately to hold onto it, and refuse to accept the full consequences of the fact that the whole universe has again become a paradox.

During the Enlightenment physics set itself up as the avowed enemy of metaphysics. It came to be asserted finally that if we would only cease to bother about the "why" and confine ourselves exclusively to the question "how," there would no longer be any permanently disputable subjects. To this day the positivist philosophers try to dispose of the traditional problems of philosophy by declaring that they are devoid of meaning and do not need to be asked. But one obvious result of the "new" physics and the "new" psychology has been to reintroduce them—often in almost identical form—and to make them crucial in any attempt to understand even the "how." Thus if the terms "Psyche" and "unconsciousness" are more than metaphors and therefore really science rather than mere poetry, they raise again the whole problem of the relation between body and mind, thought and chemistry.

No metaphysical question is more traditional, more elusive, or more thorny. None presents more persistently that evidence of its genuineness which consists in the fact that it arises no matter on what level of subtlety one operates. To the naïve it used to be simply the question of how the Soul got into the body, or what intercourse the one had with the other, and in what form the one persisted after the other had ceased to function.

But the problem continued to plague the subtlest and most abstract analysis when it reappeared in the form of the question what sort of traffic "thought" could have with "matter"; how the *Idea* of an object could be produced by the object itself.

The Idea is self-evident to the mind which is aware of it; the material object is merely inferred from the presence of the Idea. But the two realities—if indeed the second is assumed to be real at all—are qualitatively and absolutely distinct; seem to have their being in discontinuous realms. And it was this fact which drove Berkeley to the famous paradox which has often been dismissed but never logically resolved. For Berkeley did not deny that matter exists. What he did maintain was that *if* matter existed *merely* as matter, we could not possibly be aware of it, since the "ideas" which we have of matter are obviously not material and cannot be part of it. If, therefore, these ideas do arise out of and do correspond to the thing called matter, then matter itself must be dual. It must, in accord with the Platonic notion, be ideal as well as material and the only contact which our minds can have with it must be via that ideal aspect which corresponds to our own idea.

Now the most curious and most important fact is that while the "new" psychology calls renewed attention to the body-mind problem, the "new" physics suggests a different approach to that problem by its own novel solution of what looks like an analogous problem. To common sense and to classical physics alike the fundamentally different realities called Matter and Energy seem as absolutely different in their nature and substance as Mind and Body, or Mind and Matter. Every elementary textbook used to begin by defining the two as ultimates, each to be accepted without further analysis and impossible in any way to equate. That both exist and that both are primary is insisted on with the same lack of qualification that one would expect to find in the case of Mind or Soul and Matter as defined in the first paragraph of a popular treatise on religion.

The question how Energy or even Force could operate upon Matter involved a metaphysical question closely analogous to that of the Mind-Matter question. Long before the almost apocalyptic proclamation of Einstein's conversion formula the concept of Gravity had troubled the thoughtful and come to seem actually as incomprehensible as Dante's Love and superior to it as an explanation of what moves the material masses of the universe only because it could be mathematically formulated, not at all because it seemed to mean any more. Here was a Force—the most all-pervasive of all Forces—and yet one which not only affected the material without being itself material but was, in other ways, even more mysterious than other forces because it was omnipresent, invariable, and not to be modified. Indeed, many began to suspect that Gravity was not a Force at all, that the fact that we had to call on it to explain the universe indicated some radical error in our conception of the real universe in which Gravity might be not a separate thing but something inherent in the nature of Matter existing in space-time.

But the possible solution of the special problem of Gravity seems relatively quite unimportant by comparison with the solution of the whole Matter-Energy problem. The formula $E = MC^2$ (now repeated in many popular discussions almost as a kind of incantation) actually does have implications sensational beyond those of any other formula whatsoever. What it says is that the only two supposedly primary, discontinuous, fundamentally different realities of the physical universe are not discontinuous or fundamentally different at all, that instead of being qualitatively different they are actually quantitatively convertible. Moreover, the operation of the atom bomb is said to give empirical evidence of the truth of the revolutionary pronouncement. Thus the writing of the formula followed by the practical experiment makes the whole situation very much like the one which might arise if it were suddenly announced that so much body was the equivalent of so much mind, or so much Matter the equivalent of so much Idea, and if the possibility of the conversion of one into the other were then demonstrated by the disappearance of part of an object when some mind became aware of it.

Inevitably a new possibility now suggests itself. Perhaps the positivists who argue that we ask meaningless questions are right in a way they did not suspect. Perhaps the questions how mind can occupy a body or how a force can operate upon matter are meaningless questions because they are based on the false assumption that in both cases two different kinds of reality are involved. Perhaps the materialist and the idealist, the mechanist and the vitalist are not disputing about anything which is real. What is the use of declaring that Man is a Machine or that Man is a Spirit; that thought is a chemical process in the brain, or that thought cannot be reduced to physical processes; what is the meaning of such disputes if the distinction between the material and the nonmaterial is as unreal as the distinction between matter and energy.

If this is not a universe composed of Matter *and* Energy but of Matter-Energy why should it be assumed that it must remain, nevertheless, one which is either Material or Ideal? To suppose that it may, on the contrary, be both; that what we call "matter" is one manifestation of "thought," is no more repugnant to common sense or experience than the declaration that matter and energy are different manifestations of the same thing. It is ridiculous for anyone to say that he is a materialist or a vitalist when we cannot know what the distinction between the two is unless we are sure, as now we are not, what matter may be capable of.

That the so-called Galileo-Newton revolution was not a revolution at all in the same sense that the Einsteinian revolution genuinely is, can be easily illustrated by a comparison of a formulation typical of each. Such a formulation will show very well how the one stayed within the bonds of common sense and the other did not.

$S = \frac{1}{2}gt^2$ describes the way in which a falling body—for instance the legendary apple of Newton's tree—falls. It states that the distance which it falls in a given time is equal to one half the square of the number of seconds it has been falling, multiplied by a number "g" which varies slightly at different points on the earth. Everyone who had ever used his senses to observe the phenomenon knew that such a body fell faster and faster the longer it fell. All that this formula does is to describe more accurately, by reducing to quantitative terms, what experience had taught. To extend it as Newton did to the whole solar system involves nothing paradoxical. All you have to do is to state that wherever in the universe two bodies are falling toward one another they do so in a manner described by the same law—"g" in every case being taken to be a constant defined by the mass of one body in relation to the mass of the other and by the distance between them. The only effect of this announcement is to make the universe seem more regular, more uniform, and more dependable than it was previously known to be. It is not at all to violate the common sense but rather to confirm it.

On the other hand, to say with Einstein that $E = MC^2$ is to say something entirely different in its effect. To assert that matter can be turned into energy, that a given mass is equivalent to an amount of energy equal to that mass multiplied by (of all things!) the square of the speed of light, is to fly in the face of all ordinary experience. In Newton's case the novelty consisted chiefly in reducing the thing to exact measurement. In Einstein's case the startling fact is not the statement how much matter is equivalent to how much energy but simply the assumption that the two are somehow equivalent—which is an assumption common sense would never have made.

To be told that on the deserts of New Mexico and in the air above Japan certain lumps of matter simply ceased to be, is to be told something which common sense—confirmed by all science which could claim to be merely an extension of common sense—would call impossible nonsense. To be told further that the process is no doubt reversible, that matter may disappear and then be created again, is to be compelled to reconsider our most fundamental assumptions concerning the nature of reality. What was once ultimate is ultimate no longer. What we once thought of as the inexplicable and never-to-be-repeated first creation of matter may be taking place every day. Newton told us that the mysterious heavens were as knowable to common sense as our own backyard; Einstein tells us that our own backyard is as mysterious as the heavens were ever supposed to be.

Samuel Johnson was once asked whether he thought that anybody believed the truths of religion *in the same sense* that he believed the facts of everyday life; and Dr. Johnson, profoundly religious though he was, replied with a categorical "No, sir." The incident reminds us that "levels of belief" are very real and that Animal Faith is usually stronger than belief of any other kind. Does anybody, one must therefore ask, believe the truths of the newest science in the same sense that he believes the facts of everyday life? And the answer should be an equally categorical "No."

Probably most of us do not even believe that the sun is ninety million miles away in the same sense we believe that the post office is five blocks from our front door. But our difficulty in believing that is only the difficulty of believing something quantitatively outside our experience rather than contrary to it. Most of us therefore probably do believe it in some sense which may be less than our belief in what Animal Faith consents to, while it is nevertheless stronger than our belief in things like the matter-energy transformation which are not only outside of, but also repugnant to, experience.

Nevertheless the fact remains that the more different levels of belief on which the mind is compelled to operate and the less clear the distinctions between them, the more difficult it becomes for us really to "know our own minds." And though the scientific age began with the determination to eliminate as far as possible all those levels which could not be reconciled with Animal Faith, it has ended by reintroducing them, so that our position has become more analogous to that of the fifteenth-century man who did not know whether or not he believed in Hell, than it is to that of the nineteenth-century scientific mind which was far more certain of what it genuinely believed and far less given to asserting belief in what it was actually only trying to understand.

Of course no one can be sure that this state of affairs is permanent.

Certain of the most ineffable conceptions of mathematical physics, like curved space and spherical time, may someday again be dismissed as impossible fancies. But it is not likely that the backyard universe will ever be re-established unless civilization and the human mind should devolve to some condition where much that has been discovered and thought is lost.

Moreover, and what is more important for the moment, the probabilities are that at least for some time to come, science is going to be less and less translatable into common-sense terms. It seems reasonable to conclude that the man who wishes to understand the world in which he lives will do well to accept the fact and to stop attempting, as he so often does attempt, to understand more of it in terms of common sense and old-fashioned science than can actually be understood in those terms.

Our inconsistencies are most glaring in such areas as those of politics, sociology and morals, where the methods employed are least clearly defined. There, empirical snap judgments, the prejudices of Animal Faith, and scientific pretensions of some sort, all meet. And the fact that they all do meet there helps explain why these so-called Sciences of Man, even when they are scientific at all, tend to lag so far behind the physical sciences—not only (as is generally admitted) in their results, but also (as is not so generally admitted) in respect to the very premises on which they are founded. It explains why, to put the thing as bluntly as possible, the theories and methods most prevalent among social scientists are mechanistic, deterministic, and materialistic; why they cling so stubbornly to old-fashioned prejudices against admitting the existence of intangibles and unpredictables; why they continue to do so when the actual sciences dealing with a physical world much less complicated than the human world have completely abandoned the attempt to describe or deal with it in any such way. Many physicists have given "free will" back to the atoms, but many sociologists still seem to deny it to the human being.

It is those who profess to describe, predict, and control human behavior that speak with outdated contempt of what they call mystical notions and are prone to deny that there is anything which cannot be accounted for without recourse to any concepts less mechanistic than instinct and conditioning. They insist on treating even the world of consciousness as though it were analogous to that billiard-ball universe which was long ago abandoned by the sciences that deal with "dead" matter, and they would make the Science of Man simpler than physics. They refuse to grant to the individual human being that degree of individuality and unpredictability now granted to the atom and they insist on remaining materialists in a world where matter, as an ultimate persisting reality, has ceased to exist.

That the paradoxes of physics are possibly only provisional is irrelevant. It is true, for instance, that Einstein himself, having done so much to make the universe mysterious, has expressed the conviction—admittedly a pure act of faith and certainly not agreed to by many physicists—that somehow and at sometime the paradox of the atom will be resolved in such a way as to re-establish determinism at least to the extent that energy and matter will be demonstrated to behave in a completely predictable manner. But the important point is that in physics the most useful working hypotheses at this moment seem to be those which freely acknowledge an unpredictable element as well as various other things that would have seemed absurdly paradoxical two generations ago. The suggestion made here is that the Sciences of Man might do well to accept a little more freely than they seem inclined to do the possibility that man himself is at least as mysterious as a lump of uranium.

Despite the large claims which are made, it is not completely self-evident that the most generally accepted methods of these sciences have been entirely successful in, say, the education of the young and the prevention of crime. It has already been pointed out that the crime rate admittedly rises, and it has already been remarked that we cannot logically take it for granted that it would have risen still faster if the methods used to prevent it had been less completely those which the social sciences have recommended. But leaving aside the debatable question of the extent to which they have been successful in controlling human behavior, it seems even more legitimate to question whether their assumptions have contributed to the psychic health and comfort of the human being who cannot very well accept their mechanistic implications as valid for others unless he accepts them as valid for himself also.

When he does so accept them, he finds himself living in a human society where he must surrender for himself as well as for his fellows certain rights, privileges, and dignities which, nevertheless, continue to seem real in the world of his own intimate experience. If the deepest convictions of others are always or even chiefly the results of their conditioning, so must his be. His sense of right and wrong, his standard of value must be, like theirs, not convictions won by his own independent mind but the predictable results of the environment in which he has lived. Even his decision to do or not to do what seems to him wicked or criminal is not really his decision; and if he agrees that others can and should be molded and manipulated into convictions as well as into patterns of conduct which social scientists have agreed to find desirable, he must himself submit to such moldings and manipulations. Quite literally his soul is no longer his own.

Moreover, and even if he believes that he is willing to consent to all this, it will still be as an autonomous individual capable of making his own decisions that he will continue to appear to himself in his own consciousness. And it may very well be that another reason why this age is an Age of Anxiety is to be found in the contradictions inevitably incident to a life in two irreconcilable worlds—the worlds of intimate experience and that world of abstract convictions in which the validity of intimate experience is categorically denied.

The purpose of this book is to examine certain aspects of the prevailing mood and temper. Inevitably that examination has involved at various points the influence of the assumptions and methods of those social sciences which directly attempt to affect the mood and which also, incidentally and indirectly, influence it still further simply by virtue of the fact that many people have pretty generally accepted certain of their assumptions and approved of their methods. The belief that, for instance, the most important thing about a human being is the fact that he has been "conditioned" may affect a human being more profoundly than any deliberate "conditioning" to which he has been subjected.

For this, as well as for other reasons, it may be that the social sciences would have served mankind better and would have more successfully promoted even that "adjustment" they lay so much store by if they had been as willing as the physicists have shown themselves to admit the unpredictable, intangible and paradoxical aspects of nature and behavior. Their attempts to minimize and disregard the importance of conscious process, to deny the autonomy of the individual mind, to reject as without real significance the hard facts of direct intimate experience, and to insist on regarding consciousness itself as a deluding epiphenomenon, has done more than encourage a split between the two worlds in which moderns try to live. It has also resulted in a theoretical picture of the human universe which is both fantastically complicated and startlingly inadequate: complicated because its attempts to explain away the apparent reality behind such concepts as free will and the ethical sense are necessarily very elaborate; inadequate because the most ambitious mechanical man remains obviously a very incomplete one.

The suggestion is not that we must return to theology, to simple Christian belief, or to anything else. But the suggestion, or rather the insistence, is that the old-fashioned Science of Man is as inadequate to account for man himself as Newtonian physics is inadequate to account for the universe in which man has his physical being. Behind the ancient and possibly quite unsatisfactory concepts of free will, individual responsibility and the validity of value judgments, lie some realities without the recognition of which it is not possible to manage a world in which human beings will be either successful or happy.

The minimum responsibility of the social sciences is to recognize this fact freely and to make some serious attempt to find out what those realities are. They will never help us solve our problems as long as they continue to go on the assumption that whatever is true of a rat is true of a man. Indeed they will not be able to solve them so long as they assume that even a rat is adequately accounted for on the basis of mechanistic premises.

If it should turn out, as it probably will, that they cannot investigate the reality behind the key concepts without reconciling themselves, either permanently or temporarily, to paradoxes not resolvable by common sense, then they had better follow the physicists who have already done just that. There is certainly no reason for assuming that the human being is both simpler and more mechanical than the ultimate particles out of which actual machines are made. If Matter can become Energy, there seems no great difficulty in believing that the physical stuff of the brain may become Mind—in some sense as different from the protoplasm of a cell as the energy released over Japan was different from the matter which disappeared when that energy came into being.

## The Function of Discourse

If the sense of making choices and of entertaining preferences, along with all the other components of conscious life, are, like consciousness itself, merely epiphenomenal and therefore in some sense illusory, then we are creatures who owe our whole past history, who owe the very state of being human at all, to our extraordinary capacity for being more at home among illusions than among realities, and we are in some curious way epiphenomenal ourselves. But if—and it seems at least possible—all of what seem to be human capacities and human traits have somehow either always existed or at some time struggled into being by becoming genuine phenomena in their own right, then a large part of the whole modern effort to achieve what is commonly called an understanding of reality may be in fact an attempt to destroy what has been slowly emerging or slowly coming to be recognized. It may be a deliberate turning away from the most significant realities and a stubborn refusal to recognize them.

In that case, what is commonly called "the fallacy of origins" takes on an added significance. It involves something more than the usually recognized error which we make when we assume, for instance, that patriotism is "nothing but" a determination to profit from the prosperity of our tribe, that honor is "nothing but" a reflex action in accordance with the pattern to which we have been conditioned, or that love is "nothing but" the biological urge to reproduction. Such errors are commonly assumed to be, at most, a failure to distinguish between the parts of a continuous series of essentially similar phenomena. But if the series is actually discontinuous; if, for example, honor becomes at some point something new, something radically different from the conditioned reflex which seems to be all that can be discovered in certain aspects of behavior, then the fallacy is much more monstrous than was supposed and the consequences are far more serious.

Perhaps the time has come to reconsider the whole problem of the cart-and-the-horse to which the Platonic tradition gave one positive answer and modern thought has tended to give, even more dogmatically, an opposite one. Because of the long-fixed habit of our minds it seems to us almost self-evident that the simpler, grosser, most obviously material and most mechanistically explicable manifestations of any phenomenon are the realest and the most fundamental. Even when we admit, for example, that love may manifest itself in a form we can usually distinguish from simple sexual desire, that honor may evolve into something equally distinguishable from a simple code of class behavior based on class interest, and that, in general, morals are not quite identical with mores, we still usually tend to regard the one as having its origins at least in "nothing but" the other.

The suggestion that the true explanation might begin at the other end; the notion that, for instance, sexual desire might be regarded as the simplest and crudest manifestation of an equally fundamental reality called "love," and that we might, therefore, speak of sexual desire as "nothing but" a manifestation of love—all such suggestions strike us as childish and mythological. Yet on purely a priori grounds the one explanation is no less tenable than the other, and the chief reason why we prefer our usual one is simply the fact that the physical sciences have accepted it as a master key.

Once we try, merely as an experiment, the alternate hypothesis, we discover that everything we have explained to ourselves in one way can be explained in the other. When Freud says that the human need for a trust in God the Father is "nothing but" a projection of the need for an earthly one, a theologian might reply that, on the contrary, the human need to repose trust in the head of a natural family is "nothing but" the analogue, on a lower plane, of his even more fundamental need for that God who is the father of all. Indeed one may go even further and argue that when the materialist begins by assuming the reality of the physical world and concludes, therefore, that consciousness must be somehow the product of it, he is less justified than the idealist who assumes that, since mind is the fundamental reality, then all of what we call the material world must be some sort of projection from consciousness. After all it is consciousness alone of which we have direct evidence; everything else exists only by inference from it.

Perhaps the real truth is that our statement of the cart-and-horse problem is itself based on a misconception. Perhaps the relationship between mind and matter, as well as the relationship between sex and love, is not as simple as the metaphor suggests or as either Platonic idealism or scientific realism suppose. In medicine the emergence of psychosomatic theories signals the breakdown of simpler concepts of the relation between body and mind in much the same way that the concepts of the new physics signalize the breakdown of simpler physical theories, and the importance of psychosomatic concepts is just that they abandon the assumption that there must be a cart and a horse—that either mind must rule body or body mind. It proposes instead a more difficult assumption: more or less independent realities so correlated that, instead of a cart and a horse, we have two independent movers. Inject adrenalin into the blood stream and an animal will grow tensely apprehensive. If that were all we knew, then it might seem logical to assume that apprehension is "nothing but" adrenalin in the blood stream. But it is not all we know, since it is equally true that, if an animal becomes tensely apprehensive, adrenalin in unusual quantity will appear. Obviously something more than a simple, one-way relationship of cause and effect is involved. Body and mind are connected in some manner for which simple rationality has no name and which is difficult for it to conceive.

Perhaps, then, it will prove in general true that neither Platonic nor realist theories are adequate. Perhaps there is some sort of psychosomatic relationship which exists, not merely within the human body, but in the universe at large. Perhaps man is a microcosm in some sense more significant than that implied in medieval philosophy. Perhaps the whole human world of consciousness and value is related to the whole world of physical fact in some fashion analogous to that of the relationship between the soma and the psyche in the individual man.

If the mind may produce effects on the body as surely as the condition of the body can affect the mind, why should it be difficult to believe that, for example, a moral conviction may sometimes determine what will happen to a man just as surely as what has happened to him may sometimes determine what his moral conviction will be? Perhaps we are not compelled to choose between the belief that human beings are completely autonomous and the belief that all their mental experiences are physically determined. Perhaps both beliefs are incomplete. Perhaps both conduct and our conscious attitude toward it may, like the physical condition of the body, be determined either by society or the autonomous individual.

In almost every age there have been those who bewailed the corruption of manners, the decay of morality, the loss of standards, the prevalence of some moral disease. To that extent nearly all ages have been, like the present one, sometimes haunted by a sense of guilt as well as sometimes oppressed by anxiety. But if ours is, nevertheless, unusually anxious, it seems also more than usually convinced that some disease is epidemic. What professional moralists, professional preachers, and perhaps the querulous aged have always professed to believe is proclaimed today by a larger, more heterogeneous group. The young as well as the old frequently confess anxiety and a sense of some guilt which they do not know how to purge. That we are in some parlous state is often taken to be self-evident, even by those who agree on nothing else and who sometimes propose panaceas as irreconcilable as "return to God" on the one hand and communism on the other. Seldom have doctors seemed to disagree more completely on everything except the fact that the patient is ill.

Behind the seeming completeness of this disagreement there lies, nevertheless, a common concern—from two irreconcilable points of view— with what we have called the human world of freedom and the importance of those illusions or realities which make up the realm of morals. To many political, sociological, and psychological "realists" it is the lingering persistence of our unscientific concern with this human world which is the cause of the disease. According to them what we need is to surrender the illusion completely and enter boldly upon that phase of social development which will begin when we have acknowledged without reservation the mechanical determinants of all human behavior; the unimportance of everything except behavior itself; and the meaninglessness of such concepts as honor, decency or fair play except as rationalizations of class interests. According to a minority of others, of course, what this first group calls the source of the disease is, on the contrary, the last protest of health against the morbidity which has all but destroyed it.

One thesis of this book seems therefore to receive support from both sides. The most general and inclusive account of the decision which our world is in the throes of making is that which describes it as an attempt to decide what attitude it will take toward all those phenomena which exist and have for so long existed in the consciousness—whatever may be their relation or lack of it to anything outside the human consciousness itself. In the simplest possible terms, the question is whether we have paid too little or too much attention to them; whether we have been too much or too little concerned with the failure of sociological and psychological accounts of the world in which we live either to satisfy us or to seem quite adequate to our immediate experience. If the answer to which we incline is "too little," then the problem becomes that of discovering how we might go about the business of paying more.

One solution which has today a respectable number of proponents is, of course, the simple "return to" God, religion, perhaps to the specific tenets of some historical Christian church. Another less often formulated than implied is merely the continuing search for some unified and scientifically based "world view" in which, for instance, the paradox of human bondage and human freedom is resolved by a science of psychology more adequate than that of any of the schools most popular today. The fact remains however that comparatively few either wish for or find possible any simple "return to," and that the science capable even of establishing any sort of comprehensible continuity between the phenomena of consciousness and those of matter seems a long way off. Meanwhile the consequences of our increasing tendency to dismiss as merely irrelevant whatever has not been incorporated into the so-called social sciences seem to many disastrous, to be in fact the ultimate cause of the anxiety and the hopelessness as well as of the disorder of our times.

At least one physical scientist, aware of the situation and at the same time professionally concerned with the fact that physics and chemistry have come to the point where they must accept the paradoxes that result from their inability to reconcile observed phenomenon with any consistent hypothesis concerning the nature of reality, has suggested the possibility that the Science of Man should reconcile itself to analogous paradoxes. Thus President Conant, in the course of the same discourse that was previously quoted, does pass from an exposition of the situation in his own science to a very brief consideration of our moral crisis and he writes:

> Scientific theories . . . have little or no bearing on the age-old problem of good and evil. . . . Inquiries into the nature of this meaning would be inquiries about what I have called spiritual values.
>
> The dialectical materialists and also some agnostics would question whether the universe of inquiry I have just postulated is more than a name for mythology. . . . Almost certainly these people would maintain that advances in the social and biological sciences would eventually result in the final substitution of value judgments based upon science for those now accepted as part of our Judaic-Christian tradition, that it would be possible someday for psychiatry, social psychology, biology and anthropology to occupy this whole area of inquiry. Yet they would hardly challenge the statement that a vast number of value judgments today contain elements that have no connection with science. The question then appears to come down to this: Can those value judgments that do not now involve scientific concepts be replaced in principle by those that have originated in scientific investigations?
>
> As to the unifying, materialistic World Hypothesis, my doubt stems from its manifest inadequacy. . . . On the other hand, the formulations that attempt to include spiritual values, modern physics, biology, and cosmology within one total scheme attempt, to my mind, too much. . . . My preference would be for more adequate exploration of special limited areas of experience; one of these would include those experiences which can be ordered in terms of a system of spiritual values.

So far as the present discourse is concerned the key sentence in this quotation is the last, and the key phrase is "adequate exploration of special limited areas of experience."

Metaphysics no less than science has, to be sure, unity as its ideal. The philosopher and the moralist, no less than the physicist, would like to eliminate all "limited areas" by extending his comprehension of each until the boundaries between them disappear. Einstein's increasingly inclusive "field theory" is a highly specialized illustration of the attempt in physical science to reduce the number of unique manifestations with which the scientist has to deal.

But the physical sciences have never refused to recognize or to investigate "limited areas" of physical phenomena when they could do no better. Physics and chemistry pursued their separate investigations until the very recent past when the boundaries between the two sciences were broken down. No one, to take an extreme example, ever proposed to disregard electricity until it could be shown, as Einstein has been attempting to show, that a generalized statement of the laws describing its operation is identical with a similarly generalized statement concerning gravity. But we are, on the other hand, faced with something not wholly unanalogous to such an absurdity when a psychologist or social scientist refuses to recognize as in any way significant the conscious phenomena which cannot be understood in terms of the concepts and methods of his mechanistic scheme. He insists on a unity which can be achieved only by disregarding what appear to others to be perfectly legitimate data.

When, at the beginning of this chapter, it was suggested that we might try the effect of refocusing our attention and of paying more rather than less attention to the realities of our conscious life, one intention was to suggest what President Conant implies in his dry and precise recommendation of a "more adequate exploration of special limited areas of experience." Such areas include some—like the whole area of sensations as distinguished from the physical cause of sensation—which only by the broadest definitions of the terms "can be ordered in terms of a system of spiritual values. But like "spiritual values" they also can be studied only if—and this is perhaps the most important fact of all—their ineluctable reality be admitted on the basis of the primary evidence of the consciousness rather than denied because they cannot be accounted for in some physical-chemical scheme. Moreover, if we do decide to study them as a real if limited area of experience, then we must do so in their own terms rather than in those borrowed from sciences which, by definition, they do not concern.

What this means is that morality must be discussed in moral terms, and metaphysical questions, like the nature of value, in metaphysical. The "special limited areas of experience" cannot be adequately explored except by methods appropriate to, and on the basis of hypotheses consistent with, the character of the area itself. We shall get nowhere if we insist on translating even the very terms of our discussion into those appropriate only to some other special limited area explored by a given science to which the very existence of the consciousness is irrelevant. If, for example, the areas covered by aesthetics and ethics are limited and to some extent discontinuous areas, then they cannot be well explored except by the acceptance of concepts and terms similarly limited and similarly discontinuous with the concepts and terms which have been found most useful in dealing with other limited areas. "Value" and even "Evil" have significance for the organization of these areas even though they cannot be defined in such a way as to be useful in any other.

In connection with this proposal it is certainly relevant to remember that a "new psychology" sprang into being when its founders boldly adopted a similar program. As long as psychologists confined themselves to the investigation of phenomena which obviously lay within the area of other sciences and dealt only in concepts regarded as legitimate by those exploring these other areas, their results were singularly unimpressive. To read today about "Wundt's Law" or even the vast palaver over such elementary things as the distinction between perception and apperception— in fact to read any pre-Freudian textbook—is to be oppressed by the triviality and aridity of the science as it then existed and to realize that they were relieved only when a William James permitted himself the liberty of reflecting and moralizing in a fashion more in the tradition of Montaigne than in that of any formal science. Thus perhaps the most important of Freud's achievements was not the formulation of any of the specific theories associated with his name but simply the freedom which he won for psychology when he frankly introduced a novel set of concepts, beginning with that of the Psyche itself, and including the whole now familiar repertory of Suppression, Repression, Transformation, Transference, etc.

That he did so was, of course, the cause of much violent opposition on the part of the more orthodox. They accused him of merely inventing a mythology and demanded that he either demonstrate the neurological aspect of each of the phenomenon he discussed, or in some way or other provide a means for translating his concepts into familiar ones. But Freud, however much he may have wished that such translation could be accomplished, recognized the reality of phenomena which could not be studied or discussed except in such terms as he invented. Here, in other words, was a limited area of experience which had to be either ignored or recognized both as limited and as to some extent discontinuous with the areas which physiological psychology explored.

Freud preferred not to disregard it. But there are many persons, including no doubt some by now reconciled to Freud, who will not recognize an analogous situation. They would rather deny the importance, the meaning, the very existence of limited areas of experience than examine them in terms of concepts foreign to whatever science they, as individuals, are professionally committed. They will not, for example, allow us to urge a pupil or a citizen to choose Good rather than Evil because they do not see how a machine can choose or how Good and Evil can be defined.

Even to enumerate the most important of the limited areas of experience which we tend to disregard and to suggest the terms and the concepts which might be employed in investigating them would require another volume as substantial as the present. One single example may, however, be given to illustrate what is involved and the kind of consequences which might result from a genuine study of such an area by methods which are, and to some extent were found in the past to be, genuinely fruitful.

The most obvious example of such an area is the area of morals. That such a realm exists and is of great importance has been taken for granted by most thinkers throughout most of human history. Traditionally it was discussed in terms of certain concepts like those of Right and Wrong, Individual Responsibility and the sense of Guilt or Innocence—all of which did, at least, correspond to something in conscious human experience and therefore appeared to be meaningful to those who entertained them. Without using these terms or some equivalents not yet invented no effective consideration can be given to the realm of morals as it presents itself to the conscious experience of the human being.

That the conclusions reached by those who did employ such terms varied greatly at different times and in different societies has been recognized at least since the time of Herodotus who anticipated Lecky's nineteenth-century *History of European Morals* by noting with wonder that what certain peoples regarded as a sacred duty appeared to others as an impiety of which they could not imagine themselves guilty. Yet most men at most times nevertheless still continued to believe either that different systems of morals were more or less valid attempts to formulate some True Morality or, at the very least, that they were rational formulations of a given set of mores without which those mores could not be successfully perpetuated.

To nineteenth-century science, on the other hand, it seemed evident that any area of so-called knowledge, or even any realm of discourse, within which no positive or generally accepted conclusions were reached was one upon which no time should be wasted, and science therefore proposed that the attention once given to moral questions should be devoted instead to the study of the objectively observable behavior which history records. Characteristically, the fact that this would involve the abandonment of all value judgments unless science itself could formulate them, was either overlooked or welcomed. So too and no less characteristically was the fact that the whole area of human experience within which the sense of Right and Wrong, of Guilt and Innocence, and of many other concomitants of conscious life are primary realities was dismissed as insubstantial or shadowy, and the human being was urged to accept a situation in which it becomes his duty to disregard, dismiss, even to feel ashamed of, some of the most vivid of his experiences.

Meanwhile, however, even science itself was compelled to recognize that conduct or behavior has important social consequences, and it soon found itself faced with the necessity of devising some way of dealing in its own terms with the problems which it took over when it dismissed as incompetent the moralist who had previously assumed responsibility for them. If social stability is impossible unless most men behave in accordance with some pattern, then you must discover what that pattern should be and you must find some sanctions for it, some method of persuading men to follow it. But, since no value judgments except those assumed to be self-evident could be evoked, the attempt to describe a desirable pattern of behavior had to lead to the statement that whatever has survival value is desirable and that nothing which cannot be shown to have such survival value is of any importance. And since no "moral sense" or any freedom to follow its dictates could be invoked, the method of promoting conformity to the pattern could not be other than of "conditioning."

Thus, if we follow this line, then, sooner or later, the ideal which we have to accept and the principles on which we must attempt to operate actually do come down to those described in *Walden Two*. Neither the ideal nor the methods used to realize it can be mitigated except by the admission, recognized or unrecognized, of some sort of freedom for the individual and some sort of validity for value judgments other than those called self-evident.

Even supposing that such a society could survive—and we are already half way to it—it would be one in which the whole experience of living had become different from any formerly called human and, happily or unhappily, a large part of what has been the conscious life of the individual would have disappeared—as indeed some believe it is already tending to disappear in societies like our own where many admit, sometimes with distress, that they no longer can give intellectual assent to tastes, desires, impulses and reluctances which they have nevertheless not wholly succeeded in banishing from their consciousness. Thus even Communist revolutionaries sometimes confess that it is only after a struggle that they conquer moral scruples which they nevertheless believe to be scientifically indefensible.

But it is by no means yet certain that a society which believes in nothing except survival is actually capable of surviving; that the mere pragmatic usefulness and convenience of other ethical systems, even of very diverse sorts, are not such as to give them in practice a greater "survival value" than any general principles which could be accepted in such a society as that of Walden Two. It may very well be that those who believe in nothing but survival will always ultimately be conquered, or in some way superseded, by those who believe in something else.

## It May Not Be Too Late

However limited human freedom may be, the freedom, if it exists at all, is unique, and, given a lever with which to operate, there is no guessing how powerful a force the free man may exert. To say this is not to say that rulers, educators, publicists, and social workers should henceforth rely on nothing except man as a free moral agent and therefore on his power to choose his values and govern his conduct. But it does mean that they must not leave any of these things out of account.

Because the human intelligence is weak, and because the pressure of events is always forcing it to choose some method and some principle for dealing with its problems, it is perpetually tempted to simplify too much. One of the simplifications to which it is especially prone is that which attempts to avoid the distinction between the *sine qua non* and "the one thing necessary." But the distinction is vital here as so often it is. Belief in the reality of values and in man's ability to recognize or to establish them is a *sine qua non* for any world which is to remain what has previously been thought of as human. It is not, however, all that is necessary for the management of such a world.

Five thousand years of history demonstrate how far noble ideas, exalted faiths, and stern codes of morality are from actually guaranteeing wise, just, or even decent conduct. Obviously, these ideals and codes are not enough; despite them, human history has seemed to some no more than a record of crimes and follies. Men who profess, sometimes sincerely, to put honor above everything have by no means always acted honorably. But it is no less true that it is because of what some men have professed, and to some extent been influenced by, that human history is not "nothing but" crimes and follies.

Past history shows that beliefs and professions are not all that is necessary. It shows also that the other necessary things include more than that sincerity and consistency which were lacking often enough. These "other things necessary" include intelligence and knowledge, and knowledge includes much of what we know about science and technology. But the lesson of the most recent history is something quite different from that of the past. It is that the thing we have recently neglected is also a *sine qua non*.

How else can one explain the fact that, knowing so much more than our forefathers knew, and having, possibly, even more good will than they, we should nevertheless be failing so conspicuously; failing even to the point of coming sometimes to doubt that we are good enough to survive or that our problems are solvable? If, on our premises, they seem not to be, then a very good case is emerging for the contention that a time has come for trying others.

Unless something of the kind is possible, then we really are helpless, no matter how much we may talk about "planning" or "intervening in the process of evolution." Just as the ideal of a "free society" is absurd unless individuals are somehow free, so, even more obviously, we cannot "plan" if what we think we are planning is actually only the inevitable result of what has already happened. Unless the unpredictable and the undetermined is possible, then the society which we talk about "building" is actually being built willy-nilly and all our resolutions and efforts are the mere illusions which some Marxists seem to assume that they are. As one of them is reported to have admitted in the course of a debate in the Soviet Union, it is highly unphilosophic even to urge: "Workmen of the world, unite!" The most that can reasonably be said is merely: "The workmen of the world are uniting."

Some may be hearty enough to reply that evolution—or the dialectic of matter, if they prefer to call it that—has done pretty well by us so far, and that they are content to trust the future to it. So far, they think, it has led us upward and onward. Why doubt that it will continue to do so?

Actually there is no real assurance that it will unless we surrender to it our own hopes and desires and define "upward and onward" to mean no more than whatever changes may take place. There is certainly no assurance that a mechanically evolving universe will move in any direction which we, by our present standards, regard as desirable. Indeed a very pretty case could be made out for the contention that it is actually headed in a contrary direction.

Leaving Man out of account for the moment, we observe that the most recent plants are the members of the composite family which include many of the most pestiferous weeds. The "highest" insects—*i.e.,* the most recent—are the group to which the ant belongs. By the criterion proposed by Professor Skinner—prolonged and flourishing survival—these two classes of organisms are the most successful of living creatures. Yet the composites have achieved their success partly because they have learned to produce a prodigious number of seeds without wasting much strength in the production of flowers. More obviously the ants have achieved theirs because they have solved their social problem so perfectly that they do not even need to practice the techniques for "conditioning." They are born properly conditioned, and they would no doubt argue, if they were capable of arguing, that a reflex which has become fixed by heredity is "higher" than one which must be impressed by society upon each new individual.

Taking their condition as evidence, it would seem that the ultimate condition to which evolution tends is that of a dull and even hideous efficiency. And if to some it seems that human society is tending in that direction, then it is not really fantastic to suggest that the cases are parallel and that the few thousand years which are to us the history of human civilization actually constitute no more than a brief interlude of inefficiency which intruded between the time when the nervous system of the human animal reached a certain unprecedented degree of complexity and the time—now approaching—when that complexity will achieve a more stable organization and all the phenomena associated with what we call civilization will disappear.

If the true situation is anything like that, then the disappearance of man's belief in his own autonomy will signalize a decisive crisis in the course of evolution. All that part of the human past which we know anything about then represents the phase of development during which the delusion that he is more than a machine influenced the character of his conditioning and was one of the factors of which he was a product. The future will be that accelerating phase during which this factor no longer operates. Gradually he will be conditioned to accept the fact that he is nothing in himself, and even the epiphenomena associated with consciousness and the delusions regarding choice and value will disappear.

Perhaps they have already begun to do so. Perhaps there is nothing which can alter or even delay the process. But if the so-called epiphenomena are actually something more, if the very ability to imagine that we may be something more than "products" is something new in the universe and something which corresponds to a reality, then we may be having our last chance to make something of it. We should think twice before we consent to dismiss the possibility from our minds. If we do not, we may never be able really to think again.

[Above chapters, "The Loss of Confidence," "Grand Strategy," "The Minimal Man," "The Old-Fashioned Science of Man," "The Function of Discourse," and "It May Not Be Too Late," from *The Measure of Man*. Reprinted by permission of the publishers, The Bobbs-Merrill Company, Inc.]

>=====0====0====0====0====0====0====0====0====0====0====0====0====0====0====0====0====0====0====0====0====0====<

IN "HUMAN NATURE AND THE HUMAN CONDITION" (1959) I MADE A NEW
approach to one of the same problems in a chapter reproduced below.

>=====0====0====0====0====0====0====0====0====0====0====0====0====0====0====0====0====0====0====0====0====0====<

## The Not So Blank Slate

No offhand saying is more familiar than "You can't change human nature." Nevertheless, we are today much more likely to proceed upon the
assumption that you can; and the whole of the prevalent, Marxist-tinged
social philosophy takes it for granted that "human nature," far from being a constant, is nothing but a determined and predictable reaction to
"society."

Moreover, that old-fashioned minority which says and really means,
"You can't change human nature," is generally dismissed as reactionary
and cynical. What they are usually assumed to mean (and what they very
often do mean) is merely that man is incurably self-centered, selfish, envious, grasping, combative, greedy, mischievous, and cruel.

The possibly encouraging aspects of the assumption that there is something permanent about human nature and that it is changeable only within
limits, is curiously overlooked. If man is incurably this or that unamiable
thing he may also be, incurably, this or that admirable or even noble
thing. When liberals consider what the Nazi and Communist totalitarians
have made the condition of millions to be and when they assume that this
condition will prove intolerable in the end, they sometimes say that
"sooner or later human nature will rebel." But it won't and it can't unless human nature is, indeed, an independent reality, not merely a product.

Even in the United States the same unanswered question arises in a
milder form, because all proponents of a completely "planned society" also
go on the assumption that human nature can be made to become whatever
the social, political, and economic organizations are designed to make it.
To say to them that "you can't change human nature" *may* mean, as it
often does, that you cannot condition man to the abandonment of all desire for personal profit, personal possessions, "status," and all the other
prizes given to excellence. But it may also mean, perhaps, that you cannot
make him the pure conformist and pure materialist which many "planned
societies" seem to want to make him.

Considered thus, "You can't change human nature" may be an expression of the last best hope for an age which has lost faith in man as, in any sense, the captain of his soul. And since it does seem to suggest such a hope, then surely there is good reason to re-examine the so generally neglected assumption that there is, after all, some such thing as human nature, or, to put it in another way, that what we are born with is not a completely blank slate.

One had best begin by remembering that just such a reexamination of the theory was made during the eighteenth century for exactly the same reason that we would like to make it, and also that those who, for a time, did confidently reassert the reality of human nature were worsted a few generations later by that new wave of destructive criticism of which so much of today's thinking is a part.

The nihilistic conclusions which inevitably follow from the Hobbesian premise had been drawn by Hobbes himself and eagerly embraced by the intellectuals of his time, who felt themselves emancipated from the traditions of a soberer generation much as those of the nineteen twenties felt themselves emancipated from Victorianism. But after hardly more than a generation of exuberant Hobbesism the early eighteenth century began to put up its own fight against the nihilism to which, like us, it could no longer oppose traditional religious assumptions.

Its answer to the question, "To what shall we turn for guidance now that we no longer have God's revealed word?" was the concepts of nature and of right reason.

If, so it argued, the good cannot be defined as "that which is in accord with God's will" it is at least "that which is in accord with nature." And it proposed a simple criterion by which it thought that nature might be distinguished from custom or mere fashion. Whatever tastes, customs, or convictions vary radically from time to time and from place to place were recognized as mere matters of fashion. Whatever all men tended to agree upon was accepted as "in accord with nature."

The *Iliad,* for example, exemplified the natural laws of aesthetics because all men who had ever known it found it admirable. Because a belief in God seemed to be a universal characteristic of all societies this belief must also be natural, though none of the theological creeds which are so wildly variable and inconsistent are. Thus nature (including human nature) was presumed to set up its own absolutes.

What men should do was not, to them, whatever men do do, but rather what men have always thought they *should* do. Education was not, as we now think it should be, an "adjustment" to the prevailing or fashionable mores but to a life "in accordance with that right reason which understands and accepts the laws of nature." The best literature or music was not, as we now tend to think, whatever is at the moment preferred by the greatest number of people but what, in the long run, nature is seen to be striving toward.

Unfortunately, perhaps, this fight against the nihilistic implications of the blank slate and the relativism which follows logically from it turned out to be only a delaying action. Presently, the concept of nature was criticized out of existence just as that of God had been. There simply is not, said its critics, *anything* in religion, or morals, or art upon which, in actual fact, all men, or even nearly all men, have agreed.

The support and factual amplification of this criticism became one of the chief tasks of anthropology and sociology during the nineteenth and twentieth centuries. Before the first of these centuries was over, William Lecky in his very influential *History of European Morals* could write that there is no act which cannot be shown to have been forbidden as a sin at one time and place and enjoined as a duty at some other. And so, after the heroic struggle of the eighteenth century Lecky brought us back once more to the conviction that morals are merely mores; that neither God nor any permanent human nature gives sanction to one system of ethics rather than another. We were, in other words, given back the blank slate upon which anything can be written, and, on the whole, the twentieth century has accepted it.

Professor Leo Strauss, a present-day defender of the now usually discredited concept of natural right, has recently pointed out that the collapse of the eighteenth-century argument based upon "general consent" does not logically invalidate the concept itself:

" 'Consent of all mankind,' " he writes, "is by no means a necessary condition of the existence of natural right. Some of the greatest natural right teachers have argued that, precisely if natural right is rational, its discovery presupposes the cultivation of reason, and therefore natural right will not be known universally: one ought not even expect any real knowledge of natural right among savages."

This defense is applicable, not only to the concept of natural right, but equally to all the other phases of the more general concept of the natural as some sort of reality. But it is not likely to be very effective with most contemporary relativists because it assumes that reason, as distinct from rationalization, is possible and because it rules out as irrelevant the opinions and practices of the savage, the uncultivated, and the stupid upon which the relativists lean so heavily in drawing their conclusions concerning what is "natural" and "normal"!

Nevertheless, the fact remains that in a world which has so definitely rejected all transcendental sanctions for either codes of behavior or standards of value, "nature" and "human nature" seem to be the only possible place to look for a norm which is not merely an average or a concept of an "ought" which is more than a description of usual conduct. The question whether or not there is such a thing as human nature therefore remains for us the grandest of all living questions and makes it necessary for us to ask whether the usual negative answer really is justifiable and permanent or whether we shall some day swing again in a different direction and discover evidence now neglected that human nature really is something in itself and does provide certain absolutes, valid at least in the human realm.

Have the anthropologists been so preoccupied with the collection of materials to demonstrate the *differences* between cultures that they have overlooked some things which really are common to them all? Have the experimental psychologists been so busy conditioning both animals and men that they have paid little attention to the resistance to conditioning which both can put up?

One little straw blowing in the winds of psychological doctrine seems to point in that direction. Some skeptics have begun to wonder whether instinct on the one hand and the conditioned reflex on the other really can account for all the behavior of living organisms. A brain which carries written upon it even a system of instincts is far from being a blank slate. But that is by no means all. Certain other sufficiently obvious facts have recently been emphasized: (1) Birds know by instinct how to fly and do not have to be taught. (2) Seals do not know instinctively how to swim but are very easily taught by their mothers to do so. (3) You would have a very hard time indeed teaching most songbirds to swim.

*There are, in other words, not just two classes of animal behavior (inborn and learned) but also a third—that which is not inborn though the ability to learn it easily is.*

Some to whom these facts have come home have begun to wonder whether the same may not be true, not only of skills, but throughout the whole psychic realm of beliefs, tastes, and motives. The thesis of the moral relativists is—to take an extreme case—that since no one was born with the "innate idea" that dishonesty and treachery are evil, then the conviction that they are evil can be nothing but the result of social education. The opposite, so they say, could just as easily be taught. Value judgments are therefore merely the rationalized prejudices of a given culture.

May not, in actual fact, the contrary be true, namely, that certain ideas are more *easily learned* than others; that what the eighteenth century called natural law, natural taste, and the rest is real and consists in those beliefs and tastes which are most readily learned and also most productive of health and happiness?

Perhaps you can condition an individual or a society to think and behave "unnaturally" just as you might possibly teach a robin to swim. But men who have been conditioned to think or behave unnaturally are as unhappy and as inefficient as swimming robins. As the biochemist Roger J. Williams puts it, "There are blanks and blanks. The blank brain of the child is capable as time goes on of accepting, digesting (perceiving), and acting upon a multitude of impressions that the brain of a rat is quite incapable of handling."

Is this belaboring the obvious? At least it is not anything so obvious that the implications have not been for long disregarded by those who preferred to disregard them. Perhaps no ideas are innate; but if the capacity to entertain readily some ideas and not others is innate, then it all comes down to much the same thing. Professor Williams has led us back by a new route to the eighteenth century and to one of the most discredited exponents of its ideas. "Nature affords at least glimm'ring light;/ The lines, tho' touch'd but faintly, are drawn right."

What Pope thought of as a metaphor may be an accurate biological statement. On the not quite blank slate the lines are touched too faintly to constitute an automatic instinct. They are much like the latent image on a photographic plate—imperceptible until developed. But what development will reveal already exists. There is such a thing as human nature. What we are born with is not a blank slate but a film bearing already a latent image.

No doubt—as Pope went on to say elsewhere, as experimental psychologists prove in the laboratory, and as educators as well as dictators have all too often demonstrated—the lines may be "o'er laid," and the unnatural cease to seem a creature of hideous mien. But the conditioners have to work at it—hard. Men believe in, for instance, the reality of Good and Evil much more readily than they can be made to accept cultural relativism.

Such an assumption is at least one which no valid science forbids, and if we make it, we are saved from the nihilism of present-day cultural and moral relativism as the eighteenth century was saved from the nihilism of Hobbes. In a sense, God—or at least a useful substitute for Him—exists. We have again some point of reference now lacking in every inquiry which sets out to determine what kind of society, or education, or culture would be best for us. One thing is no longer as good as another provided only it can be shown, or made, to exist. We need no longer talk only about what can be *done* to men or what we might be able to *make* them into. We can talk again about what, in themselves, they *are*.

That involves what is certainly no easy inquiry. One of the most terrifying of Pascal's *Pensées* seems to range him with the enemy: "They say that habit is second nature; perhaps nature is only first habit." To distinguish correctly between the one and the other is one of the most difficult tasks we could set ourselves. But perhaps it is also the most important.

More than two thousand years ago when Herodotus was inventing cultural anthropology he noted a fact which anthropologists still make much of. Inquiring about funeral customs, he discovered that those who burned their dead were shocked when told that some peoples buried theirs and that the latter were no less shocked to learn that other human beings were so impious as to consign human bodies to the flames. On the basis of this fact Herodotus was already almost prepared to conclude what the nineteenth century hailed as a great and novel discovery, namely that morals are, after all, only mores. When in Rome you should do as the Romans do—not merely because that is the courteous way to behave but because the customs of the Romans are, in that latitude, what is truly right, seemly, and proper.

Does this necessarily follow in any such unqualified and unlimited sense? True, history may give us no reason to suppose that burying one's dead is more in accord with human nature than burning or that burning is more in accord with it than burying. But there is, nevertheless, a fact which neither Herodotus nor most recent cultural and moral relativists seem to have noticed: There is a good deal of evidence to support the contention that an enduring characteristic of the nature of man does bid him dispose of human remains in *some* traditional and ritual fashion. Burial customs of one kind or another appear so early in human prehistory that their existence may be one of the criteria for distinguishing between men and mere half-men, and some sort of respect for his dead may have been part of the nature of man for as long as there has been man to have a nature.

All such imperatives (if there are any) as originate in human nature itself must be, like that which bids man pay respect to his dead, highly generalized rather than specific. But even such highly generalized imperatives can have important consequences. The pure relativist who denies the existence of *anything* permanent in human nature and who then finds himself shocked by, let us say, the "atrocities" committed against the dead by Nazi authorities is logically bound to tell himself that he is merely reacting according to a prejudice unworthy of one who has come to understand intellectually that custom is never more than custom and that there is no reason why, for instance, corpses should not always be made into useful soap—as they were in Germany during the Second World War.

But such "mere prejudices" may not be prejudices at all. They may be rather a revulsion against a practice which violates something fundamental in human nature, namely, that something which does not require burial rather than cremation or cremation rather than burial but does require ritual respect for the dead. Similarly, other Nazi attitudes toward, say, the victims of genocide may not be merely part of the unfamiliar mores of another race but one of the clear signs that Nazism consists of a whole complex of principles and practices repugnant not merely to "prevalent ideas of right and wrong" but to the nature of man himself. Perhaps, indeed, the fundamental horror of Nazism may be just that it follows further than we have yet followed the implications of the relativism we profess without yet having so consistently implemented them.

If it is true that human nature does require some ceremonial respect for the bodies of the dead as a testimony of respect and an expression of awe in the face of death, then that fact will suggest another generalization. It may be true that cultures exhibit such a bewildering variety of actions and attitudes as to give a superficial air of probability to the conclusion that *all* moral ideas and all ideas of what constitutes propriety are no more than what limitlessly variable custom has established. Yet men almost invariably believe that *some* beliefs and *some* customs are right. However diverse and irreconcilable specific moral judgments are and have been, moral judgment itself has been a constantly continuing activity of the human mind. What no society has ever been able to believe for long is precisely the doctrine which ours has embraced—namely, that morals are no more than mores.

A sense that right and wrong (however difficult to determine) are nevertheless both real and tremendously important seems to be part of fundamental human nature. In simple societies no sanction other than custom may be needed to justify what is done or what is not done, because custom itself is naïvely accepted as the final arbiter and is not regarded as "mere" custom. The more intellectually sophisticated a society becomes, the more complicated the questions involved are seen to be, the more subtly they are investigated, and the less clear the answers.

But the conviction that the difference between right and wrong is tremendously important persists and has hardly been got rid of even in those societies which profess the most unqualified relativism. To state the proposition in the most general possible terms, it comes down to this: An obvious characteristic of the nature of man is his inveterate habit of making value judgments. Perhaps he is the only animal who can give rational form to his preferences or is capable of calling them by such names as The Good and The Beautiful. But he cannot be better defined than by saying that he is the animal which *can do* and *does insist upon doing* just that.

Yet this is the fact which the cultural relativists most strangely overlook, both when they profess to be purely objective and when, as has often been the case, they draw lessons or "morals" of their own. They point out how irreconcilable different sets of customs and different sets of values can be. What is "good" in one primitive tribe is "bad" in another. They bid us therefore recognize the relativity of all such judgments and then, in the light of our understanding, divest ourselves of the "prejudices" of our own culture.

What they fail to notice is the most striking fact of all: that no enduring society ever has been "unprejudiced" in that sense. Even if they insist upon denying what is here maintained—namely, that to have "prejudices" is a necessary consequence of the nature of man—they should at least admit that such "prejudices" obviously have a tremendous "survival value."

A current college textbook of psychology gives a conveniently simple statement of the relativist position. "Moral conduct," so it says, "is conduct of which a given society approves," and by the absoluteness of its statement it clearly implies that "moral conduct" is also "nothing but" just that. If the author is convinced that this is a truth which it is his duty as a scientist to promulgate, he should at least add also the simple warning: "Undeniable as this fact is, no society which limited itself to this definition has ever endured for long." To try to live without "moral prejudices" (i.e., without making value judgments) is to try to live in a condition so fundamentally repugnant to our nature that it cannot long continue.

Unless we admit that man is a creature to whom moral judgments are "natural," we cannot ask a great many meaningful questions such as, for example, what is the good life, as distinguished from a "high standard of living." We cannot ask them because they can be asked only in connection with some conviction concerning what kind of life it is in the nature of man to lead. And it is because we cannot discuss the good life that it has not become either so unqualified or so accessible as our mastery of the physical environment should make it.

We can ask what are the "needs of industry." We can debate the relative merits of laissez faire, socialism, and any economic system in between —but only so long as we confine ourselves to the question which of them most successfully promotes abundant production, not which makes a good life most accessible. We can also ask what laws and what system of education best meet the needs of either technology or pure science. But we cannot ask *what would best meet the needs of man* or consider the question whether or not, in any specific instance, the "needs of industry" (or even the needs of science) may require some modification in the interests of the possibly conflicting needs of man. We cannot ask any such questions because we have ceased to believe that man has any nature and believe instead that, since he has no needs of his own, he will "adapt" or "adjust" to whatever conditions are most favorable to industry, technology or science, or what not.

The only categorical imperative we accept, almost the only inescapable obligation we feel, is the obligation to realize all the potentialities inherent in technology. Whenever the possibility of moving faster, of producing more, or of exercising any increased power presents itself we accept the duty of moving faster and of wielding more power. What can be done must be done. But we feel no such responsibility toward the potentialities of human nature and we cannot do so as long as we continue to assume that such potentialities do not exist except in so far as they consist in an almost limitless adaptability to the conditions which the non-human can create.

That eighteenth century which believed so confidently in the law of nature and appealed so frequently to it fell often into a folly the opposite of ours. Instead of denying that the "natural" or "normal" had any meaning, it was very ready to proclaim that almost any attitude or custom with which it was thoroughly familiar and sympathetic was "in accord with nature" and any conflicting attitude or custom "contrary to nature." It was insufficiently aware—as we certainly are not—that to distinguish between the natural and the merely customary is often extremely difficult, perhaps sometimes impossible.

Against their sometimes fatuous pronouncements "cultural relativism" is in part a protest. Yet the difficulty was never really forgotten even when the reality of the distinction was most unquestioningly accepted. That habit is "second nature" is an idea so old that it fills our literature, and John Donne can refer to "that demi-nature custom" without implying that custom is more than a simulacrum. Most certainly it behooves those of us who undertake to assert again that man does have a nature to be fully aware of the difficulties. The nature of man is something which may be inferred, not directly demonstrated, and the more specific any alleged characteristic of that nature is, the less certain it will be that it actually is "nature" and not what Donne called "demi."

We must begin with the minimum assertion that human nature, though enormously variable and exceedingly plastic, is not infinitely so; that though men readily believe and want to do a great variety of different things, they are not readily or very often conditioned to believe or want to do certain others; and that though the discoverable traits of their nature can generally be described only in very general terms our history is sufficiently well known to support the inference that some of the generalities can be stated.

One such probably permanent characteristic of the nature of man has already been mentioned: namely, the persistence with which he makes value judgments of some kind and thus persistently raises the very questions which relativists dismiss as either demonstrably unanswerable or radically meaningless. He insists upon believing that right and wrong are real, that justice and injustice do exist, even though he is not certain what any of them are.

Even if we could get no further than that, we would have already gone a long way. We would have demonstrated that "cultural and moral relativism" is a doctrine repugnant to the nature of man and that the attempt to build a society upon such relativism is certain to reduce him to a condition which he can come to accept comfortably only insofar as he succeeds in dehumanizing himself. Anxiety, tension, and the other forms of malaise whose prevalence so many have observed with alarm are in part the penalty paid by those who have not been completely conditioned into accepting comfortably their condition. The mass-man is the creature who has to some extent escaped the malaise by ceasing to be a man at all.

About the nature of man we shall perhaps never have much detailed knowledge. The very fact that habit can imitate nature so cunningly may forever prevent the development of any body of positive, detailed knowledge comparable to that which has accumulated around other subjects in themselves less important. Perhaps there can never be a real science of man, however much those who are trying to dehumanize him may believe that they have already founded it. The objectivity of science is possible only because it does involve a subject (man) and an object (the external world). But a science of man proposes that the subject—call him the observer, if you like—should be also the object; and that is impossible. Man can observe other men "objectively" only insofar as he excludes from his observation the fact that they are men like himself. Therefore what is nowadays called the science of man is, in actual fact, only the science of man-considered-as-something-less-than-man.

We shall never see ourselves other than through a glass, darkly. For that and for other reasons there will always be disputes over the question whether or not some specific law or custom is or is not "in accord with nature." But to say that is to say only that right and wrong or the beautiful and the ugly must continue to be, as they have always been, to some degree outside the scope of positive knowledge. Yet no matter how inconclusive any discussion which involves them may be, the very fact that the discussion does take place is sufficient to set any society which takes the discussion seriously significantly apart from any society which tends, as our own does, to consider it not worth engaging in. No disagreement concerning *what* is right or wrong is so fundamental as that between those who believe that *some* value judgment is valid and those who believe that none is more valid than any other. Similarly, on a lower level, no two societies can differ so greatly because of what they consider "good manners" as either differs from a society in which no such thing as "good manners" exists.

The appeal to nature will, then, never settle the dispute between the big-endians and the little-endians in any Lilliput. Perhaps, for instance, monogamy is not "natural" and polygamy "unnatural," any more than burial of the dead is the one and cremation the other. But again it may well be true nevertheless that it is "natural" to accept *some* code rather than none at all in governing the relations of the sexes—just as it is natural to feel that some ceremonial disposition of the dead is "right and proper."

Should we, however, ever come again to believe that the question whether or not something is "in accord with human nature" is a meaningful—perhaps the most meaningful—question, we shall want to explore this permanent human nature in many directions and test the extent to which it is possible to determine, with some degree of probability at least, characteristics of that nature somewhat more specific than any so far suggested. Are there any which seem pretty obvious in the light of what we already know about the histories of cultures?

I myself should confidently say, "Yes, at least one other"; and it is this: Man is not by nature a pure materialist or satisfied with what are called common-sense value judgments. One of the most evident constants of human nature is the desire for Goods other than the material, and the vast majority of cultures have put something else first. They have sought God as the ancient Hebrews did, or, like the Greeks, beauty and wisdom. Below those levels they have sometimes put the highest value on glory, courage, personal prowess, or military success and believed that comfort as well as security were well sacrificed for them. Even the belief that a large collection of shrunken human heads is the thing most to be desired testifies to the fact that to believe something more worth having than material wealth is as nearly universal as the belief that some things are Good and some Evil. A society which, like ours, defines the good life as identical with the high standard of living is running contrary to a fundamental characteristic of the nature of man.

In *Notes from the Underground,* Dostoevsky asked: "Does not man, perhaps, love something besides well-being?" and then he half-answered his own question with, "Perhaps he is just as fond of suffering." This answer is no doubt an exaggeration—even what we are fond of calling a "neurotic exaggeration." But perhaps it is only an overstatement of the true reply. Perhaps the animals do not desire anything except well-being. That we cannot know. But that man does desire something else is part of his humanity. Call it perversity or call it the determination to transcend the most obvious Goods. In either case it exists and is important, so important that we might well hesitate before trying to "condition" him out of it. Should we succeed, we might find that we had turned man back into an animal again.

Could we at this moment get no further than the two statements already made, namely, that man is (1) inveterately a maker of value judgments and (2) not by nature a pure materialist or utilitarian, we should already have called attention to the fact that in at least these two important respects the present condition of man is one to which he cannot "adjust" without violating his nature.

Thus the ideal of the welfare state has its dangers unless we are willing to raise seriously the question, "In what does total welfare for a human being consist?" And that question cannot very well be raised without some concept of "normality." Why could we not follow the lead of Shaw's oculist and recognize that the criterion should be what an eye (or a man) *can be* rather than what either most often is? By any such definition a "normal human being" is some kind of individual, while the "average human being" is little more than a mass-man. Today we are obsessed with origins and must stretch a point to consider even potentialities. Perhaps we shall have again to recognize the meaning of entelechy—to ask, that is to say, not merely what was the origin but also what is the destiny of man; not merely what is he but what is he striving to become?

From the two statements already made about normal human nature one might well proceed to raise at least two questions—not to be answered confidently, but upon which would in turn depend the answer to the question whether or not, in two other respects, our society is organized upon "unnatural" assumptions.

Do men naturally desire justice as well as believe that it is a reality? The ancient philosophers thought they did, whereas we moderns have decided that what they desire is only their individual or their class interest instead. Should it turn out that the ancients were even partly right, that might make a great difference in our way of dealing with our fellows —beginning even in the nursery and the kindergarten.

Some child psychologists insist that what children need is "uncritical love" and that they should be made to feel that they can count upon it no matter how "naughty" they may be. Yet it is a common observation that what the unsympathetic call "spoiled" children seem very often extremely unhappy. Can that be because the expectation—the desire, even—that acts should have consequences and that the way one is treated should depend to some extent upon the way one behaves is latent on the not quite blank slate and constitutes the most primitive form of that idea of justice which, in some way and to some extent, all "normal" men do love. Perhaps a world which violently disappoints this expectation is seriously disturbing even to a child. Perhaps the best way to deal with delinquency and crime would be not to assume as we now tend to do that "society" is wholly to blame, but to mix some justice with "understanding." Perhaps if we did so both the delinquent and the criminal would be less "mixed up" just because they found themselves in a society which, to that extent, met one of the expectations of normal human nature.

The second question would be whether the technology which has made the environment of most men who live in every "developed" country one almost wholly man-made has not placed them in what seems to fundamental human nature an abnormal environment. Perhaps the natural context for the human being is the context of the natural world. Once he was surrounded by other living things and his most intimate relations were with other men, with animals, and with plants. Now his most usual and intimate business is with machines. Does that tend to make him machine-like? Is it ultimately responsible for the fact that he has become a mechanist as well as a materialist and thus tries to believe things contrary to his nature?

Both the behavior of man and the condition of man have been exhaustively investigated in our century. Any attempt to investigate his nature would certainly involve such questions as those we have just been raising and they cannot be answered so easily as questions concerning his condition (What proportion of homes has a telephone?) or his behavior (What is the average number of hours he spends in watching television?). But they are more significant. The attempt to study the nature of man would involve both what, on the evidence of history and anthropology, seem to be the constants and perhaps also an attempt to apply that reason which, as Professor Strauss pointed out, may be more important than "common consent" in any successful attempt to discover what "the natural" really is.

Neither method will be easy for us to apply. The first will not be easy because of the inherent difficulty in distinguishing between the habitual and the natural; the second because it must assume the validity of reason despite the fact that of all the faiths which modern man has lost the most disastrous may well be his loss of faith in reason itself. When the eighteenth century ceased to believe in revelation it proclaimed its faith in reason. We dismiss reason as no more than the rationalization of individual interests, class interests, and the prejudices of a particular culture. Unless the lost faith is to some degree recovered no true humanism is possible.

But do we, many will surely ask, dare embark seriously upon any such difficult, even dubious, enterprise? Has it not already been admitted that only when all such enterprises had been abandoned and Western Europe had turned its attention to no questions except answerable questions addressed to external nature, did progress begin? To return again to questions of another sort might jeopardize our technological civilization and open the way to all the gossamer nonsense of metaphysics, the miasma of superstition, and the opiate of dogma.

Such an objection might have been easy to defend no more than a few generations ago, when it was assumed on what seemed to be a solid base of experience that the new world of increasing comfort would continue indefinitely and when, therefore, inner confidence accompanied outward prosperity. But the world, while continuing to grow richer and more powerful, is now restless and apprehensive within. The Age of Confidence has, as no one denies, given way to the Age of Anxiety. The richest and most powerful civilization which ever existed is also the most frightened.

There must be some explanation of this paradoxical situation. If it is not that an exclusive concern with wealth and power do not lead to peace, plenty, and happiness, then what is it? If we have achieved what we thought we most wanted to achieve only to find ourselves threatened by extinction as well as plagued by less concrete anxieties and fears, what explanation is more reasonable than the assumption that what we thought we wanted was not what, or was at least not all, we actually do want? And if that is, indeed, the answer, then what decision could be more reasonable than the decision to ask again, and as searchingly as possible, what we *do* want, what it is in our nature to want and to be satisfied with? If we refuse to ask such questions is there any conceivable program other than that to which, explicitly or implicitly, we are actually committed—namely, the program which aims principally to achieve still more wealth and still more power?

Those who deny that our program is merely this, point out that it includes also a more equitable distribution of the wealth and a wiser use of the power. Thus they try to make the great issue of our time a political issue. But the conflict between those who call themselves democrats and those who advocate one or another variety of totalitarianism is not actually as fundamental as is usually assumed. It is hardly more than a dispute about (a) the method to be followed in achieving similar ends and (b) the rigidity and consistency with which various general assumptions should be insisted upon.

In their most familiar forms, communism, socialism, and liberal capitalism all tend to assume that wealth and power (in one way or another achieved, distributed, and controlled) are both the *sine qua non* of a good society and also the only things necessary, since all other goods (in so far as there are any) may be trusted to emerge spontaneously from them. All three either dogmatically assert or tend to assume also that since society makes men, human nature is whatever a given society makes it.

Because society is organized on these assumptions, man is becoming the mere tender of those machines which he believes are serving him so well. But as he more and more completely submits himself to their needs, as he stands on the production line, drives his car along endless miles of concrete highway, or even guides his jet at speeds beyond the speed of sound, there lie at the back of his mind the nagging questions, "Is this the thing for which I, with my sense of beauty, my passion for justice, my desire to create, and my gift for contemplation was born? What has become of that opportunity to become more fully human which 'the control of nature' was to provide? At what moment did things climb into the saddle and begin to ride me? Am I doomed henceforth to be ridden; or could I somehow once again *use* rather than *be used by* the things which I once hoped to command? I have subjected all living creatures to my will. What is this mere *thing* which is mastering me in its turn? Am I the lord of all creations except of my own? Do all these questions arise because I know everything except myself? Would they be answered if I knew as much about what I am as I know about what I can do?"

Our prophets often describe the "new world" which lies just ahead when atomic power has been harnessed to peaceful uses; when we can travel across space instead of merely through air; or even when the work week has been reduced to twenty-five hours. But there is in actual fact nothing really *new* about this new world. It would be merely one which had taken another step in the direction which many previous steps had taken. New worlds never were and never will be created except by new ideas, or aims, or desires, or convictions. Christianity created a new world and so did the seventeenth century's new faith that a knowledge of the laws of nature could change rapidly and radically mankind's condition. To some slight extent our own age is still part of the new world Christianity created and it is still very much part of the new world which faith in science created. But there will be no newer world as long as there is no idea or ideal newer than that of the seventeenth century.

If we should ever decide that we do want a new world we shall have to find first the faith which could make it. As long as we believe that the only human reality is the human condition there will be no fundamental change in that condition. If we should become convinced again that man has a nature and that the greatest of his needs is to create a condition suited to it, then a really new world might come gradually into being.

[From *Human Nature and the Human Condition*. Reprinted by permission of Random House, Inc.]

# · II ·

# Life, Art and Peace

ONE CHAPTER OF "THE MODERN TEMPER" HAD BEEN CALLED "LIFE, ART AND Peace," in which it was argued that literature might be a refuge from the torment of modern Existentialist despair, but that one could not live by it because we had come to realize that it was always, in one way or another, not an account of the real world, but a fantasy in which reality had been remolded nearer to the heart's desire. In *Experience and Art* (1932) I elaborated that thesis, writing:

"The world of art is a mimic world, superficially resembling the natural one but fundamentally quite different. For even when it seems most literally imitative, even when it is most determinedly realistic, it is conceived in accordance with the laws and limitations of the human mind. In it the emphasis is the emphasis of an unescapable human prejudice; the very order of events is an order logical according to the system of human logic; and the meaning is a meaning humanly comprehensible instead of being, as the meaning of Nature may very well be, quite beyond the understanding of man, who is only one of Nature's innumerable children. Nor can even the most desperately 'naturalistic' art escape the fact, for it is, at its most literal, Nature passed through a human mind, Nature probably distorted by desire, and Nature certainly modified to whatever extent is necessary in order that it may be comprehended by reason which can operate only within its own limitations. Philosophers may dispute concerning the extent to which the actual universe is a *thinkable* one, but the distinguishing feature of the Universe of Art is just the fact that it is perfectly and readily thinkable—for the very reason that it came into existence by being thought; that it is everywhere molded by the human mind."

In his *Events of Life,* Havelock Ellis had popularized a gentle version of the doctrine (preached by Anatole France and many others) which proposed that we consider living an "art" and substitute aesthetic preference for moral imperatives. But it seemed to me then (and it still does) that freely to choose whatever ethical principles one decides to prefer inevitably leads to the conclusion—old as gnosticism and new as atheistical existentialism—that no act is inherently better or worse than any other and that we are, for example, free to choose treachery as no less admirable than loyalty if we wish to do so.

"Many solutions of this dilemma have recently been attempted. Thus certain philosophers of science—Bertrand Russell for example—proclaim their faith in the ability of science itself to conceive and enforce a unity entirely satisfactory to a reeducated humanity and they propose to throw overboard all those values which they dismiss as merely literary. Certain others—like I. A. Richards—seem to envisage a permanently bifurcated universe clearly divided into a world of facts which we believe and a world of fancies with which we are pleased to amuse ourselves. But if Mr. Russell's reeducated man exists at all, he is at least very rare; and Mr. Richards' dilettante can, on the other hand, hardly hope to achieve more than dilettantes usually do.

"That 'poetic faith' which he bids them cultivate usually is, and usually needs to be, ambiguous. Poetry affects us most strongly when we are so carried away as to forget the distinction between the two kinds of faith and when, for the time being at least, we mistake the one for the other. But Mr. Richards bases his whole solution of the dilemma which he is considering upon the proposal that we should deliberately cultivate our sense of the distinction between the two, and prepare ourselves for the enjoyment of literature by remembering that it is completely 'unreal.' Surely it is yet to be proved that genuine 'poetic faith' can co-exist with a vivid sense of the fact that it is merely poetic, and surely, for that very reason, Mr. Richards' esthetic system can serve at the very most only as a temporary device by means of which lost souls may still manage to 'appreciate' what they can no longer enter into. It has provided them with an ingenious instrument for literary analysis but it is hardly adequate as a philosophy of life."

The artist, so I argued, can be a guide rather than merely a refuge only when he manages to convince us that the universe he presents is a real not a fictitious one. He cannot supply us with the moral standards we desperately need unless we believe that he has revealed rather than merely invented them. And that is exactly what great artists once succeeded in doing for their contemporaries. But the only poets or novelists of our own day in whom we really believe are those who tell us that there is neither good nor ill but thinking makes it so.

"Dust lies thick upon countless epic poems composed by poets who knew what the *genre* required and were perfectly willing to put themselves in Homer's place. But that is hardly enough, and civilizations are at least as difficult to compose as epics. The one does not come into being when the muse has been invoked and the other cannot be coldly created out of a few fragments carefully selected from amidst the wreckage of various creeds. Each is an organic whole in which some faith has breathed the breath of life and the mere will to believe, the mere conviction that belief is necessary, will not do.

"About each there is something spontaneous, something apparently inevitable. Shakespeare wrote as he did and Raleigh lived as he did because to them it seemed the only way to write and the only way to live—not because the one coldly selected a style and the other came to the conclusion that, since it was necessary to believe in something, he might as well believe in Honor, Adventure, and England. We still understand that the latter believed in these things; we still understand to what that belief led him. But we have lost the sense that such (or any other) beliefs are inevitable.

"Nor is this analogy between the kind of affirmation which makes poems and the kind which makes civilizations merely an analogy. The poem and the civilization are parallel phenomena—one occurring in the realm of thought and the other in the realm of action, but each is the result of some passionate faith inclusive enough to give form either to living or to contemplation. Each implies an imagination powerful enough to interpret in humanly usable terms the data present in the consciousness, but each implies also that these data shall be capable of such interpretation. Hence the first question which inevitably arises in connection with contemporary conditions is the question whether or not the data of the contemporary consciousness are susceptible of such a humanly usable interpretation . . .

"The artist himself, hardly less than the scientist, has peered into many dark and unlovely corners. He too has the passion, perhaps ultimately fatal, for knowing; and that passion has led him on, horribly fascinated, from discovery to discovery. The satirist and the realist, no less than the astronomer and the biologist, stand between us and any Homeric conception of the world amidst which we live. Zola, Baudelaire, and Ibsen;

Gissing, Hardy, and Dostoevsky—these men, hardly less than Darwin and Freud, have disillusioned mankind with the universe and with itself. Though perhaps none of them actually discovered anything, all called our attention to much and made it an inescapable part of our consciousness. Doubtless there are, in all their works, few ugly facts which Shakespeare did not in some sense know. But there was a meanness in human nature and a sordidness in human fate which he could somehow disregard, which he could blithely ignore in a fashion no longer so easy. This meanness and this sordidness have been examined with a care and described with a force which rendered them no longer negligible. Art has acknowledged them; and for that reason they have become, not merely facts, but facts which have taken their place solidly in the human consciousness.

"For this reason, also, they must be dealt with, and an imagination which proposes itself as competent to make Art out of the modern world must find a place for them, whether the work which it is endeavoring to create be literary or social. There is no golden age of faith, of simplicity, or of ignorance to which we can return—unless, indeed, society as we know it should suffer some overwhelming catastrophe which would break the whole continuity of its development and return the few straggling survivors to savagery. Those eccentric converts to fifth century paganism, thirteenth century Catholicism, and seventeenth century Anglicanism, who propose to live and write as though they were in the heyday of the culture which they have chosen, are mere refugees whom few will follow. They have acknowledged the defeat of their imagination and taken refuge in a world which, however substantial it may once have been, is now no more than a world of phantasy ...

"It is only in the sense which has here been implied that there can be any meaning to the statement that Life is Art and that Esthetics can take the place left vacant by Religion and Morality. To say that is to say only that one work of art may be replaced by another; but the other must still be found. Some unified aim, some hierarchy of values, some sense that something is supremely worthwhile, must impose itself upon us with a self-justifying inevitability.

"What we seem to have is an embarrassing profusion of almost equally unsatisfactory possibilities. What we lack among the advocates of each is an imagination strong enough to make that possibility seem inevitable. Nor is it, so long as this is true, worthwhile to affirm any abstract faith in art. If Love and Honor and Duty can be salvaged, then some one must write about them in a fashion which carries conviction. If we are to get along without them, then someone must describe a world from which they are absent in a fashion which makes that world seem still worth the having. And it is just its failure to do either of these things quite adequately which reveals the weakness of contemporary literature . . .

"Only one thing is certain. We shall know what artist we ought to accept when we find ourselves accepting him and we shall know what Authority ought to be obeyed when we find ourselves obeying it. Life may be an Art—but only when it is characterized by Art's spontaneous inevitability."

[Above quoted material from *Experience and Art,* Harrison Smith & Robert Haas, Inc., 1932; reprinted Collier Books, 1962.]

*Experience and Art* attracted less attention than any of its predecessors. In part that was, perhaps, because the shock of the Depression had distracted interest from abstract speculation; also, perhaps, because the most frequently accepted aesthetic (if it could still be called that) had become the exact antithesis of that which I had expounded. Valid art was now destined by the communist theoreticians to be a literally accurate picture of reality as Marxism perceived it. Its function was social criticism; even, as some insisted, as a weapon to be wielded in promoting revolution.

In Moscow (1928) I had first come to realize that the aim of communism was not merely to create a new political and economic system but also to reject in toto the whole culture of the past to which I was far more firmly attached than to any political or economic system. In an interview with Serge Eisenstein, creator of the films *Potemkin* and *Ten Days That Shook the World,* he expounded to me the new philosophy in its most extreme form.

"Eisenstein received me in his very modest lodgings littered with books and scraps of film. A large, heavy man, with a head of flying hair like that affected some years ago by the youth of Italy, his bearing and his conversation alike suggested very strongly the Italian Futurists with whom, as a matter of fact, he had been allied, and they prepared one for the fact that his communistic ideology was superimposed upon the Futurism which was at its full tide in Russia when the Revolution broke.

"Like most people brought up in the Futurist school, Eisenstein began by sweeping nearly everything that *is* into the junk heap with one wave of the hand. The theater, of course, is dead and done for. Art should strike with the direct impact of a physical blow, and only the cinema can do that. The only good play in Moscow is *The Humming of the Rails,* and it is good only because it is killing the theater. In fact, its perfectly literal naturalism is not theater at all—it is merely inferior cinema. The people of the future will want only actualities and the movie is much more actual than the stage.

"The legitimate function of art is a purely practical one; its purpose is solely to produce convictions and to lead to actions. During the Revolution, for example, its duty was to provoke revolutionary acts. People went from the theater or the cinema to the barricades. Now that the Revolution is accomplished it has, of course, other work to do. Religion, for example, has not been completely destroyed and for that reason the thing which he likes best in his new film *October* (shown in America as *Ten Days That Shook the World*) is the attack upon religion." [From *More Lives Than One,* 1962.]

Perhaps, so I said half seriously to myself, he is speaking for those self-confident, believing barbarians I had predicted in *The Modern Temper.* A few years later I was surprised to discover how many of my formerly liberal friends and acquaintances had undergone an astonishing conversion and now rejected toleration, skepticism and sincerity in favor of a militant and ruthless orthodoxy, including conspirational double-dealing defended on the ground that the end would justify the means. The directors of the Civil Liberties Union declared that civil liberties were inappropriate in Russia: and, as one erstwhile liberal explained to me, "we Communists believe in free speech until five minutes after the revolution." I reacted with a small volume called *Was Europe a Success?,* in which I argued mildly for the cultural heritage of the past without undertaking to defend its social system.

For my pains I was dismissed by Lincoln Steffens as merely an example of those who were incapable of understanding what he had meant when he said after a visit to Russia, "I have been over into the future and it works." By the English left-wing politician John Strachey I was explained as a typical exponent of a dying culture, while Lord Russell explained his own paradoxical position in a letter to *The Nation:* "I do not disagree with Mr. Krutch as to what I like and dislike . . . but we must not judge the society of the future by considering whether or not we should like to live in it; the question [which he answered in the affirmative] is whether those who have grown up in it will be happier than those who have grown up in our own society or those of the past."

To my defense of the older tradition I added the following expression of my incredulous wonder at the swiftness of many liberal conversions, and I would have been even more astonished if I had known how many of those then prominent presently underwent another conversion and went as far to the right as they were then to the left.

## Communism and the Old Pagan

The spread of Christianity as described by Gibbon, Dill, Hodgkin, and the rest has always had for me a peculiar fascination. For many years I attempted without great success to imagine what it must have been like to live in the days when Conversion was a common phenomenon, and I tried, especially, to put myself in the place of some cultivated Greek or Roman who discovered with amazement that his most intimate friends were turning, one by one, to the strange new delusion.

For years, I told myself, he and they had read the same books, discussed the same questions, and recognized the same dilemmas into which experience and knowledge had led them. When they met their conversation began where it had left off before, and they understood one another in that fashion which is possible only to men whose vocabularies coincided both as to meaning and connotation. And then, quite suddenly, everything was changed. "I have been saved," announced one of them, and though he was never able to explain exactly what "salvation" meant, he had acquired along with it a new set of terms which replaced the old and made communication impossible.

Words like "grace" and "faith" and something called "truth" supplied the framework of his discourse. They seemed to render meaningless all the terms which the two friends had been accustomed to use and they had the magical power of making him forget everything which had seemed most obvious before. For him all doubts had been laid to rest, all questions had been answered—but not, unfortunately, in any communicable fashion. No one had previously been keener in his analysis of other faiths, no one more ready to grant the dubiousness and ambiguity of all things. But suddenly he had become impatient of every hesitation, irritated by every inquiry. And at the same time every value had been transvaluated. "Philosophical," "intellectual," "balanced," "detached," "skeptical," and the rest had become terms of reproach; "simple," "uneducated," "ignorant," "poor," and the like, terms of praise. He could no longer answer arguments but he no longer needed to answer because he had become at the same time incapable of understanding or even, perhaps, of hearing them.

Still further—and strangest of all—he had ceased to value the things which he had formerly held most dear. The culture which had seemed the one really precious heritage of mankind was suddenly of so little account that all the literature which embodied it had best be destroyed, and the sensibilities which that literature had developed were suddenly so despised that no one still tainted with them could hope to be accepted into the new congregation or really to understand how its members felt. What he had discovered was not an idea to be discussed like other ideas. Neither was it a plan and a hope to be tried out like other plans and entertained like other hopes. It was Revelation, and Revelation is exempt from the possibility of error or the need for growth. It does not require, like human things, to be criticized and tested and developed. It is not subject to the doubts which are appropriate to human conceptions and it is not to be judged in accordance with what we have learned by experience with other philosophies or other faiths. They were products of fallible humanity, while this comes straight from God. One has faith or one has not, and nothing else matters. To him who has it, all things are possible; from him who has it not, nothing is to be expected.

Something like all this, I told myself, must have happened; yet I was still unable to feel myself in the place of the student of Aristotle and Plato who was thus confronted, not with an ignorant man, but with an intimate friend who had suddenly transformed himself into a creature capable of holding beliefs with a kind of intransigence hitherto observed only in men ignorant of history and untrained in speculation. I concluded that the phenomenon was one never likely to be witnessed again, and I should probably have continued in that opinion if I had not seen it unexpectedly repeated and found myself in a position strangely like that of the Roman or Greek whose perplexity I had been unable to imagine. I, too, have now witnessed the process of conversion. I, too, have now found myself faced with friends whose mental processes have come, over night, to be quite incomprehensible and to whose vocabularies have suddenly been added magic words obviously rich with meanings which elude all my efforts to comprehend them.

I am referring of course to the spread among intellectuals of the communist faith; and I am interested for the moment, not in the doctrine itself, but in the way in which it is held. In the former I have, indeed, at least a sympathetic interest. I recognize the plight of contemporary civilization even as, I imagine, some Roman pagan may have recognized the plight of ancient Rome. Like him, I suspect that it needs revivifying ideas and I am more than a little inclined to suspect that my converted friends are in touch with some likely to prove of value. But it is the process of conversion, the psychological effects of Salvation that I cannot understand, and I am bewildered by the way in which the new faith renders unrecognizable the minds which I thought I knew so well. Surely there must be other Old Pagans like myself, and it is for their benefit that I set down these reflections. Can we formulate our attitude in such a way as to explain ourselves to the baptized and saved? Probably not. But perhaps, at least, we can define for our own benefit those doubts and those hesitations which no longer seem respectable to those from whose companionship we once derived so much pleasure and profit.

I realize, of course, that even the most enthusiastic of Communists bitterly resent the suggestion that theirs is a religion or a faith. I have, moreover, no desire to quarrel over words since it seems to me that one of the most conspicuous weaknesses of my friends is just the tendency to settle an argument by the application of some damning label like "capitalistic" or "bourgeois." But if communism is not a religion, its effect upon those who embrace it is, in many respects, like the effect of a religious conversion, and it is this effect which disturbs and alienates one who cannot imagine himself accepting it in quite that way.

I think that I understand in some fashion what the abolition of capital would imply. I can even imagine a possible and perhaps relatively satisfactory society based entirely upon public ownership. Several times during the course of human history there has been a distinct change in the social system and, since several of these changes seem to me to have been for the better, I think it quite possible that another might be made. Each has, nevertheless, been accompanied by its own abuses and revealed defects not apparent until the new system had actually been put into operation. Perfection is not characteristic of any political institution. Yet communism seems inspired by a kind of mystical faith. It does not propose itself as better, but as perfect; and it repels those who might be interested in it as an economic system by insisting at the same time that it is much more than that—by proclaiming the imminence of a complete rebirth and by demanding instanter a totally new man. Communist art, Communist love, Communist science, and Communist philosophy already exist in theory if not in actuality, and it is assumed that to break with the economic organization of the past is to break at the same time with the whole tradition of human sensibility. Men are not only to work differently but, because of that, to *be* different, and thus what begins as an economic system ends as something essentially religious in the sense that it is supposed to remake life in its entirety and to affect those things which appear to have no immediate connection with it.

Communism has its bible of course and, say some, its congregation of saints. Like Christianity, it proposes the sacrifice of many immediate goods for the sake of a better life to be led in some future; and though its adherents profess to be materialists of the most uncompromising sort, they are, nevertheless, willing to accept the acknowledged deprivations attendant upon life in the only Communist country now existing because of compensations which appear to be wholly spiritual—because, that is to say, of the sense which that life gives of being led in harmony with a unified mass intent upon the same achievement and accepting the same standards. "Better is a dinner of herbs where love is, than a stalled ox and hatred therewith" is a fine saying, but it seems hardly more appropriate to a materialist than does the promise of plenty some five years, ten years, or a generation hence to those who once so bitterly ridiculed the preacher's promise of "pie in the sky, by and by, by and by."

But the most striking of all the effects of communism is the way in which those who embrace it lay down their burdens at the foot of some cross. Just as the earliest Christians justified their refusal to concern themselves with the world as they found it by announcing this world's imminent destruction, so the Communist dissociates himself from every effort to ameliorate conditions as they are and prophesies the immediate doom of capitalism. He rejoices in the sufferings of his fellows because those sufferings are calculated to wean them away from any lingering hope in the possibilities of this world and, like the Christian again, he proclaims that society must die before it can be born anew.

Likely enough the convert is a man with considerable previous knowledge of the history of political experiment. He has been immersed in the details of economics and sociology. He has seen how the most admirable political institutions have been perverted in practice. But when the light breaks upon him he seems to forget his previous knowledge. Though he is willing to grant that half the failures of democracy are the results of the human weakness of elected officers, he refuses to admit that the human element would interfere with the perfect working of the communistic institutions, and if pressed with the inconsistency he will probably be ready with an essentially religious reply—namely, that men are corrupt only because of the false philosophy encouraged by false political institutions. Like Rousseau, he believes that human nature is perfectible and he differs from Rousseau only in proposing communism instead of a Return to Nature.

Moreover, since communism is essentially sacred, any complete acceptance of it involves also the acceptance of the idea of blasphemy; and the Communist is almost invariably sincerely shocked by the expression of any doubts concerning even a minor detail of his theology. Before conversion he had probably himself specialized in doubts. While still a mere progressive, he had prided himself upon his ability to make and to meet all sorts of criticism. He had even believed passionately that opposition was healthful for the thing opposed and he had celebrated dissent as such, arguing that the very crank was necessary to the well-being of society. But as soon as he has been converted honest doubt becomes blasphemy, and that protestantism which he had previously so much admired becomes the most dangerous of perversions.

Persecution he justifies exactly as it was justified by the early Church, and he bases his justification upon the same contention, namely, that though toleration was admirable so long as the final and absolute Truth had not been discovered, it becomes a crime as soon as one knows beyond the possibility of a doubt that one is tolerating an error. And if any further illustration is needed of the essentially religious and mystical character of the communist faith, it may be found in the cleansing, magic, and sanctifying effect of the adjective "communistic" when it precedes a noun which would, by itself, suggest something distasteful or evil. A pagan might have found it difficult to perceive any important difference between that persecution which his newly converted friends hated and that "Christian severity" of which they approved. But anyone who hopes to understand the new religion must learn to make similar, rather difficult, distinctions. For years his friends thought, for instance, that they were opposed to war. They even went so far as to ridicule the whole idea that it could be justified by the ends in view. But now they have discovered that only "capitalistic war" is evil and that even propaganda—once the most contemptible of all activities—is noble if only it is understood to be a communistic propaganda. To tell only one's own side of the question, to refuse admission of any reporter known to be unsympathetic, and to censor all publication in one's own interest, is now only common sense. Nor is even this all, for the very social and intellectual tendencies which seemed most lamentable become highly desirable when they can be appropriated by the simple process of attaching the sanctifying label. "Capitalistic standardization" is evil, but "communistic unity" is delightful. If a hundred thousand cinema theaters show the same "capitalistic" movies, then the very standardization of the emotions is sickening; but if a hundred thousand cinema theaters show the same communistic films, the solidarity of the communistic society is assured; and if, in a word, the capitalistic goose-step is degrading, the communistic goose-step affords an inspiring sight.

Now to such objections as these last, the Communist replies, of course, that they are merely liberal platitudes. Though he loudly demands in present-day society the civil rights which he himself proposes to abolish, he is frank in acknowledging this apparent inconsistency which he justifies as merely tactical, and his contempt for "liberty" is as open as the contempt of an Italian fascist or a French disciple of Maurras and Daudet. Nor can it be denied that such a position is perfectly tenable, since it has, as a matter of fact, been held by far more people and proclaimed by far more governments than ever paid even lip-service to opposite opinions. But it is, again, the suddenness of the conversion, the apparent *non sequitur* of the steps which led to it which baffle those who must proceed step by step without the benefit of a sudden illumination.

At least those of the American Communists who were intellectuals first seem to have approached their present position by going in the opposite direction. They became critics of present-day society because it granted so little liberty and put so heavy a penalty upon any deviation from the accepted pattern. They were feminists before the War, pacifists while the conflict was on, and protesters ever since against all the disciplines and censorships of their time. Moreover—and unless I completely misunderstand their professed principles—their attitude was predicated upon the assumption that freedom and individuality were ultimate goods in themselves. They did not oppose one particular war because they thought its aims absurd or one particular censorship because they thought its principles narrow. Some of them, at least, even wrote pacifist novels in which war was condemned purely because an individual hero found its brutalities disgusting and, if I remember aright, all of them who were already opposed to a capitalistic society cited its lack of freedom as one of the chief reasons for finding it unsatisfactory. And yet, when communism was discovered as a possible alternative, convictions which had previously seemed fundamental fell away with an almost miraculous suddenness, completeness, and celerity. The convert became almost unrecognizable to his most intimate friends because, over night, the physiognomy of his mind had been transformed. He did not merely, and as one might have anticipated, regretfully surrender liberty and individualism as a necessary sacrifice to some greater good. He began to revile them as enthusiastically as he had once celebrated their value and to proclaim that repression and uniformity were goods in themselves. On the road to some liberal convention he appears to have heard a voice which proclaimed, "Saul, Saul, why persecuteth thou *not* me?"

Such a sudden and apparently irrational about-face, such a spontaneous and complete revision of values is, of course, characteristic of conversion. One becomes *convinced* by a slow and logical process in the course of which one gives up previous convictions painfully and one after another;

but one becomes converted by a sudden, joyous impulse which results in a transformation only later (if at all) to be rationalized. Generally it comes as a result of an intolerable strain, and very often at least it involves the surrender of ordinary rationality which the convert abandons, not because it has solved the difficulties which it has raised, but because difficulty and doubt have become intolerable. Tortured bodies faint when pain can no longer be borne, and tortured minds seek a similar escape. When the mind swoons visions come, and the communist faith in the possibility of a perfect society in the immediate future seems to be the result of such a vision. The exhausted skeptics used to enter the Catholic Church; to-day the "tired radical" embraces the communist faith.

He is weary of disappointments and doubts. He can no longer endure the heartbreaking frustrations which are the lot of any idealist who undertakes to concern himself with society. Hence he abandons with relief every conception whose defects experience has revealed to him and joyously embraces the conviction that a magic formula has been discovered. Hitherto, justice and equity were goods achieved only piecemeal and for a time. They seemed to be ideas and, as such, by very definition to be represented on earth only by imperfect and corruptible shadows of themselves. But this, he now realizes, is only because the true philosophy has not been discovered, and the time has almost come to put off corruption.

Nor is he, unconsciously perhaps, too sorry that his faith cannot be immediately put to the test. There is very little that he has to do about it right now, and he can confidently predict what *would* happen because he knows that he is not likely very soon to have an opportunity to put his experiment to the test. Like the convert to primitive Christianity, the death which he is so anxious to embrace still lies far ahead and he can proclaim with all the more willingness his impatience to surrender all the pleasures of this world, for the very reason that the kingdom of heaven is not quite at hand. When the time comes he will be only too glad, not only to share the hard lot of a revolutionary workman, but also to surrender the freedom of his movements and the right of private judgment. *Then* he will do what he is told to do and think what he is told to think. *Then* orthodoxy will be easy because by that time orthodoxy will be, of course, his doxy. Meanwhile he enjoys the immemorial privilege of the sanctified which makes it lawful for him to take advantage of what the heathen make possible. He does not sell all his goods and give to the poor because the time has not yet come when it is possible to do that in the right way. He does not do as he is told because the right people are not yet telling him what to do; but he is convinced—against the evidence of all that previous observation of human nature would indicate—that the whole of his fundamentally dissenting and protesting psychology will change when communism triumphs.

He knows that he has always, and in accordance with his temperament, been among the "outs"; he knows that seeing the other side has been his specialty; and that organizing minorities has always been his joy. He has always held the opinions which would shock his milieu and read the books that his college library kept on the reserved shelf. Indeed he is doing something like that right now. But communism is going to come and it is going to come in just the form which he envisages. Hence when it does, he will be the perfect cooperator and he will be ready always to accept the official doctrine. It will represent truth in the form of scientific certitude, and there will be no excuse for dissent. At last, in a word, Christianity's two-thousand-year-old dream of the absolute rule of Absolute Authority will be realized in a surprising way. Everything will be tolerated except error, and man will at last enjoy that freedom which the Church has always called the only true one—namely the freedom to do only what is right.

We Old Pagans fall short of the requirements for salvation chiefly because we insist upon regarding the Communist State with the same detachment we employ when we consider the virtues or the defects exhibited by monarchy, fascism, and democracy. In them we perceive a distinction between the logic of their theory and the results of their practice. We are aware of the extent to which their working is affected both by the character of those who put their principles into operation and by the operation of certain forces whose influence was not accounted for in the theory itself. We even remember with some misgivings the fact that universal suffrage was not the panacea which it once seemed that it would be, and hence we consider communism as a political philosophy which may be the best ever proposed but which is, nevertheless, no more than a political philosophy and, as such, not exempt from those defects characteristic of all human things. Hence we cannot perceive in it that easy road to perfection which we must proclaim it to be before our Communist friends are willing to regard us as other than benighted tools of oppression. To us it appears that the converts refuse to give their vision that critical examination which alone would give promise of making it useful; to them it appears that we refuse to acknowledge the transcendent, the apocalyptic nature of that vision. We should be willing to examine their proposals coolly and rationally. We should be willing to be convinced that, all things considered, a society based upon the common ownership of wealth and a centralized control of production would be an improvement over any society hitherto organized. But we are not capable of religious conversion, and without that we cannot be saved.

Nor is it worthwhile to deny that, being men of little faith, we are not yet willing to give up as completely as the true believers demand the goods which this and all past societies have afforded. We do, it must be confessed, still refuse to believe that this wicked world is composed exclusively of pomps and vanities and we are no more willing to break completely with all the past than the Roman philosopher was willing to renounce his Plato and his Virgil merely because he was offered a Bible at last. Clumsy, inefficient, and cruel as all societies have been, some joys have been snatched and some good work has been done in the midst of them. Even those refinements of feeling, even those artistic sensitivities, which the Communist denounces as so many products of decadence seem to us to be, in themselves, far from contemptible; and we are not willing to renounce them forever without being shown more conclusively than we so far have been shown, either that our economic system cannot be improved unless we *are* willing to renounce them, or that the benefits of the new system would satisfactorily compensate for their loss. Saint Jerome learned in a vision that he must cease reading Virgil or be damned; we have not yet been convinced that Economics need be a God as jealous as Jehovah. As true pagans we want some liberty to worship at various shrines. We must insist upon the right to value some things which have no bearing upon either production or distribution and we turn aside from the economist because he proclaims—in too familiar an accent—"thou shalt have no other God but me."

We are—Heaven help us—still liberals. We still, that is to say, believe not only that criticism and protestation are necessary accompaniments to the development of new ideas, but also that individuality, and nonconformity, and freedom, are goods in themselves. We do not believe that an amelioration of the economic system is impossible unless we surrender all of those goods which the last thousand years have painfully achieved and even if we did believe that, then we should prefer a chaotic economic system to one in which man had given up art and philosophy and individuality in order that he might be well fed and well housed.

The world certainly needs to be saved but it is less evident that it needs to be Saved. To a skeptic at least it seems that there are very few things worth paying for at the rate which a genuine conversion demands, and he is afraid of what, specifically, a conversion to communism would entail.

Already he has heard even literary critics make remarks which seem about to shape themselves into the formula of the servant of the Prophet before the library of Alexandria: "If these books agree with the Koran they are unnecessary; if they disagree they are pernicious." He wonders, moreover, that his converted friends never seem to wonder how great the danger is that ambitious and powerful men might turn the institutions of communism into tools for achieving unexpected ends. What if the Communist State should reinterpret the Gospel of Marx as successfully as the Church succeeded in reinterpreting the Gospel of Jesus?

[From *Was Europe A Success?*, Farrar & Rinehart, Inc., 1934.]

BEFORE THE DECADE OF THE THIRTIES CAME TO AN END MOST OF EVEN THOSE who called themselves left-wing had ceased to advocate double-dealing as a necessary technique and were inclined to assume that a new society would not reject all the values and all the moral assumptions of the economic system it was to replace. But the old attitudes still had a few defenders as witness this reply to one of them.

## Cant, Candor, and the Class War

Some months ago I read in the New York *Herald Tribune* a statement attributed to a very successful playwright with political interests. Its vertiginous implications have troubled me ever since, and I have lost some sleep trying to think my way through them. The tentative conclusions I now put up to *Nation* readers, for the problem is important. A good deal of what people like this playwright call "the confusions of our time" is certainly exposed.

The occasion was a dinner in honor of the Reverend Howard William Mellish, and the subject was our proper attitude toward Russia. The speaker was denouncing those liberals who criticize the alleged defects of the Soviet system and he said, still according to the *Herald Tribune*, that "the concept of intellectual honesty does not apply when peace is at stake." Now this is at least refreshingly frank, and it struck me first because contempt for intellectual honesty is more often exhibited than openly defended as a principle. Even more striking, however, is the implication that the more crucial a problem becomes, the more reprehensible honest consideration of it is.

A good many different roads to peace have been widely advocated. Some believe that it is possible only when supported by overwhelming military might, and some only when law is universally respected. There are those who put their faith in world government and others who hope for the gradual spread of the Christian principle of nonviolence. But never before have I seen it suggested that intellectual honesty is the great impediment and that what is needed is neither armaments nor love but simply a rigorous determination not to look facts in the face.

Why, I wonder, should we confine the benefits of the new method to Russia? Since we want to live in peace with all the world, a universal "Dishonest Neighbor policy" would seem to be called for. Nor do I, for that matter, see why the benefits of the method should be confined to international affairs. We have domestic problems too and some of them are quite pressing.

It is here that the vertigo begins. Once international peace has been solidly founded on intellectual dishonesty, we pass to the labor front and begin to be thoroughly dishonest about industrial monopolies as well as about union racketeering. Unless it be insisted that in relatively trivial matters intellectual honesty should be maintained as some sort of curiosity we might then get rid of it in our private lives. For all I know, it may be not only a threat to international peace but also one of the principal causes of divorce and the real secret of the housing shortage. Perhaps what all these problems need is some good, hard crooked thinking of the sort which promises such admirable results in our relations with Russia.

We may, I think, take it for granted that intellectual dishonesty, like most other virtues, becomes easier and easier to attain the more we practice it and that we should soon learn to shut our eyes almost automatically. If, as I have been told, there is no difference between morality and *mores,* then the truth about anything would soon come to seem genuinely shocking, and once people were thoroughly ashamed of it in connection with anything at all we should be in sight of our goal. Utopia would be complete as the last shred of intellectual honesty had been rooted out of the humblest citizen. Peace, plenty, and universal happiness would be realized in a classless society where all men were liars but where no one knew that he was—because no one would ever think the truth even in the depths of his soul.

At present this Utopia is only in the dimly foreseeable future. Meanwhile, we live in a world not only complicated by abnormally acute differences of honest opinion but infested at the same time by people who practice dishonesty as a deliberate method. They invite us to battle over fictitious issues and pretend to defend hotly principles for which they have the utmost contempt. There seems only one thing which those of us who belong to the past can do—attempt to recognize them as promptly as possible and treat them in some appropriate fashion. But what is the appropriate fashion?

As a drama critic I shall probably be called upon to review future plays by the dramatist whose incautious confession furnished the text for this discourse. Shall I, in that case, feel compelled to ask myself first of all how important he seems to consider the subject of the particular play, and then, if it appears to be intended merely as a trivial amusement, give him the benefit of the doubt by assuming that he means what he says? And if I am right in understanding him to maintain that there is a certain critical point at which a subject becomes important enough to make sincerity a vice, shall I therefore conclude that his most serious plays will be intellectually dishonest? Shall I have to ask what ulterior purpose has persuaded him to avoid the truth as he sees it, and what it is that he is trying to achieve by pretending to believe the things he is saying?

Naturally, I should prefer to deal with the work of a man who professed to believe that sincerity is a virtue even when a good deal is at stake. But my problem is minor by comparison with that of those whose business it is to deal with action in the political and social fields. The only hope I can offer them is the hope that intellectual dishonesty is ultimately self-destructive. Those who practice it usually end by deceiving themselves, and they generally begin to deceive one another even sooner. It was Plato who pointed out that even thieves cannot succeed unless they behave honorably toward one another. And usually they don't—for long.

[*If You Don't Mind My Saying So,* 1964.
First published in *The Nation,* 1949.]

# · III ·

# Miscellanea

━━━━━━━━━━━━━━━━━━━━━━━━━━━━━━━━━━━━━━━━━

WHEN I MOVED TO TUCSON, ARIZONA, IN 1950 I FOUND MYSELF READY TO ATTACK again the problem of the modern temper and to answer my own earlier statement of it. One result was *The Measure of Man* from which solutions were offered earlier in this volume. Thanks to the new leisure I was enjoying I also permitted myself, almost as an indulgence, to comment on all sorts of political, social, moral and literary subjects in essays whose relaxed and tentative spirit was reflected in the titles of the two volumes into which some of them were later collected: *If You Don't Mind My Saying So* and *And Even If You Do*. They fall naturally into three groups to each of which I have given a subtitle.

━━━━━━━━━━━━━━━━━━━━━━━━━━━━━━━━━━━━━━━━━

# ▪ Morals ▪

## No Essays, Please!

Every now and then someone regrets publicly the passing of the familiar essay. Perhaps such regretters are usually in possession of a recent rejection slip; in any event there are not enough of them to impress editors. The very word "essay" has fallen into such disfavor that it is avoided with horror, and anything which is not fiction is usually called either an "article," a "story," or just "a piece." When the *Atlantic Monthly,* once the last refuge of a dying tradition, now finds it advisable to go in for such "articles" as its recent "What Night Playing Has Done to Baseball" it is obvious that not merely the genteel tradition but a whole literary form is dead.

I am sure that the books on how to become a writer in ten easy lessons have been stressing this fact for a long time now. If *I* were writing such a book I certainly should, and I think that I could give some very practical advice. To begin with I should say something like the following:

Suppose that you have drawn a subject out of your mental box and you find that it is "Fish." Now if you were living in the time of Henry Van Dyke and Thomas Bailey Aldrich, your best lead would be: "Many of my friends are ardent disciples of Isaac Walton." That would have had the appropriate personal touch and the requisite not too recondite literary allusion. But today of course no live-wire editor would read any further, not because this sounds like a dull familiar essay but simply because it sounds like *a* familiar essay. But "Fish" is still a perfectly usable subject provided you remember that salable nonfiction "pieces" almost invariably fall into one of three categories: the factual, the polemic, and what we now call—though I don't know why we have to deviate into French—*reportage*.

If you decide to be factual a good beginning would be: "Four million trout flies were manufactured last year by the three leading sports-supply houses." That is the sort of thing which makes almost any editor sit up and take notice. But it is no better than certain other possible beginnings. The polemic article ought to start: "Despite all the efforts of our department of wild life conservation, the number of game fish in American lakes and streams continues to decline steadily." Probably this kind of beginning to this kind of article is best of all because it sounds alarming and because nowadays (and for understandable reasons) whatever sounds alarming is generally taken to be true. However, if you want to go in for the trickier *reportage* start off with a sentence something like this: "'Cap' Bill Hanks, a lean, silent, wryly humorous down-Easterner, probably knows more about the strange habits of the American fisherman than any man alive."

Of course, no one will ever inquire where you got your statistics about the trout flies, whether the fish population really is declining, or whether "Cap" Bill Hanks really exists. In fact, one of the best and lengthiest "Profiles" *The New Yorker* ever ran turned out to be about a "character" at the Fulton Fishmarket who didn't. Whatever looks like official fact or on-the-spot reporting is taken at face value and will be widely quoted. The important thing is that the editor first and the reader afterward shall get the feeling that what he is being offered is not mere literature but the real low-down on something or other—whether that something or other is or is not anything he cares much about.

Fling your facts around, never qualify anything (qualifications arouse distrust), and adopt an air of jolly omniscience. Remember that "essays" are written by introverts, "articles" by extroverts, and that the reader is going to resent anything which comes between him and that low-down which it is your principal function to supply. "Personalities," the more eccentric the better, are fine subjects for *reportage*. Manufacture or get hold of a good one and you may be able to do a "profile." But no one wants any personality to show in the magazine writer, whose business it is to be all-knowing, shrewd, and detached almost to the point of non-existence. This means, of course, that your style should have no quality which belongs to you, only the qualities appropriate to the magazine for which you are writing. The most successful of all the magazines functioning in America today seldom print anything which is not anonymous and apparently owe a considerable part of their success to the fact that nearly everything which appears in them achieves the manner of *Life, Time,* or *Fortune,* as the case may be, but never by any chance any characteristic which would enable the most sensitive analyst of style to discover who had written it.

The ideal is obviously a kind of writing which seems to have been produced not by a man but by some sort of electronic machine. Perhaps in time it will actually be produced that way, since such machines now solve differential equations and that is harder to do than to write the average magazine article. Probably if Vannevar Bush were to put his mind to the problem, he could replace the whole interminable list of editors, assistant editors, and research assistants employed by the Luce publications with a contraption less elaborate than that now used to calculate the trajectory of a rocket. Meanwhile the general effect of mechanical impersonality can be achieved by a system of collaboration in the course of which such personalities as the individual collaborators may have are made to cancel one another out.

This system works best when these collaborators are divided into two groups called respectively "researchers" and "writers"—or, in other words, those who know something but don't write and those who don't know anything but do. This assures at the very outset that the actual writers shall have no dangerous interest in or even relation to what they write and that any individuality of approach which might tend to manifest itself in one of them will be canceled out by the others. If you then pass the end-result through the hands of one or more senior editors for further regularization, you will obviously get finally something from which every trace of what might be called handwork has disappeared. One might suppose that the criticism of the arts would be a department in which some trace of individuality would still be considered desirable, but I am reliably informed that at least at one time (and for all I know still) it was the custom to send an "editor" along with the movie critic to see every film so that this editor could tell the critic whether or not the film should be reviewed. This disposed of the possibility that the review might in some way reflect the critic's taste.

Obviously, few publications can afford the elaborate machinery which the Luce organization has set up. However, a great many strive to achieve something of the same effect by simpler means, and they expect their contributors to co-operate by recognizing the ideal and by coming as close to the realization of it as is possible for an individual to come. The circulations achieved by these publications seem to indicate how wise from one point of view their policy is. Those which still permit or even encourage a certain amount of individuality in their writers—even those which still offer a certain amount of nonfiction which is to some extent personal and reflective as opposed to the factual and the bleakly expository—must content themselves with relatively small circulations. Moreover, since they also print a good deal of the other sort of thing they create the suspicion that they survive in spite of rather than because of their limited hospitality to the man-made as opposed to the machine-made article.

No doubt the kind of essay which the *Atlantic* and the old *Century* once went in for died of anemia. It came to represent the genteel tradition at its feeblest. No one need be surprised that it did not survive. But what is significant is the fact that, whereas the genteel novel was succeeded by novels of a different sort and genteel poetry by poetry in a different manner, the familiar essay died without issue, so that what disappeared was a once important literary form for which changed times found no use. And the result is that there disappeared with it the best opportunity to consider in an effective way an area of human interest.

Because the "article" is impersonal it can deal only with subjects which exist in an impersonal realm. If its subject is not ominous, usually it must be desperately trivial; and just as the best-selling books are likely to have for title either something like *The World in Crisis* or *My Grandmother Did a Strip Tease,* so the magazine articles which are not heavy are very likely to be inconsequential. I doubt that anyone was ever quite as eccentric as almost every subject of a *New Yorker* "Profile" is made to seem; but if a topic cannot be made "devastating" the next best thing is "fabulous."

Perhaps what disappeared with the familiar essay was not merely a form, not merely even an attitude, but a whole subject matter. For the familiar essay affords what is probably the best method of discussing those subjects which are neither obviously momentous nor merely silly. And, since no really good life is composed exclusively of problems and farce, either the reading of most people today does not actually concern itself with some of the most important aspects of their lives or those lives are impoverished to a degree which the members of any really civilized society would find it difficult to understand. Just as genuine conversation—by which I mean something distinguishable from disputation, lamentation, and joke-telling—has tended to disappear from social gatherings, so anything comparable to it has tended to disappear from the printed page. By no means all of the Most-of-My-Friends essays caught it. But the best of them caught something which nowadays hardly gets into print at all.

Somehow we have got into the habit of assuming that even the so-called "human problems" are best discussed in terms as inhuman as possible. Just how one can profitably consider dispassionately so passionate a creature as man I do not know, but that seems to be the enterprise to which we have committed ourselves. The magazines are full of articles dealing statistically with, for example, the alleged failure or success of marriage. Lawyers discuss the law, sociologists publish statistics, and psychologists discuss case histories. Those are the methods by which we deal with the behavior of animals since animals can't talk. But men can—or at least once could—communicate, and one man's "familiar essay" on love and marriage might get closer to some all-important realities than any number of "studies" could.

No one is, to take another example, naïve enough to suppose that all the current discussions of the welfare state are actually as "objective" as most of them pretend to be. Personal tastes, even simple self-interest, obviously influence most of them but only insofar as they introduce distortions between the lines. Everybody who writes for or against the competitive society tries to write as though he did not live in it, had had no personal experience of what living in it is like, and was dealing only with a question in which he had no personal interest. This is the way one talks about how to keep bees or raise Black Angus. It is not the way either the bees or the Black Angus would discuss the good life as it affected them, and it is a singularly unrealistic way of considering anything which would affect us. Even the objective studies would be better and more objective if their authors permitted themselves freely to express elsewhere their "familiar" reaction to conditions and prospects instead of working in these feelings disguised as logical argument or scientific deduction.

All the sciences which deal with man have a tendency to depersonalize him for the simple reason that they tend to disregard everything which a particular science cannot deal with. Just as medicine confessedly deals with the physical man and economics confessedly deals not with Man but with the simplification officially designated as The Economic Man, so psychiatry deals with a fictitious man of whom there would be nothing more to be said if he were "normal," and one branch of psychology deals with what might be called the I.Q. man whose only significant aspect is his ability to solve puzzles.

Literature is the only thing which deals with the whole complex phenomenon at once, and if all literature were to cease to exist the result would probably be that in the end whatever is not considered by one or another of the sciences would no longer be taken into account at all and would perhaps almost cease to exist. Then Man would no longer be—or at least no longer be observed to be—anything different from the mechanical sum of the Economic man, the I.Q. man, and the other partial men with whom the various partial sciences deal. Faced with that prospect, we may well look with dismay at the disappearance of any usable literary form and wonder whether or not we have now entered upon a stage during which man's lingering but still complex individuality finds itself more and more completely deprived of the opportunity not only to express itself in living but even to discover corresponding individualities revealing themselves in the spoken or the written word.

That the situation could be radically altered by the cultivation of the familiar essay I am hardly prepared to maintain. Its disappearance is only a minor symptom. Or perhaps it is just a little bit more than that. At least there are a number of subjects which might profitably be discussed by fewer experts and more human beings. They might achieve a different kind of understanding of certain problems and they might lead to more humanly acceptable conclusions. "Most of my friends seem to feel that . . ."

[*If You Don't Mind My Saying So*, 1964.
First published in the *Saturday Review*, 1951.]

## The Search for a Rule of Life

When some developments in nineteenth-century science aroused the apprehensions of Charles Kingsley he communicated them to Thomas Henry Huxley, and Huxley struck an attitude: "Sit down before fact as a little child . . . follow humbly and to whatever abyss nature leads or you will learn nothing."

Even today it would hardly do to reverse this injunction. We can't always refuse to face a fact before we know where it is going to lead or whether we want to go there. But so many abysses, physical and moral, have been opening since Huxley's time that we can't quite share his Victorian confidence and we might well add a *caveat* more often than we do: "Be quite sure that it really is a fact before you follow it too blindly and too far." Even science revises its facts from time to time, and sometimes it happens that we fall into an abyss between the time when a "fact" is announced and the time when it is discovered to be an error. Science is not so nearly infallible that the warnings of instinct can always be disregarded.

Just how blindly and just how far should we follow what, for instance, we can read as a fact in a textbook called *Psychology and Life?* This bulky work by a professor of psychology at the University of Southern California is described as "intended to meet the needs of students without sacrificing scientific rigor." Of its more than six hundred pages little more than one is devoted to "morals," and here is the definition propounded: "Morality is the quality of behaving in the way that society approves. . . . When a person obeys the rules and laws of his society we say that he is moral or good."

If this is a fact, then obviously "moral" and "immoral" have no meaning except in the context of a particular society, and it must be meaningless to say either that one society is morally better than another or, what is probably more important, that any individual is morally superior to the society in which he lives. Moral *excellence* is a phantom, because you cannot exceed the standard. In Nazi Germany, for instance, the torture and murder of Jews and of political opponents constituted "moral" conduct because it accorded with "the rules and laws" of that particular society. Any individual German who refused to take part in such activities was judged to be immoral by the other members of his community, and therefore he *was* immoral according to our California professor.

Is this conclusion an inevitable consequence of a "scientific rigor" which we should follow "no matter to what abyss it may lead"? Or is it merely a reckless opinion to be distrusted just because it has already led Nazi Germany and other societies into what many men regard as a very black abyss indeed? The question is of considerable importance in view of the fact that what *Psychology and Life* states with unusual clarity is what has been widely taught by many sociologists and anthropologists as well as by psychologists, none of whom calls it "moral anarchy" (which is what it is) but "cultural and moral relativism" (which sounds not only innocuous but laudably broad-minded and tolerant).

As an esoteric doctrine "cultural relativism" can well serve the purposes of the rulers of a totalitarian state raising up a generation of mass-men fanatically devoted to "ideals" which the rulers alone know to be neither good nor bad except in relation to secret power aims. But what will the effect be in a democracy like our own, committed to popular education and to the widest possible dissemination of "the truth"? What line of conduct will a thoughtful man in possession of such a method follow? How will he order his own life in the light of such facts as "scientific rigor" compels him to accept? And to what abysses will he follow these facts?

These questions I have recently been asking myself, and it seems to me that there are only two logical life-plans between which I could choose. The first and most obvious is a Machiavellian egotism. Since what is called "right" is merely the law or the custom of my community, I need have no concern with anything except what the community knows about. I will be careful to retain its good opinion while secretly taking advantage of every possible opportunity to violate law and custom with impunity. As Machiavelli said, the wise man will by no means always tell the truth but will take care to preserve his reputation for truth-telling because he can't take advantage of others unless they trust him. If, for example, you have a chance to take candy from a baby, ask only how likely it is that you will be found out. Conscience will then become nothing but what Mr. Mencken once called it: "That still small voice which whispers, 'Somebody may be looking.'"

The only other possible rule of life consistent with an acceptance of the supposed fact is less sensational but will also lead in the long run to consequences less than desirable. Should I be so timid or—by heredity or conditioning—so "group minded" that I cannot face even in the secrecy of my own heart the knowledge that I am violating the mores of my community then, for me, virtue will have to consist in the completest possible conformity to those dominant opinions which, for that community, define the meaning of "good." I can never aspire to be better than the average except insofar as I am better because I deviate less than most of my fellows from the norm. I can never hope to raise the standard of my society, because "raising the standard" is a meaningless phrase if the highest possible standard is, by definition, that generally accepted at the moment. Only an absolute conformist on the one hand and an anarchistic individualist on the other can be said to "follow the facts."

Is there no *tertium quid?* I have searched without finding one. Any society which actually accepts and acts upon what "scientific rigor" is said to compel us to believe will presently be composed of a certain number of absolute conformists plus a certain number of unscrupulous "men of *virtu.*" And there are, of course, those who say that it is precisely toward such a society that the Western world as well as the world behind the Iron Curtain is tending.

If we have not quite got there yet, it is because we have not yet followed Huxley's advice with resolute consistency. But we are on our way. As soon as enlightenment has overcome the effectiveness of residual prejudices, in favor of various traditional notions, we will get there. *Psychology and Life* says that philosophy and literature have long concerned themselves with morality but that only recently has science taken over. And it is no doubt because of literature that, for the present, most of us act sometimes as though we believed that "vice" is somehow recognizably a creature of hideous mien no matter how persistently custom or laws may describe it as divinely fair.

As Pope himself knew, his couplet is not always a safe guide. Vice does not always strike us as hideous because, so the next two lines warn us, the customs of a civilization do sometimes make us callously familiar with her face. But the abysses to which too confident a reliance on the moral instinct have led mankind are neither so numerous nor so deep as those toward which the moral anarchists (pardon me, the cultural relativists) invite us to plunge. And there is one striking cultural phenomenon they seem never to have noticed.

The most antithetical standards of value can, they are fond of telling us, serve equally successful societies. One flourishing race may believe that taking human heads is the most laudable act that any man can perform. Another, like the American Hopis, may live by peace. Competition may be the very breath of life in one place and so frowned upon in another that any sort of personal distinction is almost a disgrace. As Lecky said, there is no possible line of conduct that has not been condemned as a sin at one time and place, enjoined as a virtue at some other. But there is at least one doctrine which no successful culture seems ever to have accepted. And that is cultural and moral relativism!

No matter how outlandish the ways of some may seem, if there is anything to be learned from anthropology it would appear to be that the only really deadly social philosophy is that which holds that one way is as good as another. At the present moment we are hardly more sure than we were a generation ago where to look for a valid "ought." But we are growing notably less sure that we can get along without one.

[*If You Don't Mind My Saying So* . . . , 1964.
First published in the *Saturday Review,* 1956.]

## A Commencement Address

When an old man has an opportunity to address a youthful group on such a traditional occasion as this, it is certain that many platitudes will fall on impatient ears. You will then not be surprised if I begin with some very familiar platitudes. My excuse for doing this is that I would like in the end to make at least one deduction from these platitudes which is not as commonly emphasized as I think it should be. Unfortunately, however, the platitudes must come first.

This, as you are well aware without being told as often as you have been told, is a great age of science; also one in which science has come to mean more and more the techniques for acquiring power. We call it the power to control the forces of nature, but we are becoming increasingly aware that it means also power over human life including, unfortunately, the power to destroy life on an unprecedented scale—on so large a scale that it may just possibly involve the destruction of ourselves as well as of our opponents.

In one way or another these platitudes will be the theme of a large proportion of the commencement addresses delivered this week in hundreds of schools and colleges. Thousands of young men and women will be urged to devote themselves to science as the great need of our time and urged to do their part in making our nation strong. At the same time a lesser but still immense number of young people will be warned of the dangers as well as the promises of technology and not a few will be urged to avoid an exclusive stress upon it. They will be told that philosophy, ethics, religion and the arts are an essential part of the human being and that we neglect them at our peril.

Those who stress the dangers as well as the promises of technology are not always either querulous old men or professors of the humanities, though the latter are sometimes suspected of merely defending their shrinking classes. Among those who sound a warning are some who have been themselves very deeply involved in expanding science and technology. Here, for instance, is a singularly brief, trenchant statement from a great atomic physicist, J. Robert Oppenheimer:

"Nuclear weapons and all the machinery of war surrounding us now haunt our imaginations with an apocalyptic vision that could well become a terrible reality: namely, the disappearance of man as a species from the surface of the earth. It is quite possible. But what is more probable, more immediate, and in my opinion equally terrifying, is the prospect that man will survive while losing his precious heritage, his civilization and his very humanity."

Now what is this "humanity" which Mr. Oppenheimer is afraid we may lose? Is it simply poetry and music and art? Can we keep from losing it by insisting that all students, even in scientific institutions, take courses in the romantic poets and music appreciation? Well, it is partly that and the proposed remedy is good as far as it goes, but that isn't very far.

The issue is much larger. It has, of course, something to do with our increasingly greater, our almost exclusive stress upon wealth and power as the only things worth having; upon, for instance, our willingness to accept what we call "a high standard of living" as necessarily the equivalent of what philosophers used to call "the good life." It is, to use a platitudinous word, "materialism." To be human certainly means to be capable of valuing some nonmaterial things. As we lose interest in things other than the material, we are at least becoming that much less like human beings of the past and, in that sense, are indeed losing our humanity.

What I want to talk about this evening is something which seems to me even more characteristically and exclusively human than art or letters. You may call it "morality." I prefer to call it a strong clear sense that the difference between good and evil is, for the human being, the most important and fundamental of all distinctions.

As I say this, I hear from you an almost audible protest. "You don't mean to imply," I can almost hear you exclaim, "that we are not today deeply concerned with morality! Surely ethical questions are among those of which our society is most deeply aware. Has any other age ever talked so much about social justice, ever professed so much concern for the submerged common man? Has any other ever appeared to take more seriously human rights, political and economic rights, the rights of racial minorities, the rights of colonial peoples? Do we not acknowledge, as no age before this ever did, our responsibility for what we are for the first time calling 'one world'? Isn't ours the great age of social consciousness as obviously as it is the great age of science?"

All this I readily grant, but I am also aware of a strange paradox. It is often said, and my observation leads me to believe it true, that this seemingly great growth in social morality has, oddly enough, taken place in a world where private morality—a sense of the supreme importance of purely personal honor, honesty, and integrity—seems to be declining. Beneficent and benevolent social institutions are administered by men who all too frequently turn out to be accepting "gifts." The world of popular entertainment is rocked by scandals. College students, put on their honor, cheat on examinations. Candidates for the Ph.D. in social, as well as in other studies, hire ghost writers to prepare their theses.

The provost of one of our largest and most honored institutions told me just the other day that a questionnaire was distributed to his undergraduates and that forty percent of them refused to say that cheating on examinations is reprehensible. Again I seem to hear an objection. "Even if this is true, haven't these things always been true? Is there really any evidence that personal dishonesty is more prevalent than it always was?"

I have no way of making a statistical measurement. Perhaps these things are not actually more prevalent. What I do know is that there is an increasing tendency to accept and take for granted personal dishonesty. The bureaucrat and the disc jockey say, "Well, yes, I took presents, but I assure you that I made just decisions anyway." The college student caught cheating does not even blush. He shrugs his shoulders and comments: "Everybody does it, and besides, I can't see that it really hurts anybody."

Recently a reporter for a New York newspaper stopped six people on the street and asked them if they would consent to take part in a rigged television quiz for money. He reported that five of the six said "Yes." Yet most of these five, like most of the college cheaters, would probably profess a strong social consciousness. They may cheat, but they vote for foreign aid and for enlightened social measures.

Jonathan Swift once said: "I have never been surprised to find men wicked, but I have often been surprised to find them not ashamed." It is my conviction that though men may be no more wicked than they always have been, they seem less likely to be ashamed—which they call being realistic. Why are they less ashamed? I think the answer is to be found in the student's reply: "Everybody does it, and besides, I can't see that it really hurts anybody."

Precisely the same thing was said in many newspapers about the TV scandals. If you look at this common pronouncement, you will see what lies behind the breakdown of private morality as opposed to public, of personal honor as opposed to social consciousness. If everybody does it, it must be right. "Honest," "moral," "decent" mean only what is usual. This is not really a wicked world, because morality means mores or manners and usual conduct is the only standard.

The second part of the defense, "It really doesn't hurt anybody," is equally revealing. "It doesn't hurt anybody" means it doesn't do that abstraction called society any harm. The harm it did the bribe-taker and the cheater isn't important; it is purely personal. And personal as opposed to social decency doesn't count for much.

Sometimes I am inclined to blame sociology for part of this paradox. Sociology has tended to lay exclusive stress upon social morality, and tended too often to define good and evil as merely the "socially useful" or its reverse.

I open, for instance, a widely-used college textbook of psychology to a chapter headed "Morality." It is a very brief chapter and in it I read: "We call a man moral when his actions are in accord with the laws and customs of his society." No qualification follows, no suggestion that a thing may be evil even though sanctioned by law and custom. Certainly no hint that under certain conditions a man should be called moral only when he refuses to do what a bad law permits or an evil custom encourages.

If you accept this psychological concept of morality as no more than mores, then you are logically compelled to assume, for instance, that in Nazi Germany a man who persecuted Jews was a moral man, that one who refused to do so was immoral since persecution was certainly both the law and the custom in the country of which he was a part. I doubt that the author of this textbook would have followed his logic to that extreme, but he gives no reason why one should not do so. He certainly implies that a student may cheat on examinations and a public official take bribes without ceasing to be moral if cheating and bribe-taking are the common practice of his group or his colleagues.

What social morality and social consciousness sometimes leave out is the narrower but very significant concept of honor as opposed to what is sometimes called "socially desirable conduct." The man of honor is not content to ask merely if this or that action will hurt society, or if it is what most people would permit themselves to do. He asks first of all if it would hurt him and his self-respect. Would it dishonor him personally? He is not moved, as the cheater often is, by the argument that cheating would not do society any harm and even, perhaps, might enable him to "do good" because it would help him to get a job in which he would be "socially useful."

Two generations ago the world was genuinely shocked when the Imperial German Government dismissed a solemn treaty as a "mere scrap of paper." Today we only shrug when a government breaks a treaty. Statesmen are not expected to be men of honor, only to do whatever seems advantageous to their government.

The cheating student has come to believe, perhaps even been taught, that immoral means simply "socially undesirable," and that what everybody does is permissible since, after all, "moral" means no more than "according to custom."

When some scandal breaks in government, or journalism, or business, or broadcasting, the usual reaction of even that part of the public which is still shocked by it is to say that it couldn't have happened if there had been an adequate law supervising this or that activity. College examinations, government bureaus and television stations should be better policed. But is it not usually equally true that it could not have happened if a whole group of men, often including supposed guardians of public morality, had not been devoid of any sense of the meaning and importance of individual integrity? May one not go further and ask whether any amount of "social consciousness" plus any amount of government control can make a decent society composed of people who have no conception of personal dignity and honor, of people who, like students, don't think there is anything wrong in cheating?

It was a favorite and no doubt sound argument among early twentieth-century reformers that "playing the game" as the gentleman was supposed to play it, was not enough to make a decent society. They were right; it is not enough. But the time has come to add that it is nevertheless indispensable. The so-called social conscience, unsupported by the concept of personal honor, will create a corrupt society. Moreover, I insist that for the individual himself, nothing is more important than this personal, interior, sense of right and wrong and his determination to follow it rather than to be guided by "what everybody does" or by the criterion of mere "social usefulness." It is impossible for me to imagine a good society composed of men without honor.

I shall not labor the point further. But I will assume the privilege of a commencement speaker to give advice; and what the advice comes down to is this: Do not be so exclusively concerned with society and social conditions as to forget your own condition. You are your own self and you cannot shift the responsibility for that self to world conditions, or social conditions, or the mores of your civilization. That you cannot shift this responsibility is your burden. It is also your ultimate resource.

The time may come when you lose hope for the world, but it need never come when you lose hope for yourself. Do not say "I will do what everybody else does." Be, if necessary, a lonely candle which can throw its beams far in a naughty world. And I say this not only because I think that in the end that is best for society. I say it first of all because I'm sure it is the best and happiest course for yourself. If you must be pessimistic about the world, if you must believe that society is corrupt, then do not see in that any reason why *you* should be corrupt. Be scornful of the world if you must, but base your scorn on the difference between yourself and that world which you think deserves your scorn. Some will say that if you do this you run the risk of spiritual pride. I think the world could do with a little more spiritual pride because there seems to be so little of it about.

You will be told that you risk thinking yourself wiser and better than the common run of men. I hold that this, too, is preferable to being content not even to try to be better and wiser and more honest than they are. You may think that personal integrity and self-respect are not what you want more than anything else. You may say to yourself that putting them first would make it too difficult to get along in the world and that you want to get along in the world; that you would rather have money, power and fame than personal self-satisfaction. You may even say that you want money, power and fame so that you can "do good in the world." But if you do say any of these things, you will be making an unwise choice. You will be surrendering something which cannot be taken away from you to gain something which can be taken away from you and which, as a matter of fact, very often is.

We hear it said frequently that what present-day men most desire is security. If that is so, then they have a wrong notion of what the real, the ultimate, security is. No one who is dependent on anything outside himself—upon money, power, fame or whatnot—is, or even can be, secure. Only he who possesses himself and is content with himself is actually secure. Too much is being said about the importance of "adjustment" and "participation in the group." Even cooperation—to give this thing its most favorable designation—is no more important than the ability to stand alone when the choice must be made between the sacrifice of one's own integrity and adjustment to, or participation in, group activity.

No matter how bad the world may become, no matter how much the mass man of the future may lose such of the virtues as he still has, one fact remains. If you alone refuse to go along with him, if you alone assert your individual and inner right to believe in and be loyal to what your fellow men seem to have given up, then at least you will still retain what is perhaps the most important part of that humanity which Mr. Oppen-heimer fears we may lose.

[Delivered at the University of Arizona, June 1, 1960.
*And Even If You Do,* 1967.]

## What Is Modernism?

There are not many nations given so indefatigably to honoring their men of letters that a cabinet minister would preside over a ceremony in which the principal speaker eulogized a *poète maudit* upon whose newly erected monument was engraved the poet's own clarion call to his fellows: "We have set out as pilgrims whose destination is perdition . . . across the streets, across the countries, and across common sense itself."

The cabinet minister was André Malraux; the sculptor was Picasso; and the poet, Guillaume Apollinaire—successively the champion of cubism, of dada, and of surrealism. His own best-known works are a volume of poems called *Hard Liquor* (Alcools); a novel, *The Assassinated Poet;* and a play, *The Breasts of Tiresias.* The twentieth century, so he predicted, "will be the century of de Sade" and that prophecy seems well on the way to fulfillment.

Even if we had a Minister of Arts in this country, we cannot quite imagine him officially honoring a poet who urged painters, as well as men of letters, to set out resolutely on the road leading to that pit of Hell, of which an elder poet said the descent is easier than the road back. No, one can't imagine an American Minister of Culture doing that and, in fact, the proponents of government support to the Arts are most likely to fear that, officially at least, we would be oppressively pure, genteel, and middlebrow.

But if we are not yet quite up to the French in this respect, there is no doubt about the fact that the avant-garde, even when perverse and sadistic, is no longer without honor even in rather surprising quarters, and that mass-circulation magazines give their most frequent and extensive treatment to movies, plays, novels and poems which in one way or another—extravagant concern with usually abnormal sexuality, violence and cruelty, or at least the nihilism of the absurd—seem to be headed along the road which Apollinaire bid them take.

Earlier this year (March, 1966) Cyril Connolly, a leading English critic, was commissioned by the certainly ultra-respectable London *Sunday Times* to make a list of the hundred literary works which best presented various aspects of Modernism in intellectual literature. He headed his list with that same Guillaume Apollinaire whom the French Minister of Culture was so eager to honor, and though it is true that his list does include certain works which are neither beatnik, sadistic, existential or sexually perverse, at least a half, or perhaps two thirds of them, might, I think, be classified as guideposts to perdition. Among them (and remember these are not merely offered as striking works of literature but as typical of the modern spirit) are *Nadia* by the surrealist André Breton; *Journey to the End of Night* by the pro-Nazi and violently anti-Semitic Celine; Gide's *The Immoralist;* Huysman's *Là Bas;* Villiers de L'Isle-Adam's *Cruel Stories;* Rimbaud's *Les Illuminations;* and many others more or less in the same spirit of world weariness, world hatred, or perverse indulgence. And he finds the quintessence of modernity in Baudelaire as translated by Robert Lowell.

> Only when we drink poison are we well—
> We want, this fire so burns our brain tissue,
> To drown in the abyss—heaven or hell.
> Who cares? Through the unknown we'll find the new.*

Commenting on the list and Connolly's explanatory notes, *Time* magazine (which certainly does not appeal to minority interests only) remarks that, though to many the list will seem perverse, it is nevertheless "an achievement in taste and learning."

Readers curious enough to consult the full text with Connolly's own comments on individual works will find that he calls Baudelaire's poetry "a beam of light glowing for posterity," even though, it would seem, the poet himself declares that he does not care whether it points the way to a heaven or a hell; also that André Breton, one of Connolly's heroes, proposed to "wring the neck of literature" and that Connolly himself quotes with apparent approval the following sentence of which it is said "nothing more surrealist has ever been written": "Beautiful as the chance encounter on a dissecting table of an umbrella and a sewing machine."

I do not believe that more than a very small fraction of *Time*'s readers really shares the convictions or admires the enterprises of such writers. Yet they are obviously much interested in them and timid about expressing any doubts. If they give deserved praise to, say, Tennessee Williams for his theatrical skill, they are half afraid of not taking seriously enough the implications of his extraordinary notions concerning sexual abnormality,

---

* Reprinted with permission of Farrar, Straus & Giroux, Inc. from *Imitations* by Robert Lowell. Copyright © 1958, 1959, 1960, 1961 by Robert Lowell.

and they are half convinced that their own normality needs to be apologized for. If a whole school of novelists (now a bit démodé) defines its conception of the good life as driving a stolen automobile at ninety miles an hour after a revivifying shot of heroin, almost nobody says merely "Pooh" or "Don't be silly."

Those of us who read not only the mass-circulation magazines but such highbrow weeklies as *The Nation* or *The New Leader* have come to expect a curious contrast between the front and the back of the book. The opening pages are full of schemes for improving the condition of this or that; but the section devoted to the Arts is occupied mostly by reviews of books, movies, paintings, and musical compositions, most of which are bitterly cynical, pessimistic, and by old-fashioned standards, obscene. Moreover, this seems to reflect truly a similar contrast in taste and preoccupation between the two groups of what we still call intellectuals. Most of them are either do-gooders or, on the other hand, ready to entertain the possibility that the road to perdition is the wise one to take. If you are not a potential member of the Peace Corps, you are almost certainly a devotee of The Absurd. You want either to rescue the underdeveloped countries or explore once more the meaninglessness of the universe or the depravity of some vision of the *dolce vita*. If *Time* (as it recently did) puts Sartre and Gênet on its "best reading" list for a single week, neither of them can be said to be, by now, attractive only to the few.

Do I exaggerate either the violence, perversity or nihilism of most of the most discussed modern writers, or the tendency of even the mass magazines to select specimens as either the best or, sometimes, only the most newsworthy books? Let us look at a few excerpts from two or three publications to illustrate what I am driving at. Let us look first at the leading review in an issue of *The New Leader*. It concerns James Baldwin's newest so-called novel and was written by the magazine's staff critic Stanley Edgar Hyman who, though far from approving of the book, writes as follows:

> As an enthusiastic admirer of his two earlier novels, I am sorry to find this, his most ambitious effort, a very mixed bundle.
> The protagonist of *Another Country*, a young Negro jazz drummer named Rufus Scott, kills himself on page 88, and the rest of the book is taken up with the adventures and misadventures, mostly sexual, of the half dozen people who had been close to him. Of the important characters, only Rufus and his sister Ida are Negro, but almost everything in the book that is powerful and convincing deals with Negro consciousness.

That consciousness, as the novel shows it, seethes with bitterness and race hate. Let the liberal white bastards squirm is Rufus's most charitable feeling towards Vivaldo, his best friend; his less charitable feeling is a passionate desire for the extinction of the white race by nuclear bombs. Ida is even fiercer. She regularly affirms, in language not quotable in this family magazine, the total sexual inadequacy of whites, as well as their moral sickness and physical repulsiveness. . . . The other Negroes in the book share this bitterness and hatred without exception. A big Negro pimp who lives by beating up and robbing the white customers of his Negro whore clearly does it out of principle; before robbing Vivaldo he stares at him with a calm steady hatred, as remote and unanswerable as madness. The Silenski boys are beaten up by Negro boys unknown to them out of simple racial hostility and Richard, their father, automatically comments: Little black bastards. Rufus's father, seeing his son's mangled corpse, remarks only: They didn't leave a man much, do they? A musician who had been Rufus's friend, finding Ida out with a white man, calls her "black white man's whore" and threatens to mutilate her genitals twice, once for himself and once for Rufus.

Though *The New Leader's* critic is by no means favorably impressed, the jacket of *Another Country* is able to cite the even better known and academically very respectable critic, Mark Shorer, as calling *Another Country* "powerful." Is that the adjective he would have chosen if this almost insane outburst of racism had been the work of some Southern Ku Kluxer—as it might easily be made to seem by reading "white" where Baldwin says "black" and "black" where he says "white"? Why is black racism "powerful," white disgusting?

Now for a movie, as admiringly described in *Time*:

*Naked Prey* spills more beauty, blood and savagery upon the screen than any African adventure drama since *Trader Horn*. Squeamish viewers will head for home in the first twenty minutes or so, when producer-director-star Cornel Wilde swiftly dooms three last century white hunters and a file of blacks, attacked and captured by a horde of warriors from a tribe they have insulted. One victim is basted with clay and turned over a spit, another is staked out as the victim of a cobra.

The only survivor is Wilde. In a primitive sporting gesture, the natives free the courageous white man without clothes, weapons or water— and with ten stalwart young spearsmen poised to track him down. Hunted now, the hunter begins to run, and *Prey* gathers fierce momentum as a classic, single-minded epic of survival with no time out for faint-hearted blondes or false heroines.

It used to be said that the theater was often more searching, more bitter, and more "adult" than the movies ever dared to be. Today it can hardly keep up with them. But it tries, as witness an account of the latest play by the man generally regarded as Britain's leading playwright:

> *A Bond Honoured,* British playwright John Osborne's adaptation of an atrocious horror show by seventeenth-century Spaniard Lope de Vega, has a hero who commits rape, murder, treason, multiple incest and matricide, and blinds his father—after which he is crucified in precise imitation of Christ. London's critics cast one look at the tasteless mayhem at the Old Vic and held their noses. Whereupon Osborne, 36, flipped his Angry Aging Man's lid, firing off telegrams to the London papers. Osborne declared an end to his "gentleman's agreement to ignore puny theater critics as bourgeois conventions. After ten years it is now war, open war, that will be as public as I and other men of earned reputations have the considerable power to make it."

This account is again from *Time* but its pooh-poohing of Osborne's masterpiece got an angry reply from Kenneth Tynan, the drama critic who was for a time the regular reviewer for *The New Yorker*:

> Of the twelve newspaper critics, at least four held their breath. Herald Hobson in the *Sunday Times* said of Osborne: "He is not only our most important dramatist; he is also our chief prophet." According to Randall Bryden of the *Observer*, "The effect of *A Bond Honoured* in performance is marvelously theatrical." Allen Brien of the Sunday *Telegraph* thought it "a serious, ambitious and valuable play which matures in the memory and fertilizes the imagination," while for Milton Shulman in the *Evening Standard* it was "a stunning parable with a magnificent theatrical impact."

Having glanced at a conspicuous American novel, a conspicuous movie, and a conspicuous play, let's look now at two serious American critics, taking Leslie Fiedler first. His contention that the best American fiction from *Huckleberry Finn* to Hemingway and Faulkner is always concerned with a repressed homosexuality, is well known. In his most recent book, he comes up with the following opinions:

> [On the suicide of Ernest Hemingway]: One quarry was left him only, the single beast worthy of him; himself. And he took his shotgun in hand, probably renewing his lapsed allegiance to death and silence. With a single shot he redeemed his best work from his worst, his art from himself.

[Of President Kennedy and the Arts]: John F. Kennedy, as Louis XV, seemed up to the moment of his assassination the true symbol of cultural blight; not only our first sexually viable president in a century, after a depressing series of uncle, grandfather and grandmother figures, but the very embodiment of middle-brow culture climbing.

I have been leaning heavily on *Time* because it seems to be the publication which best gauges the interests if not necessarily the opinions, of the largest number of literate Americans. But for a second critic, and incidentally an excellent example of the schizophrenia of the liberal weeklies, I will choose an essay by the most "in" of contemporary avant-garde critics, namely, Susan Sontag published in *The Nation,* which has been for long the very paradigm of do-goodism. The article takes off from a discussion of Jack Smith's film *Flaming Creatures,* which she describes thus:

A couple of women and a much larger number of men . . . frolic about, pose, posture, and dance with one another. Enact various scenes of voluptuousness, sexual frenzy, romantic love and vampirism—to the accompaniment of a sound track which includes . . . the chorale of flutish shrieks and screams which accompany the group rape of a bosomy woman, rape happily converting itself into an orgy.

It also, says Miss Sontag, includes "close-ups of limp penises and bouncing breasts . . . shots of masturbation and oral sensuality." "Of course," she continues, "*Flaming Creatures* is outrageous and it intends to be. But [or should it be, therefore] it is 'a beautiful film.' . . ." [It is] "a triumphant example of an esthetic vision of the world—and such a vision is perhaps always, at its core, epicene."

Just why an aesthetic vision of the world is perhaps always at its core homosexual is not explained, and it suggests the same reply which Chesterton made to the aestheticism of the nineties. The art of those who professed it, so they claimed, was morally neutral. But, said Chesterton, if it really were neutral it would often find itself dealing favorably with respectability, virtue, piety and conventional behavior. The fact that it never does treat of any of these things in a neutral manner was sufficient proof that the art of its practitioners was not morally neutral but actually (to come back to Apollinaire again) an invitation to take the road to perdition.

If Miss Sontag does not explain why an aesthetic vision must be epicene (i.e., homosexual) she does undertake to explain why modern art must be "outrageous." "Art is always the sphere of freedom. In those difficult works of art we now call avant-garde, the artist consciously exercises his freedom."

That argument is obviously the same as that favorite of some Existentialists, namely the contention (a) that the unmotivated act is the most positive assertion of freedom, and (b) that the best unmotivated act is one of arbitrary cruelty. Why this should be so, I have never understood, and I understand no more why the freedom of the artist can be demonstrated only by the outrageous. In the atmosphere of the present moment, the boldest position a creative or critical writer could take would be one championing not only morality but gentility and bourgeois respectability. Even this article which I am writing at this moment will probably be more contemptuously or even vituperatively dismissed than it would be if I were defending sadism, homosexuality, and nihilism.

How square and fuddy-duddy the management of the American Telephone and Telegraph Company must be to take, as it recently has, full-page advertisements in mass media to ask and answer a question in headline type: "What can you do about obscene, harassing, or threatening phone calls?" Doesn't AT&T know that one of the easiest ways to demonstrate one's freedom in a splendidly unmotivated act consists in making an obscene telephone call? From that, one can easily work up to the various vandalisms now so popular among teen-agers and, finally, to unmotivated murder. Who else demonstrates so triumphantly an existentialist freedom as the killer for kicks?

What precisely is the road, or roads, which have led to the state of mind illustrated by the quotations which make up so large a part of this article? I do not think that any analysis ending in a satisfactory answer to that question has ever been made. Someone with the stomach for it might undertake a study as nearly classic as Mario Praz's *The Romantic Agony*, which traces so brilliantly the origin and destination of 1890 decadence —to which last, Modernism is more closely paralleled than is usually admitted, and of which it is, perhaps, only another phase. Cyril Connolly (in the discussion already quoted) has this to say:

> [It] began as a revolt against the bourgeois in France, the Victorians in England, the Puritanism and materialism of America. The modern spirit was a combination of certain intellectual qualities inherited from the Enlightenment: lucidity, irony, scepticism, intellectual curiosity, combined with the impassioned intensity and enhanced sensibility of the

Romantic, their rebellion and sense of technical experiment, their awareness of living in a tragic age.

All that is true enough and familiar enough without going far enough.
It does not explain why the most obvious and unique characteristics of the
current avant-garde are not any of the characteristics of the Enlightenment
or of any except the decadent Romantics. How, for instance, do lucidity,
irony, skepticism or even intellectual curiosity become preludes to "the
century of de Sade"? How did an assault upon Victorian complacency
and hypocrisy end by practicing a sort of unmotivated vandalism?

I suppose that anyone who undertook to trace that development would
have to begin by asking whether or not there is a single dominating
characteristic of this latest development of the modern spirit, anything
which by its frequent emphasis seems to distinguish contemporary Modernism from the movement out of which it is said to have grown. This
Modernism seems, indeed, to be compounded of many simples and not all
who represent it include all of them in their mixtures. Is the distinguishing characteristic a tendency to elevate raw sexual experience to a position
of supreme importance so that the Quest for the Holy Grail has become
a quest for the perfect orgasm? Is it homosexuality, nihilism and the
impulse to self-destruction as typified in the cult of drugs, or is it that
taste for violence which, as in the case of Baldwin, becomes unmistakably
sadistic?

If I had to answer the question, I would be inclined to say that this
taste for violence, this belief that it is the only appropriate response to an
absurd world is indeed the one element most often present in any individual's special version of the moment's avant-gardism. Psychiatrists say
that suicide is often motivated by the desire for revenge against some person who will be made to suffer by it. They are inclined to call this motive
irrational, but in modern literature and modern criticism it is sometimes
accepted as the ultimate rationality—as in the following two examples. In
Friedrich Duerrenmatt's much discussed play *The Visit* the principal
character explains her conduct by saying: "The world made a whore of
me, so I am turning the world into a brothel." In *The Nation,* the reviewer of a novel calls the self-destruction of its hero "an alcoholic strike
against humanity." In commonsense terms all such retaliations and re-
venges come under the head of biting off one's nose to spite one's face,
but that seems to be what some modernists advocate.

Seldom if ever before have any of the arts been so dominated by an all-
inclusive hatred. Once the writer hated individual "bad men." Then he

began to hate instead the society which was supposed to be responsible for the creation of bad men. Now his hatred is directed not at individuals or their societies, but at the universe in which bad men and bad societies are merely expressions of the fundamental evil of that universe itself.

It was once hoped that the iconoclasts who flourished during the early years of our century would clear the ground for higher ideals and truer values. Somewhat later it was argued that Existentialism, having demonstrated that the universe was in itself morally and intellectually meaningless, now left man free to construct meanings and morals for himself and in his own image. What that has come down to, the Baldwins, the Burroughses, and the Jack Smiths have demonstrated in our language—the Apollinaires, the Gênets in theirs.

Of course there is always the literature of social protest to which one may turn if one has had enough of sadism and the absurd. But sometimes the reviewers sound as though they were getting the same sort of sadistic kick in a less open way. Here, for example, is the way in which a recent novel is praised in (of all places) *Vogue*:

> *The Fixer*, a brilliant new novel by Bernard Malamud, is harrowing. It is a dreadful story that cuts and lacerates without relief; it is a drama of ferocious injustice and then more injustice.

If anything except unrelieved violence in one form or another is "escapism"; if human nature, the world and even the universe itself are what so many esteemed artists declare them to be, then what can any reasonable man choose to do, except escape in either life or literature—if he can.

Perhaps that is why in London recently, thousands crowded an exhibition of memorabilia of the creator of Peter Rabbit.

[*And Even If You Do*, 1967.
First published in the *Saturday Review*, 1967.]

## Honor and Morality

Many years ago I read a short piece by H. L. Mencken about honorable men (whom he admired) and moral men (whom he did not). It wasn't, I think, more than a paragraph and it didn't give him much room to maneuver. But if I have remembered it for so long he must have made it pretty clear what he meant by the distinction. Reduced to the simplest terms it was that an honorable man is one who keeps his word; a moral man one who insists that he always does "what is right under the circumstances."

From the first you at least know what to expect and you can count upon him. The second seems to cover a lot more ground and assumes a larger responsibility. He would do what is "right" even if it isn't (as is all too often the case) exactly what he said he would. He is strong for the spirit rather than the letter, for equity rather than legality, and he puts the greatest good of the greatest number above the promise of the contract. Though that sounds persuasive, one trouble is that equity and the greatest good so often turn out to be what is most convenient for him.

Now I realize of course that "honor" and "morality" are both concepts inadequate to cover so large and shifting a concept as those we try to indicate by them. But the distinction I follow, and Mencken is trying to make, is very important and it is easier to discuss when you are willing, for the moment, to adopt the two words as I define them. Moreover, it is evident that if you do accept them, then the relative importance which a civilization puts upon honor on the one hand and morality on the other has a great deal to do with the special quality of the civilization. To me, at least, it is equally evident that ours is so ready to give precedence to morality that honor is easily brushed aside when one seems to come into conflict with the other.

If this seems obscure let me give a simple example. I still remember my shocked realization of the seemingly irreconcilable conflict between honor and morality when Franklin Roosevelt (whom I nevertheless continued to admire and to vote for) announced the abandonment of the gold standard while I held in my hand a twenty-dollar certificate on which was beautifully engraved the statement that "the faith of the United States Government is pledged" to redeem this note in gold.

Please do not misunderstand me. I am not saying that we ought to have risked bankruptcy. Frankly I don't know whether we ought or ought not have done so. But if the action we did take was necessary and in the interest of the greater good, it still shocks me (and I think it should shock anyone who would like to believe that honor and morality are inseparable) that the pledged word of our government should have been so calmly broken.

I am well aware that when honor is placed above everything else it is likely to become no more than a personal and ruthless pride which can lead to such obviously immoral acts as killing your opponent in a duel or even arranging for his assassination for no reason except that personal dignity is offended; or even to such absurdities as the famous suicide of Louis XIV's cook when the fish failed to arrive on time—despite the fact that, at least in Mme. de Sévigné's version, he had been assured by the king himself that the contretemps need not be taken seriously. But if the concept of honor can grow malignantly wild like a cancer, the too easy disregard of it brings practical difficulties as well as moral shames. When there is honor even among thieves (and there sometimes is) we at least know where we stand; when there is none among governors or nations we approach anarchy.

One of the relatively—but surely not trivial—side effects of justifying broken faith by invoking "the higher good" is the encouragement it gives to sophistical invasions and the blurring of actual facts. A generation before we found it necessary to break the pledged word of the United States Government in the matter of the gold certificates Woodrow Wilson announced conscription in preparation for World War I by proclaiming that "this is not conscription but a nation's volunteering as a whole." I am not opposed to conscription. Under the conditions of modern war, to refuse to invoke it would probably be to accept inevitable defeat in advance. But is there in *1984* any more perfect example of "newsthink"? And should a government sink to the level of a Madison Avenue copywriter or the Soviet Politburo?

Newsthink, like everything good or bad, is of course not a new invention. In that line, Tertullian's "It is true because it is impossible" has never been improved upon; and I sometimes think that the Miltonic conception of "true freedom" as consisting only in the freedom to do right, not in the freedom to do wrong, must regretfully be put in the same class as the Russian definition of a People's Democracy as one in which the people have nothing to say about what happens to them.

But if newsthink is not a modern invention it certainly is one we have learned how to exploit more exuberantly than ever before. (Incidentally it might be added that Anna Louise Strong once wrote an article in which she resolved the paradox of the People's Democracy by maintaining that though the Russian people probably would not have voted in favor of many of the regulations imposed upon them these regulations did nevertheless implement "their deepest desires.")

Once you accept the premises that any sort of misrepresentation is justifiable if it helps us to achieve a desirable end, and that befuddlement of the people in their own interest is moral if not entirely honorable, you run into another difficulty: just who has a right to befuddle and who has not?

Consider for example the case of our own government which attempts to restrain misrepresentation in the advertising of business enterprises but is less severe in regard to its own domestic propaganda. On the one hand the FTC recently filed a complaint against one of the large phonograph companies which had been advertising a special offer of "any six of these superb $3.98 to $6.98 long-playing 12-inch records for only $1.89." "In truth and in fact," said the FTC, "the amounts set out . . . were not and are not now the prices at which the merchandise referred to is usually and customarily sold at retail." In other words the advertisement disregarded the fact that most record shops are now "discount houses."

Is the record company's advertising any more misleading than that which the government itself sponsors for Savings Bonds? Does anyone responsible for them really believe that if you start now buying bonds to pay for the future education of your infant child on the basis of what education now costs, you will actually be able to finance it twenty years hence out of the accumulated funds? Isn't it nearly as sure as death or taxes that the value of the dollar must continue to decline, that, in fact, our ability to deal with an expanding public debt depends in part upon the assumption that we will pay it off in a depreciated currency? Also that, therefore, either the investor in Savings Bonds will be left holding the bag or the nation will go bankrupt? It may be a patriotic duty to buy Savings Bonds. But to do so is not to insure your children's future.

Such consequences of newsthink and the habit of putting morality (i.e., expedience) ahead of honor (or truth-telling) are relatively minor by comparison with the great fact that nations have come all but openly to recognize that solemn covenants are solemn frauds. Word-breaking by nations is of course also no new thing; but at least it used to be called "treachery" not "realism" and the famous World War I pronouncement that a certain treaty was merely "a scrap of paper" came as a genuine surprise as well as a shock. It remained for a younger generation to come very near to accepting the assumption that all treaties are no more. The most inclusive generalization is that attributed to Lenin: "There is no such thing as morality in politics," though "honor" might be a more accurate word than "morality."

Chamberlain justified the sacrifice of Czechoslovakia on the ground that it would serve the greater good of the greater number by assuring the peace of Europe. But as is so often the case it turned out that dishonor didn't actually create the greater good and, even had it done so in this case, it would still have remained true that the basis of international agreements upon which, in the long run, peace must depend had been destroyed. Shortly thereafter the French began to shout "don't die for

Danzig," and now in our own country it is "better Red than dead." No doubt I shall be told that I am idealizing the past; that individuals and nations are as honorable as they ever were; and that the only change lies in the fact that we now more frankly admit that pledges are seldom kept if they work seriously to the disadvantage of those who make them. But there certainly is less honor among individual soldiers. When we read in history about this or that captured officer who "gave his parole" and was released to go home, does not that seem merely quaint? Who would be given such a privilege today, and who, if he were given it, would not consider that violating the parole was serving the higher morality if it enabled him to render more probable the ultimate achievement of that general good for which his country was fighting?

Just before the First World War broke out, *The New York Times* printed a now famous editorial in which it regretted what it recognized as the probability of large European conflict but expressed also the comforting conviction that a war between great powers was certain to be fought with due regard to the laws and protocols of existing international agreements. Probably most people accepted the optimistic assumption of the *Times* that honor was something which nations were still anxious to preserve and that necessity, the tyrant's plea, would not be accepted as sufficient excuse for any amount of treaty breaking.

Does everything which I have been saying seem priggish and self-righteous, or, as we are more likely to say nowadays, "unrealistic"? Perhaps it will seem less so if I admit that I do not know how to resolve the problems I have been trying to face. I wish I could believe that there never is a genuine rather than a merely hypocritical conflict between the honorable and the moral. But that such a conflict can exist is exactly the most troublesome aspect of the whole subject. I am—to return to one of the simplest examples I have given—not by any means ready to say that Roosevelt was wrong in taking us off the gold standard or even that Wilson was not justified, if, at a time of crisis, he helped unify the nation by his willingness to employ that outrageous bit of newsthink about "a nation's volunteering as a whole."

The problem is even more thorny when it takes the form so usual today: "Shall I keep faith with an enemy who, I am quite sure, will not keep faith with me?" But it still remains true that of all the moral decisions a statesman has to make none is more difficult than that which seems to require him to sacrifice either honor or the general good. Even when the latter seems clearly of overriding importance there are always two dangers—the first inherent in the fact that human nature weighs the scale in favor of personal advantage; the second that you never know how much you are losing when you demonstrate the untrustworthiness of your word.

Machiavelli had a rule: "Get a reputation for truth-telling and promise-keeping by being scrupulous about both when there isn't much at stake: then, having established that reputation, you can take advantage of it when a really important piece of treachery is in the making." That solution, though eminently realistic (and seeming not sufficiently considered even for practical purposes by the Russians), can hardly be called either moral or honorable. The most I can say is only that if in certain other ages both individuals and sometimes governments too readily resolved the dilemma in favor of what they called honor, ours leans too strongly in the opposite direction and that we would all be better off today if the greatest good hadn't been so readily accepted. Lord Tennyson is responsible for the somewhat fusty Victorian paradox: "His honor rooted in dishonor stood, and faith unfaithful kept him falsely true." I only wish that some equally talented modern would describe as pointedly the opposite situation where a high morality and a greater good are rooted in faith-breaking.

I hold to the opinion that our own country has, on the whole, behaved more honorably in recent years than some of its allies as well as most of its enemies, though I am well aware that many intellectuals would hoot at this as a bourgeois prejudice. I am, on the other hand, less sure that we are any better than others when it comes to the individual's willingness to accept as a rule of private conduct that everybody does it so it must be all right.

Certainly the recent investigations of cheating in schools and colleges and the prevailing attitude toward it suggest as much, and I recently met with an extraordinarily complicated example, both of the practice and the attitude. The high school son of a Tucson friend came to his father with a problem: pressure was being put upon him by a group of his fellows, all among the top students of the class, to join them in an elaborate scheme for falsifying the grades of some low-ranking members of the class. The conspirators would gain nothing scholastically—their grades were high already. But they would win the favor of those whom they benefited, many of the latter being among those "regular fellows" who, alas, have in the school society more status than the bookworms or the teacher's pets.

Accept honor as the decisive consideration and there is no problem;

otherwise it is quite a thorny one. If you can both help the poor lame ducks along and at the same time make it easier for everybody to "adjust to the social situation," is that not achieving perhaps the greatest good for the greatest number? And isn't it therefore obvious that honor should be sacrificed to morality—that is, if honor be defined as it now so often is as no more than "that which is socially useful."

[*If You Don't Mind My Saying So*, 1964.
First published in *The American Scholar*, 1963.]

## Challenge to an Unknown Writer

"When half-gods go the gods arrive." So at least said Emerson in words which summed up well the attitude of the Victorians. They were reeling under the impact of their century's multiple skepticisms but they were still able to believe that it must all be "somehow good."

We who were young in the twenties did not quote Emerson very often but we were very busy getting rid of half-gods and we believed in our job because we assumed—without always bothering to say so—that the gods were waiting to take their place. First of all, we said, let us get rid of Puritanism and Provincialism, the two great enemies of the freedom to be ourselves. And we were sure that we had selves which deserved to be free.

Almost every work of literature in any form was iconoclastic. Edgar Lee Masters and Sherwood Anderson we admired because they destroyed the idyllic image of the village; Sinclair Lewis because he did the same for the image of the small town. We admired Lytton Strachey because he revealed the clay feet of heroes and we imitated him clumsily in biographies which degenerated into that vulgarest form of idol-breaking which we all too appropriately named "debunking." If we were at least hectically cheerful that was because we cheerfully assumed that our gods (pagan gods, we hoped) would come. The new world was to be a merry one.

Freud we greeted with enthusiasm; and by selecting only the negative portions of his doctrine we assumed that he, too, was important chiefly because he exposed errors and seemed to encourage us to scrap the long-accepted patterns of behavior. Those critics and philosophers who dealt with concepts more abstruse than Puritanism and Provincialism were also largely concerned with clearing the ground. Remy de Gourmont—once much read but now apparently almost forgotten—popularized the general term "the dissociation of ideas," by which he meant the most radical possible dissolution of the habitual patterns associating one idea with another. Consciously or unconsciously, Proust was following him when he undertook to "dissociate the ideas of love and permanence"; Pirandello, when he attempted to dissolve the concept of a continuous personality or ego. When Eliot wrote "April is the cruelest month" he was dissociating one of the oldest associations, spring and renewed hope. Aldous Huxley was doing the same thing rather more obviously when, for instance, he described his lovers "quietly sweating palm to palm."

Incongruity rather than congruity became the accepted form of the metaphor and "the moon shook like a piece of angry candy." In much fashionable poetry, syntax was thrown to the winds. James Joyce all but destroyed language by making it a succession of incongruous puns. In Paris they proclaimed "the revolution of the world" and dadaism went the whole way by insisting upon radical meaninglessness. But just as the gods were expected to step in when the half-gods went, so, too, new associations were supposed to form once the old had been broken.

Like Emerson, Matthew Arnold also had tried to believe that though one world was dead there was another waiting to be born, and we, who thought ourselves so new, were unconsciously echoing him also. But the new world has not been born and the true gods are slow in arriving. Sinclair Lewis could expose Provincialism but he failed to create "a cultured heroine" who convinced anyone. We were no longer Puritans and we hoped that we were no longer provincials. We were free. But we did not know what we were free for. When the ground was cleared only Eliot's wasteland was left. We are now waiting, not for God, but for Godot. And even he is not expected to arrive.

The most obvious aspect of the new freedom was, of course, the sexual; and it was to some extent a sort of symbol of all the others. He who rejected in that department the mores of a preceding generation would be prepared, we thought, to reject all the others. Dissociation was again the method. If we could dissociate the ideas of love and permanence we could also dissociate "sex" from "domesticity," from "fidelity," and, of course, from "sin." Freed from all the arbitrary associations which had resulted in the frustrations, repressions, and guilty misery of the Victorians, it would form other and happier ones. Ultimately, so we believed, the idea of sex would associate itself cheerfully with such ideas as playfulness, joy, fulfillment, and even just plain fun. In certain previous ages it had at least come somewhere near doing just that. And we assumed (a bit unhistorically perhaps) that pagan Greece represented an even more desirable synthesis and set of associations.

If we were ever actually successful pagans during some years of the twenties, we did not remain such for long. If one may take today's novels as evidence, we get precious little joy, fulfillment, or even fun out of sex. The heroes of Tennessee Williams are more bedeviled by it than the Pilgrim Fathers ever were. If there is anything which the heroes of contemporary fiction in any form most assuredly are not, it is happy pagans.

Just how those who neither write nor read fare in this respect is harder to know. "Popular culture" is certainly not timidly puritanical in its exploitation of "sex appeal." Almost all popular songs treat of love. The most improbable products—toilet paper, for example—cannot be advertised without the cooperation of some voluptuous female. The moving pictures try desperately to outdo one another in being "frank, explicit, free," or, as they say, "adult"—this last being, curiously enough, the exact opposite of what the marriage counselors call "mature." Moralists are prone to assume that all of this means that we are abandoned devotees of the Venus Pandemos and that the man in the street, unlike the intellectual, is reveling in pagan orgies. But I am not quite sure that this is what all this desperate emphasis upon the delights of sex really means.

Anthropologists tell us that in primitive societies fertility cults involve erotic dances, and the exhibition of realistic or symbolic representations of the sex organs. But some of them, at least, add that this means, not that primitive people are obsessively attracted by sexual activity, but that they are not. The purpose of the rites is to work up an interest in something they tend to forget all about.

I am now about to ask a question rather than to make a statement. But I cannot help wondering if the dutiful wolf whistle and mammary fetishism do not suggest a similar state of affairs. If we were really so randy as we pretend to be, would we need all this stimulation? Certainly the names of and the publicity for the more expensive perfumes suggest that women are compelled to use desperate means to provoke even the most libertine of proposals. After all, the night clubs, the musical shows, and the "continental" movies are only Barmecide feasts. Do most of the spectators proceed from them to their private games or (depending upon age) do they either resume their longing for a sports car or their perusal of the *Wall Street Journal*?

So far as intellectuals are concerned, their plight seems to be, in part at least, due to the fact that instead of finding any idea which can be pleasantly associated with any other, they go from dissociation to dissociation. Once we were content to say that we did not understand the universe. Now we declare that it is radically incomprehensible. Mr. Mencken set out to prove only that the "American Way of Life" was absurd; now, as Existentialists, we have given "absurd" a technical meaning and accept it as the primary characteristic of the universe.

"Only he who has chaos within," said Nietzsche, "can give birth to a dancing star." But though we have chaos aplenty the dancing stars are few. "Nonconformity" is, I suppose, a middle-brow rather than a high-brow ideal but it, too, is characteristically negative. Like "freedom" it is meaningless unless you know for what purpose you refuse to conform. "Mother," runs a current quip, "why aren't you a nonconformist like everybody else?" If "existential," "absurd," and "alienated" are the three most fashionable adjectives, the phrase which will best establish you as "projecting a contemporary image" is "the search for identity." And that is the latest way of saying that you feel lost. Being lost is the inevitable result of being free and nonconformist without knowing what you are free or nonconformist for. To have an identity it is necessary to know what you belong to as well as to what you do not.

Ideally, the business of the "intellectual"—in the special, narrow sense of that word—is to define ultimate values. The business of the statesman, the sociologist, the economist, and the lawmaker is to devise the means by which they can be made to prevail. But rarely have the two groups paid so little attention to one another. The first are still predominantly icono-clasts verging toward, if not actually accepting, a nihilistic despair. Many, at least, of the second are full of hopeful plans to abolish racial and eco-nomic inequality, to raise still further the standard of living in our own country, to develop the undeveloped countries, and thus to fulfill the hopes of the world.

In a recent issue of a scholarly magazine the director of a large founda-tion addressed himself to the question of "Our National Purpose." What aim, he asked, lies beyond the immediate, almost solved problem of se-curing the benefits of our affluent society to all citizens of our republic? And the answer which he finally came up with was this: "Why, to confer upon the inhabitants of the whole earth the benefits of our own prosperity and our own way of life." But are we so sure that we Americans lead not only a good life, but the very best life, and that an adequate national pur-pose is simply to spread it far and wide? To some of us it seems that we could do with some of the kind of fundamental questioning which in-tellectuals are supposed to provide but which we do not get much of in any usable form. It is hardly fair to blame the doers for not consulting the thinkers if the latter will tell them only that a Good Life is impossible in an "existential" and "absurd" universe.

The two groups are literally poles apart. At one pole is the social engineer who relies upon economic reform and "proper conditioning," which latter is to be achieved by the application of those methods of manipulation that "the behavioral sciences" have developed and which (when applied by our enemies) we call "brainwashing." At the other pole are the intellectuals who recommend only that we strive toward that existential resignation which makes the absurd acceptable. If the former actually are on the right track; if society makes men and if most men would be happy in a world where they would find "things" sufficient if only we have enough of them, then we seem to be headed for a civilization in which everybody will be content except the thinkers—who have grown desperate.

Perhaps that is, indeed, the civilization we now have. The consciously "alienated" are certainly a very small minority. The majority may be, as the minority insists, vaguely and subconsciously anxious and discontent. But so far as I can observe, those who have fast cars to drive, TV sets to look at, and cake as well as bread to eat do not consider their world "absurd" and if they long for anything it is not usually something the intellectuals promise them. Nor is this to be wondered at. If the only choice is between a sort of comfortable barbarism and despair, then I suppose that the first is a wiser choice.

Would it be reasonable to hope that literature might do something to rescue us from nihilism on the one hand and from thoughtless adjustment to a kind of life which is abundant without being good? Would it be reasonable to ask, even, that it should make some effort to do so?

Many will reply that to ask such a question is to bring out into the open at last the Philistinism they had suspected from my first paragraph. The business of the writer of fiction is, they say, to describe life as it is lived. All art "expresses" or "reflects" the world in which the artist lives. If contemporary literature is confused, dispirited, and ugly, why, so is the modern world. It embodies the spirit of the age. To do anything else would be to betray its function.

Before we accept that answer as final we might dare to question two of its assumptions. Does contemporary literature adequately describe life as it is led in the twentieth century? If it does, then is this all that the literary art should be expected to do?

Actually, of course, no literary work in any form describes all the kinds of life being lived at any time. The writer could not, even if he would, do that, and he rarely attempts to do so. He selects aspects, puts his emphasis on one thing rather than another, describes what he himself finds most interesting or even, in some quite respectable instances, what is most readily marketable. The heroes of our O'Haras, to say nothing of our Mailers and Joneses, may be, as their creators would maintain, the most characteristic and the most significant of our age. But they are certainly not the only kind of people who exist. William Dean Howells has been often ridiculed for saying that it was the business of the American novelist to describe only "the more smiling aspects" of American life. But absurd as that was, it is no more absurd than the assumption that he should describe only those which grin and grimace and gnash their teeth though they never smile. A generation ago G. K. Chesterton defended Dickens against a charge that his geniality and optimism were exaggerated by saying that they undoubtedly were; but no more exaggerated than the gloom of Dostoevsky. It merely happens, he added, that today exaggeration in one direction, but not in the other, is regarded as reprehensible.

More crucial is the question whether to "express" or "reflect" the spirit of the age is indeed the only proper function of literature. Does it not also, and should it not also, at least influence if it does not create that spirit? We still use the phrase "creative writer" but if he only "reflects" and "expresses" then what does he create?

Perhaps the almost unquestioning acceptance of the theory that art is "a reflection" is another example of the extent to which Marxist theories have tended to dominate the thinking even of these who would not call themselves Marxists. If all philosophies and all convictions are mere "ideologies" and therefore mere reflections of the dialectic of an evolving society, then a reasonable corollary is that literature is, in turn, a mere "expression" or "reflection" of both the society and the ideologies that society has generated. But if one believes that art leads some kind of independent existence, that men make the societies they are in turn made by, then the creative writer, like the thinker of every kind, is not merely acted upon. He also acts. "As a man thinketh so he is" embodies at least as much truth as any Marxian assumption that what he thinks depends merely upon what he (and his society) are. To a considerable extent, at least, we see life as it has been presented to us in the books we read. The spirit of the age has been created by its artists at least as much as it has created them.

"If it were not for poetry few men would ever fall in love." So declared La Rochefoucauld in one of the most often quoted of his proverbs. If you understand "love" to mean an emotion which grows out of the association of a whole complex of ideas with nascent sexual attraction, then the epigram is as true as an epigram need be. The poets whom La Rochefoucauld had in mind made the associations. His saying is also rather truer than what is implied by those who maintain that literature can only "reflect." No man can write love poetry, they seem to say, because nobody falls in love any more. But perhaps more modern intellectuals would fall in love if more of their favorite poets taught them how.

If this really is a meaningless universe—and I am not Existentialist enough to be sure that it is—then one thing is certain: great literature describes life in terms which confer meaning upon it. Twenty-eight years ago, when I myself had recently ceased to believe that getting rid of half-gods was sufficient to assure the arrival of the true ones, I wrote in a book (*Experience and Art*) a paragraph by which I will still stand:

> If Love and Honor and Duty can be salvaged, then someone must write about them in a fashion which carries conviction. If we are to get along without them, then someone must describe a world from which they are absent in a fashion which makes that world seem worth having. And it is just the failure to do either of these things quite adequately which reveals the weakness of contemporary literature.

At the end of a recent and much admired play by Ionesco the hero proclaims that he himself, all alone if necessary, will refuse to turn into a rhinoceros. That is a good beginning. But what is it that he intends to remain? Just not being a rhinoceros isn't enough.

[*If You Don't Mind My Saying So*, 1964.
First published in the *Saturday Review*, 1962.]

# ▪ The Two Cultures ▪

### Is Our Common Man Too Common?

The Age of the Common Man is not merely a phrase; it is also a fact. Already we are definitely entered upon it, and in all probability it is destined to continue for a long time, intensifying its characteristics as it develops in some of the directions which it has already begun to take.

Most people welcome the fact, but we have only begun to assess it or even to ask ourselves what choices are still open to us once the grand decision has been made, as by now it has. How common does the common man need to be? Does his dominance necessarily mean that the uncommon man will cease to be tolerated or that the world will become less suited to his needs, less favorable to the development of his talents than it now is? Will excellence be looked upon as in itself unworthy or "undemocratic"? Can we have an Age of the Common Man without making it an Age of the Common Denominator? Do any dangers lie ahead?

One way to approach these questions is, of course, to ask what has happened already, what changes in attitudes have demonstrably taken place, how the culture of the first era of the Age of the Common Man differs from that which preceded it. What, in other words, is the culture of present-day America like, and are there aspects of it, directly traceable to the emphasis on the common man and his tastes, which are not wholly reassuring? And if there are, then to what extent are the defects corrigible, to what extent are they necessary consequences of the premises we have already accepted?

Unfortunately, but not surprisingly, there is no general agreement concerning the real nature of the situation at the present moment, though it does seem clear enough that most Americans judge both the present and the future a good deal more favorably than many observers from the Old World do. Thus, in his recent book *The Big Change,* Frederick Lewis Allen summed up very cogently the case for contemporary American culture. Hundreds of thousands read the selections of the book clubs; hundreds of thousands more attend concerts of serious music; millions listen to debates, symphonies, and operas on the radio. Never before in the history of the world has so large a portion of any population been so interested in and so alert to intellectual and artistic activities. Ours is the most cultured nation which ever existed.

Compare this with any one of the typical fulminations which proceed at regular intervals from European commentators and the result is both astonishing and disturbing. In Europe the prevalent opinion seems to be that this same civilization of ours constitutes a serious threat to the very existence of anything which can properly be called a culture.

We are told, in the first place, that for every American who does read the Book of the Month and attend a symphony concert there are a dozen who live in a vulgar dreamworld induced by a perpetual diet of soap operas, comic books, torch songs, and "B" movies. Moreover, the material prosperity and political power of this majority of sick barbarians enable them to become, as no cultural proletariat ever was before, a threat to every civilized minority. They rule the roost, and they are becoming less and less tolerant of anyone or anything superior to them.

In the second place—and perhaps even more importantly—the culture of even the minority is described as largely an imitation. It consumes but does not produce art. The best of the books it reads and the music it listens to is imported. Its members are really only parasites feeding upon European culture, and their sterility will in time kill it completely. Even their power to "appreciate" is essentially shallow—the result of superficial education, propaganda, advertisement, and a general pro-cultural hoop-la, all of which produce something very different indeed from that deep, personal, demanding passion for Truth and Beauty which has always been the dynamic force in the production of any genuine culture.

Now it is easy enough to dismiss this European view as merely the product of ignorance, prejudice, and envy. But it is dangerous to do so. To look candidly at the two pictures is to perceive something recognizable in both of them. Nobody really knows what the American phenomenon means or what it portends. And the reason is that it is actually something genuinely new. Whether you call it the Dawn of the First Democratic Culture or call it the Triumph of Mediocrity, the fact remains that there is no obvious parallel in human history. Mr. Allen and those who agree with him are obviously right as far as they go. But the unique phenomenon which they describe can stand further analysis.

A college education for everybody and two cars in every garage are ideals not wholly unrelated. An even closer analogy can be drawn with the earlier, more modest ideal of universal literacy. America was the first country to teach nearly everybody to read. Whether we are quite aware of it or not, we are now embarked upon the pursuit of what is really an extension of the same ideal, namely, a minimum cultural literacy for all. There is vast difference between being barely able to spell out a newspaper and being able to read in the full sense of what the term implies. There is a similar and probably no greater difference between, say, being able to get something out of the movie *The Great Caruso* or the latest volume dispatched to the members of a book club by editors who have trained themselves to understand the limitations of their average subscriber, and a genuine grasp of either music or literature. The term "literacy" covers a large area whether we are using it in its limited sense or extending it to include what I have called "cultural literacy." A few generations ago we pointed with pride to the fact that most Americans "could read"; we now point with pride to the fact that an astonishing proportion of them "read serious books" or "listen to serious music," and in both cases we take satisfaction in a mass capacity which exists only if we define it in minimum terms. In neither case does the phenomenon mean quite as much as those who celebrate it most enthusiastically sometimes seem to assume.

But, what, one may ask, is either disturbing or surprising about that? The minimum remains something more than any people as a whole ever before achieved. Is it likely that fewer people will read well just because a larger number can read a little? Is not, indeed, the opposite likely to be true? Is anything but good likely to come from the establishment of a broad base of even a minimum cultural literacy?

Any hesitation in answering "no" to the last question might seem at first sight to spring inevitably from nothing except arrogance, snobbishness, and a desire to preserve the privileges of an aristocracy. Yet a good many Europeans and an occasional American do seem inclined to take the negative position. The wide spread of our minimum culture does seem to them to constitute some sort of threat.

At least one fact or alleged fact they can cite as possible evidence on their side of the argument. So far, the number of recognized masterpieces produced by native-born Americans does seem disappointingly small when compared with the number of literate citizens we have produced. Is that because American art is inadequately recognized, or because we just haven't had time yet to mature? Or is it, perhaps, somehow connected— as some would say it is—with mass culture itself. Is the Good always the friend of the Best or is it sometimes and somehow the enemy? Is Excellence more likely to lose out to Mediocrity than it is to mere Ignorance or Nullity?

The line being taken in Europe today has a good deal in common with that of the twenties. To some extent indeed it may have been learned from our post-World War I intellectuals; the disdainful European conception of American society is a good deal like Mencken's Boobocracy. At the present moment, however, the current of opinion at home is running in the opposite direction, and it is no longer unusual for the confessed intellectual to defend the culture which his predecessor of a generation ago despised and rejected. But complacency has its dangers too, and it may be worthwhile to examine a little further what can be said in support of the European's thesis.

This, he hears us say, is the Age of the Common Man. But we as well as he are not quite certain what we mean by that. Insofar as we mean only the age of universal opportunity, what was once called simply "the career open to talents," nothing but good could seem to come of it. But many people do, sometimes without being entirely aware of it, mean something more. When we make ourselves the champion of any particular group we almost inevitably begin to idealize that group. From defending the common man we pass on to exalting him, and we find ourselves beginning to imply not merely that he is as good as anybody else but that he is actually better. Instead of demanding only that the common man be given an opportunity to become as uncommon as possible, we make his commonness a virtue and, even in the case of candidates for high office, we sometimes praise them for being nearly indistinguishable from the average man in the street. Secretly, no doubt, we hope that they are somehow superior, but we feel at the same time that a kind of decency requires them to conceal the fact as completely as possible.

The logical extreme of this opinion would be the conviction that any deviation in either direction from the statistical average is unadmirable; even, to take a concrete example, that the ideal man or woman could best be represented, not by an artist's dream, but by a composite photograph of the entire population. And though few would explicitly acknowledge their acceptance of this extreme position, there is a very strong tendency to emphasize quantitative rather than qualitative standards in estimating achievement. We are, for instance, more inclined to boast how many Americans go to college than to ask how much the average college education amounts to; how many people read books rather than how good the books are; how many listen to the radio rather than how good what they hear really is.

Argue, as I myself have argued, that more can be learned about almost any subject from ten minutes with a printed page than from half an hour with even one of the better educational programs and you will be met with the reply: "Perhaps. But so many *more* people will listen to the radio." In a democracy quantity is important. But when the stress upon it becomes too nearly exclusive, then democracy itself threatens to lose its promise of moving on to higher levels. Thus the Good really can become the enemy of the Best if one insists upon exclusively quantitative standards.

Certainly one of the striking—some would say one of the inevitable—characteristics of our society is its penchant for making widely and easily accessible either substitutes for, or inferior versions of, a vast number of good things, like the vile substitute for bread available at any grocer's. That bread can be come by without effort, and it may be true that fewer people are in want of bread of some kind than ever were in want of it in any society before. But that does not change the fact that it is a very inferior product.

Another and related tendency of this same society is its encouragement of passivity. A generation ago moralists viewed with alarm the popularity of "spectator sports": the fact that people gathered in stadia to watch others play games for them. But we have gone far beyond that and today the baseball fan who takes the trouble to make a journey to the Polo Grounds instead of watching the game on his TV set has almost earned the right to call himself an athlete. One wonders, sometimes, if the popularity of "discussion" programs does not mean very much the same thing; if most people have not now decided to let others hold remote conversations for them—as well as play remote games—even though the conversations are often no better than those they could hold for themselves.

As John Stuart Mill—certainly no antidemocrat—wrote a century ago: "Capacity for the nobler feeling is in most natures a very tender plant. . . . Men lose their high aspirations as they lose their intellectual tastes, because they have not time or opportunity for indulging them; and they addict themselves to inferior pleasures, not because they deliberately prefer them, but because they are either the only ones to which they have access, or the only ones which they are any longer capable of enjoying."

In the history books of the future this age of ours may come to be known as the Age of Statistics. In the biological and physical as well as the sociological sciences, statistics have become, as they never were before, the most important tool of investigation. But as every philosophical scientist knows, the conclusions drawn by a science depend to a considerable extent upon the tools used. And it is in the nature of statistics not only that they deal with quantity but that they emphasize the significance of averages and medians. What usually exists or usually happens establishes The Law, and The Law is soon thought of as identical with The Truth. In all the arts, nevertheless, it is the exceptional and unpredictable which really count. It is the excellent, not the average, which is really important. And there is, therefore, one aspect of the cultural condition of a civilization to which statistical study is curiously inappropriate.

No one, it may be said, needs to accept the inferior substitute or hold himself down to the average level. But simple and complete as that answer may seem to be, there are facts and forces which do tend to encourage an almost unconscious acceptance of mediocrity. One, of course, is that the inferior substitute—whether it be baker's bread or the movie show playing at the neighborhood house—is so readily accessible and so forced upon one's attention by all the arts of advertising as well as by the very way in which our lives have been organized. Another and more serious one is the tendency of the mass media to force out of the field every enterprise which is not based upon mass appeal. Whatever the reason may be, it is a generally recognized fact that it is becoming increasingly difficult, economically, to publish a book which is not a best seller or produce a play which is not a smash hit. More and more, therefore, artistic enterprise must be abandoned to the movies and to television where the mass audience is sufficient to defray the staggering cost.

Besides these economic reasons why the new media tend to concern themselves only with mass appeals, there is the additional technical reason why the two newest of such media tend to confine themselves to it. Since TV and radio channels are limited in number, all the arguments in favor of democracy as it is sometimes defined justify the existing fact that these channels should be used to communicate what the greatest number of people seem to want. That is the argument of the great broadcasting chains, and on the premise assumed it is a valid one.

The only mechanical instrument of communication which can make a reasonable case for the claim that it has actually served to increase the popularity of the thing communicated on its highest level of excellence is the phonograph, and it is significant that the phonograph is the only such device for communication which—especially since the invention of tape recording and LP—has found it economically feasible to cater to relatively small minorities. The fact that it does not cost much to produce a record may well have an incalculably great effect upon American musical taste.

What the question comes down to in the simplest possible terms is one of those which we asked at the very beginning of this discussion: Can we have an Age of the Common Man without having also an Age of the Common Denominator? That question has not been answered, probably cannot be convincingly answered, at the present moment. But it is a fateful question and the one with which this discussion is concerned.

One must not, of course, idealize the past to the extent of assuming that the best works were always, inevitably, and immediately the most popular. Two years ago James D. Hart's thorough and amusing *The Popular Book* (Oxford University Press) demonstrated conclusively that since colonial times there have always been absurd best sellers. The year that Hawthorne earned $144.09 royalties in six months was the year his own publisher paid Susan Warner $4,500 for the same period and another publisher sold 70,000 copies of one of Fanny Fern's several works.

Neither, I think, should it be supposed that any society ever has been or ever will be so organized as to favor exclusively the highest artistic excellence. As a system, aristocratic patronage is absurdly capricious; capitalistic democracy tends to favor vulgarity; socialism would probably favor official mediocrity. The question here is not whether contemporary America provides ideal conditions for cultural developments on the highest level, but whether it renders such development unusually difficult instead of making it, as the optimists insist, almost inevitable.

Of the unfavorable influences which I have mentioned, it seems to me that the most serious is the tendency to confuse the Common Denominator with a standard of excellence. The mechanical and economic facts which tend to give the purveyors of mediocrity a monopoly—highly developed in the case of radio and TV, probably growing in the publishing business —may possibly be changed by new developments, as they have already been changed in the case of the phonograph. But to confuse The Best with the most widely and the most generally acceptable is to reveal a spiritual confusion which is subtle and insidious as well as fundamental. It could easily nullify any solution of the mechanical and economic problems created by the Age of Mass Production. How real and how general does this confusion seem actually to be?

More than one sociologist has recently pointed out that as technology integrates larger and larger populations into tighter and tighter groups the members of these groups tend inevitably to work, live, and recreate themselves in the same way and in accordance with the standardized patterns which the facilities provided for these various activities lay down. For ill as well as for good, "community living" becomes more and more nearly inevitable and individual temperament or taste finds less and less opportunity to express itself.

One result of this is that the natural tendency of the adolescent to practice a desperate conformity is prolonged into adult life and the grown man continues to want what his neighbors have, to do what his neighbors do, to enjoy what his neighbors enjoy. This is one of the things which the European may have in mind when he calls us a nation of adolescents, and commercial interests take advantage of our adolescent characteristics by stressing, through all sorts of publicity, the fact that this is the kind of cigarette most people smoke, the kind of breakfast food most people eat, and the torch singer or crooner most people like. The best-selling book is not only the easiest one to buy, but it is also the one we must read unless we are willing to be made to seem somehow inferior. What is most popular must be best. As a broadcast official recently said, to call the most popular radio programs vulgar is to call the American people vulgar. And that, he seemed to imply, was not merely nonsense but pretty close to treason. The voice of the people is the voice of God. God loves the common man. If the common man loves Bob Hope then God must love Bob Hope also. In musical taste as in everything else the common man is divine.

It is this logic which, unfortunately, the purveyors to the mass audience are very prone to follow. Undoubtedly, it leads them to the line of least resistance at the same time that it provides them with a smug excuse for both inanity and vulgarity. They are, they say, servants of the public and have no right to doubt that the people know not only what they want but what is good for them. The age of the common man has no place for any holier-than-thou attitude. It believes in government "by" as well as "for" the people. Totalitarianism is what you get when you accept the "for" but not the "by," and the attitude of, for example, the British Broadcasting Corporation, with its notorious Third Program, merely demonstrates that England has not yet learned what democracy really means.

No doubt the questions involved are too complicated to be discussed here. A few years ago, Charles A. Siepmann in his *Radio, Television, and Society* fully and impartially reported on both the policies and the arguments as they affect the media with which he was dealing. But at least one conclusion seems obvious. If there is any such thing as responsibility on the part of those most powerful and best informed towards those whose appetites they feed, then no provider of movies or records or television programs may escape the minimal duty of giving his public the best rather than the worst it will stand for. Mr. Mencken once declared that no one had ever gone bankrupt by underestimating the taste of the American public, but there is an increasing tendency to believe that, by dint of long trying, certain commercial exploiters of the mass media have succeeded only too well in underestimating it considerably.

What is obviously called for is a public opinion less ready than it now is to excuse the failure to meet even minimal responsibilities; but that public opinion is not likely to arise unless those responsible for public thinking play their own parts, and there is a tendency for them to yield rather than protest. Unfortunately, the fanatical exaltation of the common denominator has been taken up not only by the common man himself and by those who hope to profit by his exploitation but also and increasingly by those who are supposed to be educators and intellectual leaders. Instead of asking "what would a good education consist of?" many professors of education are asking "What do most college students want?"; instead of asking "What books are wisest and best and most beautiful?" they conduct polls to determine which the largest number of students have read with least pain. Examination papers are marked not in accordance with any fixed standard, but in accordance with a usual level of achievement; the amount of work required is fixed by the amount the average student does; even the words with which the average student is not familiar are edited out of the books he is given to read. How, granted such methods, is it other than inevitable both that the average will seldom be exceeded and that the average itself will gradually drop?

As David Reisman and his collaborators pointed out two years ago in their brilliant analysis called *The Lonely Crowd* (Yale University Press), the ideal now persistently held before the American citizen from the moment he enters kindergarten to the time when he is buried under the auspices of a recognized funeral parlor is a kind of conformity more or less disguised under the term "adjustment." "Normality" has almost completely replaced "Excellence" as an ideal. It has also rendered all but obsolescent such terms as "Righteousness," "Integrity," and "Truth." The question is no longer how a boy ought to behave but how most boys do behave; not how honest a man ought to be but how honest men usually are. Even the Robber Baron, who represented an evil manifestation of the determination to excel, gives way to the moneymaker who wants only to be rich according to the accepted standards of his group. Or, as Mr. Reisman sums it up, the American who used to be conspicuously "inner-directed" is now conspicuously "outerdirected."

According to the anthropologists, many primitive societies are based almost exclusively upon the idea of conformity and generate what are, in the anthropologist's meaning of the term, remarkable cultures. It may, of course, be argued that America and the whole world which follows in America's wake is evolving in the direction of this kind of culture. But if by "culture" we mean something more narrowly defined, if we mean a culture which is continuous with that of the Western world since the Renaissance, then it is my contention that it cannot flourish where the stress is as nearly exclusively as it threatens to become upon "adjustment," "normality," or any of the other concepts which, in the end, come down to mean that the Common Denominator is identical with the Ideal. Especially, it cannot flourish under these conditions if the result which they tend to produce is intensified by the fact that ingenious methods of mass production and mass propaganda help impose upon all the tyranny of the average.

Salvation, if salvation is possible, may be made so by technological developments like those in the phonograph industry which tend to break monopoly and permit the individual to assert his preferences and his tastes. But the possible will not become the actual if in the meantime the desire for excellence has been lost and those who should be leaders have willingly become followers instead. If the Age of the Common Man is not to become the Age of the Common Denominator rather than what it was originally intended to be—namely an age in which every man had the opportunity to become as superior as he could—then the cultural as well as the political rights of minorities must somehow be acknowledged. There is not really anything undemocratic about either the desire for, or the recognition of, excellence. To prove that ours is the most cultured nation which ever existed will constitute only a barren victory if we must, to prove our point, use nothing but quantitative standards and reconcile ourselves to the common denominator as a measure of excellence.

One might sum up the situation in a series of propositions. (1) The Age of the Common Man has begun. (2) Despite all the gains that it may legitimately claim, they are threatened by those confusions which arise when the common denominator is consciously or unconsciously allowed to function as a standard of excellence. (3) The dominance of mass media almost exclusively under the control of those who are little concerned with anything except immediate financial gain does tend to debase taste. (4) Ultimate responsibility for the future rests with the thinkers and the educators whose most important social task at the moment is to define democratic culture in some fashion which will both reserve a place for uncommon excellence and, even in connection with the largest masses, emphasize the highest rather than the lowest common denominator.

[First published in the *Saturday Review,* 1953.]

## Are the Humanities Worth Saving?

In his sentimental moments even the tycoon sometimes puts in a word for the good old days, and he may, like Henry Ford, support a museum to preserve their relics. In somewhat similar fashion nearly everybody professes to regret "the neglect of The Humanities." Any discussion of education or of contemporary civilization is likely to include a formal bow in the direction of Culture, much like the equally formal bow in the general direction of Religion. "Oh yes, I almost forgot. There is also God and the humanities—very important things of course, though I haven't time to discuss them now."

Nevertheless, the tycoon is not anxious to bring the good old days back, and relatively few people are actively interested in the humanities, no matter how seriously they profess to take them. Compare the contents of any "class magazine" with that of a corresponding publication of the nineteenth century. Compare, for example, the modern *Harper's* or *Atlan-*

*tic* with the same magazine two generations ago. Politics, sociology, and—to a lesser extent—science have now almost a monopoly. Any sort of writing whose appeal is primarily to what are still somewhat vaguely called "cultural interests" is almost nonexistent. Yet it was the staple of these same magazines not so very long ago. About such things their public has obviously ceased to care very much.

If, despite the parlousness of the times, there really is a case for The Humanities, why does the public continue indifferent? Can it be because that public, though willing to support liberal arts colleges much as it is willing to support churches, is not very clear in its own mind what the humanities are about or what they are for? Would it be wise for a time to talk less about their sad neglect and more about what, if anything, they are?

The word itself is exceedingly vague. Interpret it broadly as "whatever concerns the human being" and there isn't much it cannot be made to include. Interpret it as narrowly as it is sometimes interpreted and it ceases to mean much more than "polite accomplishments," analogous to the needlework and flower-painting which ladies were once supposed to dabble in, principally in order to demonstrate that they really were ladies rather than something economically and socially inferior. Those—and there are many—who unconsciously define the word thus, quite properly relegate all the activities it implies to idle upper-class ladies and to those timid, ineffectual males who are tolerated in a realistic society because of the entertainment they provide for these same refined ladies.

A subtler approach is the attempt to give real meaning to the concept "humane" by a process of elimination. In contradistinction to *what* are certain pursuits so described? To that question the Renaissance scholars who gave us the word would probably have replied something like this: "Why, humane learning is so called to distinguish it from divine learning or theology; also, of course, in contradistinction to those 'illiberal' studies merely mechanical or immediately utilitarian in their aims. More specifically, 'humane' means what you find in the writers of Greece and Rome."

Unfortunately, time has tended to destroy the usefulness of these definitions without supplying us with a good one that is currently workable. "The humanities" does not mean merely the Greek and Roman classics because, however valuable or even indispensable they may be, they do not now contain all humane knowledge. "Humane" does not mean merely "profane" as opposed to "sacred," because nearly everything with which the modern world concerns itself is "profane" in that sense. And, though the term still does mean "without immediately useful application," the development of the sciences has raised a new confusion. They are no longer necessarily "illiberal" and they are not always merely immediately practical in their aims.

Deny the adjective "humane" to all scientific knowledge and you impoverish the concept of the humanities to a point where it is even more likely to suggest little more than "elegant accomplishments" plus "a pious concern with the notions and achievements of the past." You encourage the idea that the humane is not merely nonscientific but actually antiscientific; that it implies a flight from modern knowledge, and that therefore "the humanist" is necessarily some sort of old fogey, a quaint and curious adherent of a lost cause, worth tolerating only because he embodies some charm to which we make a faint nostalgic response.

At the other extreme is the position taken up in the late nineteenth century by those who followed the lead of Huxley. To them modern science is simply the form that humane learning has assumed in our time. Chemistry and physics and biology *are* Culture. To study them is not only to master specific facts but to reap at the same time all the benefits supposed in the past to accompany the study of the classic curriculum.

When we lament today the neglect of the humanities, or discuss solemnly what should be done about it, we get nowhere, partly because we do not define what we mean by the term and frequently vacillate between several possible meanings. Even when we try to face the crucial question of the relation between, and the rival claims of, "the sciences" and "the humanities," we seldom get beyond two vague notions: First, that the sciences are "humane" when they are taught as "cultural" rather than "professional" subjects; and second, that "the humanities" include also certain considerations and concerns which science cannot, or at least does not yet, take into consideration. But neither of these notions is very precise or very helpful. What are "the cultural aspects" of science and what, if anything, are the realities with which science cannot or does not deal?

Of these two questions the second seems to me the more important as well as the more difficult. Unlike certain nineteenth-century educators, we are aware that the physical sciences are not merely utilitarian. We no longer dismiss college courses in chemistry as "stinks" or assume that physics is merely something which the future engineer must learn. Science has influenced philosophical, ethical and religious thinking so profoundly that even those who regard the so-called scientific philosophies, religions and systems of ethics as erroneous, must recognize that any "cultured" man needs to know something about them as surely as a cultured atheist needs to know something about Christian doctrine and history.

But there is much less agreement on the other question. If the modern humanities are still to be something more than "science taught in such a way as to emphasize its cultural values" along with, perhaps, a certain amount of historical and antiquarian lore, then what is this something? What is its hard core? Is it anything except some knowledge of those irresponsible fancies with which the prescientific age permitted itself to dally and which we try to regard with condescending tolerance? Are there any important "humane truths" which are nonscientific?

Most of us who call ourselves humanists do believe that we deal with such truths. But we have not succeeded very well in making them seem real to others. Discuss the humanities with any scientifically-minded person. Even though he is one of those who will grant, at least for the sake of peace, that "the humanities ought not be neglected," the chances are that he will find it very difficult to say why, or to imagine what these same humanities may be, unless they are, essentially, not much more than a game some find it nostalgically agreeable to play with the naïve, disorderly, and usually erroneous notions which amused the childhood of our civilization. That there are any realities that can only be investigated by nonscientific methods, he can hardly believe. Yet unless there really are some such, then we take the humanities too seriously rather than not seriously enough.

Sometimes—though not often enough—official science admits that its field, though large, is limited; that its methods are not applicable to every subject of investigation; that it is not, in a word, omnicompetent. Yet it has extended its range so widely and produced results so impressive that neither the scientist himself, nor the public which he has so properly impressed, pays much attention to disclaimers. Both are prone to believe that the limitations of science leave little reality unexplored. And since we can hardly expect the scientist, even at his most modest, to define for us what he does not claim as part of his province, we must define it for ourselves, and what I propose is simply this: Let us examine the positive claims rather than the negative admissions of science, and see what that leaves over as a possible subject with which the humanities alone may deal, in their admittedly less positive manner.

By science's more modest practitioners we are sometimes told that its subject matter is *all objectively verifiable truth,* and that its method is *experimental verification.* It deals with what can be proved and, especially, *with what can be measured.* Could we then define the humanities by stating a simple opposite? "Humane learning and humane studies are those which concern themselves with what cannot be experimentally verified and is not susceptible of measurement." That, I think, would clear the air.

Science has often misled the age when scientists have claimed scientific authority for statements which were not based upon any experiments and did not involve any accurate measurements. The humanities have often done themselves a disservice when, as often, they have rejected genuine scientific truths or when, as is nowadays more common, especially in connection with fiction and drama, they have claimed a kind of scientific authority for their own productions. But unless we are willing to affirm boldly that there is a large area of elusive truth which it would be fatal to neglect, but which nevertheless cannot be dealt with by any scientific method; unless we are willing to admit also that in this area doubt and dispute must rage, perhaps forever, because what is included within it cannot be measured or subjected to controlled experiment, then there is little use in "defending the humanities," because there is little left to defend.

Most of what are called "the cultural aspects of science" lie within the area of the humanities as here defined. So also do so many other vastly important matters that it is the field of science rather than the field of the humanities which seems, by comparison, restricted—so restricted indeed that science itself comes to seem only an astonishingly effective method of dealing with very limited subject matters. If we permit ourselves to contemplate the truths which cannot be verified and the values which cannot be measured, we may well wonder that any age dared to neglect them. Yet neglect them we did, and it may be for that very reason that a civilization which has made so many careful measurements and performed so many triumphant experiments is, nevertheless, a civilization which has come justly to fear that the human race itself may have no future.

Since the days of Francis Bacon there have always been individuals who maintained that only "facts"—positive and verifiable knowledge—are worth bothering with. But never before our own, has there been an age when most people made this assumption so uncritically, that they ask in all innocence for so much as a single example of something important and knowable which cannot be measured or made the subject of an experiment.

Suppose we consider, for example, that reality which is called "happiness." Pope described it as "our being's end and aim," and though there have always been some—Bernard Shaw is a modern instance—who dismissed happiness as unimportant, even scientists usually admit that most of us continue to pursue it whether we ought to or not. Yet "happiness" is something which falls almost completely outside the purview of science. Its various degrees cannot be measured. The conditions which produce it cannot be controlled. We cannot demonstrate that an individual man either is, or is not, happy. In fact, his emotional state cannot even be safely inferred. We know perfectly well that many a man who "ought to be happy" and many a man who "acts as though he were happy," isn't.

To banish these undoubted facts the positivist is forced into an absurd and disastrous subterfuge. Knowing that science cannot deal with subjective states and being committed to the contention that only scientific knowledge is useful, he cannot escape the conclusion that such subjects as happiness are not worth thinking about at all. We should, he says, devote ourselves instead to those objectively measurable and controllable factors which, so he blandly assumes, determine subjective states. Since we can make some sort of approximate measurements of "the standard of living" we will adopt the convenient assumption that happiness varies directly with the standard of living. Hence, though we cannot profitably talk about happiness, we can talk (and how!) about welfare. The two ought to be, approximately, the same thing.

No assumption could, of course, be falser: Literature may be unscientific but it has never made the mistake of assuming that prosperity is the same thing as happiness, or that people are happy when "they ought to be." Yet this simple fact is in itself enough to suggest both what the subject matter of the humanities is, and one of the functions humane works of literature, or art or philosophy *do* perform.

These works concern themselves with, for instance, happiness, contentment and joy—as well as with their opposites. Their first and simplest function is to keep us human by acknowledging, as the scientists do not, that "the merely subjective" is vastly important in human life, that we are not merely "economic men" or "members of a social group" or "psychological types" but Men to whom such unmeasurable, unverifiable, uncontrollable realities as happiness are at least as important as any which can be measured, verified, or controlled; that in a word, the subjective is the very core of our being. Because the Founding Fathers were essentially humanists they asserted man's right to Life, Liberty, and the Pursuit of Happiness. If they had not been humanists, it would have been to the Pursuit of Welfare, or even of a High Standard of Living!

Totalitarian governments boast that their aim is the establishment of a scientific society. Some would-be perfectors of what we call Western democracy seem to cherish a similar ideal. But no society that based itself exclusively upon what can be learned by the scientific study of man could consistently recognize the existence of happiness as distinct from prosperity, welfare or a "high standard of living." Nor could it, for that matter, recognize as real any aspect of any man's inner life. Yet, insofar as a democracy tends to ignore that inner life, just to that extent does it obscure one of the most important distinctions between the facts and the theories of totalitarianism and the Western tradition.

Without humane learning no man can remain what we now call Man. Either he will slowly become so extraverted and adjusted that he is actually no more than one of those figments of the imagination with which scientific politics and sociology deal, or his individual awareness of his truest and vividest inner life will alienate him from his fellow beings because he will have no communication with them in terms of that inner life; because he will meet no public acknowledgment of the fact that any other human beings live any such lives, or are, indeed, human at all. Politics unites the outward actions of men; "the humanities" unites their thoughts and feelings. It draws them together in spirit.

But this is by no means all. Indispensable as is the function which consists merely in revealing that an inner life is something not unique but shared, different as mankind would be had "the humanities" never publicly acknowledged its humanity, the great creators of the humane tradition did not stop with the performance of this function.

Though they were deprived of both measurement as a tool and of experiment as a method, they went on to investigate as well as to describe the phenomena with which they dealt. They drew conclusions from observations which cannot be rigidly controlled and projected upon human beings as a whole, experiences which they knew only from their own. Even the assumption that men other than themselves have any consciousness or desire can be made only by such a gratuitous projection. And though by such methods they have not "proved" anything, they have carried conviction; and it is by the power to convince rather than by experimental verification that we test the validity of any work which claims a place among "the humanities."

As a result of such unscientific procedures as it can employ, the humanistic enterprise has built up that store of ethical convictions, moral principles and standards of value by which men live, as surely as it has created an awareness of their intimate selves and the correspondence between one intimate self and another. The body of humanistic knowledge is neither wholly consistent with itself, much less is it demonstrably true in any objective sense. But it is, nevertheless, a body of imperfect knowledge indispensable to civilization.

In a profound posthumous essay published in *The Virginia Quarterly,* under the somewhat misleading title "Americanism," Santayana recently provided an original approach to the great underlying problem of today. The modern world, he says, began in the sixteenth century when Western Europe came first to realize fully that knowledge—at least a certain kind of knowledge—is power. The determination to acquire that kind of knowledge launched the most dazzlingly successful enterprise any group of human beings ever embarked upon. And if the most recent consequence is the growing fear that power, getting out of hand, will destroy the race that released it, there was another unnoticed consequence that preceded all such fears.

The very success, so patent and incontrovertible, of the determination to pursue relentlessly the newly-opened source of power, favored the unconscious conviction that the knowledge which does confer power is the only kind of knowledge there is. True knowledge, as opposed to mere fancy on the one hand and mere pedantry on the other, comes thus to be defined as simply "that which confers power." Moral philosophy, poetry and art are as contemptuously disregarded as the theology which the new age more specifically repudiated: They do not confer power—at least no power over the physical universe so evident as the power which scientific knowledge confers. And because they do not they are, therefore, not knowledge.

Words are tricky things. At first sight it may seem that De Quincey's famous distinction between the literature of *knowledge* and the literature of *power* is a direct contradiction of everything which has here been said. "Books, we are told, propose to *instruct* or to *amuse.* Indeed! . . . The true antithesis to knowledge, in this case, is not *pleasure* but *power.* All that is literature seeks to communicate power; all that is not literature, to communicate knowledge."

From another point of view the exact opposite may be said: "All literature seeks to communicate one kind of knowledge; all writing which is not literature seeks to communicate power." But the contradiction is apparent rather than real. Because De Quincey had never submitted to the tyranny of science he was able to mean by "power" not the ability to control directly the physical environment, but the ability to carry conviction and to arouse passion. He realized, in other words, precisely what kind of power humanistic knowledge confers upon mankind. It does confer upon us a kind of knowledge or, if you insist, halfknowledge, upon which the richness of human experience and the stability of society largely depend.

Deprive the individual and the world of all the convictions which science cannot prove to be legitimate, and neither man nor his world could stand. The question whether the humanists have revealed morality or invented it, whether they have discovered "value" or created it, is less important than the fact that but for them, mankind would never have conceived of, and quite certainly never have cherished, either. And if poets have sometimes fixed erroneous and pernicious ideas upon whole sections of the human race, at least only other and better poets have ever been able to remedy the evil.

Such at least is the affirmation which any effective defender of the humanities must be willing to make. Unless there is a kind of knowledge which is not power in the sense that scientific knowledge is power, and unless that kind of knowledge can, however imperfectly, be discovered and communicated by literature and the other arts, then the humanities are a fraud at worst, a trivial amusement at best. They certainly cannot save us and they are not worth saving. We should not be disturbed by their neglect. It would be more sensible to say, "Good riddance."

[*And Even If You Do,* 1967.
First published in the *Saturday Review,* 1953.]

## Should We Bring Literature to Children?

Fifteen years ago I accepted an invitation to address an association of teachers of English. No such organization has invited me since, and there may be some connection between the two events. The announced "theme" of the meeting was something like "How to Bring Literature to Children," and I told the audience that the question was all wrong. Trying to answer that wrong question had already led to "projects" for the study of

Shakespeare, which consisted not of discussing the plays, but of pasting up notebooks with publicity pictures for the movie version of *A Midsummer Night's Dream*. What they should ask, I said, was "How to Bring Children to Literature." Literature should stay right where it was. What they proposed was not education at all, but a refusal to educate.

Since that time great strides have been made in the art of bringing literature to children of all ages, from four to fourscore. The great novels and plays, reduced to half an hour on radio or television, we take for granted; and somewhat more alarmingly we also take it for granted that soldiers should learn both the art of war and the ideology of democracy out of comic books, prepared for their instruction.

With my thesis I imagine that a good many people will disagree, but most of even those who do, will not want to deny the existence of the tendency which they approve of and I do not. More and more it is taken for granted not that all men, being created equal, have a right to the best, but that "the best" is whatever the largest number of people find immediately accessible and pleasing. Therefore, of course, men are best served when we attempt to find out what they like and to give it to them.

Educators used to assume it was their duty to select the great books of the world and to teach students why they really are great. Even today the Chicago group advocates a somewhat fanatically narrow version of this assumption, and has created something of a stir because of a fundamental premise which would once have been thought self-evident. But the tendency of the time is much better illustrated by a group of professors of education who have just recently proposed that the list of required reading in schools should be based upon a study (which they have just sponsored) of the tastes of schoolchildren.

That the list so compiled contained very few of the supposed classics and was very heavily loaded with books that would seem very trivial indeed to any one whose taste was more cultivated than that of the children themselves, seemed to the educators a fact quite irrelevant. The question of whether or not this was the proper way to select books for educational purposes was not even raised. But it is certainly, and with a vengeance, "bringing literature to children" rather than bringing children to literature. Indeed, it is difficult to see just what we are supposed to be getting in return for all the money spent on schools if school children simply spend their time reading what they would read anyway. It might be argued that the teachers were learning something from the pupils— namely, what the taste of uneducated children is. But the pupils were certainly not learning anything from the teachers and it would seem that the children are the ones who ought to be paid salaries—if anyone should.

Would any pediatrician base the diet prescribed for the young submitted to his care, simply on an effort to determine what eatables they remembered with greatest pleasure? If he knew that the vote would run heavily in favor of chocolate sodas, orange pop, hot dogs and bubble gum, would he conclude that these should obviously constitute the fundamental elements in a "modern" child's menu?

Items drawn from the newspapers over a period of only a few weeks show clearly which way the wind is blowing. One college professor proposes that colleges should cease trying to teach college students what he contemptuously calls "literary English" and teach instead only that kind of expression which has been found "acceptable" in the student's own group. Another writes to protest the use of the word "ubiquity" in a newspaper, on the ground that many people do not know what it means. A third, going the whole way at once, urges that colleges drop from their courses of study everything which does not contribute to the student's "adjustment to society." The fact is, however, that language "acceptable to the group" is precisely what one gets in communities where there is no formal education whatsoever. The fact is also that if no one ever used any words which everybody did not know, then no one would ever learn any new ones, and the common vocabulary would gradually drop lower and lower until it contained only the three or four hundred words which are said to serve the needs of the most primitive people. As for "adjustment to society," that is something which necessarily goes on. But the purpose of education is, or at least was once assumed to be, the production of knowledge, attitudes, skills and tastes, to which, on the other hand, society would adjust itself.

Mr. Alexander Pope, whose works were not on the list of the schoolchild's favorite books, once described the progress of the learner as one in which he is, as he climbs, continuously inspired by the sight of new peaks beyond: "Hills peep o'er hills and Alps on Alps arise." In contemporary theory, whether in reference to the education of children or adults, nothing is supposed to be more carefully avoided than anything that suggests a glimpse just beyond the local horizon. Books are carefully graded according to the "age level" to which they are supposed to be appropriate. Vocabulary studies are consulted to make sure there are no words which the child at that "age level" is not supposed to know. But surely the best book for any intelligent child is often the one somewhat beyond his comprehension, and if there are some words he does not know, he may just possibly be inspired to find out what they mean.

I am well aware that the tendency that I have been deploring seems to some people to be what is meant by the "democratic movement." To me it is exactly the reverse because "democracy" seems to me to be based upon the belief—or at least the hope—that the "common man" does not have to remain common and that, given the opportunity, neither intellectuality nor artistic appreciation is beyond him. To believe the contrary and to conclude from that belief that whatever is the product of practice, cultivation, training and aspiration should be discredited and discarded, is not democratic but nonsensical. Yet a colleague of mine who attended an influential national conference of so-called educators reported that "intellectual" and "intellectualist" were the favorite terms of disparagement and that they seemed, as a matter of fact, to correspond pretty closely with the current Soviet favorites, "formalist" and "formalism." He was told that "doing" and "loving," not "intellectualizing," were the activities to be cultivated in a democracy, and my friend was angrily howled down when he protested that he himself was so boundlessly democratic that he believed even intellectual people had a right to an education.

I cannot think of anything better calculated to produce a rigid two-class society, composed of the rulers and the ruled, than this assumption that both the education of children and the instruction of the adult population are aims best achieved when a small professional group of educators, publicists, commentators and whatnot, spends its time deciding what is appropriate for the average citizen to know or think and what devices of "mass communication" will work best if these bits of information and opinion are to be transmitted without requiring of him the intellectual activities to which he is supposed to be so little given. I am by no means sure that any information which can be communicated via, say, the comic-book technique, could possibly be as important to the progress of democracy as the accomplishment of the confessedly more difficult educational feat that consists in teaching people how to read and how to find in the printed word, with all its subtlety and flexibility, a congenial method for receiving communications.

A good deal has been said about the importance of the distinction between "education" on the one hand and "indoctrination" or "propaganda" on the other. Confessedly, the line is sometimes hard to draw, but confessedly also, the difference between an educated population and an indoctrinated one is precisely the difference between a democratic society and a totalitarian society. The line, then, needs to be drawn, however difficult it may seem to be to draw it, and perhaps there is no better way to make the distinction than this: Whenever an attempt is made to convey knowledge or influence opinion in such a way that the person addressed becomes, as a result, less merely passive, more capable of criticism, and better prepared to make an effort to learn and think for himself, then what has been done to him comes under the head of education. Whenever, on the other hand, the attempt to convey knowledge or influence opinion is such as to encourage his indolence and his passivity; whenever it aims to require the least possible effort on his part and confirms him in, rather than frees him from, the existing limitations of his powers of attention and analysis, then it is propaganda or indoctrination. And it is my contention that both current educational theory as it applies to school or college students, and current methods of mass communication as they are applied to adult education in most of its forms, are tending in the direction of propaganda rather than of genuine education.

Those who are now attempting to use radio and television, however good their intentions, need to be on guard against the fact that whatever the possibilities may be, those media of communication lend themselves most easily to processes which are dubiously educational. Even the most conscientious brief version of a novel or play, even the most conscientious dramatization of a historical event, is something less than the original work of art or than genuine history. And, while we are busy congratulating ourselves that at least it is reaching people who otherwise would not meet either literature or history at all, we forget to ask how many there are who might otherwise have taken to reading if they had not had thrust upon them this lazier substitute. Mr. Fred Allen, whose remarks on television have, to be sure, sometimes been interpreted as the result of an irritation at a disturbing novelty, predicted that the man of the future would have eyes the size of cantaloupes and no brain at all. It may at least be said cautiously that we know what he means.

It has also been said that there is no country in the world where it is so easy to go to school and so difficult to get an education as in the United States. I do not think that that is really true, but I am not sure it does not threaten to become so, or that we are not in danger of destroying the educational system by our very eagerness to make it easy and efficient. Carlyle maintained that the true university was merely a collection of books. That is certainly a very extreme statement of one point of view. But I am not certain that it is any further from the truth than the popular American assumption that the best school of any kind is the one most dominated by the largest number of professors of education, most responsive to the results of questionnaires, surveys, opinion polls and statistical compilations, most elaborately equipped with slide projectors, phonographs and radio sets. Some day we are going to have to realize that you cannot "give" anybody an education. The best you can do is to make it possible for him to get one.

[*And Even If You Do*, 1967.
First published in the *New York Herald Tribune Book Review*, 1951]

## Psychoanalyzing Alice

Most readers of *The Nation* must have seen in their daily paper some account of the adventures of Alice in the new wonderland of psychoanalysis. Many years ago, the late André Tridon undertook to explore the subconscious mind of the same little lady, but Tridon was something of a playboy, while Dr. Paul Schilder, research professor of psychiatry at New York University, was presumably in dead earnest when he warned his hearers at a recent meeting of the American Psychoanalytic Society against exposing children to the dangerous corruptions of Lewis Carroll. All of Carroll's ten brothers and sisters stammered; "this fact might have made the author unhappy"; and in any event his superficially pleasant fairy stories are the expression of "enormous anxiety."

According to the account of Dr. Schilder's speech printed in *The New York Times,* most of Alice's adventures are "calculated to fill her with anxieties" of a pernicious nature. "She feels separated from her feet, she is stuffed in and out of small holes, and she never knows from minute to minute whether she will be small or large. . . . There are severe deprivations in the sphere of food and drink. . . . The poem of the Walrus and the Carpenter is of an astonishing cruelty. The Lobster is cooked. Alice herself frightens the birds with tales of devourings. . . . The fear of being cut to pieces comes again and again into the foreground. The head of the Jabberwock is cut off. There is a continuous threat to the integrity of the body in general." Even worse, apparently, is the fact that Carroll plays fast and loose with language and the conception of time. The innocent child may never recover from the shock of "mimsey" or "wabe." "This is a world of cruelty, destruction, and annihilation. . . . One may be afraid that without the help of the adult the child may remain bewildered in it and may not find his way back to the world in which he can appreciate love relations, space, time, and words." Personally, I have never heard of a child who confessed to being dangerously terrified by *Alice,* or of an adult who attributed his downfall to a trauma received from the book in infancy. But no doubt that proves nothing. The fears inspired are sub-conscious also.

Now there is not, so it seems to me, any reason for doubting the large general assertion that Lewis Carroll had "complexes," or that his fantasy was to some extent at least an expression of them. Even if we leave such esoteric matters as "threats to the integrity of the body" in the hands of specialists like Dr. Schilder, it ought to be evident that his nonsense, like so much nonsense and so much wit, was a device by means of which his intelligence protested against various kinds of cant which his priggish and conventional temperament would not permit him to flout openly. I see nothing farfetched in the assumption that queens are absurd puppets in *Alice* because Carroll outwardly accepted the absurd legend of Victoria, or that the farce of the trial is largely unconscious satire of the pompous procedure of courts. Nor do I see how anyone can ponder the dilemma in which Alice is placed when she tries to choose between the Walrus and the Carpenter without perceiving a submerged La Rochefoucauld in the mild-mannered don who found his chief delight in photographing little girls. Alice, it will be remembered, thought she liked the weeping Car-penter best because he seemed a little sorry for having betrayed the oysters. But when she was told that it was he who had eaten the most and tried to shift her sympathy to the Walrus, she got a crushing retort—the Walrus had eaten as many as he could get. Only a man who had hidden somewhere in his soul a very cynical conception of human behavior could, I submit, have conceived that incident.

If we go that far we may also, I suppose, take it as a matter of course that Alice's fantastic adventures are none of them quite sane. But that is not the point. Why, of all people, should a psychoanalyst be shocked to find complexes in an artist, or afraid to have children ("polymorphically perverse" by Freudian premise) introduced at an early age to a literature the very secret of which is its successfully playful catharsis of certain all but universal obsessions? As for the satire and the cynicism which Dr. Schilder does not mention, I should say that any child is ready for it as soon as he is capable of recognizing its existence and that he is never too young to begin to laugh at those morbid fears which, the psychoanalyst himself is ready to assure us, he is never too young to feel.

In America the Philistine used to be above all else a moral man. The arts had nothing to fear from his fury except when he could discover that they were "impure." Nowadays he is more likely to discover in the most unexpected places some defiling trace of either "bourgeois prejudice" or "psychological abnormality," and to look askance upon anything that does not combine the obsession of a social worker with the "normality" of a boy scout. Some years ago when I first met a certain distinguished psychoanalyst I told him that I had observed in his many books what appeared to me to be a rather serious *non sequitur:* The first eight chapters were usually devoted to showing how abnormal most of the distinguished people of the world had been, while the last always concluded with a "Therefore, let us endeavor to be as normal as possible." I asked him if he did not suppose that a too thorough psychic housecleaning might be undesirable for those who aspired to be something more than merely "normal," and I received a remarkable if somewhat pompous reply. "I would not," he said, "like to give a categorical answer to that question, but I will say one thing. Dr. Freud and I are the only two prominent psychoanalysts who have never themselves been analyzed—and I think we have made the greatest contributions to the science."

[*And Even If You Do,* 1967.
First published in *The Nation,* 1937.]

## The Infatuation with the Primitive

A few weeks ago I stood with a small group of other tourists at the mouth of the cave-sanctuary near Lascaux in southern France. Presently we were admitted through the iron doors which now close it. We walked down a concrete ramp and by the light of electric bulbs gazed at the polychrome zoo painted on the uneven walls, one picture sometimes superimposed upon an older one. The pictures date from the last ice age when glaciers covered most of Europe. The pictures are also, according to the pronouncements of many art historians, greatly superior to those executed by other races thousands of years later; so superior indeed that anthropologists were for a time reluctant to believe they could be as old as they actually are. And not only were the artists more accomplished than those who succeeded them in prehistoric times; their feeling, again according to the art historians, was more "modern" than that of the academicians of the eighteenth and nineteenth centuries. They were closer to Picasso than to Landseer.

At least, "modern" is what we now call it. But I could not help thinking that it was lucky for the reputation of these anonymous painters that their work was first discovered in 1940 instead of in, say, 1840. Had it come to light in the nineteenth century it would have excited anthropologists, but not critics of art. Ruskin for example would have seen it no more than the faint beginnings of artistic ability, for the adjective "primitive" had at that time connotations entirely derogatory; whereas today it implies, as often as not, admiration and praise. "Primitive," said our grandfathers, "and therefore barbarous." "Primitive," say we, "and therefore beautiful."

Has anyone ever suggested that this preference today for what used to be called barbarism may have chilling implications? After all, it is one thing to say that "progress" in the arts is not, as in technology, obvious. It is another to accept as simple fact that in certain fundamental respects art regressed until only a generation ago, when it found again in "the modern" a true rôle. Could it mean that we are looking back in some far from desirable way; that we admire primitive art, not because it is like us, but because we are becoming more like it; that we are determined, not to go forward along a true road newly found, but back and back and back until we are wholly barbarous ourselves? In any case, all the recent enthusiasm for the primitive surely represents a revolution too startling to be merely accepted without further inquiry.

In painting and sculpture we seek our inspiration either in the very ancient, or among those living people who, like the African tribes, have remained in a primitive state. We admire and imitate the masks and other carvings of peoples who not too long ago would have been called hardly human. This taste for the primitive, either archaic or surviving, until recently would have seemed sheer perversity.

Yet if it actually is perverse, the perversity is, to at least a minor degree, widely shared even by those of us not wholly committed to the modern primitive. Though much of the latter does not please me greatly, I am—to take a very mild example—more moved by Giotto than by Raphael, which is usual enough today, but even a hundred years ago would have been generally regarded as merely silly. Nor is there any reasonable doubt that a great part of our best art—even though some of us are not entirely comfortable with it—does look backward for its inspiration.

As for modern literature, it is certainly not classical, and though some would say its tone is barbarous, its form does not, like that of the plastic arts, obviously suggest the primitive. Joyce's *Ulysses* does not immediately remind us either of the epic of Gilgamesh, or of some creation-myth still current in some primitive tribe—at least not as directly as a Modigliani portrait will now always remind me of a flattened statue of a Cycladic mother goddess (carved about 2000 B.C.) which I happened to see in Athens shortly after my visit to the Lascaux caves.

But if literature seems headed down some road which is neither that of the civilized nor the primitive, some of the other arts definitely look back to the barbarous. Jazz, which at least many take so seriously that they call it the only "modern" musical idiom, is mostly derived from savage Africa, and in its own way much "serious" modern music also re-emphasizes elements once very prominent in the primitive. The graceful tinkle of sixteenth-century lute music is certainly far more "civilized" than the aggressively primitive "Rites of Spring," often taken as a landmark in the development of the modern idiom.

Consider also the case of the drum—presumably the most ancient of musical instruments, just as rhythm is presumably the most ancient of musical elements. As far back as the emergence of the classical orchestra, it played a rôle of increasing prominence. It first began to crash out in Beethoven and Berlioz, and in the late Romantics, it thundered.

Nevertheless, it was not until very recently that "percussive" came to be an adjective with usually favorable connotations. The piano was played "percussively," and composers either emphasized this quality in instruments not purely percussive or, more and more frequently, wrote music for whole groups of percussive instruments. As for popular music, of the more "advanced" sort, many of the best-selling phonograph records are now labeled only "percussive" this or "percussive" that. In the early eighteenth century, John Byron invented the terms "tweedle-dum" and "tweedle-dee" to ridicule what he thought absurd distinctions between one composer and another. Today it is more likely to be the difference between "bum-bum-bum" and "bum-*bum*-de-bum."

Is it possible that atonality is not a new freedom but merely a relapse into some pre-Greek period before any kind of mode of tonality had been discovered? And why has architecture, too, moved away from Greek grace and Roman dignity toward the great monolithic mass which suggests the Inca and the Aztec rather than either the classical or, for that matter, the Gothic? What in general is the origin of this feeling of kinship with the primitive, and why has its meaning been so seldom questioned? Perhaps it has, in writings with which I am not familiar, but I can recall only such casual references as that in Aldous Huxley's *Along the Road,* and the frontal attack made upon modernism some forty years ago by Wyndham Lewis in his queer (and queerly interesting) *Time and Western Man.*

Wrote Huxley:

> Barbarism has entered popular music from two sources—from the music of barbarous people . . . and from serious music which has drawn upon barbarism for its inspiration. . . . Composers seem to forget that we

are, in spite of everything, and though appearances may be against us, tolerably civilized. They overwhelm us not merely with Russian and Negroid noises, but with Celtic caterwaulings on the black notes, with dismal Spanish wailings, punctuated by the rattle of castanets and the clashing harmonies of the guitar.

Wyndham Lewis's thesis was that our eclectic culture—which is so proud of its appreciation of the art of various epochs, of a cosmopolitanism which permits us to turn with ease from Michelangelo to Hiroshige and from Palestrina to Rimski-Korsakov—actually means that we have no more than a hurried, tourist's familiarity with anything and that what he called "time-trotting" is as absurd as the globe-trotting some of us indulge in with so little profit. Some time after his book was published, Lewis asked me to meet him in Regent's Park where we would not be overheard by spies. He invited me to join him in a counter-conspiracy against all those who were engaged in propagating the primitive in art and thought—D. H. Lawrence and Sherwood Anderson being prominent among the villains—in order to undermine the basis of civilized society.

It seemed pretty absurd at the time, and the "conspiracy" is so typical of the fanatic (which Lewis certainly was) that it reminds me of an acquaintance who was unshakably convinced that the Kinsey Report had been subsidized by the Communist party in order to undermine the moral character of Americans and thus soften them up for conquest. But I am not quite so sure as I was then that there does not actually exist a drift in a somewhat disturbing direction, all the more alarming just because there lies behind it something much harder to deal with than a Machiavellian conspiracy.

To designate the feeling experienced by the American of another generation when he made contact with European culture, Edmund Wilson borrowed from Melville the phrase "shock of recognition." Is, then, the excitement with which moderns view the primitive a shock of recognition, an ominous sign that a barbarism that was, has made contact with a barbarism to be?

There are, of course, various other possible and less sensational interpretations, even if one rejects the simplest and most current, which is that Picasso is primitive or even prehistoric, rather than Renaissance or classical, simply because all of what used to be called civilized art moved further and further away from its true aims and methods. We had learned all that could be learned from it and found that it had led us astray. We then sought true inspiration elsewhere.

At the other extreme from this prevalent interpretation, one might say that the more extravagant aspects of primitivism are no more than a fashion destined to pass because fashion always is, as Oscar Wilde said, "a form of ugliness so intolerable that we have to change it every six months." For this interpretation there are plenty of historic parallels. The aesthete in *Patience* objected to an artistic effort on the ground that "it isn't medieval; it isn't *even* Japanese." One of his present-day successors might similarly object that "it isn't prehistoric; it isn't even African." The nineteenth century did learn something from both the medieval and the Japanese, but it absorbed what it could learn and then returned to its own proper business, which was not to be completely either.

Somewhere between these two possible interpretations—the one which sees primitivism in the arts as self-justifying, and the other which dismisses it as a fad exaggerating a modicum of truth into a stupendous revelation—there is a third, which would call it a kind of neurotic syndrome, understandable but unhealthy and the consequence of the prevalent, not unjustifiable alienation of the intellectual and the artist from the world in which he finds himself. Technology has created a physical environment which he finds uncongenial, and modern thought has created a mental and spiritual environment no less repugnant to him. He rejects the civilized and the rational because he feels that both have betrayed him. He goes off in search of D. H. Lawrence's "dark gods" and discovers that the plumed serpent acknowledges important truths to which Socrates was as blind as Herbert Spencer, or as any of our own exponents of the rational and the utilitarian.

Under remotely similar circumstances the eighteenth century, weary of its tame virtues, invented the Noble Savage (not as artist, because it never admired except in literature any painting, sculpture or architecture more ancient than the so-called "Gothic") as an embodiment of benevolence and stern, simple virtue. The actual savage has long been known not to have resembled even remotely that innocent paragon; so far as I know, it is as artist only that the primitive man is now admired. He was, we admit, ignorant, cruel, dirty, and bedeviled by senseless taboos. But he created works of art unrivaled in modern times except by those who have sat humbly at his feet—as he still lives in Africa, in Polynesia and elsewhere, or as his ghost lingers in the caves at Lascaux.

Some years ago Gerald Heard propounded the ingenious theory that civilization, though always developing, rises along a spiral rather than on a simple upward curve. At different times it looks back with sympathetic understanding at this or that earlier stage of its development—now sensing a kinship with Greece and Rome, now with the Gothic, now with the Byzantine as it spirals over them. As a highly speculative explanation of a fact which might otherwise seem to have only the meaningless meaning of erratic fashion, this theory has its attractiveness. It is also somewhat reassuring. But I cannot help wondering whether this spiral may not be descending rather than rising and if, therefore, the "eternal recurrence" may be not so much an actual recurrence as a repassing from above.

I hope that my own fears are unfounded. But developments in the arts have often been paralleled in other fields and as I contemplate political, social and military events rather than those merely artistic and cultural, I find them suggesting the gloomier alternative. Hitler, Mussolini and Stalin represent phenomena which, before World War I, we believed to have been banished from the Western world forever. Now we know that they and their like are something the possibility of which will always face us. The anthropologists' pet theory, that customs are the only basis of a moral code, is very up-to-date, but it is also a return to the concept of the tribal god whose rules and regulations are valid only for his chosen people.

This Sunday morning, just before I wrote these lines, my radio, tuned to Tucson's FM station, played an hour of music built around the beat of drums and the thumps of bass viol strings. As I listened to it—and not without pleasure as I am somewhat ashamed to confess—I couldn't help wondering whether I was merely paying reasonable tribute to the dark gods whom it behooves us still to recognize; whether I was a time-trotting tourist in Wyndham Lewis's sense; or whether I was sliding down the spiral toward an African prehistory far more remote than even the caves at Lascaux, and was indeed experiencing a shock of recognition.

[*And Even If You Do,* 1967.
First published in the *Saturday Review,* 1962.]

## The Prosperity of a Jest

Everybody seems to be interested nowadays in what is called "communication." The lowest of the lowbrows dropped radio for television because they recognized TV as "a new medium of communication"—even if they did not call it that. The highest of the highbrows go in for semantics because that is the most esoteric aspect of the same grand subject. Meanwhile, all the in-betweens who busy themselves with World Problems talk about nothing more earnestly than mass communication.

There are—they will tell you—good reasons for all this. Never before were there so many things which the world needed to know. Never before was it so important that everybody should understand what was once the business of the ruling class alone. Intellectuals must study semantics so they can communicate with one another. Educators and publicists must study mass communication so they can reach the Common Man. And if you object that the quality of the thing communicated seems to vary inversely with the ingenuity of the means used to communicate it, they reply that it need not be so.

Perhaps television drama is not so good as legitimate drama or, for that matter, so good as the movies. In fact, perhaps it has nothing to recommend it except (a) its accessibility and (b) the charm of novelty plus the wondering admiration that the invention arouses. But, they say, it *could* be first class. There is no reason why Sophocles instead of Milton Berle, and Plato instead of Arthur Godfrey should not be piped into every home.

"Propaganda" and "advertising" are sometimes recognized as dangerous influences. They employ the techniques of communication to serve the selfish interests of individuals and groups. But that, we are told, is merely because the propagandist and the advertiser have got way ahead of everybody else when it comes to understanding how to communicate. The educator must wake up and catch up. He must take the instruments away from his opponents. They sell toothpaste and soap. They boast of creating "psychological wants" which nobody had until he was taught to have them. It is up to us to sell tolerance, good will, the scientific attitude and even perhaps wisdom itself, by similarly proved methods.

That there is a catch in all this, nobody seems to be very much aware. But there is a catch and the catch is this: The methods of the advertiser and the propagandist are not really usable for any purposes other than their own. They want their audiences to be as passive and uncritical as possible. Their methods are calculated not merely to make that audience believe what it is told, but also to believe just because it has been told. Their aim is to hypnotize and condition. The last thing they want is any thinking-for-yourself. Like the Bellman who went hunting for the snark, they have almost convinced even themselves that "what I tell you three times is true." Hence, what they are engaged in is not a kind of education but the direct opposite of education. The end result of their skill in one kind of communication is a group of listeners and "viewers" who are less than ignorant; it is a group which knows things that are not true and has become increasingly incapable of learning anything.

Nothing more clearly distinguishes a method of education from a technique of indoctrination than the fact that education demands from the subject some effort, especially some effort of attention, while propaganda does not. The advertiser will go to any length to make everything easy. The educator will see to it that something is expected of his pupil. He knows that no one can learn anything worth knowing unless he is willing to learn, as well as willing to be taught. He knows that learning how to learn is more important than any specific thing he can "communicate." And the grand question has now become whether or not the new techniques of mass communication inevitably and by their very nature weaken the power to learn at the same time that they make being taught so easy.

What so many enthusiasts of communication will not realize is that there is a point beyond which everything should not be made varied, vivid, picturesque, dramatic and "interesting." A time is sure to come when something which needs very much to be learned cannot possibly be made as vivid, picturesque, dramatic and interesting as certain other things. And when that time comes, only the individual who can turn his attention to what is most important, rather than allow it to be captured by what is most interesting, is capable of being educated.

Some years ago Mr. Clifton Fadiman used—and for all I know may have invented—the phrase, "the decline of attention." Nearly everyone seemed to recognize its aptness. It covered everything from the schoolteachers' complaint that children would no longer take the trouble to learn arithmetic, to the publishers' discovery that "condensations" sold better than original masterpieces and that pictures which could be glanced at were increasingly preferred to articles which had to be read. The college student plays the radio while he studies because he cannot keep his mind on his books; vacationers at the beach take along a phonograph, a deck of cards and various other pieces of paraphernalia because neither the sea itself nor any one of their other diversions can hold them for long. Even the magazines that professedly address the more intellectual audiences find it continually necessary to become more "striking." The newspapers' discovery that bigger headlines paid off was followed by the magazines' discovery that only an arresting makeup would enable them to survive. No one can be expected any longer to open a monthly simply because he has learned from experience that it will contain something interesting. His attention has to be caught by a snappy title, a striking picture, a teasing promise held out. Even among more intelligent and better-educated people it can no longer be assumed that they will *give* their attention. It has to be *caught.*

Some who are mildly disturbed by these phenomena explain them by saying rather sourly that we all "have too much," and that we are like a spoiled child who can never be entertained because he has too many toys. Others, refusing to be disturbed at all, explain rather complacently that ours is merely a world which is richer, livelier and more vivid than it used to be. But is it? Does a child who comes home from a school where he has had his "natural interests" nervously catered to, who then goes out to the movies and comes home again to a television set (this is precisely the usual routine of my friends' children) really lead a richer life than the nineteenth-century child who had nothing to do after school except read *Robinson Crusoe?* Does the adult who glances through a picture magazine, skims a news-weekly, watches ten minutes of a Senate investigation on TV, and then hears the *scherzo* movement of a symphony on the "Ford Hour" really live a richer life than his grandfather who actually read the *Atlantic Monthly?* It is not what you have available but what you take in that counts. And there are a great many adults as well as a great many children who don't seem to have time to take anything in.

Recent advertisements of a well-known encyclopedia make their pitch on the number of illustrations that this still valuable work contains and on the fact that it is "as interesting as a picture magazine." Perhaps it is. Perhaps it ought to be. But that isn't, and ought not to be, the most important thing about it. What kind of public buys an encyclopedia not because it is full, authoritative and accurate, but because it is "as interesting as a picture magazine"? It is more expensive than a picture magazine, and to buy it for the pictures is a waste of money. Is an encyclopedia wise to enter into such competition on such terms? Should a college compete with TV on approximately the same level? Or should colleges and encyclopedias alike assume that there still exists some audience for what only colleges and encyclopedias can give? Just how much should either know or care about certain techniques of communication?

Many of those who are advocating fuller use in education of "the mass communication media" seem ready to accept not only the limitations of those media but the very techniques which most outrageously pander to those who cannot or will not really attend to anything.

Suppose we listen for a moment to a spot commercial. Our advertiser knows that his hearers cannot be expected to listen for even thirty seconds while being told about the wonderful new toothpaste which, for the tenth time during the past decade, has "revolutionized tooth care," and which is now urged upon him "for your toothbrushing pleasure." Since thirty seconds is too long for the audience's span of attention, the message must be broken up thus: three seconds of instrumental music followed by some odd sound, preferably one never heard before; ten seconds of a jingle set to nervous music; then a male speaker who makes one of the large claims which Dr. Johnson already knew as the essence of advertising. He is interrupted by a female voice that gurgles, "Yes siree, that's true! That new element Abradabracan really did make my teeth sparkle!" Then the male announcer takes over again, and there is a reprise of the jingle.

Now take a step up to one of the semi-serious commercial interview programs. Stripped of the various announcements and commercials, it may last ten or possibly even twenty minutes. Yet the chances are that there will be at least two visiting celebrities as well as the interviewer. Move another step up to one of the longer, more ambitious entertainment programs. It may be studded with "names," but no one stays on much longer than is necessary to prove to the listener that he was actually there. Turn finally to a serious, noncommercial discussion program. The chances are three to one that it will present a "panel." But why? Is it primarily to promote an exchange of opinions, develop the sharpness of debate, et cetera? Perhaps. But isn't it also because no one speaker could hold the attention for that long? It takes at least two to tell about a toothpaste in thirty seconds; it takes quite a group of contrasting personalities to hold a "serious" audience for thirty minutes.

It seems to me (if you don't mind my saying so) that we have reached a point where "failure to communicate" is more often the result of a failure of attention—which no one seems to think we can do anything about— than of those imperfections in our techniques of communication which everybody seems determined to remedy, even if it means teaching patriotism through comic books, mathematics by moving pictures, and the principles of ethics as they can be expounded in a jingle set to music. Though most educated people seem to have agreed some years ago that the "commercial" is one of the ugliest and most humiliating phenomena of our civilization, some of these same people do not seem to realize how close they come to wanting to make what they call "popular education" one long commercial designed to sell science, culture and right-political thinking to people less and less willing to make any effort of attention.

Are what our school principals grandly call "audio-visual aids" usually anything more than concessions to the pupils' unwillingness to make that effort of attention necessary to read a text or listen to a teacher's exposition? Can anything be said in favor of most of them except that they are, at best, a surrender to the delusion shared by children and adults alike that the mechanical techniques of communication are interesting in themselves, no matter what (even if it happens to be genuine information) is being communicated? Are they not, at worst, merely devices for "catching" an attention which can never be given freely or held for long? How often can it be said that any movie, film strip, or recording teaches the so-called student—who has dwindled into a mere listener or viewer—more than could be learned in the same time with a little effort, or that the mechanical method has any virtue other than the fact that such effort is not required? Is there anything a picture can teach the pupil which is worth as much as that ability to read, which he stands in very great danger of losing?

What those who so earnestly discuss the problems of communication seem to forget is that its success depends upon the sensitivity of the listener as well as upon the efficiency of the transmitter. Or, as Shakespeare knew, the prosperity of a jest lies in the ear of him that hears it. What is the use of trying to make the jests simpler and simpler if the ears for which they are destined are to grow duller and duller? It is not a little learning, but a little capacity for learning, which is a dangerous thing.

At the moment, various educational institutions are making a new effort to use radio and, more especially, television for their own purposes. Perhaps, if it is not too late, they may succeed. But if they do succeed, it will be because they are more interested in what they have to communicate than in what it seems easily possible to communicate within the limitations the medium imposes. To those interested in the method itself there is nothing less suitable than a mere lecture. For purposes of true education it may very well be that there is nothing better. Fewer people will listen, but those who do will actually be getting what they might get at the college itself. On the other hand, try to use either radio or TV not as a mere mechanical means of diffusion, but as an institution which has developed its own methods, standards and techniques, and you will get a substitute for instruction as obviously inferior to what it has replaced, as most TV drama is inferior to the stage play and most radio concerts inferior to what could be heard in a concert hall.

Colleges are among the few surviving institutions that sometimes put quality above quantity, that are not yet quite convinced that when you spread something wide that is all to the good, no matter how thinly you spread it. They may make use of the media of mass communication, but it is at least as likely that these media will make use of them. I am not at all sure that we ought to take the instruments of mass communication away from the advertisers. Perhaps we should let advertisers keep them. Perhaps we should have a little more faith in the media which are our own and which we know how to use.

[*And Even If You Do,* 1967.
First published in *The American Scholar,* 1955.]

## The Uses of Literature in an Age of Science*

Let me immediately call your attention to the fact that my title refers to the function of literature rather than merely to the function of the writer in an Age of Science. That the writer has such a function is seldom doubted. He can act as an independent middleman between the scientist and the uninstructed layman. Sometimes he is little more than a ghost writer, who on the one hand, shares enough of the scientist's knowledge to have some idea of what he is doing, and at the same time, enough of the ignorance and other limitations of the uninstructed layman to know how to tell this layman as much as the layman will be able to understand. Such a writer is useful; in fact, he is desperately needed by both the scientist (who needs the financial and political support as well as the confidence of the layman if science is to play its full part in society) and by the layman if the layman is not to regard science as a form of black magic which must remain totally incomprehensible.

This importance of the writer is, then, great and beyond dispute. But is there such a thing as literature which is not anti-scientific on the one hand, nor mere popular science on the other; something which concerns itself often with the same subject matter as science but in some different way? And when I say literature, I am thinking not only of fiction and drama and poetry but also, perhaps especially, of expository writing, which deals with the same facts and themes as pure science but with an approach and emphasis which is different.

Now I am not, I hasten to assure you, about to launch upon a defense of the humanities of that familiar sort which consists of vague reference to literature as a graceful ornament and relaxation, as a home of lost causes to which we pay sentimental deference, or as a land of "dreams" to which we retire when reality is too much for us. What I am trying to define for myself is a function, or rather a group of functions, which literature per-

* Speech delivered at the Rockefeller Institute.

forms when it is neither an escape from scientific truth nor a mere popularization of such truths but a way of looking at science which is not, and need not be, the scientist's way, but which makes it easier for many of us to live comfortably in that world of science which is so different from the world our imagination gave us back in the days when imagination was free to imagine pretty much what it pleased about nature, about human nature, and about a God made in man's own image.

Because literature, unlike science, is at least as much subjective as it is objective, because it is so distinctly man-centered rather than centered outside man around some concept of absolute truth to fact, literature constitutes a continuous reminder of something the man of letters believes to be true and believes that the scientist sometimes denies or forgets, namely, that science exists to serve man, not man to serve science. The man of letters is not so ready, as many scientists are, to say that we must never ask whether this discovery or that machine is likely to be a blessing or a curse to mankind and that we must be prepared, if necessary, to perish for the Glory of Science, much as Jonathan Edwards said he would be willing to be damned for the Glory of God.

The inventor of an airplane in Samuel Johnson's romance, *Rasselas,* refused to make his invention public, because he believed that man should not be able to fly until he had first become virtuous. We are not likely to, and perhaps should not, take quite that position. But we may appropriately accept the reminder that the power which science so abundantly supplies us with is good only so far as it is used for good ends; that if we are not willing to refuse to fly until we have become virtuous, we ought at least to realize that being able to fly will not make us either virtuous or happy —which is what the more extreme proponents of technological progress seem to assume. If mankind really does presently enter upon a scientific and technological Utopia—instead of either perishing in a catastrophe or being reduced to a mere slave of his own machines—it will be because he has remembered what many scientists who have a touch of literature in them and literature itself have in many different ways reiterated, namely, that unless man sees science as his servant rather than his all-demanding god, he may end by immolating himself on that god's altar, as the victims of religious superstition have immolated themselves upon the altars of their own, not stranger gods.

Hardly less obvious, or less often recognized, is that thorny question of values. Can science establish them and, if not, are they then necessarily either merely arbitrary or merely fictitious? To the first question, "Can science establish values?", scientists themselves give sometimes a "Yes" and sometimes a "No" answer. And if the answer is "No," those who give it sometimes answer the second question, "Are values then merely arbitrary or fictitious?" with a "Yes." And if they do answer "Yes," then they fall into the completest possible moral relativism, where the monster is as admirable as the saint.

Because this question has been so often discussed, I am not going to discuss it at length but make only two comments. So far as I myself can see, science as such cannot by its very definition establish values. I rest my case on a very simple statement made some years ago, not by a man of letters but by an official scientist of great repute, Dr. Vannevar Bush. "A value," he said, "cannot be deduced from a statement of fact." That seems to me to be conclusive: Science is concerned only with facts, and a statement of fact cannot define a value.

If the methods of science cannot define a value, then it may be asked, "Can anything else?" Certainly neither literature nor philosophy has ever succeeded in establishing values as statements of fact, accepted as such with that degree of unanimity with which scientific statements of fact have been accepted, for a time at least. But though a given science may reach a very high state of development without concerning itself with values either directly or indirectly, literature might almost be defined as an attempt to give some account of human life on the assumption that values are of supreme importance. Literature, which deals with the scientific subject matter, may sometimes legitimately raise again and again the question whether or not the universe outside of man is actually morally neutral. I certainly would hesitate to say that neutrality has been conclusively demonstrated and I see no reason why the question should not be asked again and again as searchingly as possible. But even if you dismiss such attempts to find a human meaning in the external universe, one fact seems to me to remain. All civilizations have rested upon the explicit or tacit assumption of some system of hierarchy of values, however arrived at and however different from that accepted in other and perhaps equally successful civilizations. And it is literature in one form or another —literature oral or written—which transmits the civilization's value system, however arrived at. If science cannot establish a system of values and if civilization can't survive without one, then civilization cannot survive without literature. In an Age of Science, it is important that this literature should not be anti-scientific or ignorant of science. To be either is to make certain that the literature will be discarded—as the fundamentalist theology was discarded in the old war between science and religion. But literature should have its own way of treating the facts and themes of science.

Let me now try to say something concerning a theme neither so easy to state, nor quite so frequently explored, as either of the two I have just been touching upon.

It used to be said that science was merely systematized common sense. Such it obviously was in the days of Galileo and such it still was, to a considerable extent, well into the nineteenth century. But no one would maintain that it is that today. Over the portal that marks the entry to modern physics and modern biology (which is coming more and more to unite with physics and chemistry) is written a sort of parody of Dante's *Inferno*: "All common sense abandon, ye who enter here."

If science began in the Renaissance, when men began to put more trust in the evidence of their senses than in logical and metaphysical arguments, modern science demands that we reverse the process. In the first place, our senses are of little use because the facts that we are pursuing lead us into the realms of the small, smaller, and yet smaller where first our unaided eye cannot follow, then where our optical microscopes cannot take us, and at last into the realm which even the electron microscope cannot wholly penetrate. At best we have only to deduce or infer what we can never expect to see or hear or feel. What is even worse, we are now used to being told that the real but invisible world, which we cannot reach with our senses, is also not capable of being reconstructed in our minds—even that ultimate reality is not only not understood but quite possibly not understandable. The paradoxes of the metaphysicians, like that involving fate and free will, are no less unsolvable than is, say, that of the wave and the corpuscle. Yet it was to that dilemma that the enterprise of common sense ultimately conducted us.

As far back as the nineteenth century we began to realize that things were not what they seemed: that, for instance, when our five senses told us that the chair we sat on was a solid object, all five of them were lying. By now all the ordinary phenomena of the world we seem to inhabit are mere fantasies, created by senses and intellectual concepts which, one and all, are united in a conspiracy to deceive us.

And yet most of our lives is necessarily lived in the realm of appearance. Call it animal faith, if you like. But whatever you call it, our active, our emotional, and a large part of our intellectual life continues (and probably will continue as long as we are recognizable as the kind of creatures we now are) to have its being in the world of seeming rather

A KRUTCH OMNIBUS

than in the world of scientific facts. Even if you are inclined to dismiss literature as no more than an account of the universe as it really isn't, such is the universe of appearances which is in many ways more real to us than any other. If we did not have animal faith, we could not survive; and, at a minimum, literature helps us to retain an animal faith by which we can live in our human world.

The last claim I have to make is the most inclusive of all, perhaps indeed includes all the others. It is based upon the simple fact that man is, or at least always has been so far, a creature of emotions as well as of intellect. But pure science has to do with the intellect only. It is concerned exclusively with knowing and through knowing, with doing. The phrase "coldly scientific" has become a cliché. And science thus performs its special function when it is cold, in the sense that it refuses to allow its conclusions to be influenced by its emotions. But the man who is nothing but "coldly scientific" (if indeed such a creature has ever so far actually existed) is hardly a man at all.

All literature is, on the other hand, emotional. To a greater or lesser extent it also may be concerned with what we believe to be the facts of life, but it inevitably involves (as science does not) an emotional reaction to those actual or supposed facts. And this is very significantly the case with that special sort of literature with which I am concerned this evening; with that sort, I mean, which deals with the facts and the themes of science in some literary way. You may call it impure science, if you like. I am aware that some scientists despise it more passionately than they despise even the literature which is admittedly an escape from fact into the realm of fantasy and dreams. To them it seems not only childish but dangerous, something capable of disturbing and corrupting the vision of science itself. But surely it is no threat to that vision so long as it acknowledges what it is and does not pretend to be pure science.

Perhaps I can put the same thing in another way by saying that man needs not only to know but also to wonder and to love, and that science, as such, has nothing to do with either wonder or love though those two are perhaps the essential concern of the kind of literature I have been trying to defend.

I am aware that certain extremists would reject everything I have said and maintain that what I have called the function of literature has turned out to be purely the attempt to preserve certain of the all-too-human weaknesses which the true scientists have by now got rid of for themselves and which they believe are destined in time to cease to cripple, as to date they have always crippled, all attempts to create a thoroughly rational and scientific civilization.

A few months ago I came across a very clear statement of this position in an imaginary conversation written by J. Bronowski in which he celebrates the macromolecular biologist as the man who has at last enabled pure science to answer all the needs of the human being. "He is," and I quote, "the man who unravels the secret of life by using the tools of physics. He shows—we have shown—that the structures of biology become intelligible when we treat them, not as a string of mysteries but as strings of molecules. That is the universal unity in which we believe."

Bronowski then goes on to compose a scientific poem which is quite as bad as Erasmus Darwin's famous "Botanical Garden" and proclaims that when he regards biology not as a string of mysteries but as a string of molecules, "an icy sweetness fills my mind."

If this is indeed not only all we know on earth and all we need to know, then I have this evening talked nothing but foolishness. But so far as I am concerned, I still do not see how treating biology as a string of molecules removes all the mystery and wonder and, if it did, then I would fall back upon the contention that an "icy sweetness" is not enough for me and that I do not believe mankind as a whole would be satisfied with it.

Neither do I see how an understanding of the macromolecular structure of the living cell can throw any light on any question involving either ethics or aesthetics. If such knowledge is indeed all we know on earth and all we need to know, then the only conclusion which can be drawn is one which some positivist philosophers have drawn already—namely, that all questions involving ethics or aesthetics are, as they are fond of saying, "meaningless questions."

If they are not meaningless but fraught with meanings and consequences of tremendous import, then we must attend to even those often contradictory hints which literature in various forms has attempted to communicate.

We may *say* that good and evil, like ugliness and beauty, are merely the prejudices of a given society but few people have ever consistently acted upon that assumption and no society which as a whole acted upon it, could last for long.

Of all scientists the physician is perhaps the one who is most aware of ethical problems and he sometimes says that medicine has an ethic, but I do not see how it can be deduced from the science of medicine itself.

Consider the case of those Nazi physicians who thought it ethical to perform upon human beings experiments which shocked those physicians who adhered to other political (not other scientific) creeds. Their scientific training was the same. They knew the same facts of anatomy, physiology and pathology. They would have agreed upon the diagnosis and treatment of any suffering patient—assuming that they wanted to relieve him. Whatever made the difference between them was the result of beliefs and attitudes derived ultimately from nonscientific literature.

The ultimate concern of all science is an answer to some question *how* this or that happens or *how* this or that can be done. The question whether or not something *should* be done is one to which science as such can give no ultimate answer. Science is concerned with know-how not with know-what or know-whether.

Shortly after the end of the Second World War Dr. Robert Oppenheimer entered upon the current discussion of that threat to the human race which the discovery of atomic fission had raised. He concluded by saying that what he most feared was not the physical destruction of mankind, not that the race of human beings would lose its life, but that it might (and the phrase is his) "lose its humanity."

Ever since I first read that statement I have wondered just what he meant by it and the only answer to that question that I can arrive at is simply this: "Man will have lost his humanity when and if he has become concerned exclusively with questions concerning *how,* not at all with questions concerning *what* and *whether.*"

During the Middle Ages, when science was popularly confused with magic, it was assumed that it came from the devil and that those learned in it had lost their souls or, to return to Mr. Oppenheimer's phrase, their humanity. At the very least, science was a black art and therefore a very dangerous one.

Today, so it seems to me, the scientist is necessarily *exposed* to a similar danger. While acting in his professional or specialized capacity he must ask no question to which there is not, potentially at least, a scientific answer. He must be unemotional, objective, and neutral. He must not instinctively prefer one answer or another, must not allow himself to be swayed by prejudice, not even by prejudice in favor of what, as mere human being, he feels to be the good and the beautiful. If he abandons this kind of objectivity he risks perverting his science.

But there is nevertheless in this necessary attitude something which I am tempted to compare to the risk of trafficking with the devil.

It is opposed to certain aspects of human nature. And the scientist can save his soul only if he leaves complete scientific coldness, objectivity and neutrality in the laboratory where it belongs and, when he leaves it, resumes interest in what I would call other aspects of truth and other methods of searching for it even though he may, if he likes, call them merely human prejudices. And it is, of course, literature which tries to persuade him to do just this.

[*And Even If You Do,* 1967.
Published in abbreviated form in the *Saturday Review,* 1964.]

# ▪ The World We Live In ▪

## Why I Am Not Going to the Moon

It was, I believe, a mountain climber who invented the phrase "because it is there" to explain why he wanted to climb a particular peak. Because ours is an age devoted to all sorts of unexamined enterprises his phrase has passed into popular speech and the very frequency with which it is invoked is a striking indication of the fact that many of the things we do, many of the ends we pursue, cannot be justified except by saying that, after all, these things can be done and these ends can be pursued.

Yet we cannot, after all, study everything that could be studied or do everything that could be done. Wisdom would seem to suggest that we ask not only what can be done, but what is most worth doing—but that is exactly what the "because it is there" philosophy refuses to recognize. As Thoreau said, it is not worthwhile to go halfway round the world to count the cats in Zanzibar. But there are, I presume, cats in Zanzibar and they could be counted. Better yet, the number could be pretty accurately estimated by a scientifically planned sampling. But before approving such an enterprise as one we ought to undertake, I would want some sounder reason than simply the fact that the cats are, presumably, there.

When President Kennedy was asked why our government was so eager to get someone to the moon, even he could think of no better answer than the catchphrase "because it is there." Now, I am willing to believe that there may be better reasons. They may be military, and if there are sound military reasons I somewhat reluctantly yield to them. But I dismiss as mere foolish excuses most of the others I have heard—such as the prestige value of beating the Russians or, most farfetched of all, von Braun's suggestion that colonization of the bodies in outer space is the best solution to the population problem.

At the risk of provoking the scorn of all the proponents of pure science, fundamental research, and so forth (as well as of all the "because it is there" boys), I would like to say that I have not yet heard any argument that seemed to me to justify the enormous expenditure of time, money and brains upon this particular enterprise. Henry Adams said that the Middle Ages believed building cathedrals the thing most worth doing, just as the mid-nineteenth century in the United States gave the same sort of priority to railroad building. In our own time, exploration of space seems to have won a similar priority. We seem to regard it as not only worth doing but even more worth doing than anything else and, therefore, worth anything it may cost. But there is, it seems to me, no doubt that this inevitability means less time, less money, and less available brainpower to be spent on other things that, in addition to being there, seem to have stronger claims upon our attention.

That we should be dazzled by the sheer wonder of what man has been able to do is not surprising. The technical problems solved are surely the most difficult ever attacked by science. Out of nowhere has suddenly appeared a whole new race of experts who seem to move easily in a realm of thought and practice that most of us cannot even enter. Within a few years they have accomplished what the most extravagant follower of Jules Verne would not have dared imagine except for some distant future. Yet the very wonder of it makes it difficult for us to maintain any sense of proportion. To question its value is likely to seem mere impudence. Yet it ought to be at least questioned.

I am not thinking exclusively in terms of the argument that the money spent might be better used to relieve the sufferings of the poor, although that is itself an argument not quite so easily disposed of as Philip Morrison, professor of physics at Cornell and formerly a group leader at Los Alamos, assumed when he wrote recently in *The New Leader*: "The claim of each act we carry out in common must rest on its merit and not on the general thesis that no rich, strange, useless thing can justly be bought while some men lack necessities. . . . Those who built the Acropolis forgot the Helots; those who sailed the Indies thought nothing of the landless peasants."

The poor we have always with us and those who cite that text do not always seem to remember the context—which might seem to make it support Professor Morrison's thesis. The comment was made as a reply to those of the disciples who had rebuked a stranger woman for pouring upon the head of Jesus a rich ointment which, they pointed out, might have been sold and the proceeds given to the poor. "The poor ye have always with you but me you have not always with you." But the question is not merely whether *any* rich, interesting, or beautiful thing can justifiably be bought while some men lack necessities. It is whether, in this particular case, the enormous expenditure is justified when it means neglecting, not only many men, but many other things with at least as much claim to being "rich, strange" and (possibly) useful as well.

Like the poor, this problem has always been with us and in one form or another probably always will be. But in times past men did have one guide in deciding *which* rich and strange thing was worth spending time and brains and money to create or do: They believed (as we do not) that one thing was intrinsically and absolutely better, wiser, or more to be admired than something else. They did not have to fall back on any "because it is there" argument because they had not, like us, been reduced by moral and cultural relativism to a sort of impotence that leaves us powerless to defend one choice as opposed to another and that therefore encourages us to do whatever can be done and to offer no reason more persuasive than the simple "because it is there to be done."

If we do indeed do some things that should have been left undone and do others less worth doing than those we neglect, none of that can be blamed on science itself. The great but limited field of its competence is knowing (pure science) and doing (technology). It cannot—as the wiser of its practitioners admit—evaluate. Though it can teach us how to get to the moon, we need something else to tell us whether or not we ought to go there.

Hence it is that if science is not to blame, some scientists are—just insofar as they encourage the now almost universal belief that science is omnicompetent and that any problems that cannot be solved by the scientific method (and that means all questions involving evaluation) are simply unsolvable or, essentially, meaningless. The tendency to fall back upon "because it is there" as the only answer to the question why a certain thing should be done is simply a demonstration of the inadequacy of science alone as a guide for either society or for the life of an individual.

Three centuries and a half ago Francis Bacon wrote in *The Advancement of Learning*: "We are much beholden to Machiavelli and others, that write what men do, and not what they ought to do." This was perhaps a useful observation at the time; but the situation in the intellectual world is now by no means what it was in Bacon's day. And of all the

threats to civilization perhaps none is greater than that which leads sociology to ask only what men do do and technology only what can be
done, or, to use again the popular phrase, "what is there." By banishing
"ought" from the vocabulary of our sociology, and by asking of our tech-
nologists only what they can do rather than what is worth doing, we are
making ourselves passengers in a vehicle over which no critical intelligence
pretends to exercise any control and which may, indeed, take us not only
to the moon but to destinations even less desirable.

Some will no doubt answer that many of the advances of science are due
to boundless curiosity concerning things that seem to have no possible
application. But such curiosity is much safer when it leads us to know
whatever we can know rather than to do whatever we can do. We have
a tendency to rush from knowing to doing without pausing for reflection.
Technology, if not science, has sometimes entailed penalties when it has
taught us how to do things better left undone. This fact was seldom
noted even by a few until quite recently when a minority began to wonder
whether or not it would have been better for everybody if the secret of
the atom had never been penetrated. Curiosity, even scientific curiosity,
can open a Pandora's box as well as a treasure chest. And one should use
a certain amount of caution in lifting the lid of any box whose contents
are unknown.

Primitive man suffered from both a lack of knowledge and a lack of
know-how. He believed a great many absurd and often troublesome
things that were not true. He had a very limited knowledge of how to
do what he wanted to do. But this last limitation was also something of a
safeguard, even if a rather unsatisfactory one. He could not destroy his
environment as disastrously as we can destroy ours, and he could not kill
as many of his neighbors as he would have been glad to kill if he had
known how. Perhaps his intentions and desires were even worse than ours,
but he didn't know as well as we, how to implement them. We know only
too well. Know-how continues to leave know-what and know-whether
further and further behind.

I do not know just how military expenditures compare with those in-
curred in connection with the exploration of space. But except for defense, no other single enterprise of the government is financed on so lavish
a scale. This surely suggests that those responsible for giving it this un-
questioned priority assume that of all the achievements possible in our
generation this is the one most important. But does anyone seriously believe that this is true? That if a good fairy should grant us one wish we
should say, "Let me get to the moon, and beyond"?

Consider, for example, the population explosion: not only what it has already done to make life difficult and ugly, but also what it threatens to do in the future. In the minds of many thoughtful people it is a danger to mankind that may be as great as that of atomic warfare—the one threatening us with too many people, the other with a world in which there will be none at all. One could easily fill a book full of statements by responsible persons that say just this in one way or another. One moderate comment from Dr. Walter Hoagland, president of the American Academy of Arts and Sciences, will suffice. In a recent *Bulletin of the Atomic Scientist* he described experiments that demonstrate to his satisfaction that in animal populations overcrowding produces various pathological conditions, including a fatal adrenal malfunction called the Stress Syndrome. He believes that the same thing will happen to human beings under similar circumstances, and this seems to dispose of the assurance that the feeding of a monstrously overgrown population will present no serious problems to an ever-advancing technology.

Dr. Hoagland went on to suggest that we can "do nothing and just wait for the Stress Syndrome or a new virus to do its work," or we can "leave the solution to some trigger-happy dictator with a suitable stockpile of atomic weapons." On the other hand, so he suggests, we might just possibly "decide on an optimum population for the world and by education and social pressure try to see that it is not exceeded."

Admittedly, that last suggestion, though the only sensible one, involves problems to which the solutions are not at the moment by any means obvious. But it is to President Johnson's credit that he has given, more clearly than any other high government official ever has, recognition to the fact that the population explosion should be reckoned with somehow, sometime. Not long after his inauguration the foreign aid bill contained this sentence: "Funds available to carry out this provision may be used to conduct research into the problems of population growth." True, the implication seems to be that no such problems exist in our own country. And the very fact that so timid a statement should mark an epoch is itself enough to demonstrate how casually, almost as a parenthetical afterthought, we approach what is, in actual fact, the second if not the first greatest threat to the future of mankind. Suppose that we had got no further in our plans to explore space than the provision in an omnibus bill for funds "to conduct research into the problem of space travel." Would that not suggest that we didn't think it very important—just something that might be looked into some day and at leisure?

Historians of ancient Egypt say that what we would call its "national income" was, during its days of greatness, very high. But the standard of living endured by the majority of its population was very low indeed because all of the income above what was essential to the barest existence went into the pyramids and other extravagances.

Now, no one could say that such a situation exists today in the United States. A good deal of our national income goes, not only into welfare, but into the pockets of citizens who buy with it what they like—whether that be education for their children, books and pictures and music for themselves, or (in somewhat more numerous instances) the most expensive automobiles their income (plus available credit) will get them. But future historians (if there are any) may wonder that we put into our rocket motors and all that goes into the making of them so large a slice of the national income.

Once, for several centuries, the Western world was united in the belief that the most important task it could possibly accomplish would be the recovery of the Holy Sepulcher. It sacrificed thousands of lives, to say nothing of vast wealth and a large part of its manpower, in the attempt to achieve something that few of us today can regard as having been more than an irrational obsession. Yet to a large section of the intelligent men of that time the enterprise must have seemed as obviously important as landing on the moon seems to us. But is not the moon, like the Holy Sepulcher, a mere symbol? It is not even in the hands of the infidel— though I suppose that if the Russians get there first it will be considered to be. And I wonder if, at some not too distant date, our crusade will not have come to seem no less incomprehensible than that of our forefathers.

Why don't we devote to the problem of overpopulation an effort as determined as that we are making to get to the moon before the Russians? Why, even at long last, do we do no more than to say that a small part of a large fund may be used to "conduct research into the problem"— but not to take any action?

The most important of the answers to this question is not the opposition of moralists or the indifference of those who see in what they call a "bumper crop of babies" an ever increasing market for the baby foods it will eat and, a little later, for the cigarettes it will smoke. The most important reasons are, first, the fact that this problem is far more difficult than the problem (stupendous though it is) of how to get to the moon; and, second, that the solution, if there is one, cannot be reached by the methods that have yielded such astonishingly successful results when applied to all the problems that do not involve human nature and that therefore yield to mechanical solutions. That the technological problem of birth control has been solved, that our so triumphant know-how includes the know-how of contraception, is quite typical of our age's greatest strength. That we do not know how our know-how can be applied to promote a good life is equally so. If a Cousteau suggests that we build underseas cities and a von Braun gives the even more preposterous suggestion that we colonize the planets; if, moreover, these are taken seriously by some, it can only be because these are purely technological solutions and it is upon technology that most of us rest whatever hopes we may have for a decent future.

I remember having read, some fifteen or more years ago, a book by Willy Ley in which was discussed the conditions that would have to be created before a rocket could break away from the earth's gravity and proceed indefinitely toward whatever object in space it had been pointed at. To do that, if I remember correctly, the rocket would have to be capable of a speed twice what it had been possible to achieve up to that time. This critical speed was named "the escape velocity." And though the ironic implications of the term did not strike me then, they do strike me now. Perhaps one of the reasons we are so attracted by the problems of space exploration is that absorption in them helps us forget the more difficult problems lying right at our feet and that an "escape velocity" is precisely what we have achieved.

A good many science-fiction stories have been written about the survivors, sometimes the last surviving couple, on a depopulated earth. If I were to try my hand at that kind of fiction I should imagine a pair of astronauts who had escaped to the moon and who looked back at an earth where the Stress Syndrome produced by overcrowding had at last involved, not only the exchange of the Russian and American overkill stockpile, but also the smaller but effective contributions from what are now called— but by then wouldn't be—the undeveloped countries. Our astronauts had brought along the equipment necessary for the return journey. But it did not take them long to decide not to use it.

[*And Even If You Do,* 1967.
First published in the *Saturday Review,* 1965.]

## Invention Is the Mother of Necessity

We are all aware (and we are all very frequently told) that technology has created a world that even our own parents would not have believed possible and that many of them would have contemplated with alarm. Most of this new world we take so completely for granted that we merely turn switches, dial telephones and board jet planes without asking questions and certainly without any vivid sense of their novelty or of the fact that we really know almost nothing about how they work or how they came to be.

The vast majority of us had nothing whatever to do with their creation and certainly were never given any chance to say whether or not we wanted them. We have been carried along on a tide and, although for the most part we have been willing to believe that "progress" really does represent a progression toward something desirable, it can hardly be said that we *willed* any of the things that have happened to us. In a very real sense, the telephone, the radio, the television, the automobile and the airplane were thrust upon us. And as the newest developments come to involve more and more esoteric principles and problems, the proportion of our citizens who can comprehend, much less work creatively with them, must become smaller and smaller.

One need only read the popular magazines and those advertisements that reflect even more accurately the attitudes of the popular audience, to perceive that most of the members of this audience have, so far, felt no doubt concerning the desirability of our new world and have not ceased to believe that even faster transportation, more completely automatic conveniences, and still stranger machines will create a still happier world of tomorrow, of the day after tomorrow, and of that future that lies ahead "as far as thought can reach."

On the other hand, it is surely a fact of possibly enormous significance that a minority began a few decades ago to doubt the common assumption that "progress" means progressively greater happiness and to suspect that there is a danger in machines which we seem to control but which show an increasing tendency to control us. On a somewhat lower level, it is obvious to anyone who, like me, has read even a very few science-fiction stories that the Wellsian dream has turned into a nightmare.

Not long ago the statement was made, complacently rather than anxiously, that if all of the telephones now functioning in the United States were operated as they were only a few years ago, then the entire female population of working age would be insufficient to manage the switchboards. Just how accurate that statement may be I have no way of knowing. But, accurate or not, it suggests the undeniable fact that we are more and more dependent upon mechanical devices and that this makes our whole civilization very vulnerable. Hundreds of different and complicated machines must continue to function or a paralysis followed by death would soon ensue. What happened last November [1965] when one small piece of electrical equipment failed will be long remembered—but not, I am afraid, long enough. In fact, on second thought I am not sure that it would do much good to remember it.

One of H. G. Wells's early stories had to do with a giant brain encased in a glass box from which it controlled world society. Break that glass and chaos would ensue. This is very nearly the situation in which we find ourselves. If there is a next world war—and it seems hard to believe that man will suddenly abandon an activity that he has persisted in since long before history began—it may well be by far the most destructive ever known; not only because of our vastly increased power to kill, but also because even a few small bombs could break so many links in the intricate chain of technology, every part of which is dependent upon every other part, that the loss of a few links would make the whole useless. We would be reduced to a simplicity we have forgotten how to live with.

Years ago when I happened to be reading a volume of late Roman history I realized suddenly that the ancient world ended and the Dark Ages began when the army of Belisarius cut the Roman aqueducts and, overnight, turned Rome from a community with a water supply, said to have been comparable to that of a modern city, into a Dark Ages town where a few wells and cisterns had to serve a large population. A calamity even greater, but no less easy to imagine, might introduce us to a new Dark Age.

Evolutionists always point out that any animal species that comes to be dependent upon a particular feature of its environment is in danger of extinction. The ivory-billed woodpecker disappeared because he could not survive without that abundant supply of decaying trees that had been eliminated from our well-managed forests. On the other hand, the un-demanding English sparrow survived even the near-disappearance of the horse whose droppings he had so successfully exploited. He was adaptable enough to do without horses or, for that matter, without almost any other usual feature of his environment.

For a few hundred years it seemed as though the machines man had invented made him more secure, less at the mercy of nature's caprices. He was ceasing to be (as the English farmer complained in describing his occupation) "too dependent on the Almighty." But conveniences and facilities, which begin as no more than convenient and useful, turn rapidly into necessities as the population increases and as our life is more and more organized in ways that take them for granted. Cities got along without electricity for thousands of years. In many remote parts of the world, large areas are still so little dependent upon it that to cut it off would not create a major catastrophe or even a serious inconvenience. But suppose that bombs or sabotage were to deprive a major part of the United States of its technological lifeblood by making electricity unavailable, not only for a few hours, but for months. Goods could not be moved in; garbage could not be moved out. Before long we would be in a situation almost as impossible as that of the ivory-billed woodpecker deprived of his decaying trees.

Because I have already lived a little longer than the average man does, I have witnessed rather more than he of the recent accelerating take-over by indispensable machines. The automobile, radio, airplane and even the telephone were either invented or permitted to become indispensable to our society within my memory. I can imagine, as the majority of today's citizens cannot, what life was like without them. But the memory would do me no good if they were to disappear.

It is significant, moreover, that the newer technological devices depend upon principles more and more esoteric. The internal combustion engine, the telephone, the moving picture, the acoustic phonograph and even the airplane could be understood by the average child. In fact, three of these marvels were invented by tinkerers rather than by scientists. But if the laws governing the application of nineteenth-century physics were relatively simple, electronics, as distinguished from electricity, belongs to experts only. You and I know how a moving picture or a telephone works. But if we read an account of the way in which our television set works, it is hard to credit. And just insofar as our elaborate technology depends upon highly trained experts, just to that extent does the dependence make us more vulnerable. Once we needed little more than arithmetic to get along with our world. Then, unless we depended entirely upon others, a smattering of calculus was necessary to know what our betters were talking about. Now, within a very few years, anyone who cannot program a computer is as dependent upon those who can as primitive man ever was upon his witch doctor. What is perhaps even more alarming is the fact that even the experts depend upon other experts and, also, upon the existence of machines which they could not make for themselves if these machines happened to be destroyed.

In grammar school I learned (but of course long ago forgot) how to extract a cube root by the arithmetical method. Recently I have asked several professional mathematicians if they could perform that operation, and was told with a smile, "Of course not. You extract a cube root with a slide rule, a logarithm table or, nowadays, with the aid of a computer." But since most engineers could not calculate a logarithm table (a very lengthy job, by the way) or improvise a slide rule, much less construct a computer, even engineers would not know how to reconstruct the machinery of our civilization if it somehow collapsed or was destroyed.

A grim joke, current just after the end of World War II, consisted of the remark that, whereas the most important weapon of the next war would be the atom bomb, the most important weapon of the war after that would be the bow and arrow. This is as good a way as any of stating the fact that a calamity could so destroy all the mutually dependent features of our technology that generations, perhaps even centuries, would be required to build them up again by beginning at the bottom of the pyramid which rests upon a hundred primary tools and materials, none of which are available to man in the state of nature or, for that matter, were available to, say, Periclean Athens. What could an electrical engineer do on a desert island if he didn't have any copper wire?

Many people must be wishing that the secret of atomic fission had never been discovered. Some may even suspect that the invention of the airplane was a misfortune. Without it we would have much less reason to fear Russia or China, and would be spared the enormous expense and effort of defense—to say nothing of the possibility that such defense may prove inadequate. But we are saddled with the airplane and the atom bomb, and it looks as though we would have to live—or die—with them.

In a book written some years ago I compared the forces we have summoned up to the bottle imp in an Oriental story. The all-powerful imp will obey all commands except one. He will not get back into the bottle no matter how sternly he is commanded—and we cannot get rid of the powers we have acquired. Not long thereafter I met (I believe in the pages of the *American Scholar*) a perhaps more telling comparison that Thomas Mann suggested, between modern man and Dr. Faustus. Having sold his soul to the Devil, Faustus has what appears to be a completely obedient servant. But the time comes suddenly when the servant will obey no longer. Instead of doing what Faustus bids, he carries his onetime master off to Hell.

Could anything short of the nearly total destruction of our civilization and, along with it, most of the inhabitants of all the "developed countries," rescue us from our own dangerous devices? Is there any possibility that we may voluntarily stop short of either complete dependence upon machines or, worse yet, a war in which both sides would suffer to an extent probably unparalleled since the days when conquerors, as a matter of course, put the conquered population to the sword?

Some sort of change of heart would certainly be necessary before we could begin to arrest, or even slow down, our increasing dependence upon increasingly complex machines. And although the man in the street still thinks of a brighter future only in terms of more, rather than less, technology, there are at least a few who are beginning to ask if we are not becoming more and more dependent and vulnerable rather than more and more independent and safe. That is, at least, fairly encouraging. But the problem of deactivating atomic weapons is even more difficult because a prerequisite seems to be an increasing consensus that appears less, rather than more, likely than it did only a few years ago.

Dr. Johnson (here, as my readers have learned to expect, he comes again) was once asked if *anyone* believed in the truths of religion in the same sense that one believes in the facts of everyday life. Johnson closed what was evidently an uncongenial topic to an uneasy Christian like himself by a firm and simple, "No, sir." Now, if most of those who say that mankind seems about to destroy itself really believed that statement "in the same sense" that they "believe the facts of ordinary life," we might manage somehow to escape the danger. But it is all but impossible for us to do so, and until the threat is seen to be more real than we can actually believe it to be, we will not take it seriously enough to help us find a way of avoiding it.

[*And Even If You Do,* 1967.
First published in *The American Scholar,* 1966.]

# The Age of Violence

"I very much like to torture animals," so writes Salvador Dali in his modest *Diary of a Genius.* One of his deepest regrets is, as he goes on to say, that he has never had the pleasure of watching a lion die of starvation.

Now lions are expensive luxuries, but rats and other small animals come cheap, and a modest equivalent of the experience denied Dali is enjoyed by many adolescents in high schools that buy from one of the largest biological supply houses complete starvation kits that include various deficient diets and thus provide for a refinement which only modern science has made possible. The victims eat, but they die even more slowly than if they were entirely deprived of food. Thus the pleasure of watching them is prolonged, and it may be justified on the ground that it is "educational."

A century ago Charles Darwin told a Royal Commission that experiments involving cruelty to animals were "damnable" unless they contribute important knowledge unobtainable in any other way. And when Thomas Henry Huxley heard of a vivisectionist who said that he might give his victims an anesthetic to keep them quiet but not to spare them pain, Huxley wrote, "I would willingly agree to any law which would send him to the treadmill." Certainly high school students have no need to prove for themselves that dietary deficiencies can be fatal, and they learn nothing but hardness of heart from either these experiments or from some of the others now popular—such as, for instance, the inoculation of rodents or chicks with cancer. In their literature class they probably read "The Ancient Mariner" and are asked to comment upon:

> He prayeth best who loveth best
> All things both great and small.

But a bright student might be inclined to reply that praying in schools is forbidden anyhow, and at least one teacher is reported to have brushed criticism aside by explaining that students were sternly forbidden to regard their victims as pets or to take any interest in them as individuals. Another teacher, when asked why it was necessary to perform actual experiments when published accounts and photographs were available, replied that "using live animals fascinates the youngsters." He added that it wouldn't do to stop the experiment before death ensued because death made it "more dramatic" and "the children are not convinced unless the critters die."

There are, of course, laws against cruelty to animals, but I have never heard of a case where they were invoked to prevent any torture that claimed to have a scientific purpose. In fact, many, though not all, laboratory physiologists have bitterly opposed all the various bills introduced (chiefly, so far, without success) that would set up standards governing the treatment of laboratory animals—Senate Bill S1071, for instance. But does anyone dare say that no laboratory worker could possibly have a touch of sadism in him or even that routine familiarity with torture might make him callous? The very fact that laboratory experiments are conducted behind closed doors makes it all the more desirable that some sort of control or inspection be provided for. In England, where all possibly painful experiments must be licensed by the Home Office, eighty-eight biological Fellows of the Royal Society answered a questionnaire in which they were asked whether or not they opposed these existing controls, whether they believed they prevented the highest level of medical research, and whether they found in their own experience that control seriously frustrated legitimate results. Of the eighty-eight, only one replied "Yes" to any of the three questions; the rest gave a "No" to all three. Among comments from eminent persons were:

Sir Francis Walshe, F.R.S.: "A wide familiarity with the literature of experimental neuro-physiology leads me to think that in other countries where no such rational mode of control is used, quite a few futile and unnecessarily painful animal experiments are carried out by persons not always qualified to do them."

Professor A. T. Phillipson, deputy director of the Rowett Research Institute: "I am glad to hear the Americans are trying to introduce a bill similar to our Office Act."

Professor A. Habbow, F.R.S., director of the Chester Betty Cancer Research Institute: "I have, of course, been most interested to learn of the American bill and sorry to hear of opposition to it."

Nobel Prize-winner Professor H. A. Krebs: "I am very glad indeed to support a movement to introduce in the United States legislation similar to that operating in Great Britain. My answer to all three questions which you formulated at the end of your letter is a simple 'No.'"

One similar bill was recently introduced in one of the American state legislatures, whereupon an amendment was offered specifically exempting high school laboratories from any supervision or restriction. In the Middle Ages any cruelty was justified if it could be said to be in the defense of true religion; much the same is true today, if science is substituted. But one does not have to oppose all vivisection to ask that the experimenter should be required to show not merely that he could learn something from some horrible cruelty, but that what he could learn is important enough to be alleged as an excuse. I wonder, for instance, about the experiment recently reported to determine how much fire dogs could breathe without dying. The experimenter said that the Army "wanted to know." Why it wanted to know was not explained, but perhaps it was in order to make sure that its flame throwers were sufficiently lethal.

We like to tell ourselves that civilization has made us more humane.

Our newspapers no longer carry advertisements like the following, from a British periodical in 1730: "A mad bull, dressed up with fireworks, is to be turned loose . . . likewise a dog dressed up with fireworks; also a bear to be turned loose. N.B.—A cat is to be tied to the bull's tail." Bear-baiting was officially prohibited in England in 1835, and a few years earlier, the first law making cruelty to animals an offense *per se* was passed —over, incidentally, vigorous opposition in Parliament by those who called themselves anti-sentimentalists. Nevertheless, it sometimes seems that Emerson's Law of Compensation really does work—both ways. Perhaps there is less suffering inflicted upon animals that is frankly for pleasure, but there is probably much more of it—quantitatively, at least— in the interest of scientific knowledge.

Killing for fun and death as a spectacle are not, however, unknown today. In Tucson, Arizona, the head of a certain printing organization that opposes most of the present game laws, abandoned the usually mealy-mouthed, gun manufacturers' explanation of the wholesome effects of killing animals for fun (*i.e.,* outdoor exercise, contact with nature, making fathers pals with their sons, and so forth) for the statement that children ought to make early contact "with life and death." And frank though that was, it wasn't quite completely so. What he meant was not "familiarity with death" but "familiarity with killing," which is a rather different thing. And there is surely some doubt that there are not enough opportunities today to become familiar with that. We who have had the privilege of living in the Century of Progress have, as a matter of fact, had more opportunities to take killings of one sort or another for granted than had either our fathers or our grandfathers.

Perhaps it is because there has been so much killing in our time that there seems to have been a reversal of the once-evident trend away from ritual violence. Perhaps the fun-killings, staged by some of the veterans' organizations that invite young folk to club rabbits to death, is only a survival of a concept of sport widely prevalent down to the nineteenth century. But there is no doubt that bullfighting (once regarded as decidedly un-American) has become a smart diversion. Nor is its popularity confined to the Southwest, where the *corridas* (a little Spanish adds a touch of chic) staged just across the border are not only regularly advertised in our newspapers but often given critical reviews. Hemingway's bloodlust no doubt had something to do with the rise of the fashion, and his celebration of the bullfight as the most refined expression of the sadistic impulse met with widespread response.

A few years ago, during a Congressional hearing, a witness introduced a memo from an advertising manager to the producer of a TV serial his company was sponsoring: "More violence and more bosoms." A great deal has been written in quite proper protest against the violence that runs so consistently not only through TV melodramas and through the animated cartoons, but also through even the Disney nature films, where ritual fights (often carefully staged) play a large part. How much all these things are creating a taste, how much merely responding to it, would be hard to know, but less has been written about the increasing element of violence, danger and death in the so-called spectator sports. American football (which a recent English critic called "not violent enough for a war, but too violent for a game") is relatively mild by comparison with air shows and auto races, though even in football there are some spectators whose excitement is increased by the fact that fatal injuries are at least a very real possibility. And as far as the air shows and races are concerned, their danger is frankly stressed in the advertisements.

The most penetrating discussion I have ever seen of the part played by the ever-present threat of death at an auto race occurs, oddly enough, in a Bantam paperback called *When Engines Roar*. These "nineteen action-packed true stories capture all the daring and drama of the greatest moments in auto-racing history" and are obviously directed at *aficionados*. But the volume does nevertheless include an article, "The Psychology of Auto Racing," by one Raymond de Beker, which is reprinted from *The Annual Automobile Review*.

Mr. de Beker cites a variety of appeals that the spectacle of auto racing can and does make: Speed is one of the more spectacular achievements of technology and all aspects of technology fascinate modern man; crowds, noise, and mass hysteria offer an escape from the troubled self, and so forth, and so forth. But the principal conclusion that emerges from the analysis is foreshadowed by the opening sentence: "Motor races are just as essential a part of modern life as gladiatorial combats were in ancient Rome."

After disposing rather briefly of the less obvious appeals, the author develops fully an analysis of the most powerful ones. "In no other sport . . . is the danger of death so imminent. At Le Mans death reaped eighteen victims in a matter of seconds . . . and though the spectators have every intention of running risks only by proxy, it happens that fate panders over-zealously to a taste that conscience scarcely dares to admit." Hence (as he might have added but didn't), it is all rather as though the spectator at the bullfight was occasionally tossed into the arena or the Roman fan at the Colosseum found himself, though no Christian, suddenly in the middle of the lions (which would have served him right enough).

Mr. de Beker then concludes: "Mankind has reached a dangerous corner. . . . [He] seeks to perceive what fate this machine holds in store for him and to experience vicariously the pains of death and rebirth it involves. He wants to know if he can become the superman who defies the laws of space, the mechanized centaur he visualizes in the champion, and avoid the catastrophe which alarms yet attracts him as flame does a moth."

When I began to write this piece, the moral I would have drawn from the bullring and the racecourse would have been implied in the question how far the spectator at either is from the Emperor Commodus, whom Suetonius describes as leaning over the box to stare intently into the face of the gladiator dying a few feet away. Now, however, I wonder if the auto race isn't, unlike the bullfight, something new rather than merely a recrudescence. Perhaps its chief significance is what Mr. de Beker makes it—as a ritual presentation of man face-to-face with the machine that he half hopes and half fears may put an end to him at last.

[*And Even If You Do,* 1967.
First published in the *Saturday Review,* 1965.]

## Men, Apes, and Termites

"We are, in fact, anthropoid apes trying to live like termites, and, as any philosophical observer can attest, not doing too well at it."

So wrote the late distinguished anthropologist Ralph Linton, and with true scientific detachment stopped there. Whether wisdom dictates that we should solve the problem by returning to the ape or by going further in the direction of the termite he does not say. And neither does he offer a *tertium quid.*

For the moment this caution is irrelevant. I cite him only as one example of the fact that the vision of mankind's ultimate fate as possibly that of a faceless horde united in a brainlessly efficient society does continue to turn up frequently even though it is now a cliché of science fiction and other versions of anti-Utopia.

Earlier moralists thought rather well of ants, from the time of Solomon and the legendary Aesop at least down to La Fontaine. When we first turned against this supposedly admirable insect I do not know, but some-time during the nineteenth century the tide did turn. The ant's prudence, cooperativeness, and complete devotion to the greatest good of the greatest number began to seem excessive; and it was not the sluggard but the intellectual who was advised to "go to the ant"—to be warned rather than to become wise.

The only recent example I know of a survival of the former attitude was supplied by a certain famous astronomer whose hobby is the social insects and who remarked to one of my friends something like this: "Los Angeles has appealed to me for advice on the best way of fighting the Argentine ant. Now I have a good deal of admiration for that insect. It is industrious, peaceful and socially disciplined. I can't say that I have much admiration for the people of Los Angeles. And so, between you and me, I did not give them my best advice." Still, though Los Angeles now seems to be the American city least admired except by the film-struck and a certain number of its own inhabitants, I doubt that even this waggish astronomer would really prefer the Argentine ant to the Los Angeleans.

In recent years prophets have been more fertile in imagining possible dooms than possible salvation and those who specialize in the vision of men-like-ants have cited a variety of causes and symptoms supposed to be preparing or signalizing that fate. These include the welfare state that destroys initiative; the passion for conformity; and even the simple fact that our greatest cities would, from a moderate altitude, look much like anthills at this very moment.

None of these tendencies or symptoms seems to me to indicate very clearly the real process by which man might become more like termites than like men—or even like apes. What I propose (if the reader doesn't think all this hopelessly *vieux jeu*) is to take the whole thing with a certain degree of seriousness as a kind of allegory (even if it is not a literal description) of something which might possibly happen and to come up with a suggestion concerning just where a real threat lies—a threat close enough to be worth considering as possibly operative in the not-unimag-inably-distant future.

Let us begin with a look at what Professor Linton's termites are really like. They aren't ants, of course, and they have been around many millions of years longer. Their characteristics represent a development so much further advanced in a similar direction that an ant might say (if he had any brains), "Let us pause and take thought lest the free and abundant life of our species disappear and we become more like termites than we ants want to be."

Man, so the anthropologists and the paleontologists tell us, has been a social animal for less than one million years; ants, bees and wasps for about seventy million; the termites for something like two hundred million. That certainly suggests that all these insects have had vastly more experience than we with social organization and cooperation; also, that in all of them the effect has been to move steadily in the same direction, with the result that they have become, among other things, a conspicuous example of "the survival of the fittest"—though to avoid semantic confusion, we had better remind ourselves that this misleading phrase really has no content. If you ask, "Fit for what?" the only answer is, "Why, fit to survive," and the statement then comes down to mere tautology: "Those survive who survive."

The ant, by comparison with the termite, leads a free and spacious life. Many species are not completely blind; he has elbow room, he walks over the open spaces, he sees something of the world, and he breathes fresh air. On the other hand, the vast majority of individual termites, belonging to the most highly evolved species, never leave their crowded fortress city, could not see anything if they did, spend their entire existence in the narrow chambers and narrower tunnels of a labyrinth where they were born and where they breathe perpetually the damp, carbon dioxide-heavy atmosphere and dread more than anything else being compelled to leave it, even for an instant. The lives of certain human city dwellers who spend their days in air-conditioned offices, pass from them through tunnels of the subway to narrow chambers in some housing development, may seem remotely analogous. But the analogy is still pretty remote.

Within one of the termites' closed cities there is only one imperative, "the greatest good of the greatest number," and that is not a conviction but a built-in response, as the result of which, for instance, "a soldier"— dependably and without the least hesitation—sacrifices his life in defense of his fellows. Some of the metaphysicians of the Soviet Union have discussed the meaning of freedom in a way which seems to say that the only true and perfect freedom consists in no longer wanting to be free; termites have reached that state—or perhaps have gone a little beyond it. They do not want anything. They merely react as they have reacted for millions of years.

Termites entered the popular imagination some years ago through Maeterlinck's secondhand account, to which he added mystical overtones suggesting that the termite community was governed by some sort of communal over-soul. The more usual view of the biologist is that they are actually nearer mere machines than even the less highly developed insects or than, in all probability, they themselves were in the very long ago before they took the road that has led them to a brainless and merely unconscious efficiency.

The recent but standard account of one of the most highly developed species is entitled *Dwellers in Darkness* and is based on an original study by the entomologist F. H. Skaif. It emphasizes what is to us the horror of the termites' existence. Like those survivors of atomic catastrophe described in science fiction as confined to their "shelter," the termites are compelled to pass their entire existence in the Stygian darkness of their fortresses because to venture out would be to meet immediate death, either by desiccation or by falling victim to marauding ants. The food problem they have solved by living exclusively upon decayed vegetation and by practicing an extreme form of the injunction "Waste not, want not." In fact those now struggling with the problem of life on a long-distance spaceship might take a hint from the termites' solution of a similar problem: "If you think for a moment, you will realize that the sewage problem inside the densely crowded community must be a difficult one and the insects have solved it in a bizarre but efficient manner . . . the food passes through the alimentary canal of several individuals until all the nourishment has been extracted from it and only a dark-colored sticky paste (used as a building material) remains. . . . In this city of endless night the inhabitants shed their skins six or seven times as they grow up and the narrow corridors would soon be choked with these empty husks if they were not disposed of in some way or other. The termites get rid of them by eating them. . . . It is the same with their method of disposing of the dead. A cemetery is not needed inside the crowded fortress because the dead are eaten by the living."

If you can forget some of these and other similar practices that are somewhat repulsive to us, and consider only the abstract characteristics of termite society, it does seem often to approximate the ideal of certain Utopians. There is no selfishness, and only the welfare of the community counts. There is no competition, only cooperation; no struggle for individual wealth, superiority or status. And the state (if you imagine that it ever existed) has indeed withered away. No laws are necessary because no one would do anything a law might exist to prevent. And though this is so far from being a classless society that there are many classes among certain species of ants and bees, no one is interested in social mobility because each, like the citizens of Aldous Huxley's *Brave New World,* accepts with perfect docility the role assigned him. In fact there is only one respect in which this brave world is different from Huxley's. In the latter, reproduction was controlled but sexual activity was abundantly open to all. The termites have adopted a more direct Draconian system. "About ninety-five percent of the inhabitants of a termitary are workers. These are males and females that have not developed fully and their sexual organs are vestigial and useless. As their sexual organs do not function, the workers are denied the privilege of parenthood and they know nothing of the distractions of sex."

Nevertheless, to quote Skaif again: "Apart from microorganisms, termites are far and away the most numerous of living creatures in Africa and they teem almost everywhere in the soil. It may be said that they own Africa in a truer sense than do the human inhabitants, that they were here long before man arrived and that they will probably be here long after he, through his folly, has gone." Harvard University's Professor B. F. Skinner has maintained that the only criterion to be applied in judging the desirability or undesirability of any institution or act is simply the question whether or not it will make it more probable that the society which encourages it "will be here tomorrow." By that test the termite society is triumphantly successful.

In any case, survival alone seems to be indeed the termites' only success. Though their way of life is the most elaborate known to any creature except man himself, they know neither joy nor sorrow. In all probability they are not conscious at all. They weigh no questions, they make no choices. They live but they are not aware of living. The adventure of life has reached a dead end. They have come almost the full circle from the inanimate mechanism back again to something hardly distinguishable from the mechanical.

Most of us would not like to think that even in the remote future Professor Linton's paradox of the apes trying to live like termites would resolve itself in any fashion even remotely analogous, and if we take the possibility as in any sense serious we might ask ourselves how the termites got that way and whether or not there is any lesson to be learned from them.

Henri Fabre was convinced that the answer was simple: it is merely that God had chosen to give them nearly infallible instincts instead of blundering brains. Modern biologists have, of course, only theories. But some of these theories are at least suggestive. No creature except man, so some of them insist, ever rested his hope of survival on his ability to fore-see and choose rather than upon instinct and its inherited pattern of be-havior fixed by natural selection. Yet even biologists who make such an absolute distinction between man and the other animals admit that there is also a difference in the degree to which instinctive behavior in other animals is fixed and not capable of modification by any novelty in the situation to be met. We may refuse to call it intelligence, but a cat, a dog, or any other mammal does not respond to a given situation with quite the same predictable, unvarying behavior as the termite or even the ant.

Somewhere, very far back in time, one group of primitive creatures took one road and another group took a different one.

[*And Even If You Do,* 1967.
First published in the *Saturday Review,* 1963.]

## Through Happiness with Slide Rule and Calipers

From my own childhood I remember the story of a little boy whose chief delight was in his Sunday school—until a worldly uncle took him out to the ball game. That evening he announced that he was never going to Sunday school again. He had had some real fun for the first time.

Now the lesson to be learned from this story is that you can never evaluate an experience of your own without comparing it with something else and can't evaluate the experience of anyone else at all—because you can never really know what it was. When a man tells you that he enjoys Mickey Spillane and rock-'n'-roll as much as you do Tolstoy and Bee-thoven there is no way of knowing whether this is true or not. Maybe if he ever got from Tolstoy and Beethoven what you get, he would not waste time on his present favorites.

This is one of the many reasons why sociological measurements of con-tentment, or efforts to determine what people ought to have in the way of education, employment, and "standard of living" to make them happy, are very nearly meaningless. You can't tell how much contentment they ex-pect or have ever known. This man's contentment may be what those who have been used to a richer life would call dissatisfaction or even misery. We can't even know whether or not it is true that most men lead lives of quiet desperation.

These ponderous reflections were inspired by a recent report from the National Opinion Research Center at the University of Chicago entitled

*In Pursuit of Happiness—A Pilot Study of Behavior Related to Mental Health.* I presume that it is well done as such things go and that its "methodology" would be approved by other sociologists. But my own first reaction is simply this: the war between science and religion will be settled long before that between literature and sociology. The proponents of each were born under different stars and are equally incapable of seeing the same things as either significant or interesting.

To the sociologist it seems that the poet and the philosopher deal only in opinions and guesses for which they offer no substantiating proof and that they inhabit what I once heard a professor of sociology describe as "the never-never land of the humanities." To those who, for good or ill, exemplify what is called "the literary mind," the sociologist seems, on the other hand, to pretend to define the indefinable, to measure the unmeasurable, and then to come up with conclusions that are either not demonstrated at all or, quite as frequently, so obvious that they need no demonstration.

Before I go into more detail concerning any of the charges that I make so recklessly, let me give two specific examples of, first, the laboriously demonstrated obvious and, second, the measurement of the unmeasurable.

Example 1. On the basis of answers given to a questionnaire concerning things the questioned worry about, it is stated that only 4 percent of those under fifty, as opposed to 21 percent of those fifty or over, worry about growing old. Do we need any ghost come from the grave or any researcher from a National Research Center to tell us that? Without any investigation whatever I venture to state that only a fraction of 1 percent of those under six worry at all about growing old—unless you count worrying because they are not growing old as fast as they would like.

Example 2. In an elaborate analysis of a set of figures dealing with (a) the degree to which a subject calls himself "happy" and (b) how much worrying he thinks he does, I read the following:

> Somewhat surprisingly, however, there is no relation between positive feelings and intensity of worry, 23% of both those with high and with low positive feelings and intensity of worry reporting that they worry a lot. We find also that men with high anxiety (34% as against 20% of the lows), those with high marital tension (26% as against 19% of the lows), and those with low job satisfaction (26% as against 18% of the highs) report worrying a lot. Intensity of worry is thus negatively related to well-being.

This is a real beaut. Note first the statistical proof of the obvious, namely the fact that those who are anxious and don't like their wives or their jobs worry more than those who are serene, happily married, and content with their jobs. Note second the gobbledygook. Instead of saying that those who say they worry a lot are not less likely than others to say that they are happy, you get "intensity of worry is thus negatively related to well-being." Note third that this supposed paradox is easily resolved on the basis of common-sense observation concerning the vagueness of the units of measurement and the subjective nature of the individual's estimate of his own condition. In the first place "a lot" is not a meaningful unit of measurement. In the second place, it seems obvious enough that when two individuals are asked whether or not they worry "a lot" the answer may depend upon how much worry each thinks is inevitable and how much he supposes most other people do. "A lot" may be very little to one, a great deal to another. Talk about the literary man's being merely subjective! There is no way of correlating external situations or even behavior patterns with the inner state that constitutes "happiness."

Ever since literature began it has had a good deal to say and even more to imply about happiness. Sociology is a much more recent enterprise and my impression is ("my impression"; there, says the sociologist, is the literary mind at work) that it was rather late in its development before it took up happiness in addition to more tangible subjects. Presently I shall give some examples of the kind of thing literature on the one hand and sociology on the other have had to say on this subject, but first I must insist that it seems to me (there goes the literary mind again) that an important difference between the two is that sociology (unlike literature) professes to be a science and therefore has no right to talk about anything unless it can be clearly defined. Yet when the study under consideration attempts to define what it proposes to investigate it takes uneasy refuge by saying that "the underlying assumption of this research is that there is a dimension called variously mental health, subjective adjustment, happiness, or psychological well-being. . . . At present there is neither a generally agreed upon name for this dimension nor agreement as to the appropriate methods of deciding where a particular individual should be placed on such a dimension. . . . The pilot study reported here was undertaken in the belief that much of the disagreement stems from a basic lack of knowledge about the behavior of people leading normal lives."

Was there ever such a mare's nest of definitions in terms of things not themselves defined and equatings of the dubiously equatable? What is a normal life; or is it merely an average one? If "mental health" is synonymous with "happiness," if happiness is defined as "subjective well-being" and subjective well-being defined as "adjustment" and "adjustment" defined as "that which provides a normal life," which is to say "a happy life," how do we break out of this circular series of definitions? And of course there are also all the now-familiar questions concerning adjustment as an ideal.

Even more important is the fact that the whole of the ancient dispute about the contentment of a contented hog and the discontent of a discontented Socrates pops up. The present study seems to imply that the state of the contented (or shall we say "adjusted" and "normal") hog is to be preferred to that of the discontented Socrates, or at least may be compared with it. But Samuel Johnson (a man of letters) says something on the subject which a sociologist might ponder before he attempts to penetrate the secret of content and adjustment. Boswell is reporting:

> I mentioned Hume's notion that all who are happy are equally happy; a little miss with a new gown at a dancing school ball, a general at the head of a victorious army, and an orator, after having made an eloquent speech in a great assembly. *Johnson*: Sir, that all who are happy, are equally happy is not true. A peasant and a philosopher may be equally *satisfied* but not equally *happy*. . . . I remember this very question very happily illustrated in opposition to Hume, by the Reverend Mr. Robert Brown, at Utrect. "A small drinking glass and a large one, may be equally full; but the large one holds more than the small."

Questionnaires take the replies of any subject at face value; the questioner must assume that any man's reply is as reliable as that of any other. Hence he might find himself compelled to conclude that the well-fed hog wallowing in his sty was more content (therefore "happier," "better adjusted to a normal life," and in sounder "mental health") than the grumbling philosopher. There is no place in the present study where divine discontent may be recorded.

The person being questioned is occasionally asked such a question as "Did you feel on top of the world any time last week?" But "happy" seems often to mean "not unhappy" and the key terms—"mental health," "adjustment," and "normal"—are all rather negative, while happiness is or ought to be positive. Contrast the sociologist's few drab words, all of which are assumed to refer to approximately the same thing, with the rich vocabulary of literature that recognizes an extensive hierarchy, every level of which implies a discrimination instead of assuming a dubious identity. This hierarchy might run something like this: Contentment, amusement, fun, pleasure, happiness, delight, joy, ecstasy. It is true that literature does not attempt to define these terms and the sociologists will say that they are vague. But there is a complexity that the man of letters is aware of and the sociologist obscures.

At about the same time I began to read *In Pursuit of Happiness* I found in my newspaper a reporter's account of a check-up visit to a couple that had been married for seventeen years. He found them happy (the word is his) and got the opinion of a neighbor that the marriage had turned out better than most of those in the neighborhood, even though this "happy" couple lived in near destitution in a shack on a rutted dirt road in Kentucky.

Even this would not have made them newsworthy, but another fact did: Seventeen years ago, when the wedding took place, the husband was seventeen and the wife seventy-seven. I suppose that the sociologist would find them not "normal" (*i.e.,* average) but I don't see how he could escape the conclusion that they were, by his own definition, happy and well adjusted. Moreover, they enjoy a high degree of "job (or jobless) satisfaction" since they are content to live on the wife's relief payments.

Those of us who are blessed or cursed with the literary mind would not be greatly distressed by this happy couple's failure to be "normal" since we have no prejudice in favor of what we prefer to call, not the normal, but the average. We would, however, question the significance of the broad term "happy" and ask, "Where do they stand on the amusement, fun, pleasure, joy, and ecstasy scale?" Though both we and the sociologists will probably agree that the situation of this contented couple is not the most desirable one, literature would throw more light than sociology does on the question why most of us would not change places with either the ninety-four-year-old wife or the thirty-four-year-old husband. Neither would know how to make all men happy, but I still think that a familiarity with the best that has been thought and said by men of letters is more helpful than all the sociologists' statistics.

Misguided attempts to deal quantitatively with so complex a thing as happiness are the enemies of literature and perhaps of happiness itself because they encourage us to assume both that one kind of happiness is the same as another and that they are equally valuable. In fact nothing is more important, prudentially or morally, than the realization that whether or not the pursuit of happiness is a legitimate chief aim depends upon which of the many happinesses one chooses and upon the means used to pursue it. Taken seriously, statistical studies are all too likely to teach us only how to become dismally "adjusted." Is it safe to take seriously a study in which you put in the same category everyone who says that he frequently feels "on top of the world," even though feeling on top of the world may mean anything from the friskiness of a puppy to the joy celebrated in the Ninth Symphony?

Here, chosen almost at random, are some of the things that some of the best thinkers and sayers have had to say on the general subject of happiness—which Alexander Pope called "our being's end and aim." They are wildly diverse, sometimes flatly contradictory, and range upward from the profound pessimism with which my little anthology begins. But for all their inconclusiveness they tell us more about the experience of being human than all the sociologists' demonstrations that job satisfaction contributes to contentment and that older men worry more than young ones about growing old.

"The natural progress of the human mind is not from pleasure to pleasure but from hope to hope" (Johnson); "None would live past years again yet all hope pleasure from what yet remain" (Dryden); "Call that man happy and that man alone he who can call today his own" (Horace); "Pleasures are like poppys spread; you seize the flower the bloom is dead" (Burns); "We are never as lucky or as unlucky as we believe" (La Rochefoucauld); "Pleasure and beauty are byproducts: The direct pursuit of pleasure and beauty is folly" (Bernard Shaw); "Young men spend their time anticipating the future: Old men in remembering the past" (Anonymous); "Better a dinner of herbs where love is than a stalled ox with hate" (the Bible); "Rarely, rarely comest thou, spirit of delight" (Shelley); "Many green islands there must be/In the wide sea of misery" (Shelley); "That sad word joy" (Landor); "I have known such joys as might have inspired a Homer or a Shakespeare" (Thoreau); "God's in His heaven, all's right with the world" (Browning); "I have a lover's quarrel with life" (Robert Frost).

It is true that poets have more often written odes to dejection than exclaimed with Shelley "The world's great age begins anew" or with Donne "And now good morrow to our waking souls." But even in that fact there may lie the useful suggestion that to expect joy too often is to experience it less frequently; and literature, unlike sociology, offers consolation. Isn't Frost's lover's quarrel with life more fruitful than "adjustment"?

Since I would not like to deprive anyone of legitimate aid in reaching "our being's end and aim," I will pass on to those who may find them useful a few of the conclusions based on this "pilot study" of 2,006 persons, of whom 24 percent said they were "very happy," 59 percent "pretty happy," and 17 percent "not too happy."

College graduates with incomes of $7,000 a year or more are happier than those who have had no formal education past grammar school and who make less than $3,000. But before you decide to make yourself happier by achieving some higher learning, consider a further fact: "When the income is the same, the better educated are less happy than their less cultivated counterparts. Single women are only slightly more unhappy than married women, but single men are twice as unhappy as married men." The conclusion for those who put their faith in statistics as a guide would seem to be, first, don't get too much education unless you think you are going to earn a considerable income and, second, if you are a man make every effort to find a wife, while, if you are a woman, leave marriage or single blessedness up to chance while you concentrate on goals like "job satisfaction" that are more likely to affect your happiness.

A more general conclusion is that the degree of happiness is influenced more by positive satisfactions than by dissatisfactions so that those who have many worries will nevertheless call themselves happy if they have many "positive feelings." "Happiness is a resultant of the relative strengths of positive and negative feelings rather than of the absolute amount of one or the other." These all-important positive feelings are said to be most likely to be dominant in those who are active participants in social gatherings. (This is a good place to point out that, however true this may be statistically, it doesn't mean that "togetherness" will necessarily produce results.) Thoreau—who, I suppose, was not "normal"—was one of the few men who have ever called themselves almost unqualifiedly happy. But I doubt that he would have been so if he had read a pilot study and decided to mend his ways. Statistics take no account of those who prefer to hear a different drummer.

Perhaps, indeed, the most important of all the limitations of the sociological method is the result of its usual assumption that happiness or unhappiness is principally dependent upon some external conditions; that we are as content or malcontent as our situation ought to make us. Yet all human experience, as well as most literature, recognizes that such is very far from being the case. In his book on Dickens, Gilbert Chesterton points out that this extravagant optimist became such long before he had escaped from the misfortunes which persistently dogged his boyhood, and he adds other examples to support the paradox that personal experience does not make optimists or pessimists. Even more relevant perhaps are the lines Samuel Johnson added at the end of Goldsmith's "The Traveller":

> How small of all that human hearts
>     endure,
> That part which kings or laws can
>     cause or cure.
> Still to ourselves in every place
>     consign'd,
> Our own felicity we make or find.

Little things, even trivial things, often make us happy, while catastrophes are often surmounted. We go up or down for unreasonable reasons, finding the world alternately bright or dark because we are, as Pope said, "too soon dejected and too soon elate." All things considered, we can learn more about happiness as an inner and wayward state from *Happiness Is a Warm Puppy* than from the ambitious compilation of the answers to a sociologist's questionnaire.

To those who are already pretty normal and well adjusted but who would like to be even more so, such conclusions as this study offers may prove helpful, though the already normal should be warned that even among such one man's meat is sometimes another man's poison and that in the case of any thoughtful individual his own opinion of what would make him happy may be a safer guide than statistics. Even by strict mathematics he is at least one-fourth as likely to belong to the 25 percent who react one way as to the 75 percent who react another, and if he is the kind of man who turns to books for guidance he is much more likely than the percentage would suggest to be among the minority. Only those who have none of that self-knowledge that has sometimes been called the beginning of wisdom, and that literature endeavors to communicate, should play the game of life as though it were bridge (or even poker), where the odds are the same from one person to the next.

As for me, I shall continue to feel that for all the contradictions that literature exhibits, I get most enlightenment and most help in the conduct of my own life from those who dwell in what the sociologist called the never-never land of the humanities. And I have an uneasy conviction that the more legislators and educators come to rely on the sociologists' findings, the less the society they help to make will encourage the development of those "abnormal" and "maladjusted" individuals who have contributed so much to the civilization from which they dissent.

[*If You Don't Mind My Saying So*, 1964.
First published in the *Saturday Review*, 1963.]

## If You Don't Mind My Saying So . . .

When I visited my native town in the spring of 1945, it was buzzing with rumor. At Oak Ridge, some fifty miles away, mysterious things were going on. Some said that they had to do with the disintegration of the atom, and when this guess was passed on I smiled a rather superior smile. "That," I said, "is a good many years away."

A few months later, on the morning of August sixth, my wife broke my early morning sleep. "The radio has just announced that an atom bomb was exploded over Japan. What does *that* mean?" "It means," I said, "that I am scared to death." A bad prophet I had obviously been, but like a good many of my fellow citizens I could be wise after the event.

Usually the great crises of history have not been recognized at the moment. Few seventeenth-century Englishmen knew that an apple (the most fateful since Eve's) had fallen upon Newton's head. Decades later no Londoner exclaimed to another, "Watt has just invented the steam engine—and you know what *that* means." Only three Magi and a few shepherds knew that Jesus had been born. But we seem to have changed all that.

We may be wrong in our estimate, though it does not seem probable that we are, at least so far as the momentousness of the event is concerned. But it is less likely that we have assessed it with perfect accuracy, and ever since I recovered from the first shock I have wondered whether the most obvious meanings are the only or even the most important ones.

Everyone knows that what disintegrated along with some billions of plutonium atoms was the last small vestige of physical security for the civilian which TNT and the airplane had left us. So also, however, did various other things less immediately recognized. Even ten years later, optimists and pessimists are still concerned chiefly with the question of whether the new era is bright with the prospect of new powers and prosperity, or whether it is only a new era of destruction. But two fundamental premises vanished into thin air along with those certain material particles which ceased, in that instant, to be material at all. And the two premises were these: (1) that what we called our "control" over nature really is effective, and (2) that physical science had at last made the physical universe intelligible.

The first premise is no longer tenable because a force can hardly be said to be under control if it threatens to destroy all civilization and possibly all life. The second is not tenable because the physical universe has turned out to be so different from what was confidently assumed that some leading scientists are already expressing the opinion that it is radically unintelligible—that no image we can ever form of it will correspond to what actually is. Should we manage somehow to escape self-destruction, then it may quite possibly turn out that the abandonment of these two premises will affect the future of civilization quite as much as any new power the atom can be made to release.

That there was a catch somewhere in our boasted control was suspected by some from the time when we first began to boast of it. Those few always feared that, like Faust, we were selling our souls for powers which seemed unlimited but in fact were not. Like Faust we exclaimed:

> Who would not be proficient in this art?
> How pliant is this Mephistopheles,
> Full of obedience and humility!
> Such is the force of magic and my spells.

But like Faust again, we discovered that the Devil is controllable only so long as he consents to be, and that the more of his power we acquire, the more completely we become his victim. We controlled the steam in the piston and the electric current which circles the armature, but we neither controlled nor even foresaw the effects, good and bad, which the steam engine and the electric motor would have upon civilization.

To the few who pointed this out the reply was commonly either that the end would be somehow good or that, in any event, we must go where fate is taking us. But neither of these replies will any longer do. Mephistopheles is not to be trusted. Self-destruction is too high a price to pay for power or even for the disinterested pursuit of truth. We may be glad that we invented the Bomb first. But there are few who now doubt that it would have been better if its invention had been forever impossible to any human being whatsoever.

From the beginning, science promised us two things. Besides that ability to manipulate our physical environment which reached its ultimate when the atom was rent asunder, it promised something often called more important. Science would, it was said, do much more than make our lives more comfortable, more convenient, more safe, and more abundant. It would also give us a clear insight into The Nature of Things and replace with demonstrable Truth those fragmentary, illogical, and inconsistent notions about the structure and workings of the universe which poetry, metaphysics, and religion had foisted upon us.

The first promise has certainly been abundantly fulfilled if the word *manipulate* is insisted upon and not confused with the word *control*. But the once generally accepted belief that the second promise was also being kept turns out to be a delusion when even the less radically skeptical physicists admit that what used to be called "the scientific world view" is by no means clear or consistent and that, at a minimum, the universe is very unlike what it was supposed to be. The newest "scientific world view" dissolves nineteenth-century certainties into a mist of guesses and paradoxes at least as full of inconsistencies and incomprehensibilities as any mishmash of religion, mythology, metaphysics, and poetry ever was. "I believe because it is absurd" has come again to sum up the most advanced credo.

How many angels can stand on the point of a needle? That question, so I have been reliably informed, seems never to have been asked by any schoolman and was invented by some nineteenth-century rationalist who imagined that it was the sort of thing a schoolman would ask. Modern physics, on the other hand, does ask how many atoms could be placed on that point where angels might once have stood. Moreover, physics answers it—probably correctly enough. But it has no more idea what an atom is than it has what an angel would be like. It can count atoms and even disintegrate them. But it does not know what they are. The determination to manipulate the physical world has proved astonishingly successful while the determination to understand it seems to have failed completely.

Once we were told that if some results of technological advance were dubiously desirable we ought to be willing to accept them in exchange for that enlightenment of the understanding which accompanies the march of scientific achievement. But that understanding we now know has eluded us; and it will be a grim joke on the Hero as Scientist if the final result of his efforts is to be not merely that he will blow himself to bits, but that his last moments will be those during which he is less clear in his own mind than he ever was before concerning the real nature of the universe around him. May it be that the only things to survive Hiroshima are pure technology on the one hand and, on the other, philosophy, metaphysics, and even, as a remote possibility, religion? Did Science as Guide and Savior die there at the very moment when its claim to be a master of power was most abundantly vindicated? No poet, philosopher, or metaphysician has ever done his job one-tenth so well as the scientist did his— partly, perhaps, because the job of the scientist is easier. But no one except the poet, the philosopher, and the metaphysician has ever done the harder job at all.

Some few scientists still assure us that all they need is more time. The day will come, they say, when science will establish ethics and even aesthetics on a sound scientific basis. We shall then know what is Good and what is Beautiful as surely as we now know the formula for water. When that time comes we shall be sure at last of not only what is worth having, but how to get it; not only how to blow people up, but just who, and under what circumstances they should be disintegrated. Knowing, as then we shall, what good, wise (and of course "adjusted") men really are, we shall be able to produce them as surely as we now produce metals or plastics to fit the specifications drawn up in advance.

Perhaps. But time is running out. Can we afford to wait? Since August 6, 1945, it has seemed less likely that we can.

For as long, almost, as human thought has left a record, there have been those who insist that behind all the diverse manifestations of the universe there lies but one protean substance which reveals itself to our minds under aspects as diverse as what we call "matter" and what we call "energy," "thought," and even "spirit." Instead of saying that reality is "nothing but" one or another of these, they believed it to be something capable of being them all. At the very beginning of the scientific age, Giordano Bruno was one such. But during most of the three centuries which lie between him and us, the boldest, the most active, and the most successful investigators of nature assumed a premise directly antithetical to his. Matter and energy, for instance, were not one thing but two. What is called thought and emotion must be some form of energy if, indeed, they are to be assumed to exist at all as more than by-products of energy acting upon matter.

On the basis of this premise the great triumphs of physics and chemistry were achieved. When Einstein set forth his famous conversion formula he turned his back upon the working hypothesis which for more than three centuries had worked so well; and he took a long stride backward toward monism and Bruno. The mind-body problem did not, to be sure, concern him at the moment. He did not suggest that mind, or spirit, is the same as energy, just as energy is the same as matter. But the analogy is close and the speculative extension of the one proposition to include the other seems, at the very least, not fantastic.

Had Einstein's formula remained on paper where he himself might very well have left it, most of the world would have been little impressed. Today, mathematics may carry more weight than metaphysics does, but only to the new physicists, already deep in both, did a mere formula carry much conviction. Most of us do not believe anything unless something happens when the belief is acted upon. And something did happen over Hiroshima. If a city is destroyed because a small group of men were ready to proceed on the assumption that $E=MC^2$, then we are willing to grant that matter and energy really are convertible. A general public which has never heard of monism begins to lean again in its direction.

From news items I learned that several "teams" are still busy officially investigating the various "side effects" of the first bombs. But has anyone undertaken to investigate the ideological casualties, to determine not only to what concepts radiation was fatal, but also what damage was suffered by those which survived, and perhaps most important of all, what gene mutations will reveal themselves in the next generation of concepts, philosophical as well as scientific?

Positivists are fond of assuring us that various current terms are "meaningless." But they were hoist on their own super-petard when its explosion rendered meaningless certain of their own favorite words, notably *material* and *materialistic*. If Einstein was as right as the bombs seem to have proved him, then these terms have ceased to mean anything at all.

To say "I am a materialist" is meaningful only if the concept *matter* can be defined in such a way as to distinguish matter clearly from something else. Until a few years ago such definition seemed easy. "Matter is that which occupies space and has weight." This definition distinguished it as clearly from *energy*, which occupies no space and has no weight, as it did from *life* or *spirit* or *idea*, which, having neither the characteristics of matter nor the characteristics of energy, were sometimes assumed not to exist at all. To say "I am a materialist" meant "I believe that the only fundamental reality is that which occupies space and which has weight."

But the matter which disintegrated privately over the American desert and then publicly over Japan ceased in those instants either to weigh anything or to occupy any space. At those instants, therefore, the meaning of the term *materialist* disappeared as completely as the disintegrated atoms themselves. When men fought in the streets of Byzantium over the terms

*Homoöusian* and *Homoiousian,* some shadow of meaning may have remained in them. But between the man who says, "I am a materialist because everything is material," and the man who says, "I am not a materialist because nothing is ultimately material," no definable difference any longer exists. What is material at one moment may become, in an instant, not material at all.

On the basis of this seemingly demonstrated fact, many a scientific treatise will have to be revised if the now meaningless statements are to be eliminated from them. Almost at random I opened a recent book on one of the biological sciences. There the authority of a distinguished scientist is quoted to support the contention that the appearance of life on earth can be accounted for "without the intervention of the non-material." Does this statement, in the light of the most recent knowledge, mean anything at all?

On that morning ten years ago, my first reaction, formulated while I was still between sleep and waking, was proper enough. In fact I am rather proud of it. I had then—and we all still have—good reason to be scared. But I have wondered increasingly whether that phrase sums up everything we ought to feel. The metaphysical consequences, if we survive to enjoy them, may be salutary as well as immeasurable, and we may be waking at last from a long bad dream. It may seem a pity that blessings should come as thoroughly disguised as they sometimes do. Whoever arranged this one appears to have outdone himself—if he really did wrap up a boon in that package. But who knows? They say that God works in mysterious ways. Possibly they are sometimes even as mysterious as in this instance they seem to be.

[*If You Don't Mind My Saying So,* 1964.
First published in *The American Scholar,* 1955–56.]

# · IV ·

# On Some Men and Some Books

MERE WRITING ABOUT BOOKS AND BOOKMAKERS IS ONE THING; "SERIOUS Criticism" is quite another. This I am willing enough to admit, but I have never aspired to serious criticism partly because anyone who wrote about books, plays, authors and writers as often as I did and over so long a span of years would have been compelled to revise drastically his opinions and his methods every decade or so if he was to maintain his claim to be taken seriously.

The discouraging fact is that fashions in serious criticism have changed almost as frequently as any other fashions. About the time that I first began to write book reviews for the New York *Nation* and the *Saturday Review,* Anatole France's once-admired dictum, "Criticism is the adventure of the soul among the masterpieces," was just beginning to be despised as not criticism at all but only what T. S. Eliot was presently to dismiss as the product of a re-creative impulse too weak actually to achieve an independent creation. But Eliot's star was just beginning to rise and the most respected theory of criticism then current was Benedetto Croce's Expressionism, which maintained that the true business of the critic was to discover a personal expression behind the work. Eliot soon put Expressionism to flight with his insistence that impersonality, not the revelation of a personality, was the distinguishing characteristic of real art. Following this pronouncement, the explication of a text considered without reference to either the life and personality of the writer or the spirit of the age in which he wrote became the only true method of penetrating to the significance of the novel or the poem. Then psychoanalysis, both Freudian and Jungian, intruded and works were interpreted either in terms of the creator's complexes or as embodiments of archetypical myths. Thus while some were keeping their eyes on the text, others made it their business to seek out the Oedipus complex, the death wish or the universal myth which must certainly underlie every work worthy of attention of the serious critic. The only choice which such a serious critic seemed to have was either exclusive emphasis upon one or the other of the various methods or an admission that they were all valid and that no one man could possibly deal adequately with the problems of serious criticism. Thus one very serious critic seriously proposed that no one should attempt so formidable a task alone and that in the future criticism should operate principally through panels of critics who would attack poems from every possible angle and by such a joint effort render them understandable—presumably, that is to say, understandable by other critics and possibly other poets, though the general reader would continue, as always, to read and enjoy for reasons which had nothing to do with the meaning of what he read. Thus Robert Graves announced that he wrote poetry only for other poets, and in some quarters it seemed to be assumed that a poem (and to a lesser extent all creative writing) exists primarily in order to provide a problem to be solved, and that the best poem is the one which is most complicatedly obscure. Thus some critics at least were very much like those expositors of the Bible of whom Dryden wrote: "Plain truths enough for needful use they found/ But men would still be itching to expound." And of whom he added, "Each was ambitious of the obscurer's place."

At the present moment the avant-garde seems concerned less with the dispute over the methods of criticism than with the question of what the purpose of art is or should be. The left-wing critics of the thirties insisted that the only meaningful art was devoted to social criticism, but a generation later such "now" critics as Susan Sontag and Anthony Burgess have returned to an 1890 estheticism. Thus Mr. Burgess wrote in his review of a current novel, "Where *Last Exit to Brooklyn* possibly fails as good art is in its arousal of social conscience."

My first book dealing with a writer and his works was *Edgar Allan Poe —A Study in Genius* which was clearly, if not very technically, psychoanalytical in method. Never since have I tried to fit into any school and have always been content in discussing a book or an author merely to point out whatever seemed to me most interesting at the moment. I no doubt sometimes sank to the level of attempting to describe the adventures of my soul among the masterpieces, sometimes searched for the personality being expressed, and sometimes, even, sought a hidden meaning. As a consequence, no serious critic has ever taken me seriously. But since I have never been in fashion I have also never fallen completely out of it and have maintained over the years a modest group of readers who have not been put off by the fact that I am not a serious critic.

Something of my own attitude to the seriousness with which the serious critic takes his task and himself is set forth in the little essay which follows.

## The Highbrows Are Not Always Right

Two articles in two magazines have drawn my attention to the existence of a Literary Establishment described as rather more distinct than anything of the sort that existed in my day. Members of this Establishment are said to be primarily concerned with talking to (and impressing) one another, although they also have great influence upon that section of intellectual youth that dutifully likes what it is told it ought to like and turns up its nose on cue from the noses of Establishment members. Some, at least, of the members seem tacitly, and sometimes explicitly, to accept a criterion of literary merit that seems to me highly unreliable: "Wide popularity is *prima facie* evidence of inferior quality." To me it seems that "Popular, therefore inferior" is almost as likely to mislead as "Popular and therefore excellent."

It is of course a commonplace of the textbooks that, by the middle of the eighteenth century, literacy—in England at least—was sufficiently widespread to make it possible for a writer to appeal from the patron to the public. Some persons have always regarded this as an unmixed blessing; others have pointed out that it made a great deal of trash profitable. The thesis propounded by some now seems to be that the emergence of a large public was an unmixed calamity and that since the time when it appeared High Culture has been squeezed out by Mass Culture on the one hand and Middlebrow Culture on the other; also that of the two latter, both of which now flourish exuberantly, the Middlebrow is the worse because it competes directly with the High and is likely to be mistaken for it by that large public that believes itself to be cultured when it is only vulgar.

Hence the importance of the Establishment. It alone can accomplish the task of separating the sheep from the goats or, in more elegant terms, of pointing out to the few outside the Establishment who are capable of appreciating High Art which books belong in this category and which are mere vulgar pretenders.

Now I certainly do not believe that all best sellers are masterpieces or that a novel or a play must be great if it is much admired for a month or two by what is called the educated public.

On the other hand, history will bear me out that there are many instances where time has reversed the contemporary judgment of the most solemn critics. "Who reads Cowley now?" The answer was, "Nobody," only a generation after he had been the darling of the highbrows. And of course the most notorious example is Shakespeare. If popularity damns, then there is no hope for Chaucer, Shakespeare, Dryden, Pope, Fielding, Byron, Dickens, Thackery, Trollope or Tennyson, every one of whom (except possibly the first) not only enjoyed a public larger than the elite of his day, but catered unconsciously or consciously to the large public by making concessions to it. All had at least some of the stigmata of the middlebrow: They were definitely not *avant-garde;* they appealed to the masses; they were in many respects imitative of their predecessors; and, in the case of several, definitely chauvinistic.

It is of course as easy to idealize the populace as it is to idealize the aristocracy, but to assume that the aristocratic patron necessarily had good taste is to succumb to the "good old days" fallacy. Suppose that the reputation of Gibbon's *Decline and Fall* had depended, not upon the public which hailed it as a masterpiece, but upon that prince of the royal blood who accepted a copy of the second volume with the immortal words: "Another damned, thick, square book. Always scribble, scribble—eh, Mr. Gibbon?"

Petrarch, who admired the unread and now unreadable works of Boccaccio, referred contemptuously to *The Decameron* as "Published, I presume, during your early years." But the middlebrow public of his day had given it a warm reception. In the prologue to *Don Quixote,* Cervantes says that his aim is to write so that "the simple shall not be wearied, but the grave shall not despise it." Yet for all that, he seems to have been unhappy about this masterpiece and wrote thereafter only the unreadable *Persiles and Sigismunda,* which was clearly intended to meet the standards of High Art as defined by the serious critics of his day.

I doubt that popularity or accessibility is a reliable criterion of either worth or worthlessness, especially since books perhaps not intended for the general public, and perhaps not at first accepted by it, sometimes turn out to be exceedingly popular in the long run.

Swift, it should be remembered, said that he wrote *Gulliver's Travels* to vex mankind, not to please it. That is something that the Establishment would approve of highly. He had as great a contempt for the brains, taste and integrity of the average Englishman as any member of the Establishment has for the brains, taste, and integrity of his contemporaries. But *Gulliver's Travels* was soon one of the most widely-read books in the language. As Chesterton said, there is only one thing worse than being afraid to disagree with the public and that is being afraid to agree with it.

Do members of the Establishment get nervous if a new book from their typewriters sells more than any of their previous books? Would they refuse to write for a magazine whose circulation grew beyond a certain point? And if so, then what, precisely, is that point? How widely can a book be read and still escape damnation as "middlebrow"? How does a member of the Establishment feel when he gets a favorable review in *The New York Times Book Review*?—which happens to be, of all organs of literary opinion, the one that members of the Establishment hold in greatest contempt.

Many years ago, the woman editor of what was at the time the most widely respected highbrow monthly told me that her writers, unlike those who wrote for *The Nation,* could be sure that what they said would be understood. "We have," she explained, "succeeded in whittling our circulation away until we reach only those genuinely interested in aesthetics." Not long after this remark the magazine succumbed to its success. I wonder if those members of the Establishment who occasionally contribute to such magazines as *Esquire* and *Playboy* have ever advised the editors to "whittle away" their circulation.

It has been explained to us very often (sometimes apologetically and sometimes with complacency) that ours is an age of criticism and this is, of course, one reason why the critics tend to assume that the nonprofessional reader is necessarily wrong. But the Alexandrian Age also was an age of criticism and there is something Alexandrian about much contemporary critical analysis. It seems to be assumed that poems exist in order to be explicated and that, therefore, the best poem is the one that provides the explicator with the best opportunity to exercise his ingenuity.

Similarly, novels exist in order that critics may lay bare their symbolic or mythological content (often unsuspected by the novelist himself). Thus Mark Twain certainly did not know that *Huckleberry Finn* was, as one of the best-known contemporary critics has recently demonstrated to his own satisfaction, a homosexual novel. Indeed, the tendency to discover various other hidden complexes where they have previously been unsuspected may remind some of us of the story of the psychiatrist who told a patient who had just submitted to the ink blot test that he was obsessed by sex. "I'm obsessed by sex—I am the one who is obsessed by sex!" the patient exclaimed. "Who has been showing me all those dirty pictures?"

And when a critic, instead of merely pointing out that *Huckleberry Finn,* or some other great novel, has been admired for the wrong reason, undertakes the complementary demonstration that some nearly unreadable work is really a masterpiece because its author has so obviously understood that the true function of the novel is to be ambiguous, mythic, or involved with the castration or some other complex, I am reminded of what a seventeenth-century French reader remarked when the author of an epic poem called attention to the fact that he had scrupulously "obeyed all the rules of Aristotle": "I am grateful to him for having obeyed the rules of Aristotle but I am very angry at Aristotle for having compelled him to write so dull a poem."

Even the ideal of pure poetry, pure painting and pure music seems to me to lead nowhere. So does the stated determination of the modern poets that every word shall be inevitable, indispensable and profoundly significant—that there must be, above all, no uninspired lines. If Homer sometimes nods, why should not a modern poet be granted a similar indulgence? Byron is full of commonplaces, so are Wordsworth and Tennyson. But are they destined to be regarded always as lesser than Ezra Pound and Robert Lowell? What we demand in the long run is not perfection but a rewarding whole.

Serious critics (in the special but familiar sense of the term) have never taken me seriously. Perhaps, then, it is only sour grapes to say that they have, in one sense, taken themselves too seriously—not because they are (as I have often found them) acute, conscientious and illuminating, but because they vastly overestimate their own influence upon the fate of literary works. The members of the Leavis school (who represent this kind of seriousness at its most serious) sometimes state explicitly, and they imply almost continuously, that they are aware of a tremendous and almost dreadful responsibility. Just insofar as they prevail, just thus far will righteousness prevail. On them and on other serious critics falls the task of making the proper discriminations and arranging in their proper order the hierarchy of writers past and present. Just to the extent that they do so, will the genuinely great get their due and the inferior be prevented from enjoying the attention and esteem they do not merit.

It is, these critics say (and to this extent I agree with them), tremendously important that excellence be recognized and vulgarity discountenanced. But I don't agree with their corollary that righteousness will prevail just to the extent that serious critics champion it. No man, said Dr. Johnson, was ever written down except by himself. That, I think, is about nine-tenths true; and so is what Johnson might have added but didn't: No man is ever written *up* except by himself.

Criticism is an interesting activity for the critic and often makes interesting reading for the reader. It is a stream that flows parallel to the great stream of creative writing. But in the end it will be the writer, not the critic, who determines what is High Art and what is Middlebrow Vulgarity. Not even Professor Leavis can exercise much influence upon the ultimate reputation of those whom (with such a sense of his awful responsibility) he attempts to write down or write up. Whether or not D. H. Lawrence is ultimately established as the greatest English writer of the twentieth century will depend upon what Mr. Lawrence wrote, not upon what Professor Leavis has said about it.

In favor of the outmoded and now despised impressionistic, or adventures-of-the-soul-among-the-masterpieces, kind of criticism which T. S. Eliot damned as the expression of the weak creative impulse rather than the genuinely critical, at least this much can be said: It recognizes the secondary role of the critic instead of seeming to elevate him above the creator.

Shortly after the end of the First World War a Columbia University professor published an enormously successful novel. As is so often the case when an academic or a highbrow achieves popular success, he was so delighted that he was unnecessarily insistent upon calling the attention of his colleagues to the fact that he was famous. The following story, which I believe to be true, was told: The wife of the best-selling author met on campus one of his professional colleagues and demanded excitedly, "Have you read John's book?" "Not yet," was the reply. "Oh," she said, "it is a great book; you must read it right away; it will endure." "In that case," replied the possibly envious colleague, "there is no hurry."

Critics who are too much concerned with undeserved popularity or undeserved neglect might bear this anecdote in mind. I don't say that criticism may not hasten or retard, but I do say that serious critics need not wake up in the middle of the night in terror lest they have damned some great book to eternity or enthroned some faker.

[*And Even If You Do,* 1967.
First published in *The American Scholar,* 1966–1967.]

THE FIRST CHAPTER OF "EDGAR ALLAN POE" ENDS WITH THIS SENTENCE: "Throughout the ensuing study we shall be compelled to assume that the forces which wrecked his life were those which wrote his works."

Some idea of what this implies may be suggested by the following excerpts.

### "Passions of the Head"

I have already spoken of the rôle which wounded pride doubtless had in producing his wild career at the University of Virginia, and have spoken also of certain psychic difficulties from which Poe had doubtless already begun to suffer at that period, but there occurred at the stage of his life which we have just been discussing an event which throws a flood of light upon his mental state.

Scarcely was Poe well settled in his new home when he was married to Virginia Clemm, a girl who was not only literally a child in years but was destined to remain all her life a child in mind. She was the daughter of the woman who had sheltered him in Baltimore, he had known her almost since her infancy, and she had acted as a childish confidante during the course of one of the flirtations of his obscure years. Now he married her, and to whatever reasons one may attribute the act they cannot but suggest something abnormal. As early as September 22, 1834 when the child had just completed her twelfth year he had taken out a license to marry her in Baltimore but the strenuous and understandable objections of a distant relative either postponed the wedding or kept it a secret. Mrs. Clemm, however, a simpleminded woman who was devoted with an absolutely unquestioning devotion to Poe, supported him in this as she supported him in everything else that he wished to do and now on May 16, 1836 the pair were publicly and religiously married in Richmond by a Presbyterian minister to whom the bride "seemed very young" in spite of the fact that an acquaintance of Poe's obligingly perjured himself by declaring that Virginia was of the full legal age of twenty-one years.

Poe's love affairs, both before and after this one, were usually somehow fantastic. Generally they were purely "platonic" like his boyhood worship of Mrs. Stanard, but when they tended to approach the physical they were frenetically violent. In later years, as we shall see, he went completely mad when passion touched him, and once before his marriage he had shown how dangerous love in the ordinary sense was to his mental stability. During the obscure Baltimore period he had begun a flirtation with "Mary" (recently identified as a certain Miss Devereux) and late one evening he suddenly proposed that they be married upon the instant. Startled, she refused, but not long after he appeared at her home intoxicated and behaved in a manner so insanely violent that he was forbidden the house. The incident was prophetic of the character of his conduct during a whole series of brief love affairs late in life, but none of these strange affairs was so strange as his marriage, which was, it appears, no real marriage, with the child Virginia.

The event is indeed one very difficult of explanation for those who are loath to admit that the abnormality of Poe's literary expression had its roots in the very center of his being. Such persons tend to undertake the impossible task of making this marriage romantic. Sentimentalists stress the undoubted fact that Poe was always devoted to his wife in a brotherly fashion, and they have even suggested that this extraordinary union with a child is additional proof of the remarkable purity of his character; but facts cannot be denied. If it was his intention to make her fully his wife his act strongly suggests either abnormality or brutality, and if, as was certainly the case, he intended her as a wife in name only, this deliberate renunciation of a normal life cannot but indicate the existence of some emotional disturbance of profound importance in any understanding of the nature of the strange productions of his imagination. Here is a man who was always, as one who knew him said, in love. His entire life from childhood to death was an almost unbroken series of hectic and abortive flirtations; and yet, at the very beginning of his career, he deliberately tied himself to a child with whom for some time, at least, after the marriage was arranged sexual relations would be impossible.

It so happened that prolonged illness made sexual relations with her impossible even after she reached maturity and it may be suggested that certain of Poe's psychic abnormalities were a result of the unnatural restraint that he was called upon to exercise; but in view of his temperament and his actions such an explanation seems to me to be essentially inaccurate and superficial. Poe, it is true, could not have known that Virginia would become a permanent invalid but he certainly did know when he proposed to marry a girl just over twelve that the marriage must remain for some time at least unconsummated. It must have been the sexlessness of her beauty which appealed to him and thus a temporary continence was not so much thrust upon him as deliberately chosen. Doubtless he was aware in his own mind of nothing except the charm which feminine beauty divorced from any suggestion of conscious sex had for him and he would call his admiration for Virginia a worship of purity: but when we consider the distaste which his writings reveal for the whole idea of sexual passion and the unhappy history of his constantly frustrated flirtations with other women we may guess that this abnormal absorption in purity was but one of the outward signs of a deep-lying inhibition and we may guess also the function which Virginia was to perform in his life, though he himself did not clearly understand the fascination which she had for him. Her youth would serve as an excuse for leaving her untouched and the fact that he was already married would furnish him a plausible reason why all his affairs with other women must remain, if not exactly platonic, at least unconsummated. Events to be discussed later will make it clear that the efforts to escape from a realization of his own condition was part of one of the essential processes of Poe's life, but no act reveals more clearly than this one both his abnormality and the fact that he was desperately determined that it should not be admitted even to himself.

Mrs. Susan Weiss, a member of the large company of female Poe-worshippers, endeavors to explain the whole affair by maintaining that Poe was no more than a passive victim and that the marriage was merely a trick (of which Poe made the sorry best he could) on the part of Mrs. Clemm, who wished above all else a firm hold upon the irresponsible young man to whom she had become so firmly attached. The suggestion is, in the light of Poe's adoring attitude toward his wife, highly fantastic, but it does nevertheless give an obvious suggestion of one side of the truth, which is that he did deliberately marry the mother almost as much as he married the daughter. Though he did not need women in the way that normal men need them, he was extraordinarily dependent upon them for two things—inspiration and care. Virginia, described as "like a Canova" at the time when that was considered a compliment, perfectly met the needs of his morbid imagination because her undeveloped mind and pale unhealthy face, with the high forehead characteristic of the family, satisfied his conception of an unearthly purity. But she had neither the intelligence even to feign a sympathetic interest in his work nor the practical capacity to give him the maternal care which he had to have. Poe did not hesitate in after years to use the women who were fascinated by his personality for his material advantage, and there is no reason to suppose that he failed to see the advantage to himself in drawing yet more close the capable and devoted mother whom he would acquire with his wife.

Thus his marriage may, with little exaggeration, be described as a double one. In Mrs. Clemm he both loved and used the mother whose Shadow haunted him; in Virginia he had bodily before his eyes that consumptive angel who figures in all his dreams. They were ghostly shadows whose unreality seemed to make unnecessary the physical union which he could not offer.

The judgments passed upon Virginia's physical appearance vary considerably. Some speak of her as a dream of loveliness, and if one may judge from her picture she must have seemed, as she sat beside her harp in all the unimportant purity of an undeveloped mind, the very ideal of Victorian maidenhood as we see it represented in the sentimental engravings of the period. But those who have left descriptions of her seem to indicate that she was less beautiful than strange. Her dark hair and violet eyes were set off by an expression that was a genuine reflection of her sweet and affectionate disposition, but the height of her forehead spoiled the symmetry of her face and her complexion was so completely pale as to be described by some as "pure white" and by others as merely "bad." None deny, however, that her mind was absolutely undeveloped and that the combination of dark hair, bright eyes, and unearthly whiteness gave her the appearance of something not quite human. As she grew older she became not a little plump, but she grew older only in body, and the lisping speech which issued from her pouting lips expressed the childishness of her mind.

There can be no doubt that she herself was blindly devoted to Poe and that her existence like that of her mother revolved about him. It is said that she idolized him even at the time when they were first thrown together in Baltimore, and she idolized him until her death, but her devotion was, in the words of a woman who knew the Poe ménage, the same which she would have given "to a greyhound or any other handsome pet," and the affection which he returned was of the same slightly unreal sort. We see her fetching from the desk and then unfolding in delight before a visitor one of the long scrolls upon which her husband wrote, but it was to her no more than a toy, and it was with the mother that Poe discussed both his artistic and practical affairs.

Their marriage remained, throughout, singularly incomplete, spiritually as well as physically. Significantly enough the endearing name by which he always referred to her was merely "Sis," and in all of the voluminous correspondence which has been preserved only one of his letters is addressed to her; for when he wished to communicate with her he always addressed her through her mother as he might have addressed a child. Even at the beginning of his married life he was accustomed to go into society without her, and when toward the end he began to appear in literary drawing-rooms it was usually alone. If she came with him it was only to sit in perfect silence, and when he entered upon one of his tragicomic flirtations toward the end of his life there was from her no sign of jealousy. She was, in all probability, ignorant of what flirtation means.

"I believe," said Mrs. Frances S. Osgood, who knew him well, "that she [Virginia] was the only woman whom he ever loved," and this is substantially true since he was incapable of loving in any complete sense. To a friend he wrote wishing him as great a happiness in marriage as his own had been, and he spoke of Virginia as the sole support of his life; he clung to her desperately, and after she had died his life went into complete collapse; but it was not because he loved her with the love of a husband for his wife. She was the means by which he sublimated his conflict, and when she was no more it drove him into actual insanity. She was, like his exaggerated belief in his own greatness, a necessary part of the fiction by which he lived.

So far no reference has been made to Poe's literary work because it seemed worthwhile before describing it to get some understanding of the inward life from which it sprang, but in closing this discussion of his sexual nature, one poem, written not long before his death, may be quoted for the light which it throws upon this nature. To read it even casually is to get the impression, so commonly produced by Poe's poetry, of a profound and despairing moodiness sometimes expressed in almost meaningless jargon or in rather tawdry melodrama, but to regard it a little more closely is to perceive an easily interpretable symbolism.

## ULALUME

The skies they were ashen and sober;
  The leaves they were crisped and sere—
  The leaves they were withering and sere;
It was night in the lonesome October
  Of my most immemorial year;
It was hard by the dim lake of Auber,
  In the misty mid region of Weir—
It was down by the dank tarn of Auber,
  In the ghoul-haunted woodland of Weir.

Here once, through an alley Titanic,
    Of cypress, I roamed with my Soul—
    Of cypress, with Psyche, my Soul.
These were days when my heart was volcanic
    As the scoriac rivers that roll—
    As the lavas that restlessly roll
Their sulphurous currents down Yaanek
    In the ultimate climes of the pole—
That groan as they roll down Mount Yaanek
    In the realms of the boreal pole.

Our talk had been serious and sober,
    But our thoughts they were palsied and sere—
    Our memories were treacherous and sere—
For we knew not the month was October,
    And we marked not the night of the year—
    (Ah, night of all nights in the year!)
We noted not the dim lake of Auber—
    (Though once we had journeyed down here)—
Remembered not the dank tarn of Auber,
    Nor the ghoul-haunted woodland of Weir.

And now, as the night was senescent
    And star-dials pointed to morn—
    As the star-dials hinted of morn—
At the end of our path a liquescent
    And nebulous lustre was born,
Out of which a miraculous crescent
    Arose with a duplicate horn—
Astarte's bediamonded crescent
    Distinct with its duplicate horn.

And I said—"She is warmer than Dian:
    She rolls through an ether of sighs—
    She revels in a region of sighs:
She has seen that the tears are not dry on
    These cheeks, where the worm never dies
And has come past the stars of the Lion,
    To point us the path to the skies—
    To the Lethean peace of the skies—
Come up, in despite of the Lion,
    To shine on us with her bright eyes—
Come up through the lair of the Lion,
    With love in her luminous eyes."

But Psyche, uplifting her finger,
   Said—"Sadly this star I mistrust—
   Her pallor I strangely mistrust:—
Oh, hasten!—oh, let us not linger!
   Oh, fly!—let us fly!—for we must."
In terror she spoke, letting sink her
   Wings till they trailed in the dust—
In agony sobbed, letting sink her
   Plumes till they trailed in the dust—
   Till they sorrowfully trailed in the dust.

I replied—"This is nothing but dreaming:
   Let us on by this tremulous light!
   Let us bathe in this crystalline light!
Its Sibyllic splendor is beaming
   With Hope and in Beauty to-night:—
   See!—it flickers up the sky through the night!
Ah, we safely may trust to its gleaming,
   And be sure it will lead us aright—
We safely may trust to a gleaming
   That cannot but guide us aright,
Since it flickers up to Heaven through the night."

Thus I pacified Psyche and kissed her;
   And tempted her out of her gloom—
   And conquered her scruples and gloom;
And we passed to the end of the vista,
   But were stopped by the door of a tomb—
   By the door of a legended tomb;
And I said—"What is written, sweet sister,
   On the door of this legended tomb?"
   She replied—"Ulalume—Ulalume—
   'Tis the vault of thy lost Ulalume!"

Then my heart it grew ashen and sober
   As the leaves that were crisped and sere—
   As the leaves that were withering and sere,
And I cried—"It was surely October
   On *this* very night of last year
   That I journeyed—I journeyed down here—
   That I brought a dread burden down here—
   On this night of all nights in the year,
   Ah, what demon has tempted me here?

Well I know, now, the dank tarn of Auber,
This misty mid region of Weir—
Well I know, now, the dank tarn of Auber,
This ghoul-haunted woodland of Weir."

It has been suggested that this poem, with its description of hopeless hope, is merely a reflection of the poet's agony as he was compelled to watch the dying struggles of his wife who rallied only to sink again, but it is impossible to understand, if this be the case, why Diana and Astarte, never known to symbolize life and death, should play so important a rôle. Diana is, however, commonly known as the chaste goddess, and Astarte has symbolized in innumerable poems the love which is in part at least of the flesh. In the present poem it is she who tempts the poet and she who, in spite of the warning of his true goddess, leads him away only to bring him once more face to face with the tomb whose closed doors, so he now remembers, shut him forever from the possibility of further love.

Who, then, was this mysterious Ulalume or, as he had called her in more than one previous poem, this "lost Lenore"? It was not actually Virginia, for though she was dead when the particular poem in question was written, Poe had lamented the death of many a radiant maiden during the period when Virginia still lived, and Virginia was at most only a fleshly embodiment whose sexlessness enabled her to represent the lost one whose memory protected him against whoever was the "Astarte" of the moment. Were Ulalume and Lenore phantoms of that Miss Royster whom he loved as a youth in Richmond and to whom he returned after the death of Virginia; were they Mrs. Stanard whose hand he had kissed in childhood and who haunted him as the Helen of his poems; or were they rather the mother of dim subconscious memory who had, perhaps, reembodied herself in those other two women who held his fancy captive until he found in the unearthly Virginia some escape? To this question no final answer can be given. Psychiatrists may quarrel over the question of whether or not an inhibition such as his must actually arise from a previous experience and a consequent fixation or whether it may have some organic cause. But one thing is fairly certain. Poe could not love in the normal fashion and the reason lay, or at least seemed to him to lay, in the death of some woman upon whom his desire had irrevocably fixed itself. If we knew who lay behind the doors of that tomb in the ghoul-haunted woodland of Weir, we should know the answer to the greatest riddle of Poe's life.

### "You Say That I Am Mad"

It is pretty generally agreed that the attempt which Poe made in *The Philosophy of Composition* to convey the impression that all his own works were the result of logical and deliberate contrivance is either a conscious or an unconscious hoax. There are *a priori* objections to the belief that in general artistic works are created thus, but there is no writer who ever lived who seems less likely than Poe to have created in this way. In the management of his own life he was, as we have already seen and shall see again, moved almost always by prejudice, passion, or perversity and almost never by reason. His works, characterized at their best by the fantastic illogicality of dreams, are such as no man could contrive, and so uniformly similar in content and effect as to prove that they must in a sense have written themselves since no one who was struggling for bread and knew that a monotony of horror was complained of against him would willingly repeat himself so often when he could, according to his own statement, proceed to produce in story or poem whatever effect he chose to select. When it is remembered also that the characters in his stories and poems are frequently suffering from disorders of the mind of exactly the sort which might give rise to fancies such as those amidst which they are represented, that Poe's works are replete with various *obiter dicta* upon the subject of obsessions, perversions, and manias which he could have learned of only from himself, and that he gave in the mysterious wreck of his own life proof of the intimate relationship to the characters which he created, it is impossible not to see that instead of being deliberately invented his stories and poems invented themselves.

"I say to myself, in the first place, 'Of the innumerable effects, or impressions, of which the heart, the intellect, or (more generally) the soul is susceptible, what one shall I, on the present occasion, select?'" So Poe writes. But the fact remains that though he may have succeeded in convincing himself that he made such a choice, something unconscious within him saw to it he should "choose" always an effect which belonged to a very small class of the "innumerable" effects of which he speaks and which was moreover one which is rarely felt by any except persons of markedly abnormal mind. He chose perhaps but his choice was never more than between the indulgence of this or of that neurotic fantasy, between the embodiment of this or of that idealization of his own traits and capacities.

There is, however, good reason for believing that Poe, whose genius consisted, perhaps, in the possession to an extraordinary degree of the faculty of rationalization, which is one of the distinguishing characteristics of all neurotics, succeeded in convincing himself, at times at least, that he was the mere logical engine which he liked to imagine, and one may find both the roots of this delusion and the origin of the need which generated it at a time before Dupin had been created or *The Philosophy of Composition* written. The preface to the volume of collected stories called *Tales of the Grotesque and Arabesque* contains the following passage of significant self-defense:

"The epithets 'Grotesque' and 'Arabesque' will be found to indicate with sufficient precision the prevalent tenor of the tales here published. But from the fact that, during a period of some two or three years, I have written five-and-twenty short stories whose general character may be so briefly defined, it cannot be fairly inferred—at all events it is not truly inferred that I have, for this species of writing any inordinate, or indeed any particular taste or prepossession. I may have written with an eye to republication in volume form, and may, therefore, have desired to preserve, as far as a certain point, a certain unity of design. That is, indeed, the fact; and it may even happen that, in this manner, I shall never compose anything again. I speak of these things here, because I am led to think that it is this prevalence of the 'Arabesque' in my serious tales, which has induced one or two critics to tax me, in all friendliness, with what they have pleased to term 'Germanism' and gloom. The charge is in bad taste, and the grounds of it have not been sufficiently considered. Let us admit, for the moment, that the 'phantasy-pieces' now given *are* Germanic, or what not. Then Germanism is 'in the vein' for the time being. To-morrow I may be anything but German, as yesterday I was everything else. These many pieces are yet one book. My friends would be quite as wise in taxing an astronomer with too much astronomy, or an ethical writer with treating too largely of morals. But the truth is that, with a single exception, there is no one of these stories in which the scholar would recognize the distinctive features of that species of pseudo-horror which we are taught to call Germanic, for no better reason than that some of the secondary names of German literature have become identified with its folly. If in many of my productions terror has been the thesis, I maintain that terror is not of Germany, but of the soul—that I have deduced this terror only from its legitimate sources, and urged it only to its legitimate results."

It is evident from this passage that Poe resented the implication that his imagination could generate nothing except horror, and it is probable that this resentment was not unmixed with fear. Notwithstanding the suggestion that he might perhaps never write again in the same manner, he was constrained in spite of himself to do so and thus to be brought closer and closer to a realization of his perilous position upon the brink of madness. There must have been times when he knew that the "effects" which he liked to imagine himself as deliberately choosing were in fact thrust upon him, moments when he realized that in giving such vividly intimate pictures of temporary insanity in *Berenice,* of sadism in *The Black Cat,* or of mad obsession in *The Tell-Tale Heart* he was confessing to himself and others the giddy instability of his own mind. Mrs. Whitman remembered a penciled note appended to a manuscript copy of one of Poe's later poems which read: "All that I have here expressed was actually present to me. Remember the mental condition which gave rise to 'Ligeia'—I regard these visions even as they arise, with an awe which in some measure moderates or tranquilizes the ecstasy"; and while this confession gives the lie direct to his published statement concerning his mechanical method of composition it helps to explain why he himself should want to believe it.

Just as his whole life was a struggle, conducted with all the cunning of the unconsciousness, against a realization of the psychic impotence of his sexual nature, so was it a struggle also against a realization of the mental instability to which the first gave rise. It was a battle doomed to be lost from the beginning, and shortly before the final simultaneous dissolution of his mind and body Poe confessed to at least one fully developed delusion of persecution which will be discussed in its appropriate place; but doubtless he considerably postponed the final breakdown by means of the ingenious rationalization which convinced him, partly at least, that his imagination was under perfect control.

We must imagine, I think, that Poe, like many others, first turned to the practice of logic and ingenuity as an escape from feeling but that he soon found it a valuable contribution to his legend. To seem a man endowed to a super-human extent with the gift of rationality gratified that thirst for fame of an unusual sort which we have already noted, and it served at the same time an additional internal function. As the realization that he was as a matter of fact the victim of irrational and uncontrollable emotions gradually forced itself upon him, he countered this realization with the pretense that he was, on the contrary, abnormally clear in his mental processes. He demonstrated the fact as best he could to both himself and the public by his article upon the chess-player and his experiments in cryptography, and then, warming to the subject, he created the character of Dupin with whom he might imaginatively identify himself. Finally, he attempted in *The Philosophy of Composition* to convince himself that all his previous work had been the result of this same rational faculty to which he now clung desperately as the proof of his sanity, and thus the process was complete. First reasoning in order to escape feeling and then seizing upon the idea of reason as an explanation of the mystery of his own character, Poe invented the detective story in order that he might not go mad.

[From *Edgar Allen Poe: A Study in Genius,* Alfred A. Knopf, Inc. 1926; reprinted: Russell & Russell, 1965.]

>━○━○━○━○━○━○━○━○━○━○━○━○━○━○━○━○━○━○━○━○━○━○━○━○━○━○━○━○━○━○━○━<

A MORE RECENT ESSAY ON THE WHOLE PROBLEM OF THE RELATION OF PSYCHIC disturbance to creative genius follows.

>━○━○━○━○━○━○━○━○━○━○━○━○━○━○━○━○━○━○━○━○━○━○━○━○━○━○━○━○━○━○━○━<

### Genius and Neuroticism

Psychoanalysis is now one of the taken-for-granted tools of the biographer and critic, whether serious, middlebrow, or even low. It seems to me, nevertheless, that one fundamental question has never been satisfactorily answered. Exactly what is the relation between a writer's complexes, obsessions or neuroses, and his genius? An ancient gag used to run, "Photographers don't have to be crazy, but it helps." Are we compelled to say the same thing about artists?

Back in the late 'teens and early twenties when Freudianism first became a fad, an affirmative answer to this question was often implied or even given. The argument ran something like this: Closely examined, most great men turn out to have been at least a little bit queer; therefore, genius is necessarily queer. In fact, queerness and genius are the same thing. The artist's gift is the neurosis he exploits.

With shame I must confess that I was guilty of seeming to accept this absurdity in the first book I published (not counting a doctoral thesis). It was a biographical-critical study of Edgar Allan Poe, who was, among other things, a perfect sitting duck for the amateur psychoanalyst. And I chose him for that very reason. I laid great stress on his sadistic fantasies, his obsessive concern with death and dissolution, and with what seemed to be in his own life a desperate determination not to become sexually involved with any of the women whom he professed to love; also on his *Philosophy of Composition,* which maintained, despite conclusive evidence to the contrary, that he deliberately chose macabre effects, which were in fact the only ones he could produce.

I am still ready to argue that the theory I evolved concerning Poe's personality is consistent. I still believe also that the *"frisson nouveau"* which Baudelaire discovered and celebrated in Poe is a neurotic shiver. But in my enthusiasm I went far beyond this. I said, or at least strongly implied, that Poe's neuroses *were* his genius and that, if we could get all the facts, such was usually the case with great imaginative writers. They are always neurotic. Unfortunately I neglected to ask why, if all geniuses are neurotic, all neurotics are not geniuses.

What I am asking now is simply this: Granted the extravagance of any mere equating of genius with mental disorder, what actually is the relation between them, especially in extreme cases like that of Poe where at least much of the unique character of the work obviously is profoundly influenced by these disorders? That great art is essentially sane, I am convinced. But it often is the product of minds which seem to be more, rather than less, disturbed than those of ordinary men.

Perhaps the reason why the contemporary critic seems rather disinclined to face this question is simply that he (and all of us) have come to believe that what used to be called "abnormalities" are part of the psychic makeup of nearly everybody, and that the genius sometimes seems more abnormal than most men simply because he gives us a better opportunity to see his mind at work. But even so, I think my question is not completely answered. To take again the extreme case of Poe, it seems certain enough that if he had been less neurotic his work would have been quite different from what it is. Would it have been better—or would it have been less original, less interesting? What would be the answer to the same question if it were asked about some other writer much less obviously "unhealthy"?

Shortly after my own indiscretion was published, I received a letter from Dr. Beatrice Hinckle, translator of Jung and then (next at least to the Freudian, A. A. Brill) the best-known practicing psychoanalyst. She approved my diagnosis and said she had met a number of cases where the pattern was the same as Poe's. But she added a vehement protest. The neurotic genius was a genius in spite of his neuroses, not because of them. Mental illness was never anything but a handicap. This seemed to me then, and still does, as much an overstatement as my own opposite thesis. Poe would certainly not have written what he did if he had been "normal." It's there that the problem arises.

The whole question comes to my mind again because I have just been reading several reviews of the new fourteen-hundred-page edition of Beethoven's letters, many of which had never before been accessible and which, so the reviewers all seem to agree, are painful reading for those who admire Beethoven the man, no less than the music he wrote.

Here is a case far more complicated than that of Poe; the relation between the man and his abnormalities is far less simple. "Liegeia" and "The Fall of the House of Usher" (to say nothing of such astonishing productions as "Berenice" and "The Pit and the Pendulum") obviously bear so close a relation to their author's own neurotic fancies that the one seems a direct expression of the other. Though Poe has given artistic form to his obsessions, they and the stories they inspired are qualitatively almost identical. But whatever the "Ninth Symphony" may express, no one would be likely to call it obviously "sick" in the sense that Poe's writing usually is. On the basis of the works alone, the understandable image of Beethoven has been of a heroic figure struggling manfully against a cruel fate and transmuting his agony sometimes into tragedy, sometimes into a joy that transcends the suffering over which an abounding vitality triumphs.

This is the way in which he has usually been pictured by admirers who assumed (and wanted to assume) that the man and the music were identical. That element of stormy protest which is so different from anything to be read into the cheerful Haydn, or even into the plaintive discontent sometimes audible in Mozart, is sometimes explained in terms of a changed socio-political atmosphere. Haydn accepted the position of the musician as merely that of one of the higher servants of the nobility; Mozart, for all his nascent vision of democracy and brotherhood, was too gentle to be moved to anything approaching rage. But Beethoven was the child of a revolutionary era. He was less contented than either of his two great predecessors because he could not, like them, accept the status quo. Hence he spoke out violently with the voice of the genuinely committed rebel.

But whatever truth there may be in this picture, it is not the whole truth. The letters are said to confirm abundantly what some of the more recent biographers have maintained—namely, that the man whose utterances are so "noble" was in his own character and personality a sort of distressing parody of his musical utterances. It is not merely that he was quarrelsome, pettish, and given to throwing dishes at the cook. His relations with his scamp of a nephew—conventionally pictured as proof of his loving patience—actually included a dishonorable attempt to separate this nephew from his mother and to become in effect a mother himself. The lonely titan, aspiring toward fulfillment in the love of the several women he worshipped but was denied, seems, not entirely unlike Poe, to have seen to it himself that any promising relationship was broken off. All this, together with the grotesque possessiveness of his attitude toward the incorrigible nephew, invite the psychoanalyst to explore some pretty dark corridors. But even that is not all. Though it may seem odd to speak of a truly great artist as suffering delusions of grandeur, Beethoven seems to have been close to paranoid in both his sense of his own greatness and in what amounts to delusions of persecution. The fact remains that what were mere delusions in the artist are somehow transformed into convincing realities in the works which he created. Listening to them we believe what he believed about himself; reading the letters we still see a relationship between the man and his work. But it is by no means an identity.

Perhaps the best of the reviews I have read (that by Albert Goldman in *The New Leader*) puts it thus:

> "No one who has read the Sterbas' book [*Beethoven and his Nephew*] will ever forget the terrible image it contains of the great Beethoven living constantly in a kind of emotional squalor, his imagination periodically inflamed by fantasies of a paranoidic order in which he figures as the noble and innocent victim of base and evil persecutors. And no one who knows Beethoven's music could fail to connect these dreadful distortions of reality with the mythopoetic content of his compositions—allowing, of course, for the idealization of fantasy in art."

This describes, perhaps as well as possible, what seems actually to have happened. But it does not answer the question (possibly unanswerable) how anything so improbable *could* have happened. Some critics dodge the question by insisting that in the case of any work of art one should always fix one's exclusive attention on the work itself; that all "background," whether biographical, historical, sociological or whatnot, is both irrelevant and misleading; that it not only tends to explain away rather than explain, but may also make it actually impossible to take the work in question at face value—which is the only way in which a work of art can profitably be taken. We must not let Beethoven the man get between us and the works. It is only they that we have any business concerning ourselves with. Too much biography and there is danger that we will hear in the "Ninth

Symphony" only the paranoid ragings (which are not actually there) and miss the grandiose triumph of a joyously achieved victory over cruel fate (which very decidedly *is* there).

Such an attitude defines one approach to criticism and possibly the most fruitful one. But if—as seems to be the case—we must remove Beethoven from the category of the normal and healthy artist where we once pigeon-holed him along with Haydn and Handel, then we must put him among the neurotics and raise again the question with which we started: What is the relationship between works of art and the neurotic afflictions of their creators?

What is the power, which Beethoven had and Poe did not have, of using but transcending delusions of grandeur and of persecution? Would this question lead to the conclusion (not too helpful, I admit) that it is wrong to say either that neurotic abnormality is genius or that, as Dr. Hinckle protested, it is merely a disability over which the artist triumphs? Would it enable us to grant that most geniuses are neurotic and at the same time explain why all neurotics are not geniuses? Genius, in this conception, does not consist in the abnormality but in the power to transform it, and Beethoven was a far greater genius than Poe just because he could make a sane image out of what was in itself not entirely sane. Such an explanation is perhaps no explanation at all. It leaves "genius" as mysterious as ever. But it does enable us to recognize the troublesome fact that great works are often created by men less great than they, while, at the same time, it removes the temptation to fall into the error of believing that art itself is not "sane" and "healthy."

Those who read Havelock Ellis in pre-Freudian days will remember that he was concerned with our problem in a rather old-fashioned way at a time when the "abnormality" of genius was most likely to be attributed to physical causes. Max Nordau in his once-famous, but now mostly un-read *Degeneracy* argued that most modern literature was indeed neurotic and therefore simply bad art. But others were far from ready to accept this simple solution. Did the febrile excitement characteristic of the tubercular contribute to the glow of Keats's poetry? Did a moderate colony of *Spirechaeta pallida* act as a stimulus in Swift, Neitzsche and Beethoven, all of whom were suspected of playing host to it? Were geniuses most likely to appear in families some members of which were mentally subnormal, and did this suggest that the creative spirit was more closely related to feeblemindedness than to insanity?

Any theory that the artist is in some sense sick (note, by the way, that Thomas Mann seems to have at least toyed seriously with this thesis) raises a practical problem that becomes more pressing as "planning" is more and more talked of and is coming to include artificial insemination in the interests of eugenics, as Sir Julian Huxley has only recently proposed. One of Havelock Ellis's theories might suggest that syphilis should not be stamped out completely; some psychological theories, that all neuroses should not be nipped in the bud. Perhaps Beethoven would never have written any of his major works if he had been psychoanalyzed in time.

For the present, most of these are, fortunately, only theoretical questions. But there is a related and very practical one. No age before ours has been so determined to give children "all the advantages" of a good education and a happy, normal childhood. Yet the lives of great men all (or at least in numerous instances) remind us that they frequently had none of these good things, and that overcoming difficulties was a stimulus, not a deterrent. Either God or Nature seems to work in a mysterious way. Whom the Lord [or Mother Nature] loveth he chasteneth.

Who is to take the responsibility for planning these difficulties and attempting, for the benefit of humanity at large, to thrust painful greatness upon some of those about to be born? Had I been asked, as I was reaching the age of discretion, whether or not I wanted to be Beethoven at the price he paid, I am afraid I might have said: "No, thank you. I'd rather be 'normal' or even just 'average.'" But think what the world might have lost had Beethoven been given that choice.

[*And Even If You Do*, 1967.
First published in the *Saturday Review*, 1963.]

MY NEXT ATTEMPT AT A BOOK WAS "FIVE MASTERS" (1930), WHICH WAS subtitled *A Study in the Mutations of the Novel*. In it I chose three novelists who seemed to me to have introduced a new method of prose fiction. The selection which follows, like the book as a whole, was not intended to illustrate any specific theory of criticism but merely to find interesting things to say about the writer and his work.

## Samuel Richardson

During the course of the hundred and fifty years immediately following the publication of *Don Quixote* an enormous number of persons learned to read. One result of this fact was the creation of a book-buying public larger than any known before and the consequent rise of authorship as a possibly profitable profession. Another was the establishment of middle-class taste as a major factor in determining the form and spirit of fiction.

Hitherto, though the author had often belonged to the lowest class of society he had written primarily for the highest—unless of course his words had been intended, like those of Shakespeare, to be heard rather than read. Henceforward he was very likely to feel in some manner or other the influence of the solid, respectable and money-making element of the community.

In the English literature written by the contemporaries of Cervantes (and Shakespeare) there had been little evidence of any concern with this element. The citizen or "cit" had begun to appear as a usually contempt-ible character in the Jacobean drama and more frequently in that which succeeded the restoration of Charles the Second. But since, broadly speak-ing, he neither read nor wrote, his point of view had been unrepresented in literature, and from the books of *belles lettres* current even a century after the death of Shakespeare one might almost suppose that society had maintained the old pattern. The ideals which dominate them are still the ideals of the scholar, the *littérateur,* the man of fashion, or the martial aristocrat, and things are still seen from the point of view of the one or the other. Yet it was during the hundred and fifty years just referred to that England became a nation of shop-keepers and it would be a vast mistake to suppose that the small part played by the middle class in drama or fiction was any measure of its importance in the national life.

Though this class had not as yet established any contact with literature it was growing rapidly in wealth, in power, and in self-confidence. In hundreds of counting-houses merchants and tradesmen were building up a substantial order entirely outside the old aristocracy and without physi-cal or spiritual contact with it. The power of the new order was founded upon wealth instead of position; its manners were regulated by respect-abilities instead of fashions. And in the great commercial houses of the city it had a source of tradition entirely independent of the court. Some-thing of puritanism lingered in its prejudices but it was a puritanism so vulgarized by prosperity that the extravagances of any enthusiastic piety were hardly less foreign to the spirit of the cit than were the gaieties of the Restoration gallant. His was a narrow, practical, thrifty, cautious, hardworking, and inflexible order, totally new.

Humble at first and content to regulate his household in his own way, he began gradually to extend his influence into government and then to raise his voice in protest against the manners and ideals of classes with which he would not previously have dared to meddle. It was primarily through him that the movement for the "reform" of the English stage took place at the end of the seventeenth century and it is his influence also which is to be seen indirectly at work in the writing of Addison and Steele who might, as a matter of fact, very reasonably be considered as the apologists to their own class for the ideals of another. But so great was his suspicion of art—so profound was his instinctive distrust, not only of its "immoralities," but of its incautiously adventurous idealisms as well— that it was long before he realized the possibility of making it a vehicle for the expression of his own spirit. He feared that his daughter might be prepared by *belles lettres* for seduction at the hands of some fashionable gallant whose tongue had been oiled by poetry and romance, but he dreaded such a calamity hardly more than the possibility of finding himself cursed with a son who had imbibed from literature a distaste for the profitable routine of the counting-house. Art at best was a waste of time and the citizen had managed to rise because he did not like to see anything wasted.

Chivalric idealism, romantic love, and the ecstasies of mystical religion are, no less than martial or gallant adventures, essentially luxuries. They may be cultivated by the vagabonds who do not particularly care about getting on in the world and by those whose position places them above the necessity for doing so, but they are likely to be looked upon with an understandable suspicion by the members of a class which thrives upon prudence, thrift, and common sense. The merchant goes to church on Sunday, makes a suitable match, and tends to his affairs. He has no more time for metaphysics or mysticism than he has for romance, and hence, the rise of the middle class means inevitably the rise of a tepid sort of literature adjusted to his sympathies and his comprehension.

Defoe, the first great bourgeois writer, did not succeed in taking the curse off fiction just as George Lillo, the author of that dramatic homily for apprentices called *The London Merchant,* did not succeed in making the theatre entirely respectable. Defoe was as moral as he was prosy but he had had more actual experience with politicians and hacks than with respectable citizens and his tales were either of adventure or of crime. Time was necessary for the process by which literature was infused with bourgeois ideas and it remained for Samuel Richardson to discover how domestic life could be made the subject of improving fiction. Richardson happened to be—if the word has any meaning—a genius; but every detail of his experience was calculated to mould him into the exact image of substantial respectability. Only a happy accident made a novelist of him but it was obvious that if he should ever take his pen in hand it would be in the interests of virtue—as virtue is conceived by the tradesman.

■

Richardson was born, somewhere in Derbyshire, in 1689. He was a quiet boy and his father, a joiner practising his trade in London, soon began to observe in his hopeful son traits which suggested a career in the Church. In the first place the young Samuel was known to his school-fellows by the cumbersome nickname of "Serious and Gravity." In the second place he had already, when not yet eleven years old, written to a widow of fifty a hortatory letter full of quotations from scripture directed against her alleged hypocrisy.

Nor were these facts the only ones which seemed to foreshadow success in the ministry, for the youth also exhibited at an early age that capacity for lending a sympathetic ear to female confidences which was later to stand him in good stead in a secular profession but which has been the making of many a popular clergyman. Though a bashful boy, he was not, he says, more than thirteen years old when he used to frequent the sewing circles of the neighbourhood and when three young ladies who had "a high opinion of my taciturnity" came independently to him for aid in composing answers to their lovers' letters. He served them gladly and so much to their satisfaction that he had evidently already developed a capacity (later conspicuously exhibited) for writing feigned letters which seem authentically female by virtue of a certain modest ardour.

But in spite of these talents so early exhibited, financial difficulties made it necessary for the father to give up the plans he had already formed and to bind out the budding moralist to a printer. To the printshop he accordingly went and with a characteristic determination to "do the duty nearest him" he became, if we may believe his own improving account, the very model of the industrious apprentice. Though he had had only the most elementary of formal educations his scrupulosity forbade him to use either the time or the candles of his master for any efforts at self-improvement and thus the ideas which he imbibed in the establishment where he worked were uncorrupted by any thoughts or feelings unsuitable to the place. In due time he appears, as was eminently proper, to have married his master's daughter, and by easy stages he rose to be owner of his own publishing business. After bearing him six children, none of which survived beyond the age of four years, this wife died but the loss was promptly made good by a marriage in the following year to the sister of a bookseller.

Richardson was now leading what is called a useful life and it must be confessed hastily that he was not in any ordinary sense literary. He cared little for reading and at the age of fifty he had written nothing for publication except a few prefaces and dedications composed as so many articles of trade. What he had done, as financial competence and a certain amount of leisure were achieved, was simply to move into a comfortable house just outside of London proper and there to exhibit with considerable satisfaction the virtues of his class.

Nor was he by any means lacking in class consciousness for despite his eminent success in the city he believed that he "knew his place." As innumerable passages in his writings show, he looked upon those whom it had pleased God to make his betters with a suitable respect and he knew how to value, not only a lord, but a lord's second cousin as well. Yet he was far from displeased with himself because he did not see how anybody could deny the exemplary character of his career. He had never, he said, been in a "bad house" in all his life, nor ever, so far as he was aware, even in the company of a loose woman. He was honest, industrious, kindly, Christian and prosperous. That members of his circle respected him was a matter for satisfaction but hardly for surprise. He was obviously worthy of respect and since he had never set any example except a good one he saw no reason for trying to seem unaware of the fact that his company and his conversation were of a highly improving sort.

Up to 1739 he had revealed no tendencies or talents not easily predictable by anyone familiar with his boyhood character. He still wrote letters with a fluency and a delight positively abnormal and it seems that at one time he kept up a voluminous correspondence with a gentleman distinguished by nothing except his willingness to receive and reply to the epistles which it evidently gave Richardson some peculiar pleasure to compose. But beside these harmless epistolary indulgences he was remarkable for nothing except his delight in mild conversations ranging over the narrow field which lies between moral discourse on the one hand and gossip on the other.

Naturally his preference for female society rather increased than diminished. Women gave him the deference which he liked, they were more inclined than men to receive with complacency the instruction which he loved to give in matters touching either manners or morals, and in other less tangible ways they were more congenial company for a man whose habits of persistent industry had sheltered him from the boisterous world of masculine London. From women he had learned pretty much all he knew or was ever to know about "life," and even after he had become an international figure it was still women who made up the most numerous company of those who came to form a kind of court around him. They helped him to formulate that essentially domestic view of things which was the distinguishing character of his novels and they repaid his unusual respect for "women's notions" with a tender veneration which was in part filial and in part, no doubt, mildly erotic.

Thus at the age of fifty Richardson was the good man appropriately rewarded. He was also, to all appearances at least, both happy and content and it is not likely that his beneficent influence would ever have extended beyond a narrow circle had it not been for the fact that a publishing firm happened to ask him to compile a sort of "Complete Letter Writer" for the benefit of semi-literate persons.

Now the Devil himself could not have conceived a trap more appropriately baited since the proposal was one which invited Mr. Richardson to do the two things which pleased him above all others—namely to write letters and to give good advice to inferiors. Accordingly, after making the characteristic proposal that the scope of the book be enlarged so that it might instruct the humble readers "how they should think and act in common cases as well as indite," he threw himself into the task with enthusiasm and produced a collection of one hundred and seventy-three letters, advertised as the work of a man who had given particular attention to the problems of courtship and marriage, and published with the following title: "Letters written to and for particular friends, on the most important Occasions. Directing not only the requisite style and forms to be observed in writing Familiar Letters; but how to think and act justly and prudently, in the common concerns of human life."

The subjects of the letters are various and their moral tone as high as is consistent with their compiler's inveterate inability to dissociate righteousness from prudence. Most of the correspondents, whatever their sex or position, have the editor's penchant for the hortatory and the feigned recipients are accordingly advised upon all sorts of subjects—the impropriety of following immodest fashions in clothing, the dangers to which a too ardent courtship exposes the young girl, and the inevitable vexations of all processes at law. There are, besides, letters of condolence which "with small variations may be used to a husband on the death of his wife, and on other melancholy occasions of the like nature"; letters from "a young lady in town to her aunt in the country"; and letters written back and forth between humble but modest lovers. All the correspondents are assumed to be very much alike in their fondness for commonplaces of all sorts and hence all are likely at any moment either to launch into a sermon or to indulge themselves in the pleasure of making long observations not particularly original in character. "Let who will speak against Sailors; they are the Glory and Safeguard of the Land. And what would have become of Old England long ago but for them." Yet the book is almost fiction and marked everywhere by a copious though completely undistinguished imagination.

Richardson did not profess to take much pride in the compilation. It was intended, so he said on a later occasion, "for the lower class of people" and he advised a friend that it was not worth his perusal. But it gave him an idea. In composing it he had discovered a perhaps unsuspected capacity to imagine incidents and a certain talent for writing in character. These were the gifts of the writer of romance and though Richardson had a very low opinion of novels in general it occurred to him that he might turn the foolish and reprehensible taste of the generality of mankind to good account by preaching to them under the guise of fiction. One or two of the letters already written had been concerned with the conduct of a servant girl improperly importuned by her master, and when Richardson wrote them he began to remember an incident of the same kind which had been related to him many years ago and which had remained in his mind because of the instructive conclusion to which the events had led.

"I thought the story, if written, in an easy and natural manner, suitable to the simplicity of it, might possibly introduce a new species of writing, that might possibly turn young people into a course of reading different from the pomp and the parade of romance writing, and dismissing the improbable and marvellous with which novels generally abound, might tend to promote the cause of religion and virtue." No purpose less tangible or less important than the promotion of "the cause of religion and virtue" would have seemed to him sufficient to justify the expense of time necessary to read, much less to write, a story; but the case of the serving maid Pamela seemed to him so remarkably edifying that he began to write it in the form which the Familiar Letters suggested.

Certain difficulties were involved since the unfortunate girl had to be endowed with an almost superhuman capacity for epistolary composition if she was to be supposed, as is actually the case, to recount all her adventures as they occurred, and Richardson was sometimes put to such straits to explain how she obtained time and paper for her letters at certain crucial moments that Pamela is made to guard her pen and ink almost as carefully as she does her virtue and to plan means for dispatching her letters with more ingenuity than she used in her efforts to escape the violent attentions of her master. But Richardson had never written anything but letters and throughout his whole career as novelist he was accordingly compelled to make each of his characters a victim of his own epistolomania.

In this species of composition his fluency was, however, amazing. He began *Pamela* on the tenth of November, 1739, and finished the second volume (692 printed pages in all) exactly two months later. But from the beginning he had what he could never do without—female approval. "While I was writing the two volumes my worthy hearted wife and the young lady who is with us, when I had read them some part of the story, which I had begun without their knowing it, used to come into my little closet every night with: Have you any more of Pamela, Mr. Richardson? We are come to hear a little more of Pamela, etc."

Thus encouraged he proceeded with enthusiasm and the book was published anonymously in November, 1740, under the following characteristically explicit title: "PAMELA: or, Virtue Rewarded. In a series of Familiar Letters from a beautiful Young Damsel, to her Parents. Now first published in order to cultivate the Principles of Virtue and Religion in the Minds of the Youth of both Sexes. A Narrative which has its Foundation in Truth and Nature; and at the same time that it agreeably entertains, by a Variety of *curious* and *affecting* Incidents, is entirely divested of all those Images, which, in too many Pieces calculated for Amusement only, tend to *inflame* the Minds they should *instruct.*"

*Pamela* was not intended for "the lower class of people" exclusively but it was aimed straight at the great bourgeois public which cared more for respectability than for art and its success was never for a moment in doubt. Only the existence of a great hunger never before fed can explain the amazed delight with which it was received, and almost from the day of its publication to the day of its author's death Mr. Richardson, that great and good man, was immersed (though never overwhelmed) in a flood of flattery more deep and soothing than any ever enjoyed before or since by fortunate penman.

Perhaps Rousseau and Voltaire made more *noise* in the world. Perhaps their renown was greater. But by the generality of mankind they were suspect. One admired their genius while one depreciated their tendency and even as one applauded one entered caveats unnecessary in the case of the great champion of indubitably *virtuous* ideas. Here at last was a literary genius as understandable and as sound as he was brilliant—someone who could be taken to the bosom without reserve. He drew tears, not for Hecuba, but for his own readers and that was much; but it was not all. In principles he agreed with the great public against the wits. He was as right-minded as he was great. And here, for once, was a man who had not been compelled to make the choice generally considered inevitable: he was both clever *and* good.

Hence the trickle of praise which had begun with the "worthy hearted wife" gradually swelled into a torrent of admiration as persons further and further removed from the domestic circle of the author added their tributes. Shortly after publication Richardson sent a copy to Aaron Hill—a minor *littérateur* who deserves to be remembered less for any of his writing than for the fact that he named his three daughters Urania, Astrea, and Minerva—and to Hill's credit it must be said that he struck the right tone at once. On December 17, 1740 he begins coyly (while still pretending to have no suspicion as to the identity of the author) with an expression of pleased amazement. Who, he asks, would have dreamed to find under the "modest disguise of a novel all the soul of religion, good breeding, discretion, good-nature, wit, fancy, fine thoughts and morality." But who pray is the author and "how has he been able to hide hitherto, such an encircling and all-mastering spirit?" "If it is not a secret, oblige me so far as to tell me the author's name" for the book will live and "twenty ages to come may be the better and wiser for its influence."

By December 29, all pretense of ignorance concerning the author has been dropped but there is not therefore any need to moderate the fulsomeness of the flattery. Mr. Richardson will be pleased to know that not even the youngest hearts are untouched by the beauty of his work. A few evenings ago when it was being read aloud in the blameless family circle of the Hills a six-year-old child had crept under a chair and been there forgotten until "a succession of heart-heaving sobs" revealed his presence. "I turned his innocent look towards me, but his eyes were quite lost in his tears; which running down his cheek in free currents, had formed two sincere little fountains on that part of the carpet he hung over."

But even this was not for Richardson quite enough. He asked Hill for critical suggestions and Hill knew exactly what was wanted. He goes over "Pamela" twice—once "with the eye of a cynic" and once with that of "vigilant friendship"; but with neither the one eye nor the other can he "pick out anything that might not suffer by altering." "Upon the word of a friend and a gentleman, I find it not possible to go further, without defacing and unpardonably injuring beauties which neither I, nor any man in the world, but their author, could supply with others as sweet and as natural!" "Where," as he not unnaturally asks a little later, "will your wonders end or how could I be able to express the joy it gives me to discover your generous rising, not like a pyramid, still lessening as it labours upward, but enlarging its proportions with the grace and boldness of a pillar, that, however high its shaft is lifted, still looks larger at its capital."

It is true that Hill expected and received from Richardson some slight return in the form of very moderate praise of his own work. It is also true that Hill was financially obligated to the author of *Pamela*. But his laudations were hardly less hyperbolical than those of persons who owed the fortunate author nothing whatever. Mr. Pope, to be sure, contented himself with saying rather ambiguously that the book "would do more good than many volumes of sermons" and indeed it was not as yet from the literary that the author received the highest praise. But ladies of fashion were said to carry the volumes about with them just to show that they too were reading what everybody talked about and at least one preacher promptly recommended the book from the pulpit.

The further down one went in the intellectual scale the more touching were the evidences of its power to stir hearts and moisten eyes. At the village of Slough the inhabitants gathered around the blacksmith while he read the incomparable romance aloud and when he came to the place where the heroine triumphs his hearers set up an involuntary shout. Moreover, other children besides the precocious infant at the Hills' were touched, and one little girl, "not twelve years old," was inspired to compose a poem which began:

"O Pamela, thy virtuous mind
Riches and honour has resigned;
Riches were but dross to thee,
Compared with thy mod-est-y."

Without doubt the "new species of writing" had caught on, but the most remarkable feature of its vogue was the fact that the emotions which it aroused were not apparently aesthetic in character but somehow warmer and more intimate. Richardson was at once overwhelmed with personal letters. Was the story true or false? Who was the original of the incomparable Pamela? Everybody was delighted but everybody was also disposed to weep tears which seemed to be, in part at least, tears of relief. Something long awaited had been let loose upon the world. A new pattern of feeling had been created.

■

If the book which thus became, not so much a literary event, as the occasion of a crisis in the history of human sensibility, had subsequently got itself lost; if it, together with its author's succeeding works, had passed out of the range of our possible knowledge like most of the odes of Sappho and some of the books of Livy, then we might well have been excused if we had lamented our loss as one of the saddest in literary annals. But the marvellous romance—which many good judges believed unequalled by anything of its kind until the appearance of Mr. Richardson's second work—was not lost, and it remains, on the contrary, to be read by any reader curious enough to peruse the pages marked by a certain fatuity effectively concealing whatever merits they may possess.

Pamela is a lady's maid left by the death of her mistress at the mercy of the latter's rakish son, Mr. B. Mr. B. loses no time in proposing to set her up as a sort of *maitresse en titre* and when she retreats under a barrage of virtuous sentiments the young man is so impressed that he redoubles his efforts to obtain a prize made triply valuable by a resistance founded upon such honourable sentiments. An attempted rape is somewhat mysteriously frustrated by the indignation of the intended victim and the villain (drawn in lurid colours) plans a stratagem. Promising Pamela that she shall be conducted in safety to her poor but virtuous parents he has her carried instead to a farm house managed for him by a sinister female and, soon putting in his appearance, he resumes his threatening importunity.

Poor Pamela is now in the most desperate straits. Her citadel is assaulted alternately by cajolery, by abuse, and by another attempt at violence so nearly successful that the monster is at one time fairly between her sheets. Moreover her writing materials are almost exhausted when Mrs. Jewkes (the traitor's housekeeper) gives her "a bottle of ink, eight sheets of paper and six pens, with a piece of sealing wax." "This," says Pamela, "looks mighty well" and she can now continue to scribble at a desperate rate an epistolary account of her trials and a full exposition of her sentiments. Beset though she is, she will never, she assures her parents, forget either the humbleness of her position or that virtue which is her only glory. With great complacency she describes the admiration which her conduct has aroused among the better sort of people and she recounts at length the frenzy to which her exemplary inflexibility had driven Mr. B. How great are her trials but how great is her glory!

Mr. B. continues alternately to flatter, to threaten, and to rail. He calls her by every abusive name he can think of. He loads her with obloquies. But this madness is merely the sign of a defeat not quite acknowledged for suddenly, almost in the midst of his most venomous insult, he surrenders to an impregnable propriety. Will Pamela, who can be neither seduced nor violated, consent to marry him?

The reader is surprised but Pamela is not. She is immediately mistress of the sentiments which she believes appropriate to the circumstances. She remembers her place and the gulf between her and her master which nothing can really bridge. She is overwhelmed and she is grateful. Can Mr. B., rich and elegant as he is, stoop to her? It seems that he can and the remaining third of the book, devoted to Pamela's triumph, includes a full account of both her sentiments and her wedding dress. "Mr. Colbrand being returned, my master came up to my closet, and brought me the license. O how my heart fluttered at the sight of it. . . . I made bold to kiss his hand: and, though unable to look up, said, 'I know not what to say, Sir, to all your goodness: I would not, for any consideration, that you should believe me capable of receiving negligently an honour, that all the duty of a long life, were it to be lent me, would not suffice me to be grateful for.' "

Such a synopsis—and indeed any possible synopsis—can reveal only the absurdity of the story. Nor is the novel itself—redeemed though it is by Richardson's remarkable talent for creating a convincing character—likely to produce upon the reader any impression except one of amazed incredulity at the humourless obtuseness of its feeling. Mr. B. is so devoid of any reality as to make it impossible to discuss his motives or his character. Richardson knew nothing whatever of "worldly" life and his own tepid imagination was so incapable of conceiving either the nature or the effects of an unruly passion that his villain is merely a monstrous lay figure suggestive of nothing except the bugaboo which haunts the dreams of spinsters warned too often against the villainy of mankind. And if Pamela is real enough, her complacent vulgarity is so completely beyond all description that even promiscuity would seem, beside her calm determination to resist all importunities until the monster consents to buy her off, at least commendably generous.

One hardly knows where to begin to state the objections both moral and psychological which immediately rise in the mind of any modern reader and it is indeed hardly necessary to do so. One may surely venture to leave unparticularized those which have to do with the heroine's perfect willingness to accept as a compliment the proposals of a man who has just shown himself incapable of the most elementary decency and one may also safely omit speculations concerning the character of this hero who, even after his capitulation, condescends with an insufferable complacency to the girl whom he has just "raised to his level." But since the virtue of the heroine and the admirable moral to be drawn from her story were the points upon which contemporary admirers most strongly insisted they may both be given a cursory glance.

"How happy am I," upon one occasion Pamela exclaimed, "to be turned out of door with that sweet companion, my innocence" but innocence is, of all the virtues, the one in which subsequent commentators have found her most conspicuously lacking. It is true that she set a prodigious value upon what she was accustomed to call "her jewel," but innocence is surely not the word best suited to describe the quality of a mind which spent most of its waking hours in a feverish contemplation of the possibility that the body which contained it might conceivably be seduced or violated. Though the ways of the world were not known to her through experience, the defect was made good by the activity of an imagination very ready to conceive and perhaps exaggerate all the dangers which an innocent spirit would discover with surprise. Pamela anticipated every move made against her, and her "purity" was maintained at the cost of a perpetual preoccupation with fears for its safety.

Nor is it possible, as one follows with amazement the proud exposition of her principles, to discover in them anything except the logical development of a shrewd determination to get as much as possible out of the world, for if we judge her by the evidence of her own letters she is a prig at best and a designing minx besides. Richardson had set out to describe his ideal of feminine character but he had created instead a coarse-minded opportunist because he had himself achieved a cynicism more complete than is possible to any except those unaware of the nature of their own principles. The virtue of Pamela is no more than a realization of the fact that her virginity is by far the most valuable of her possessions and a wise determination not to lose what has a perfectly tangible value. The society in which she lives has agreed that a continence, broken only upon those occasions and under those circumstances sanctioned by civil and ecclesiastical law, is the *sine qua non* of that decency without which a woman has no claim to any consideration whatsoever, and while prudence thus directs her to maintain it, her creator encourages her to believe that in so doing she is rising to the greatest possible height of moral excellence.

Yet it is possible to account for every detail of her behaviour without any reference whatsoever to any principle belonging in the realm of morals. Like all maidens she had a jewel and the precious possession was one to be safeguarded with all the watchfulness of a traveller who passes through some bandit-infested waste. The thing—though to all appearances no more than a pretty trifle—has a value, thanks to which it can be bartered or sold, and therefore it must not be lost. He who allows it to be taken from him is criminally careless; he who gives it away is a fool. But in the end it must be sold. Thus, in the spirit of a dealer in precious stones Pamela goes about her business. It is not the man but his terms which she objects to and when he meets hers she accepts them. She and her parents rail against the wickedness of those who cannot hold out as she has done but by wickedness they mean folly. Skill in trade is a citizen's virtue. Pamela held out for a good price and in the end she got it. Thus is virtue rewarded.

This word Virtue slipped as easily from Richardson's pen as it did from the tongue of Pamela but there is no evidence that it had for him any awful or mysterious meaning. Usually it is merely a synonym for a technical continence mechanically maintained and it never implied anything not definable in common sense terms. Honesty, industry, amiability and even generosity find a place in his creatures as they found a place in his own character, but these qualities are always useful to those who possess them and no man was ever less capable than he of understanding anything which approached the quixotic. Perhaps he would have refused to equate virtue and prudence—to admit that honesty and benevolence and continence were virtuous *because* they brought ease and security and competence—but the fact that they did so was the outward sign of their character and the way in which God revealed his love for those who practised them.

Unable to distinguish between an inward state of soul and the conduct to which such a state was conventionally supposed to give rise he used "virtue" (that is continence) as a mere synonym for chastity and he was as incapable of imagining that a continent woman might be unchaste as he was of conceiving the possibility that chastity might be the attribute of a woman neither virginal nor married. Since Pamela resisted the seduction of her master she was inevitably both "pure" and "innocent" just as a man who gave alms was inevitably "benevolent." Thus goodness became mechanically determinable and the idea of righteousness shrank into the idea of respectability.

The character of Pamela is one so devoid of any delicacy of feeling as to be inevitably indecent. She seems to have no sense of either her own or any possible human dignity and she can be admired only if a dogged determination to resist violation is considered to be, by itself, enough to make her admirable. Despite the language of pious cant which she speaks with such fluency there is no evidence that she has the faintest conception of that disinterestedness which alone can give piety a meaning.

Yet none of the objections which are so patent to any critical reader of Richardson appeared as defects to his enthusiastic admirers since his moral feeling was distinguished from that of his middle-class fellows only because it was more perfectly typical than that of most. It was the bourgeois respectability of his century purified of all individual eccentricity, uncorrupted by any trace of either mystical enthusiasm or sceptical worldly wisdom. He thought what others thought in their most commonplace moments; he was not Bobus but Bobissimus; and his readers relaxed with comfortable security in an atmosphere so much like that of their daily lives. Among writers of robuster intellect, eighteenth-century materialism took other forms. An ironic scepticism developed in minds which had divested themselves of all concern with the transcendental and made them disturbingly critical. But the literal, unimaginative mind of Richardson stripped every idea of the aura which surrounded it and then rested complacently content with the bare formulae of a dry convention.

A little later on he could dare attempt to draw a picture of the Perfect Gentleman because Gentlemanliness—like Purity and Virtue—was not to him an illusive quality, not something evanescent and indefinable which emerges as the result of a delicate balance or a spontaneous harmony in the soul, but a simple, mechanical obedience to easily establishable canons of rectitude and decorum. Right thinking (aided a little by the precepts of a revealed but simple religion) could, he believed, determine what a man ought to do—just how generous, how forgiving, how prudent and, of course, how condescending to his inferiors he ought to be. Hence to create a model gentleman it was necessary only to invent an automaton perfectly obedient to all the rules. For him the flavour, the perfume, and that nameless grace which makes an individual charming counted for nothing, and he would have been almost as much puzzled by the suggestion that his creation lacked the personality necessary to make him appealing as he would have been shocked by the suggestion that a trace of some human failing may contribute, when nicely placed, to the charm of a character.

And yet *Pamela,* considered purely as a novel, did have one great intrinsic excellence. The central character is delineated with a dramatic realism quite independent of the moral judgment which either the creator or the reader passes upon her. She is a creature solid enough to be completely dissociated from the personality of the man who described her and to be subjected to analysis again and again as standards change. Richardson was completely helpless when he was compelled, as in the case of Mr. B. he was, to attempt the portrait of a man whose traditions, motives, and passions were outside the range of either his experience or his imaginative sympathy. His rake is ridiculous except when we see him, not directly, but as he appears in the terrified imagination of his intended victim and when we consider him, therefore, as a distorted image rather than as a real person. But Pamela herself is a masterly objectification of unconscious vulgarity, to the completeness of which her vision of Mr. B. contributes. Richardson seems to have achieved an imaginative identification with her which is admirably complete and he knew so exactly how such a person would talk, act, and feel that he drew of her a portrait seldom equalled so far as sheer realism is concerned.

It is this fact alone which makes it possible to regard the book as more than a historical curiosity. Its only absolute merit lies in the fidelity with which it represents a certain type of character and if we were to judge it as an *interpretation* of even that small section of human life with which it deals, we should be compelled to relegate it to some sub-literary limbo. Yet it is hardly to be supposed that either the enthusiastic encomiums which were heaped upon it or the international influence which it exerted is to be accounted for by the solitary and purely technical excellence which we have granted it.

Great popularity is seldom if ever the reward of mere fidelity to fact. To win it, the writer, passing beyond mere imitation, must achieve some sort of pattern in which fact is balanced against fact, emotion against emotion, and end result against end result, in such a way as to constitute an interpretation of life and its laws satisfactory to his readers. This interpretation may be profound or shallow, and it may be essentially noble or essentially vulgar; but it is the pattern (often felt rather than intellectually comprehended) which takes hold of the imagination of readers and the pattern which is taken over by subsequent writers belonging to the same school.

Now Richardson did achieve such a pattern. It was, moreover, one which had been imperfectly sketched out again and again—particularly by the second-rate playwrights—during the half century preceding the publication of *Pamela* and he had, therefore, over and above both the merit of his skill in portraiture of a certain kind and the accidental advantage of his conventional respectability, a great charm for his contemporaries—the charm, that is to say, of a new pattern which had long been struggling into existence but which had never been so nearly achieved before. This pattern is the one which is commonly distinguished by the adjective "sentimental," and though the word is so frequently and so carelessly used, the truly sentimental pattern results from an attitude very nearly as definite and inclusive as (though a great deal less exalted than) those which inspire the patterns called the Tragic and the Comic.

In the most impressive of his novels Richardson was later to achieve a work which, despite all his permanent limitations, was not only morally and technically superior to *Pamela* but characterized by a more complete mastery of a more intricate sentimental pattern. Hence we shall postpone until we come to consider this later work the attempt to understand what the pattern is, but we should note even now the fact that it is not to be confused with anything so simple as Richardson personally and his entirely commonplace acquiescence in conventional superficialities concerning the whole duty of man (which is to be respectably prosperous) and the whole duty of woman (which is to be technically virtuous). The sentimental pattern was taken over by many writers whose specific convictions, both ethical and social, would have shocked him profoundly and at least some of whom were immeasurably his superiors in intellect and taste. But the elements common to all of them are the elements necessary to compose the pattern which was destined to dominate fiction for a long time and to survive very conspicuously into the literature of today.

■

After *Pamela* had been published and praised Richardson, like the sober man that he was, made some attempt to return to the humble occupations which had formerly been his. The pen which had depicted the apotheosis of the serving-maid consented to employ itself in editing a new edition of Defoe's "Tour Through Great Britain" and the brain which had conceived so generally acceptable a reward for virtue busied itself with making analytical summaries for a volume of the diplomatic correspondence of Sir Thomas Roe. But destiny, aided by an inordinate love of praise, and an imagination doubly restless because it had been so severely curbed, again drew him irresistibly towards independent authorship.

He was now living, not far from London, in a comfortable house to which his admirers resorted to pay tribute to his genius and to contemplate with an almost religious awe the domestic life of a man whose example was universally admitted to be no less valuable than the precepts which he gave under the guise of agreeable fictions. Here he could make "ten beds" for such fortunate intimates as were permitted to spend the night under his roof and here in the garden was a summer house to which these intimates might repair to hear the latest pages of manuscript read aloud by the author himself.

The time was to come when Richardson, even though at the height of his fame, could fish shamelessly for compliments and he was ultimately to die, as Dr. Johnson bitterly remarked "for want of change among his flatterers"—to perish "for want of *more,* like a man obliged to breathe the same air until it is exhausted." But now at the period of his greatest creative activity he was living not only in a state of perfect domestic bliss but under conditions which assured him a plentiful supply of the life-giving element.

It is true that his wife was generally supposed to be of a rather self-effacing disposition and true also that one of his intimates even brought herself to observe that the daughters behaved in a manner which suggested that they might be less at ease than would have been anticipated with so perfect a father. But Richardson hastened to assure them that even this was also well. "A mixture of fear with love" was, he said, necessary to make an obliging wife and as for the "stiffness" of the daughters he could only reply that "too much reverence is not the vice of the age." "Condescension," to be sure, "becomes the character of the parent." He has done all he could to encourage them in proper freedoms. If they continue to treat him with more than daughterly reverence it can only be because of what they must inevitably feel for one who is, however undeserving, treated with so much respect by his friends.

Nor did any of these friends fail to accept as more than adequate such explanations. "Most of the ladies that resided much at his home, acquired," it was remarked, "a certain degree of fastidiousness and delicate refinement which, though amiable in itself, rather disqualified them from appearing in general society." And if this was the result of a formal association, it was not surprising that the wife who shared his bed and the daughters who had had, from earliest infancy, the benefit of his corrections, exhibited to an even greater degree this amiable inability to feel at home among more frivolous companions. But surely the constant presence of the author of *Pamela* was more than enough to compensate for the absence of less improving associates. Give "my love to Mrs. Richardson and to all who have the happiness to be under your roof," wrote Miss Fielding, sister of the author of *Tom Jones.* "Methinks, in such a house, each word that is uttered must sink into the hearer's mind, as the kindly falling showers in April sink into the teeming earth, and enlarge and ripen every idea, as the friendly drops do the new-sown grass, or the water-wanting plant."

Mr. Richardson now began, however, to extend somewhat the range of his acquaintance and sometimes consented to absent himself from domestic bliss for the sake of a short exploratory tour into that world of fashion of which he felt himself more ignorant than was wise for one who hoped ultimately to instruct it with tales of virtue in a higher place than that from which Pamela had been so deservedly lifted. Into his circle he admitted the rakish laureat, Colly Cibber, because of Cibber it could at least be said that he professed an admiration for the virtues which he admitted his inability to practise. More surprisingly still, the laureat was allowed to remain even after he had scandalized his friend by finding the latter's admiration for male virginity irresistibly risible. And upon at least one occasion Richardson paid a visit to Tunbridge Wells where he strolled with a timorous delight in the midst of a gay company and did not remember (until near the end of the letter in which the visit was described) his duty to remark that "modesty, humility, graciousness, are now all banished from the behaviour of these public-place frequenters of the sex." "Women," he concluded, "are not what they were" and he seems to have been so struck with the observation that he made it the subject of a paper which he contributed, some three years later, to Dr. Johnson's *Rambler.*

It has been shrewdly suspected that Cibber supplied some of the traits for the portrait of the fashionable rake who was to play a prominent part in the new novel and so much superior is this portrait to the previous one that the mere critic is impelled to wish that Richardson had abandoned himself more freely than he did to the society of people less ready than the members of his inner circle to agree with everything he said and to adjust their manners as nearly as possible to what he considered the ideal. But his love of a sort of flattery which only inferiors could give, his need to be immersed constantly in an atmosphere which could only be generated by the soft, almost sensual adoration of ardently inexperienced females, drew him always back to the charmed and isolated group of his most intimate worshippers.

From the outside world he could get recognition as a writer, and the approval of the rich and fashionable must have been sweet to one who never ceased to be acutely aware of all class distinction. Yet what he enjoyed most and needed most was not recognition of the sort appropriate to a man of letters but the assurance that his excellence was primarily the result, not of merely literary talents, but of the perfection of that character which he had no doubt begun to console himself by cultivating while still playing the rôle of industrious apprentice. Avid for flattery of any sort, he liked best the compliments which implied that the conspicuous virtue of his heroine was drawn from some inexhaustible reservoir of goodness within his own heart and the inhabitants of his own private little world were experts in this sort of thing. Thus the indispensable Hill had struck the right note when he wrote: "I confess there is one person in the world of whom I think with greater respect than of Pamela and that is the wonderful *author* of *Pamela*," and another correspondent (this time of the female sex) struck it again with an even surer hand when she protested that he had only given to this incomparable maiden "the virtues of his own worthy heart."

Nor is it, under the circumstances, very surprising that he sometimes turned from precept to practice when his benevolence was repaid as amply as it was, for example, in the case of one Letitia Pilkington, a literary adventuress who came to no good end but who could repay a charity with words like these: "How was I astonished to find you, like silent-working Heaven surprising oft the lonely heart with good and bounty expected, unmerited, unsought. What can I pay thee for this noble usage, but grateful praise; so Heaven itself is paid; and you, truly made in the image of God, will, I hope, accept of the low, but sincere oblation, of a thankful spirit. . . . The sin of ingratitude would lie heavy on me did I not, with the most perfect thankfulness, acknowledge your goodness. Every favor you confer receives a ten fold value from your manner of conveying it. . . .

> Angels enthroned in bliss with rapture see
> Their own divine perfections live in thee."

Richardson felt no need to deprecate the compliments paid to either his character or his work because he considered himself the champion as well as the representative of moral purity. To feign a belief that they were excessive would be to assume that Virtue could be praised more highly than she deserved and Richardson would never be guilty of such an error.

At the distance of one and three quarters centuries it may seem that the company of his adorers was more numerous than distinguished, for though his genius was generally admitted, the intimate circle never came to include a single one of the men and women who made the eighteenth century glorious and to us it may appear that the absence of Fielding, Hume, Johnson, Stern, and the rest is not entirely compensated for by the presence of any or all of those second-rate *littérateurs* and now forgotten blue-stockings who clustered about him. Surely a more intelligent man would have questioned at times just how much the flattery of persons like Hill and Mrs. Pilkington was worth; or, to choose other examples, just how much one had a right to be pleased by that of either the obscurer poetaster Thomas Edwards or a certain Miss Collier who complained with a pathetic humourlessness that Fielding's *Voyage to Lisbon* was attributed to her pen for no reason except "that it was so very bad a performance and fell so far short of his other works, it must needs be the person *with him* who wrote it."

But Richardson was pleased with all these sops just as he was pleased by the assurance given him by a mother that her son had been, at the age of twelve, inspired to compose a sermon on the text (appropriately quoted in *Pamela*) "The liberal soul shall be made fat." He was fortunate in possessing a temperament which made it unnecessary for him to consider the source of a compliment and which enabled him to judge it entirely by its magnitude. Since he readily assumed that the intelligence and the virtue of any man or woman was exactly proportioned to the admiration which that person felt for him, the value of any fragment of adulation was precisely as great as it was extravagant.

No one was ever turned away merely because he was patently silly or not entirely disinterested. "Believe me, Madam," he wrote to one correspondent, "I am incapable of flattering," and when one considers both the low opinion which he entertained of his rivals and the very moderate returns which he gave to those who flattered him, it must be admitted that the boast involves no more than a permissible minimum of exaggeration. But Richardson never kept any friend who suffered from a similar inhibition. And though he was compelled to forego intimate intercourse with equals or superiors he spent most of the time not actually employed upon his novels in either conversation or correspondence with sycophants.

Only one person seems to have seriously disturbed his complacency and that person was Henry Fielding, who was generally credited with the authorship of a burlesque which mercilessly exposed the weaknesses of *Pamela* and who later returned to the attack by beginning his own first novel as a parody of the same edifying work. Richardson never forgave a slight or an insult but so perfect was the mechanism which protected his vanity that he could indulge his rancour without any impairment of his Christian spirit for the simple reason that he never failed to discover in anyone who offended him follies or vices which deserved chastisement on their own account. Hence he never lost an opportunity to denounce both the moral and literary sins of Fielding's *Tom Jones* because its author had dared to satirize him and he never, indeed, seemed to suspect how little this nervous depreciation of his greatest rival became one who had been elevated to a height which demanded of him some suggestion of dignity.

Yet it is not, for all this, by any means certain that Richardson did not learn something from Fielding. He was not incapable of realizing from experience that the lewd were given unnecessary pretexts for laughter and he was determined that these pretexts should be wanting when he came to compose a second mirror for virtuous minds. Clarissa—for such was to be the name of his new heroine—should be placed a good deal higher in the social scale than Pamela had been, but this was not all. She should exhibit a delicacy which would have been out of place in a serving-maid and she should be inspired by the hope of a reward more appropriate to her station in life.

Richardson, no less than Dr. Johnson, considered that the "great scheme of subordination" constituted the groundwork of God's plan. He saw no reason, therefore, why anybody should aspire to anything higher than the rank and privileges belonging to the station just above his own. But while Pamela had appropriately set her heart upon rising in this world through the instrumentality of her would-be betrayer, Clarissa—whom Providence had, so to speak, been pleased to start where her humble sister had left off —might legitimately aim at higher things and be rewarded, not with marriage to a gentleman, but with Eternal Bliss.

Unfortunately there is no evidence to show exactly when Richardson first began to sketch out in his own mind the plan of the new work, but by 1745 he was far enough along with it to submit a portion of it for the approval of Hill. This latter was so rash at one time as to provoke something very near a breach in their relationship by offering a criticism of one of the heroine's actions and on another occasion he was foolish enough to take seriously the author's suggestion that he undertake the task of compressing somewhat some of the letters of which the novel was again to be composed. But from the outraged tone of the offended genius he soon realized what was wanted, and he redeemed himself twice over. "It is impossible," he said, "after the wonders you have shown in *Pamela* to question your infallible success in this new, natural attempt." And though the second masterpiece of moral fiction was, despite the simplicity of the plot, ultimately to appear in no less than seven substantial volumes "You have," he wrote, "formed a style . . . where verbosity becomes a virtue; because, in pictures which you draw with such skilful negligence, redundance but conveys resemblance; and to contract the strokes would be to spoil the likeness."

The last volumes of the new novel were not to appear until 1748 and since Hill had begun to speak of the work in 1745 it must have been much longer than its predecessor in the writing, but the most remarkable of the circumstances which surround it is the fact that the writing and the printing became public events. Richardson, no longer compelled to remain content with the encouragement of "my worthy hearted wife" and her female companions, could now call upon the members of a numerous circle for admiration, encouragement, and the assurance that nothing in all he had written could possibly be changed for the better. He was later to form the habit of having his admirers resort upon stated occasions to his house and to listen while he read aloud to them the newest chapters of the work in progress, but even now he wrote with the praises of his plan, his style, and his intentions ringing always in his ears. Nor was this all, since between the publication of the first four and the last three volumes he was still further delighted by various correspondents (to whom of course he replied at length) who not only described the ecstasy with which they were reading but either engaged in long discussions of the morality involved or implored him to arrange an outcome agreeable to the affection which they had conceived for this character or that.

While the ultimate fate of Clarissa still hung in the balance, while it was still impossible to know whether her creator intended to save her for some suitable reward as he had formerly saved Pamela, or to allow her, as the most inexorable supposed, to die at last, there were many who hardly dared to draw breath and those who enjoyed the privilege of Mr. Richardson's acquaintance hung about his study as though it were the death chamber of a queen.

Lady Bradshaigh, an aristocratic admirer, could not bear the thought of reading the final and distressing part when she learned that it was destined to describe the end of Clarissa. "Good Sir," she wrote, "do not send it, do not compel me to be ungrateful. You would not wonder at my inflexibleness, if you knew the joy I had promised myself from a happy catastrophe. I cannot see my amiable Clarissa die; it will hurt my heart, and *durably,* I know your manner, and I know my weakness—I cannot bear it." A little later when the blow had fallen she cried out again in what is either agony or a very good sentimental imitation of it: "Talk not of tragedies, I can now bear any; the deepest pain they give is momentary and trifling, compared with your long-dwelt upon, and well told story. . . . I expected to suffer, but not to the degree I have suffered. . . . When alone, in agony would I lay down the book, take it up again, walk about the room, let fall a flood of tears, wipe my eyes, read again, perhaps not three lines, throw away the book, crying out, excuse me good Mr. Richardson, I cannot go on."

From Hill no less was to be expected than that description which he gave of his family circle when he wrote "At this moment I have three girls around me—each a separate volume in her hand, and all their eyes like a wet flower in April." But even Cibber, now seventy-seven years old and, as he set off in pursuit of a reigning beauty, still incapable of practising the virtue which he had begun to "recommend" in his plays a little more than half a century before, was no less touched by a mere foreboding of catastrophe as is witnessed by an account fortunately left by Mrs. Pilkington:

"I passed two hours this morning with Mr. Cibber, who I found in such real anxiety for Clarissa, as none but so perfect a master of nature could have excited. . . . When he heard what a dreadful lot was to be hers, he lost all patience, threw down the book, and vowed he would not read another line. To express one part of his passion, would require such masterly hands as yours or his own; he shuddered; nay, the tears stood in his eyes; 'What!' said he, 'shall I, who have loved and revered the virtuous, the beautiful Clarissa, from the same motives I loved Mr. Richardson, bear to stand a patient spectator to her ruin, her final destruction? No!—my heart suffers as strongly for her as if a word was brought me that his house was on fire, and himself, his wife, and little ones, likely to perish in the flame.' I never saw passion higher wrought than his. When I told him she must die, he said, 'God d———m him, if she should'; and that he no longer believed Providence or eternal Wisdom, or Goodness governed the world, if merit, innocence, and beauty were to be so destroyed: 'nay,' added he, 'my mind is so hurt with the thought of her being violated, that were I to see her in Heaven, sitting on the knees of the blessed Virgin, and crowned with glory, her sufferings would still make me feel horror, horror distilled.' "

"These," adds Mrs. Pilkington, in a phrase which suggests anti-climax, "were his strongly emphatic words," and she continues in order to add her mite of persuasion. "I can scarcely, Sir, express the pleasure I received from the dear gentleman's warmth, nay heat, on this occasion; as it showed me at once the virtue of his own heart, and the power of the writer who could so melt, engage and fire it. But now, Sir, I must fairly own with Mr. Cibber, I cannot bear the thought of the lady's person being contaminated. If she must die; if her heart must break for being so deceived, let her make a triumphant exit arrayed in white-robed purity. . . . Spare her virgin purity, dear Sir, spare it! Consider, if this wounds both Mr. Cibber and me (who neither of us set up for immaculate chastity) what must it do with those who possess that inestimable treasure? And if the bare imagination of it is so terrible, what must it be when arrayed in the full pomp of such words as on this occasion must flow from such a heart, and such a pen as yours."

It is true that some few who had, unlike the aged poet laureat, abandoned virtuous sentiments as well as virtuous conduct, professed to feel that a tremendous pother was being made about nothing. It is true also that certain fashionable persons like Horace Walpole and Lord Chesterfield were less unqualified in their praises than simpler souls and that these judges, offended by the inordinate length of the work, failed to agree with Hill in finding the redundancy of Richardson's style a virtue. But *Clarissa* had become, even more conspicuously than *Pamela*, a public event and its heroine a personage to be discussed more fully and more ardently than any living person.

■

Richardson's spirit had been always undernourished. He had been confined to the printshop during the years when more fortunate youths were undergoing experiences far richer in their emotional content and the effect of the dull routine had been to increase the preternatural sobriety already remarked in the child. He once guardedly hinted at two or three embryonic romances which might possibly have brought some little colour into an otherwise drab existence but "a bashfulness, next to sheepishness" kept him down and there is every reason to believe that both of his marriages were the result rather of prudence than of passion. Moreover, since he read little and frequented only the tamest of all possible societies even the nourishment which he offered himself in the form of vicarious experience was of the most watery sort. The composition of *Pamela,* written when he was already fifty years old, had been his first spree—the first act of his life performed because *he wanted* to do something for its own sake, rather than because it was obviously dictated by his methodical prudence. No doubt this emotional starvation accounts for both the eager copiousness of his correspondence and the unwillingness which he exhibited to bring *Clarissa* to a conclusion. He clung pathetically to whatever contacts he managed to establish and he was in no hurry to conclude the imaginary adventures which were enabling him to live more richly than he had ever lived before. But if his verbosity was that of a man who prolongs any conversation rather than return to the undisguised emptiness of his own existence, this keen though unacknowledged hunger for some sort of emotional life was responsible for the fact that the book took on a vividness and colour not only unintended but unwanted.

Richardson still professed to believe that the art of fiction was, in itself, morally unjustifiable. "Instruction," he said, "is the pill; amusement the gilding," and he was genuinely concerned lest his characters should become so interesting as human beings that the reader would attend rather to them than to the lesson which he was intent upon preaching. Hence he provided the book with a title designed to call attention to its moral; he sprinkled the text with footnotes explanatory of the same; and he added at the end a disquisition nearly as long as the present essay. But these efforts were in vain. He could not prevent himself from becoming interested in the story he had to tell or from making it glow with a life of its own.

His personal letters reveal only the dryness, the narrowness, and the pomposity of the man. One will look in vain anywhere except in his books for any sign of his genius; but like not a few writers both before and since, he was carried further by his sympathetic imagination than his intellect could ever carry him and at least this one of his novels is richer, fuller, and deeper than the code which he professed. The moral was deduced as the result of a conscious activity; the emotions were depicted by an imagination uncontrollably eager for experiences richer than any which had been granted to the man who possessed it.

*Clarissa* is no longer much read because its inordinate length repels no less than the priggish formalism of its author's frequently obtruded judgments. But an astonishing power to captivate the occasional person who will surrender himself to it even yet remains in the seldom-turned pages. Richardson, it is true, is still concerned with persons who are unable to transcend his own limitations. He never dissociates the idea of virtue from the idea of conformity and the most admirable person is always the one who most nearly succeeds, not only in adjusting every detail of his conduct to the accepted canons of propriety, but in subduing his heart to them as well. Hence he attributes to his heroes and heroines an almost imbecilically complete submission to all the conventions. Yet they are, nevertheless, real and vivid. So completely does he enter into their emotions, so lively in his imaginative sympathy with everyone who comes within its narrow range, that his favourite characters cannot fail to engage the interest of the reader, who soon finds himself forgetting his impatience with their limitations in his concern with their experiences.

Clarissa Harlow is the model and idolized daughter of a genteel family living in the country. Addresses are paid to her by a dashing rake named Lovelace but her father, fearful lest she should become involved with him, insists upon her marrying a dull, mean-spirited man of his choice. But Clarissa, steadily maintaining her right of refusal but never asserting any right of choice, rejects him and when the duty of obedience is urged upon her in vain a family persecution develops.

At this point Lovelace reappears to beg a secret interview. Clarissa consents and he urges that, since there seems no other way in which she can escape the hated marriage, she throw herself upon his protection. At last she consents and departs with him for London where he promises to respect absolutely her freedom. What he actually does do, however, is to place her in lodgings (after informing the landlady that Clarissa is his secret bride) and then begin to put into operation an elaborate plan of seduction. Clarissa perceives it and is thrown into a panic of despair.

Now Lovelace is genuinely and desperately enamoured of Clarissa. Indeed he really intends, despite his rooted contempt for matrimony, ultimately to marry her. But he is the victim of a peculiar psychology which Richardson sometimes depicts with a surprising acuteness though at other times he allows his villain to become, like Mr. B., a purely mythological monster. Lovelace is determined to exhaust all his wiles before consenting to take his adored victim to the altar, either because (as he sometimes thinks) he wants to be sure that she is genuinely enamoured of him rather than of the safety he can assure her or because (as he at other times explains) he wants to apply the ultimate test to that virtue which must be absolutely impregnable if it is to justify the bowing of his neck to the yoke of wedlock.

Meanwhile Clarissa has come to feel a kind of love for the man whom she also despises and fears; but though he does actually ask her to marry him she refuses, partly because she cannot trust his character, and partly because it seems to her delicacy that he does not sue with either the ardour or the humility which a man ought to exhibit before the woman whom he is asking to become, forever after, essentially his subordinate. Thus the two play at cross purposes until Lovelace, maddened by disappointed and humiliated pride, tries violence and the rape (so long imminent in *Pamela*) is actually accomplished.

It was at this point that the excitement of Richardson's readers reached its height. They thrilled with horror at the violation of the heroine and they begged that she should be made to triumph at last by bringing the villain to see the error of his ways. But Richardson steadfastly resisted their importunities and he did so for several reasons. In the first place he had come (as several specific utterances show) to doubt the propriety of representing the overnight reformation of a confirmed sinner and he did not propose to have scoffers again remark with scornful glee that he had rewarded virtue by giving it the hand of a rake. In the second place he insisted that Clarissa had committed a fault when she removed herself from the authority of her parents and he did not wish to show that ultimate happiness could be the result of such an initial misstep.

Moreover, in the third place he had, though forever incapable of understanding the spirit of true tragedy, come to realize that the sentimental effect of Virtue Rewarded is less striking than of Virtue carried from one edifying distress to another. The moral would be purer and the emotion would be greater if Clarissa were compelled to die; and hence die she did, perishing of what one of the characters calls in a rather unfortunate phrase "an incurable fracture of the heart," and leaving behind her a testament which supplies the final evidence of her purity, her sweetness, and the Christian humility of her heart.

Such is the plot of the tale which Richardson requires some eight hundred thousand words to tell and which fills, in a modern edition, nearly two thousand closely printed, double column pages. Any man, said Dr. Johnson, who tried to read it "for the story . . . would hang himself." But Dr. Johnson yielded to no one in admiration for the work and it is by no means primarily "for the story" that it exists. The full title reads: *Clarissa: or, The History of a Young Lady; Comprehending the Most Important Concerns of Private Life; and Particularly Showing the Distresses that may Attend the Misconduct both of Parents and Children, in Relation to Marriage*. Nor can anyone complain that this title is either insufficiently explicit or insufficiently exact. Such is precisely the scope of the book though all these particulars are "comprehended" by being completely dramatized so that what we get is almost always genuine fiction and very seldom indeed merely a treatise.

Every important event is told two or three times over in the epistles written by the different persons involved who give accounts of it from their own individual points of view. Letters pass back and forth in all directions among the thirty-eight principal characters and the motives and feelings of each chief actor are not only described by himself but analysed and commented upon by others. Every conceivable opinion is canvassed, every transitory feeling dissected. What is the real character of the man whom the parents of Clarissa have chosen for her? How far was she justified in resisting their wishes? Should she or should she not have accepted under any conditions the honourable proposals of Lovelace once he had become her violator? May a respectable girl consort with a man of bad character in the hope of exerting upon him a good influence; to what extent is the heart a dependable guide; how far should a young lady consult her own taste in accepting or rejecting a suitor; and what should she feel upon this occasion or that? Upon these and a hundred other questions the characters all differ. Lovelace speaks for the rake, Clarissa for enlightened propriety, her confidante, Ann Howe, for the rebellious younger generation, and her father for all old-fashioned parents who are sound upon the subject of daughterly obedience.

Richardson was thus the first to make the novel an exhaustive commentary upon the minutiae of daily conduct and *Clarissa* marks more clearly than any other work the turn as the result of which the interest in a piece of fiction comes to be focused, not so much upon events, as upon the causes which lead up to and the reverberations which follow them. The older story-tellers hurry on from happening to happening. Richardson is concerned less with adventures than with the discussion of them. He does not let any event take place without examining all the antecedent causes nor does he ever pass to another until the emotional reaction of every party concerned has been fully examined. And since his mind was as conventional as it was active the result is something at once vivid and commonplace.

*Clarissa* trembles on the edge of the ridiculous. Pomposity, smugness, and fatuity are always just around the corner. And yet it would not be fair to dismiss it as merely pompous, smug or fatuous. In it there is a remarkable refinement of observation, and an amazing insight into all the corners of a small but ardent mind. Richardson's sympathies, for all the narrowness of their range, were extraordinarily acute and so completely does he live in and through the soul of Clarissa that one is compelled to admit that one at least knows what Dr. Johnson meant when he said that there was "more knowledge of the human heart" in one letter of *Clarissa* than in all of the novels of Fielding. In it readers could recognize themselves to an extent which was impossible in any previous novel. Experiences such as might possibly happen to them were here happening to people like themselves and they could live with Clarissa on the terms of an intimacy impossible in the case of any other heroine of fiction. No one could possibly *behave* like Don Quixote or Robinson Crusoe, but thousands must have asked themselves what Clarissa (or Lovelace!) would have done under these circumstances or those.

Thus their creator at once restricted and enlarged the field of fiction. He eliminated all extraordinary adventures and all passions more exalted than those within the range of the more ordinary sort of person but he examined the emotions appropriate to bourgeois existence with a minuteness never known before and he did for the middle-class heart what Defoe had done for the externals of daily life—he examined, that is to say, all its little hopes, scruples, and perturbations, with an eye which delighted to note and to respect them. Hence it was thanks more to his influence than to that of any other man that the novel could become, as it has, a dominant influence in moulding the opinions, the manners, and the modes of feeling cultivated by a very large section of any literate public.

For the upper middle class of the eighteenth century *Clarissa* became, as a matter of fact, a book of etiquette, a mirror of manners and morals. It is impossible to say how much Richardson actually imposed himself upon his contemporaries and how much his system of ethics and sensibility was something merely crystallized from the atmosphere which had been generated in the course of a social development. But the fact remains that his book seems to have established, as it were, the norm which came to be accepted by the members of the upper middle class. In *Clarissa* one saw reflected an ideal; one recognized in its characters models which instructed by example how one ought to act, to speak, to think, and to feel in social life. One realized that one was, not merely virtuous, but elegant, right-thinking, and sensitive as well exactly to the extent to which one found oneself reacting after the pattern of the more refined characters in that romance.

The fact that its author happened to be, in temperament at least, an absolute bobissimus was not for him a disadvantage but an advantage since his task was to co-ordinate the various elements which composed the spiritual universe of his fellows. Had he ever undergone any profound experience this experience would have had to find some place in his work; had he ever conceived any idea subtler or deeper than those which were congenial to the more mediocre of his contemporaries, this idea would have inevitably disrupted the vulgar harmonies which he composed. But fortunately for him neither thought nor experience disqualified him. He could codify conventional manners and he could do something still more difficult. He could give the dignity of art or pseudo-art to life as it was led by vulgar people. He could bring to its full development the sentimental pattern.

Tragedy is the form given to existence in the contemplation of great spirits. But the common man has neither the exaltation of character nor the strength of soul necessary to achieve it even if his story should ever happen to be on a scale which would justify any such grandiose interpretation of its meaning. He must see lives like his own under a form which is not that of tragedy but of something exacting less of the actors and more easily comprehended. If he must give up, as Richardson did, the idea that the motif known as Virtue Rewarded is dominant in the universal symphony, he must find in its place some conception of what constitutes success in life compatible with his timidity, his prudence, his materialism, and his ingrained regard for conventional respectability. Richardson found it and the fact that he did so is the greatest single cause of his enormous popularity.

*Hence* Clarissa *became, above all else, the model for sentimental fiction, by which term we mean here to denominate that vulgar sort of demi-tragedy produced when goodness is substituted for greatness as the necessary qualification of the hero and when, as a result, the catastrophe reveals him, not going down in rebellious defeat, but tamely acquiescent to the forces which destroy him.*

All the supremely great artists have instinctively avoided this pattern and distrusted the sort of satisfaction which it gives to an audience, but the essentially vulgar soul of Richardson felt its way slowly though unerringly toward it. To Clarissa he gave no positive or active virtues, nor even, indeed, any personality. She is no more than a slightly idealized portrait of the conventional "nice" girl of the period and the whole course of her life is determined by negative principles. Her dominant desire is the desire to achieve, despite the difficulties which surround her, a completely conventional existence and the Virtue which her contemporaries so much admired is not something which leads to any action but something which shines forth only when it resists the forces permitted to "test" it. Since her greatness is of the sort which only unusual trials can reveal, almost anyone might be generously presumed to possess it and her contemporaries took a satisfaction in her story greater than in any of the genuine masterpieces of literature for two reasons.

In the first place her excellence is of a sort which can disturb no one; and in the second place her end, brought about by her one violation of the conventional code, in no way challenges the pleasing assumption that all is fundamentally well both in human society and the universe at large. True tragedy shames and frightens. The greatness of its passions makes us blush for our own comfortable littleness and there is something terrifyingly anarchical in the refusal of its hero to admit defeat. But Sentimental Romance produces effects which are exactly the reverse. It flatters us by pretending that timid little virtues like our own are really great and that the submission which draws a pleasant tear from the eye of the beholder is the proper end of a hero.

"The writers of England excel those of all other nations in the pathetic," wrote the eighteenth-century divine Sherlock, "and Richardson is, I think, superior to all his countrymen. He makes one cry too much. By a very singular talent peculiar to himself alone, he fills our eyes almost as often by elevated sentiments as he does by tender ones. . . . He abounds in strokes of greatness, sometimes in the actions and sometimes in the sentiments of his characters, which raise the reader's soul, and make the tear of generosity spring into his eye he knows not whence. . . . He has volumes which it is impossible to read without crying and sobbing from beginning to end."

Opinions like this make it evident that Richardson's admirers recognize clearly the distinguishing character of his effects. He was credited, as another contemporary critic put it, with having "tamed and humanized hearts that were before not so very sensible." And he deliberately lent his influence to the movement which was beginning to make an ostentatious tenderheartedness fashionable by dwelling upon every scene which gave occasion for pathos. But what these contemporaries did not recognize was the fact that these effects are of a distinctly low order—that his elevated sentiments are delightful because they are commonplace and the tears which he draws sweet because they are complacent.

Delighting to contemplate a purely passive and suffering virtue, he established the vogue of a new kind of heroine whose chief distinction lies in the fact that she is ill-used, and in contradistinction to the tonic sorrow of tragedy he set up an easy pathos by placing all the emphasis, not upon the strength of the hero, but upon his blameless and pitiful helplessness.

Sentiment is merely the feminine equivalent of passion. Through its influence romantic love, mystical religion, and the thirst for righteousness are diluted and tamed. They are subordinated to prudence and respectability and thus they are made comprehensible to lesser spirits. Juliets are no less rare than Othellos but a bourgeois society cannot be other than glad of the fact. Fathers must like to believe that their own more manageable daughters are more admirable as well, and the daughters themselves, uncomfortably aware that their souls have scarcely achieved Shakespearean proportions, must like to feel that the domestic virtues are, by their very blamelessness, superior to heroism. Who could hope to live up to a Juliet's passion; who could maintain, indeed, that the shameless and disconcerting example of her vehemence is exactly edifying? But the conduct of Clarissa is as impeccable as her sentiments are comprehensible. In the very presence of death she forgives everybody. Moreover she sketches out a design for her monument and pays the undertaker's bill in advance in order that her friends may not be incommoded.

Well may her creator boast that the moral of his work is pure and that "the notion of *poetical justice,* founded upon the *modern rules* has hardly ever been more strictly observed in works of this nature, than in the present performance. For, is not Mr. Lovelace, who could persevere in his villainous views, against the strongest and most frequent convictions and remorses that ever were sent to awaken and reclaim a wicked man—is not this great, this *wilful* transgressor, condignly *punished* and his punishment brought on through the intelligence of the very Joseph Leman whom he had corrupted? . . . On the other hand, is not Miss Howe, for her noble friendship to the exalted lady in calamities—is not Mr. Hickman— for his unexceptionable morals, and integrity of life—is not the repentant and not ungenerous Belford, is not the worthy Norton—*made signally happy?*

"And who that are earnest in their profession of Christianity, but will rather envy than regret the triumphant death of Clarissa; whose piety, from her *early childhood;* whose diffusive charity; whose steady virtue; whose Christian humility; whose forgiving spirit; whose meekness and resignation, HEAVEN *only* could reward."

[From *Five Masters: A Study in the Mutations of the Novel,* Harrison Smith & Robert Haas, Inc., 1930.]

---

THE CRITICAL ESSAYS AND CHAPTERS FROM THE TWO BOOKS "SAMUEL JOHNSON" and *Henry David Thoreau* require, I hope, no commentary except perhaps the remark that the last obviously reflects my increased concern with man and his natural environment.

---

# Rasselas

It was, as has already been remarked, from the garret workroom of the Gough Square house that the final pages of the *Dictionary* had gone forth. Johnson was to remain at the same address until 1759, and it was there that he was to enter upon his next important literary projects: an edition of Shakespeare (previously proposed but temporarily abandoned), a new series of periodical essays called *The Idler,* and *Rasselas,* that Oriental fable which was perhaps admired beyond its merits by Johnson's contemporaries but is today quite unjustly condescended to by those who have either forgotten what it is like or never taken the trouble to find out.

Though *The Rambler* and the *Dictionary* had made him at last really famous, fame did not relieve him from the necessity of earning his living almost from day to day. We have already seen that the advance payments for the *Dictionary* had been spent as received, and to March, 1756, belongs a letter to Samuel Richardson which vividly illustrates how easily the sure prospect of his third dinner ahead might seem to Johnson a large measure of security. The letter reads:

> Sir,
>
> I am obliged to entreat your assistance. I am now under arrest for five pounds eighteen shillings. Mr. Strahan, from whom I should have received the necessary help in this case, is not at home; and I am afraid of not finding Mr. Miller. If you will be so good as to send me this sum, I will gratefully repay you, and add it to all former obligations.
> I am, Sir,
> > Your most obedient and most humble servant,
> > > > SAM JOHNSON.
> > > > Gough Square, March 16

Some light on the "former obligations" is thrown by a previous letter to the same person, which is dated February 19, 1756, and returns thanks for "the favour which you were pleased to do me two nights ago." Happily the letter just quoted in full is said to have borne on the margin this endorsement: "March 16, 1756. Sent six guineas. Witness, Wm. Richardson."

No doubt Johnson's need for immediate cash has something to do with the fact that the proposal to edit Shakespeare was not to bear fruit for a long time to come. It almost certainly has much to do with the further fact that a great deal of hack work—reviews, prefaces, dedications, and the like—belongs to the period immediately following the publication of the *Dictionary.* In May of 1756 appeared the first number of a new periodical called *The Literary Magazine, or Universal Review,* to which Johnson not only contributed over a period of some fifteen months but which he also, according to Boswell, "engaged to superintend." "What," Boswell continues, "were his emoluments from this undertaking, and what other writers he employed in it, I have not discovered"; but the dramatist,

Arthur Murphy (who, unlike Boswell, was already acquainted with Johnson at this period), gives an account of the latter at work as editor that is picturesque enough though perhaps not to be trusted too implicitly:

"This employment engrossed but little of Johnson's time. He resigned himself to indolence, took no exercise, rose about two, and then received the visits of his friends. Authors, long since forgotten, waited on him as their oracle, and he gave responses in the chair of criticism. He listened to the complaints, the schemes, and the hopes and fears of a crowd of inferior writers, 'who,' he said, in the words of Roger Ascham, 'lived, *men knew not how, and died obscure, men marked not when.'* He believed, that he could give a better history of Grub-street than any man living. His house was filled with a succession of visitors till four or five in the evening. During the whole time he presided at his tea-table."

Most of the hack work Johnson did at this time for the magazines was hack work and no more, but one review stands out both as a piece of extraordinarily vigorous writing and as a clear revelation of the fact that Johnson was thinking hard on one of the problems which greatly concerned his contemporaries. Such books as Thomas Birch's *History of the Royal Society of London* and Hampton's translation of Polybius he reviewed with perfunctory brevity, but when Soame Jenyns's *Free Enquiry into the Origin and Nature of Evil* came into his hands he rose to the occasion, and the ten thousand words in which he demolished that author were certainly not carelessly written.

Jenyns was a witty trifler—or at least a trifler who hoped to be witty. With the possible exception of James Boswell, who disposed of the arguments against Negro slavery in a *jeu d'esprit,* no one illustrates better the fatuousness into which feeble men could be led by the tendency of the eighteenth century to assume that a reasonable familiarity with what was called "polite learning" constituted a sufficient equipment for the solution of all problems political, moral or metaphysical. It is the glory of that century to have demonstrated more successfully than any other before or since how much common sense can accomplish and how charming a garden can be cultivated by those who are content not to look beyond the garden wall; but not even its greatest men—not even Johnson himself always—escaped fatuity when they adventured too far afield with too light an equipment.

Jenyns had formerly been a fellow contributor with Chesterfield to *The World* and he was later to aspire to a *View of the Internal Evidence of the Christian Religion.* At present he was merely endeavoring to justify the ways of God to man and performing the task with jaunty assurance.

His book, as Johnson points out, is merely an expansion in prose of Pope's *Essay on Man,* to which little is added. But while it is as difficult to criticize Pope as it would be to criticize a display of fireworks, Jenyns's attempt at a methodical exposition of a coherent system lays all the unproved assumptions, all the sophisticated arguments, and all the glaring non sequiturs open to an attack which Johnson pushes home with remorseless vigor. It is, moreover, worthy of remark that, after declaring Jenyns's book far from the impious licentiousness of Bolingbroke, Johnson attacks it, not with weapons drawn from the armory of Christian orthodoxy but with logic of the sort Jenyns himself wished to use. In one respect Johnson is a better Popian than Jenyns—in this one respect, indeed, a better Popian than Pope—for he accepts without reservation the injunction "Presume not God to scan" and what he objects to most violently is the fact that Pope before, and Jenyns after him, proceed not only to scan God but to report confidently what no man can see.

Johnson was no mystic and he did not love mysteries. He found Christianity hard enough to accept and he took no pleasure, as Sir Thomas Browne professed to do, in believing what was difficult to believe. He was too much of a rationalist not to welcome anything that would help make Christianity seem rational, anything that would actually justify to human reason the ways of God. But he was also too honest to accept specious arguments merely because they were on his side. He could advise such a man as Jenyns "to distrust his own faculties, however large and comprehensive," and he could advise it not because Jenyns was attempting to damage trust in God and not because Johnson delighted in skepticism, but solely because he would not consent to have the grave difficulties which the spectacle of human misery puts in the way of faith in God, difficulties which he himself had painfully faced, explained away with feeble argument. On one page he exposes the conception of the Great Chain of Being for the insubstantial fancy that it is; on another he demonstrates that to accept as a premise the existence of a Supreme Being infinitely powerful, wise and benevolent is to render unnecessary all the succeeding argument intended to prove that the Supreme Being does have those attributes. The story of how Johnson "refuted" Bishop Berkeley's idealism by kicking a stone is all too well known. If this review in which he met logical argument with logical argument were equally familiar to readers, Johnson's reputation as a dialectician would be considerably higher than it is.

Even in this piece, however, the strongest—or at least the most flavorsome—passages are those in which it is not so much abstract logic that is brought to bear as it is common sense supported by that familiarity with human suffering which so regularly saves Johnson from the kind of complacency more privileged members of his century too often indulged in. For many of them it was easy, as it was for Jenyns, to explain away as part of God's plan those injustices for which society was responsible and to harden their hearts with the reflection that this is, after all, the best of all possible worlds. But Johnson, for all his lack of faith in sociological reform, seldom allowed to pass unchallenged the comfortable assumption that the sufferings of the underprivileged were not only part of God's mysterious plan but probably not really sufferings at all. He clearly rebuked one of the besetting sins of his age when he wrote in this review: "I am always afraid of determining on the side of envy and cruelty," and he then proceeded to illustrate what he meant by examining Jenyns's delighted demonstration: "Poverty, or the want of riches, is generally compensated for by having more hopes, and fewer fears, by a greater share of health, and a more exquisite relish of the smallest enjoyments, than those who possess them are usually blessed with." Commented Johnson:

"Poverty is very gently paraphrased by want of riches. In that sense, almost every man may, in his own opinion, be poor. But there is another poverty, which is want of competence of all that can soften the miseries of life, of all that can diversify attention or delight imagination. There is yet another poverty, which is want of necessaries, a species of poverty which no care of the publick, no charity of particulars, can preserve many from feeling openly, and many secretly. . . .

". . . The milder degrees of poverty are, sometimes, supported by hope; but the more severe often sink down in motionless despondence. Life must be seen, before it can be known. This author and Pope, perhaps, never saw the miseries which they imagine thus easy to be borne. The poor, indeed, are insensible of many little vexations, which sometimes imbitter the possessions, and pollute the enjoyments, of the rich. They are not pained by casual incivility, or mortified by the mutilation of a compliment; but this happiness is like that of a malefactor, who ceases to feel the cords that bind him, when the pincers are tearing his flesh. . . .

"[Jenyns] imagines, that as we have not only animals for food, but choose some for our diversion, the same privilege may be allowed to some beings above us, *who may deceive, torment, or destroy us, for the ends, only, of their own pleasure or utility.* This he again finds impossible to be conceived, *but that impossibility lessens not the probability of the conjecture, which, by analogy, is so strongly confirmed.*

"I cannot resist the temptation of contemplating this analogy, which, I think, he might have carried further, very much to the advantage of his argument. He might have shown, that these 'hunters, whose game is man,' have many sports analogous to our own. As we drown whelps and kittens, they amuse themselves, now and then, with sinking a ship, and stand round the fields of Blenheim, or the walls of Prague, as we encircle a cockpit. As we shoot a bird flying, they take a man in the midst of his business or pleasure, and knock him down with an apoplexy. Some of them, perhaps, are virtuosi, and delight in the operations of an asthma, as a human philosopher in the effects of the air-pump. To swell a man with a tympany is as good sport as to blow a frog. Many a merry bout have these frolick beings at the vicissitudes of an ague, and good sport it is to see a man tumble with an epilepsy, and revive and tumble again, and all this he knows not why. As they are wiser and more powerful than we, they have more exquisite diversions; for we have no way of procuring any sport so brisk and so lasting, as the paroxysms of the gout and stone, which, undoubtedly, must make high mirth, especially if the play be a little diversified with the blunders and puzzles of the blind and deaf. We know not how far their sphere of observation may extend. Perhaps, now and then, a merry being may place himself in such a situation, as to enjoy, at once, all the varieties of an epidemical disease, or amuse his leisure with the tossings and contortions of every possible pain, exhibited together."

Why Johnson's supervision of *The Literary Magazine* came to an end we do not know, but it was perhaps to supply the loss of income from that source that he began in April, 1758, the series of weekly essays called *The Idler*. These, instead of being separate publications like *The Rambler*, appeared as part of a weekly newspaper called *The Universal Chronicle* and continued until April, 1760. Of the one hundred and three essays, all but twelve were written by Johnson himself and, again as in the case of *The Rambler*, they were later issued in book form. In its own day *The Idler* never achieved quite the degree of reputation which the earlier essays enjoyed and it is (if it be possible to compare accurately two degrees of popularity both of which are so nearly nil) even less read today, despite the fact that *The Idler*, being lighter, might be thought nearer the taste of our own time. Some of the essays, to be sure, might easily pass as *Ramblers*, but in general the proportion of pieces in a light tone is larger. The account of Dick Minim, the critic, is as near being well known as anything in either series, and one might easily choose various passages to illustrate Johnson's gift for good-humored satire.

Nevertheless, the only paragraph from *The Idler* still quoted from time to time is from the concluding number, and it is not difficult to understand why it has stood the test of time. Johnson's strain of melancholy exaggerated to a degree that made him conscious of it a certain psychological phenomenon which most readers recognize as having occurred in their own mental life after Johnson has indicated it.

"There are few things not purely evil, of which we can say, without some emotion of uneasiness, *this is the last*. Those who never could agree together, shed tears when mutual discontent has determined them to final separation; of a place which has been frequently visited, though without pleasure, the last look is taken with heaviness of heart; and the Idler, with all his chilness of tranquillity, is not wholly unaffected by the thought that his last essay is now before him.

"The secret horrour of the last is inseparable from a thinking being, whose life is limited, and to whom death is dreadful. We always make a secret comparison between a part and the whole; the termination of any period of life reminds us that life itself has likewise its termination; when we have done any thing for the last time, we involuntarily reflect that a part of the days allotted us is past, and that as more is past there is less remaining.

"It is very happily and kindly provided, that in every life there are certain pauses and interruptions, which force consideration upon the careless, and seriousness upon the light; points of time where one course of action ends, and another begins; and by vicissitudes of fortune or alteration of employment, by change of place or loss of friendship, we are forced to say of something, *this is the last*."

Johnson's style has no doubt been called "laborious" more often than it has been called anything else, but the implications of the adjective are not to be taken to include slowness of composition, for Johnson was likely to dash off at top speed even those compositions which seem heavy and involved. "When," he once observed, "a man writes from his own mind, he writes very rapidly. The greatest part of a writer's time is spent in reading, in order to write: a man will turn over half a library to make one book." And it is Boswell who tells Bennet Langton's story about the time when Johnson, on a visit to Oxford in 1759, asked him one evening when the post went out and, on being told that it would leave in about half an hour, said merely: "Then we shall do very well." He instantly sat down, composed an *Idler* (about a thousand words), and when Langton asked to read it, replied: "Sir, you shall not do more than I have done myself." He then folded the paper and dispatched it to London, where it was due at the printer's next day.

It was not until many years later that Johnson made his often-quoted remark: "No man but a blockhead ever wrote, except for money," but it is against the background of the profession of letters as he saw it at this time that the statement must be interpreted, and it is not cynical in the way that it is often assumed to be. Johnson did not love money, which he never accumulated and which he gave freely away. He put upon it the value commonly put upon it by the poor, and this is a very different thing from the value put upon it by the rich. To write for money meant, in Johnson's case, merely to write from necessity, and his statement means no more than that he could not conceive how anything except necessity could drive a man to do what he found so painful to his constitutional indolence, so much less entertaining than reading or conversation. Like many, perhaps like most, good writers, he found the process of composition disagreeable in itself even though he composed rapidly, and he spoke for many when he said: "I allow that you may have pleasure from writing, after it is over, if you have written well; but you don't go willingly to it again."

The desire to excel and to win admiration Johnson certainly had, but that desire alone was not enough to overcome his inertia, and it is noticeable that all his major works were accomplished either because he wrote under the pressure of immediate necessity or because he had previously committed himself to something from which he could not honorably escape. Thus *Rasselas* (1759), his most important work between the publication of the *Dictionary* and the appearance of his edition of Shakespeare, was composed, quite literally, to "defray the expense of his mother's funeral, and pay some little debts which she had left." The story is worth telling in full.

It will be remembered that when Johnson first established himself permanently in London some twenty-two years before, he left his mother and his wife's daughter, Lucy, with the bookshop which had lost its founder when his father died in 1731. Mrs. Johnson continued to operate it until her death, when the remaining stock was added to that of the old maidservant, Catherine Chambers, who had apparently been conducting a trade in quasi independence of the original business which Mrs. Johnson had, no doubt, allowed to dwindle as she grew into extreme old age. During all these years she and Lucy had been living in the house on Market Street where Johnson was born, and indeed Lucy continued there until about 1766 when some money left by her brother, Captain Porter, enabled her to build a house of her own.

Boswell has little to say concerning Johnson's relations with the Lichfield establishment, doubtless because of Johnson's confessed reluctance to discuss the humiliating details of his poverty, but from various sources it is possible to piece together a picture of his struggles to keep his two dependents as well as himself afloat. A surviving document dated January 31, 1740, shows that he was compelled (jointly with his mother) to mortgage the Market Street house to one Theophilus Levett of Lichfield for the sum of eighty pounds, and it is obvious from his share of this sum that he promises, in a letter to Tetty dated the same day as the mortgage, to send her twenty pounds "which I have received this night" in order that she might be able to consult a good physician concerning a serious "hurt on a tendon" from which she was suffering.

This debt of eighty pounds was to plague Johnson over a long period. More than three years later (December 1, 1743) he wrote to John Levett, the son of the original mortgager, thanking him for his "forebearance" in the matter of interest and promising to pay twelve pounds "in two months." Yet the debt evidently grew, for some eight years after that (March 7, 1752) he wrote Levett thanking him again for "the long credit and kind forebearance I have received from you" and informing him that in consequence of having sold a piece of property he can now give him "a Draught of one hundred pounds upon a Bookseller of credit payable on the first of May and realizable in the meantime." Presumably the property referred to was the rights to a portion of the collected edition of *The Rambler* of which the last number was to be printed a week later. But it was not until June 27, 1757, or more than seventeen years after the obligation had originally been contracted and only eighteen months before his mother's death, that an endorsement on the mortgage preserved in the town records of Lichfield reveals that the debt was finally liquidated—presumably out of what Johnson had recently received for subscriptions to his proposed edition of Shakespeare, though that edition was not to be published until more than eight years after he had thus spent a portion of the proceeds!

During all these years when he was struggling to keep a roof over his mother's head he does not appear ever to have seen her or indeed to have been in Lichfield at all between 1737 and her death. Writing to Bennet Langton in 1755, just after the publication of the *Dictionary* and referring to a possible journey, he said: "I have a mother more than eighty years old, who has counted the days to the publication of my book, in hopes of seeing me; and to her, if I can disengage myself here, I resolve to go." But he did not disengage himself. Nor were there lacking reasons other than his constitutional tendency to procrastination to excuse his neglect. Even the meticulous research done on his life since Boswell's time has failed to uncover any evidence that he was out of London more than two or possibly three times between 1737 and his mother's death: once when he went to Appleby in Leicestershire in 1740 to seek a schoolmaster's job; once when he visited Oxford in 1754; and, possibly, once when he appears to have been in the same place again the following year. Johnson was poor, he was often ill, and the journey to Lichfield was not to be undertaken lightly by an even more energetic man. More than a decade later he set out from London on Thursday at nine, and arrived at Lichfield on Friday night at eleven. Lucy Porter, though she had been well-off since the death of her brother, had never been to London when Johnson introduced Boswell to her in 1776.

Johnson's deep affection for his mother involved no sentimental attribution of virtues she did not have. It has already been shown that he judged almost harshly the mental equipment of both his parents and that he never concealed from himself the fact that they had neither made each other happy nor known how to avoid hurting him with the clumsiness of their affection. There was, nevertheless, more than merely a sense of duty in his devotion to his mother, and more than mere animal affection. He did, to be sure, love her because she *was* his mother and because he had ideas about what was due to parents no more or no less strict than those which he held concerning the limits of parental authority. But in addition he clung to her, to the mere knowledge that she was alive, as he clung to all old acquaintances whose continued existence afforded some protection against that sense of being alone in the world which the superficial intimacy with the great never seemed able to give him. As her end approached, some sense of guilt arising out of the fact that he had not seen her for years intruded, and it reminded him, as so many other things did, that time rolls past; and, as in one of those dreams in which we struggle desperately to do some necessary thing without making any progress toward getting it done, he was again and again overwhelmed with the sense that all his duties had been neglected. He who could not bear to have a visitor depart and leave him alone with himself was terrified whenever an acquaintance bade him an eternal farewell.

Johnson had always been thinking that he would see his mother soon. Now he knew he was either about to see her for the last time or never to see her again. Ten years before she died he had written to Lucy Porter in reply to some bad news about his mother's health that her death "is one of the few calamities on which I think with terror," and it is the noun "terror" that makes the phrase significant.

On January 13, 1759 (she was nearly ninety), he wrote the first of a series of surviving letters in connection with her last illness and death.

This first letter was obviously in reply to a communication from her which convinced him that the end was near. Three days later he writes to Lucy Porter that he has sent twelve guineas, and on the same day wrote also to his mother: "I do not think you unfit to face death, but I know not how to bear the thought of losing you. . . . I pray often for you; do you pray for me?" On January 20th he thanked her for her indulgence to him and begged forgiveness "of all that I have done ill, and all that I have omitted to do well." On the other side of the same paper he promised Lucy to come to Lichfield "if it be possible." "God grant," he added, "I may yet [find] my dear mother breathing and sensible."

His wish was not granted, for she died in his absence and was buried on January 23rd while Johnson was in London. On that day, he wrote Lucy promising to send twenty pounds "in a few days" and wrote again on January 25th: "You will forgive me if I am not yet so composed as to give any directions about anything. But you are wiser and better than I, and I shall be pleased with all that you shall do. It is not of any use for me now to come down; nor can I bear the place." On January 27th the forty-first number of *The Idler* was given over to "a letter [which] relates to an affliction perhaps not necessary to be imparted to the public," but which is printed because "I feel no disposition to provide for this day any other entertainment." The author, who is, of course, Johnson himself, remarks:

"Nothing is more evident than that the decays of age must terminate in death; yet there is no man, says Tully, who does not believe that he may yet live another year; and there is none who does not, upon the same principle, hope another year for his parent or his friend: but the fallacy will be in time detected; the last year, the last day, must come. It has come, and is past. The life which made my own life pleasant is at an end, and the gates are shut upon my prospects."

Though there can be no doubt of the depth or the sincerity of Johnson's sorrow, it is legitimate to remark that the reference to "the life which made my own life pleasant" is strongly reminiscent of things he said when Tetty died. Every person lost seemed to Johnson a final one and it may even be that, like many who suffer from apprehension and melancholy, he tended to identify its nameless cause with any event which might seem to furnish rational justification. In the Preface to the *Dictionary* he had written, no doubt with the recent death of his wife in mind: "I have protracted my work till most of those, whom I wished to please, have sunk into the grave, and success and miscarriage are empty sounds."

Now his mother seemed, as Tetty seemed then, the last person to whom he had any important tie.

As has already been indicated, Sarah Johnson's death was to be the occasion of a composition much longer and much more important than an *Idler* paper. On January 20th, just three days before the funeral, Johnson wrote to William Strahan, one of those concerned in the publication of the *Dictionary:*

To William Strahan

SIR,

When I was with you last night I told you of a story which I was preparing for the press. The title will be

"The Choice of Life
or
The History of ... Prince of Abissinia"

It will make about two volumes like little *Pompadour* [a recently published book], this is about one middling volume. The bargain which I made with Mr. Johnson was seventy five pounds (or guineas) a volume, and twenty five pounds for the second edition. I will sell this either at that price or for sixty, the first edition of which he shall himself fix the number, and the property then to revert to me, or for forty pounds, I share the profit, that is retain half the copy. I shall have occasion for thirty pounds on Monday night when I shall deliver the book which I must entreat you upon such delivery to procure me. I would have it offered to Mr. Johnson, but have no doubt of selling it, on some of the terms mentioned.

I will not print my name, but expect it to be known.

I am, dear Sir,

Your most humble servant,

SAM: JOHNSON

Jan. 20, 1759
Get me the money if you can.

"Preparing for the press" is a vague phrase which does not indicate just how much Johnson had actually written at the time, but he told Reynolds that *Rasselas* was composed "in the evenings of one week," that it was sent to the press in portions as it was written, and that he had never since read it over. The book was not actually published until April 19th, but it must have been within a few days of his mother's death that Johnson wrote the sonorous first sentence: "Ye, who listen, with credulity, to the whispers of fancy, and pursue, with eagerness, the phantoms of hope; who expect, that age will perform the promises of youth, and that the deficiencies of the present day will be supplied by the morrow; attend to the history of Rasselas, prince of Abissinia."

The form which he adopted, that of the pseudo-Oriental tale, was of course perfectly familiar to his contemporaries as a vehicle for moral instruction and Johnson had, indeed, previously used it himself in *The Rambler*. "Abissinia" was no doubt suggested by his youthful translation of Father Lobo's travels in which, indeed, occurs the title and name of one "Rassela Christos, Lieutenant General to Sultan Segued." If any specific source is needed for the thought of the opening sentence, Johnson may have found it in one of the most famous passages of one of his favorite poets, John Dryden, who puts into the mouth of Aureng-Zebe a similar reflection concerning those who "hope tomorrow will repay." The passage was, we know, one of his favorites.

Many who have never read *Rasselas* are, nevertheless, aware of the fact that it tells the story of a prince who escaped from a happy valley in order to find out for himself what men were like and how they fared. In accordance with the peculiar custom of his country (which took this means of preserving highborn persons from the temptations of political intrigue) he had been imprisoned in a sort of earthly paradise provided with every luxury and inhabited by a cultivated group of his fellow countrymen who had voluntarily agreed to commit themselves for life to this luxurious confinement.

Unlike most of his fellow prisoners, Rasselas was not content. He had some need which survived the satisfaction of every definable want and he plotted with his philosopher-guide, Imlac, to escape. Joined by his sister and her maid, they finally practised a tunnel through one of the surrounding mountains, went forth into the world, saw the unhappiness of every human condition and, in the end, decided to return to their prison because they had learned what Imlac knew from the beginning—that "Human life is everywhere a state, in which much is to be endured, and little to be enjoyed."

To Johnson's contemporaries the book was a dazzling specimen of that "true wit" which consists in achieving the perfect statement of something which "oft was thought but ne'er so well expressed." For that reason they admired it with an enthusiasm which the nineteenth century, brought up to admire novelty, paradox, perversity and eccentricity, found it difficult to understand; and insofar as we inherit the taste of that century, we too are likely to approach *Rasselas* with prejudice. But it is actually more original, or at least more tinged with the color of Johnson's own personality, than seems to have been generally remarked—possibly because in the days when it was promptly accepted as a classic there was so much less tendency than there is now to assume that individual personality, the difference between one temperament and another, is the most interesting thing which writing can reveal. Actually, Johnson did something more than merely rephrase the commonplaces which have long served to demonstrate that all is vanity. He was not content merely to indicate how men's plans go astray and men's ambitions are frustrated. His pessimism, in other words, was not merely of that vulgar sort which is no more than a lament over the failure of worldly prosperity. It was, instead, the pessimism which is more properly called the tragic sense of life, and he would undoubtedly have approved the lines of that modern poet who proclaims:

> The troubles of our proud and angry dust
> Are from eternity, and shall not fail.

Since the two things, ordinary pessimism and the tragic sense of life, are easily confused, since, indeed, they are at least mingled if not confused in *Rasselas* itself, it might be worthwhile in analyzing the tale to build the analysis around some attempt to separate them. Let us, then, begin on the lowest level.

Told in outline as it was told above, the story would seem to be no more than a device for introducing a survey of some of the various conditions of life, and its hero no more than a naïvely neutral observer. Some portion of it is, indeed, precisely that. A series of very short chapters disposes of various ways of life with almost perfunctory brevity, though often with wit. Shepherds, the travelers find, are too rude and too stupid to tell them whether or not the pastoral life is as peaceful as poets have maintained; a hermit they discover just as he is about to return to public life, a philosopher just at the moment when a personal calamity has robbed him of all his philosophy. A professional sage whose society they cultivate soon exhibits Johnson's own weakness by demonstrating that he prefers their foolish conversation to the solitary pleasure of his own wise thoughts, and when they ask him point-blank to advise them what way of life they should choose, he can only reply that he is not able to do so, since he himself has chosen wrongly. Indeed, the only person who will consent to advise them is an optimist who accepts the universe and who believes in living in accordance with nature, but who defines that process thus: "To live according to nature, is to act always with due regard to the fitness arising from the relations and qualities of causes and effects; to concur with the great and unchangeable scheme of universal felicity; to co-operate with the general disposition and tendency of the present system of things." But "The Prince soon found that this was one of the sages whom he should understand less, as he heard him longer. He, therefore, bowed, and was silent, and the philosopher, supposing him satisfied and the rest vanquished, rose up and departed, with the air of a man that had cooperated with the present system."

But by far the best chapter in the latter half of the book is one which deals with a visit to the Pyramids and includes, indeed, what is probably the finest single paragraph in the whole work. Moreover, this chapter is interesting, and one paragraph in it unforgettable, because it treats so powerfully a theme which the earlier sections had introduced but had allowed, for the most part, to remain suggested rather than systematically developed—the theme, that is to say, which has already been called the tragic rather than the merely pessimistic theme.

Rasselas, we here perceive, did not leave the valley merely in order to find out whether, in any vulgar sense, men prospered more outside it than he did within its confines. He knew that he had in the fullest measure that security and plenty and ease for which men commonly say they perform their labors and he was prepared not to be surprised that others led lives more troubled than his. Nor was it merely that he was consumed with vague curiosity. Actually he was seeking the answer to a tremendous question. "That I want nothing," said the prince, "or that I know not what I want, is the cause of my complaint," and it is the "know not what I want" that is really important. Sometimes Rasselas supposes that this sense of wanting something unspecifiable is merely the result of having had all possible desires satisfied. "I have already," he says, "enjoyed too much; give me something to desire." But Johnson is both too little an ascetic and too profoundly concerned with the ultimate nature of man to allow his hero to rest content with so simple an explanation of his infelicity. The difficulty is not merely that all desires are satisfied, but rather that man has some desire which nothing in his experience is capable of satisfying.

"'What,' said he, 'makes the difference between man and all the rest of the animal creation? Every beast, that strays beside me, has the same corporal necessities with myself: he is hungry, and crops the grass, he is thirsty and drinks the stream, his thirst and hunger are appeased, he is satisfied and sleeps: he rises again and is hungry, he is again fed, and is at rest. I am hungry and thirsty, like him, but when thirst and hunger cease, I am not at rest; I am, like him, pained with want, but am not, like him, satisfied with fulness. The intermediate hours are tedious and gloomy; I long again to be hungry, that I may again quicken my attention. The birds peck the berries, or the corn, and fly away to the groves, where they sit, in seeming happiness, on the branches, and waste their lives in tuning one unvaried series of sounds. I, likewise, can call the lutanist and the singer, but the sounds, that pleased me yesterday, weary me to-day, and will grow yet more wearisome to-morrow. I can discover within me no power of perception, which is not glutted with its proper pleasure, yet I do not feel myself delighted. Man surely has some latent sense, for which this place affords no gratification; or he has some desires, distinct from sense, which must be satisfied, before he can be happy.'

"After this, he lifted up his head, and seeing the moon rising, walked towards the palace. As he passed through the fields, and saw the animals around him, 'Ye,' said he, 'are happy, and need not envy me, that walk thus among you, burdened with myself; nor do I, ye gentle beings, envy your felicity; for it is not the felicity of man. I have many distresses, from which ye are free; I fear pain, when I do not feel it; I sometimes shrink at evils recollected, and sometimes start at evils anticipated: surely the equity of providence has balanced peculiar sufferings with peculiar enjoyments.' "

Perhaps the fact that Rasselas, when he indulges in these reflections, is dwelling in an earthly paradise tends to suggest that such thoughts are likely to occur only to a man so situated, but Johnson's own life was certainly not passed in any happy valley and yet a boredom of tragically grandiose implications was the evil always ready to assert itself even when other evils had been temporarily banished. Indeed, and as we shall see, both his theory of aesthetics and his general theory of human nature rest ultimately upon the desperate assumption that, since man never finds any really self-justifying activity, he must, if life is to be tolerable at all, fill it up with those temporary satisfactions which are gained by the gratification of the easily wearied senses and the parallel gratification of that less easily wearied but still far from limitless appetite for knowledge to which he generally gives no more exalted name than "curiosity."

But though almost the entire substance of another *Rasselas* could easily be compiled out of Johnson's recorded sayings and the identification between himself and his hero could be completely established, he nowhere else takes so definitely as he does in this tale the step which carries him from a rationalistic despair to the point where he asks the question which the Greeks had asked: "What activity is appropriate to man? In doing what does he fulfill his function and thus satisfy himself?"

Sometimes, as for instance when writing to Baretti, Johnson speaks of life as everywhere "supported with impatience and quitted with reluctance." Here his attitude seems almost Schopenhauerian, and suggests the conviction that life is endured only because the irrational will is stronger than the rational judgment. But though the passage from *Rasselas* just quoted seems at least to hint the possibility that the existence of a need must imply the existence somewhere of an answer to it, that hint has disappeared again in the later passage, which is not only the most eloquent Johnson ever wrote on this theme but perhaps, in all literature, the most magnificent tribute ever paid to the power of Boredom.

Rasselas and his companions have, in the course of their travels, just visited the Pyramids.

" 'We have now,' said Imlac, 'gratified our minds with an exact view of the greatest work of man, except the wall of China.

" 'Of the wall it is very easy to assign the motive. It secured a wealthy and timorous nation from the incursions of barbarians, whose unskilfulness in arts made it easier for them to supply their wants by rapine than by industry, and who, from time to time, poured in upon the habitations of peaceful commerce, as vultures descend upon domestick fowl. Their celerity and fierceness, made the wall necessary, and their ignorance made it efficacious.

" 'But, for the pyramids, no reason has ever been given adequate to the cost and labour of the work. The narrowness of the chambers proves that it could afford no retreat from enemies, and treasures might have been reposited, at far less expense, with equal security. It seems to have been erected only in compliance with that hunger of imagination, which preys incessantly upon life, and must be always appeased by some employment. Those who have already all that they can enjoy, must enlarge their desires. He that has built for use, till use is supplied, must begin to build for vanity, and extend his plan to the utmost power of human performance, that he may not be soon reduced to form another wish.

" 'I consider this mighty structure, as a monument of the insufficiency of human enjoyments. A king, whose power is unlimited, and whose treasures surmount all real and imaginary wants, is compelled to solace, by the erection of a pyramid, the satiety of dominion and tastelessness of pleasures, and to amuse the tediousness of declining life, by seeing thousands labouring without end, and one stone, for no purpose, laid upon another. Whoever thou art, that, not content with a moderate condition, imaginest happiness in royal magnificence, and dreamest that command or riches can feed the appetite of novelty, with perpetual gratifications, survey the pyramids, and confess thy folly!' "

According to Boswell, Mr. Strahan and Mr. Johnson bought the copyright of *Rasselas* for a hundred pounds, but afterwards paid the author twenty-five more when it came to a second edition. This seems less than what Johnson had asked in the letter published above, but Baretti told Malone that Johnson was "perfectly contented" with Dodsley's offer of one hundred pounds. In any event, the book was a great success, not only in England but abroad. Six English editions are listed in Johnson's lifetime and translations into Italian, French and German promptly appeared. A review in *The Gentleman's Magazine* for April, 1759, filled nearly five columns. Though composed mostly of excerpt and summary, the last sentence declares that Johnson's tale is full of "the most elegant and striking pictures of life and nature, the most acute disquisitions, and the happiest illustrations of the most important truths."

Voltaire's *Candide* was published the same year as *Rasselas* (probably some two months earlier). Johnson himself, says Boswell, remarked "that if they had not been published so closely one after the other that there was not time for imitation, it would have been in vain to deny that the scheme of that which came latest was taken from the other," and comparison became an inevitable topic for commentators. Johnson thought that "Candide . . . had more power in it than any thing that *Voltaire* had written"; Voltaire, acknowledging a copy of the first French translation sent him by its maker, wrote less ambiguously: *"Il m'a paru d'une philosophie aimable, et très-bien écrit."* Boswell, who of course was always ready with the correct moral sentiments, remarks:

"Voltaire, I am afraid, meant only by wanton profaneness to obtain a sportive victory over religion, and to discredit the belief of a superintending Providence: Johnson meant, by shewing the unsatisfactory nature of things temporal, to direct the hopes of man to things eternal. Rasselas, as was observed to me by a very accomplished lady, may be considered as a more enlarged and more deeply philosophical discourse in prose, upon the interesting truth, which in his 'Vanity of Human Wishes' he had so successfully enforced in verse."

Such was the line usually taken—as, for example, by one of Johnson's early nineteenth-century editors who did not hesitate to run the risk of exaggerating the effect of the printed word in order to make the contrast more vivid and who roundly announced that, while "the one demoralized a continent, and gave birth to lust, and rapine, and bloodshed; the other has blessed many a heart, and gladdened the vale of sorrow, with many a rill of pure and living water."

But such easy contrasts seem hardly worth drawing. That Voltaire is ribald and ferocious, Johnson melancholy and pietistic, is obvious enough.

Yet the very fact that comparisons are drawn seems to suggest that those who make them may have some uneasy sense that, despite the obvious contrasts, there are apparent similarities which ought to be explained away. Indeed, the two lines of argument advanced by the two moralists coincide precisely at the point where Johnson, in a passage quoted above, pays ironical respect to the special system of optimism which is the principal object of Voltaire's attack. However antithetical the temperaments of the two men may have been, they find equally absurd the proposition that this is the best of all possible worlds in the simple sense that Pope had proclaimed when he wrote:

> All discord harmony not understood;
> All partial evil universal good.

Neither is prepared to accept either Spinoza or Leibnitz, or the popular vulgarization of the two.

But the contrast between them is not the simple contrast between the cynic and the Christian, each refusing for a different reason to agree that the world is good. To afford so simple an antithesis, Voltaire would have had to be more of a cynic, and Johnson, if not more of a Christian, at least a Christian of either a more mystical or a more sentimental sort, and hence readier than he was to find a really effective consolation in the reflection that this life is merely the prelude to another. Actually, Johnson was, in one respect, more of a cynic than Voltaire, because Voltaire believed in the possibility of reform while Johnson did not. And if it is not cynicism that prevents him from insisting upon the adequacy of the pietistic solution which he makes a show of offering, it is two things which would have driven a different temperament to cynicism—namely, what he himself called his "obstinate rationality" coupled with an appetite for living which he was too contemptuous of cant to pretend to deny.

*Rasselas* does not so much end as break off. His contemporaries supposed that Johnson intended to write a continuation, but it seems equally likely that once he had written enough to fill the two small volumes he had agreed to deliver, he stopped because he did not like to write and because, in this particular case, he did not know what more to say. "It was now the time of the inundation of the Nile . . . They deliberated awhile what was to be done, and resolved, when the inundation should cease, to return to Abissinia." Thus the tale concludes, and on the basis of the final sentence one would seem justified in saying that the moral is not that no career leads to happiness and that therefore happiness should not be sought for, but rather the almost Epicurean conclusion that since the ultimate source of human unhappiness "is from eternity," the most fortunate men are those who, like the inhabitants of the Valley, are at least relieved from all the secondary causes of distress and possess in the largest measure the palliatives of security and pleasure. Rasselas and Imlac do return to physical comfort and security.

Shortly before, the sister of Rasselas has been made to say: "To me the choice of life is become less important; I hope, hereafter, to think only on the choice of eternity," and thus Johnson pays to orthodoxy, as he always does, the tribute of formal profession. But these formal professions cannot mean to him what they would have meant had they been as simply and vividly believed in as some have believed them, and here they constitute only the formal rather than the effective moral. Interpreted in the light of his own life as he lived it, the conclusion of *Candide* ("Let us cultivate our garden") would be almost as appropriate to *Rasselas* and therein, perhaps, lies one of the resemblances between the two books which made champions of English respectability so anxious to labor the obvious differences between them.

Boswell, who passed much more easily and more completely than Johnson through the series of steps which lead from the acceptance of orthodoxy to the determination to cultivate pleasantly the garden of this temporary state, could write with enviable ease:

"But if we walk with hope in 'the mid-day sun' of revelation, our temper and disposition will be such, that the comforts and enjoyments in our way will be relished, while we patiently support the inconveniences and pains. After much speculation and various reasonings, I acknowledge myself convinced of the truth of Voltaire's conclusion, *'Après tout c'est un monde passable.'*"

Johnson himself once wrote Mrs. Thrale: *"Vivite laeti* is one of the great rules of health"; and though he might well have suspected of lightness anyone who found it so easy to supply *Rasselas* with Boswell's gloss, he had no theoretical disagreement with it and in his own more troubled way attempted to put its recommendations into practice. Again and again when he is faced with the necessity either of consoling others or of facing some sorrow of his own, the steps are the same. First, the consolations of religion. Then, to others or to himself, the advice: Seek the palliatives for those ills which are susceptible of no radical remedy. That the man as well as the child can be pleased with a rattle and tickled with a straw is indeed one of nature's most kindly laws.

[From *Samuel Johnson,* Henry Holt and Company, Inc., 1944.]

## Thoreau Signs Off

Thoreau's schoolmastering was brought to an end early in 1841 when brother John, an easier, less original young man but the executive spirit of the enterprise, fell ill and the school was closed. John's malady was probably the tuberculosis to which the family was prone, but next year, before it had had time to develop, he suffered a slight accident and died in agony from a tetanus infection. Henry was deeply shaken by his brother's loss, he made no move to reopen the school, and he had probably never really considered himself so firmly settled in the profession of teaching as his mother had liked to suppose. On previous occasions he had helped his father with the manufacture of pencils, and even during his college years he had gone at least once to New York to peddle the product. Now he again concerned himself somewhat with the family business which continued to be operated throughout his life and of which, in time, he became nominally the manager. But his duties were not confining, he never devoted any considerable part of his energies to them, and he never, from the closing of the school onward, tied himself to any trade or profession. Three years after he ceased to be a schoolmaster he was called "the only man of leisure in the town."

Meanwhile, however, and beginning almost immediately after his return from college, he had set about that business of making the mental and spiritual settlements in life which seemed to him of such infinitely greater importance than any material settlements could be. In 1837, he had made the first entry in the *Journal* which he was to continue until six months before his death, and through that *Journal* he was to gain an entree into the Emerson household as well as the Emerson circle.

Sister Helen had read some of the early pages of the *Journal*. She told Emerson's sister-in-law, Mrs. Lucy Jackson Brown, that some of the thoughts resembled Emerson's own, and introductions were arranged. Soon Thoreau was frequently making one of the little company which gathered for conversation at the home of the older and already famous man; soon, also, Emerson was regarding him with respect and admiration. "I delight much in my young friend, who seems to have as free and erect a mind as any I have ever met," he wrote after a meeting in February, 1838, and a week later he was entering more praise into his diary: "My good Henry Thoreau made this else solitary afternoon sunny with his simplicity and clear perception. . . . Everything that boy says makes merry with society, though nothing can be graver than his meaning."

Before this Thoreau had begun to take some part in the intellectual life of the village, for he was a member of the Lyceum, and during the course of one subsequent winter he secured for it twenty-five lectures for a total expenditure of one hundred dollars—which included the cost of rent, fuel, and lights! Before the members of this institution—which obviously had to take what was available—he had given a talk on "Society" as early as 1838 when he was twenty-one years old and for a number of years he continued to try out on that audience observations and opinions which had previously been recorded in the ever-growing *Journal*. Presently he even—since conversation, lecturing, and publishing were, in that order, the almost inevitable activities of the group in which he found himself—managed to contribute (without pay) a few poems and some prose to *The Dial,* that famous though short-lived organ of the Transcendental movement of which first Margaret Fuller and then Emerson himself were editors.

But it is evident from both his letters and his *Journal* that Thoreau had by no means completely committed himself to the group or its activities. He had already (as he phrased it) "signed off" from the Concord church and he had no intention of "signing on" as member of any other institution. He was not sure that he wanted to assume the rôle of practicing prophet which came so naturally to Emerson, Margaret Fuller, and Bronson Alcott. Above all he was not sure that what seemed to them the good life of high-minded conversation and oracular instruction of the great public would be a good life for him, whose business seemed more with himself and with nature than with even the most select and educatable public. In what was perhaps his very first discourse before the Lyceum, he had observed that: "That which properly constitutes the life of every man is a profound secret," and had protested that society was made for man rather than man for society.

Nevertheless circumstances were to direct that his relationship with Emerson should become more intimate. He had no occupation, and when Emerson invited him to come and live in the house as handy man as well as member of the family, he came—on April 26, 1841—to stay for two years. In payment for his physical labor he received only his keep but he was brought inevitably into closer contact with the members of the Transcendentalist circle, who were puzzled by an aloofness and reserve which contrasted strangely enough with the expansiveness characteristic of at least the lesser disciples of Transcendentalism. Margaret Fuller thought him a bare hill still unwarmed by the breezes of spring, and though Emerson thought "we shall yet hear much more of him," even he objected to his brusqueness of manner, his penchant for contradiction, and his pugnaciousness about trifles. "He needs," Emerson thought, "to fall in love, to sweeten him and straighten him."

In July 1842, Nathaniel Hawthorne came with his bride to live in Concord, and he too soon came into contact with Thoreau—first, if the supposition of Sanborn is correct, not as a fellow intellectual but as the gardener lent by Emerson to prepare the grounds for the bride and groom. Probably the two men were disposed by a similar lack of social expansiveness to respect one another, and an entry in Hawthorne's notebook provides so much the best sketch of Thoreau at this period that a rather extended excerpt from it should be given.

Mr. Thoreau is a singular character; a young man with much of wild, original Nature still remaining in him; and so far as he is sophisticated, it is in a way and method of his own. He is as ugly as sin; long-nosed, queer-mouthed, and with uncouth and somewhat rustic manners . . . though courteous . . . corresponding with such an exterior. But his ugliness is of an honest and agreeable fashion, and becomes him much better than beauty . . . he has repudiated all regular means of getting a living, and seems inclined to lead a sort of Indian life. . . .

He is a keen and delicate observer of Nature . . . a *genuine* observer, which I suspect is almost as rare a character as even an original poet. And Nature, in return for his love, seems to adopt him as her especial child; and shows him secrets which few others are allowed to witness. He is familiar with beast, fish, fowl and reptile, and has strange stories to tell of adventures and friendly passages with these lower brethren of mortality. Herb and flower, likewise, wherever they grow, whether in garden or wildwood, are his familiar friends. He is on intimate terms with the clouds also, and can tell the portents of storms. He has a great regard for the memory of the Indian tribes, whose wild life would have suited him so well; and, strange to say, he seldom walks over a plowed field without picking up an arrow-point, spearhead, or other relic of the red man. With all this he has more than a tincture of literature; a deep and true taste for poetry, especially for the elder poets; and he is a good writer. At least he has written a good article,—a rambling disquisition on Natural History, in the last *Dial*, which, he says, was chiefly made up from journals of his own observations. Methinks this article gives a very fair image of mind and character . . . so true, so innate and literal in observation . . . yet giving the spirit as well as the letter of what he sees; even as a lake reflects its wooded banks, showing every leaf . . . yet giving the wild beauty of the whole scene.

Six months later Hawthorne felt compelled to add: "Mr. Emerson seems to have suffered some inconvenience from his experience of Mr. Thoreau as an inmate. It may well be that such a sturdy, uncompromising person is fitter to meet occasionally in the open air than as a permanent guest at table and fireside." Thoreau, on the whole, would have liked that.

The truth seems to be that he did not always find the high thinking which went on vocally at gatherings in the Emerson house so inspiring as it might have been. Even before going there he had declared himself a "transcendental brother," but his brethren could on occasion be silly enough —just how silly, at least when Emerson was not present, may be read in an account written to the latter by his wife in February 1843:

> Last evening we had the "Conversation," though, owing to the bad weather, but few attended. The subjects were: What is Prophecy? Who is a Prophet? and The Love of Nature. Mr. Lane decided, as for all time and the race, that this same love of nature . . . of which Henry [Thoreau] was the champion, and Elizabeth Hoar and Lidian (though L. disclaimed possessing it herself) his faithful squiresses . . . that this love was the most subtle and dangerous of sins; a refined idolatry, much more to be dreaded than gross wickedness, because the gross sinner would be alarmed by the depth of his degradation, and come up from it in terror, but the unhappy idolators of Nature were deceived by the refined quality of their sin, and would be the last to enter the kingdom. Henry frankly affirmed to both the wise men that they were wholly deficient in the faculty in question, and therefore could not judge of it. And Mr. Alcott as frankly answered that it was because they went beyond the mere material objects, and were filled with spiritual love and perception (as Mr. T. was not), that they seemed to Mr. Thoreau not to appreciate outward nature. I am very heavy, and have spoiled a most excellent story. I have given you no idea of the scene, which was ineffably comic, though it made no laugh at the time; I scarcely laughed at it myself . . . too deeply amused to give the usual sign. Henry was brave and noble; as well as I have always liked him, he still grows upon me.

Physically Thoreau must have been at this time an agreeable if not especially elegant figure. Most readers no doubt tend to think of him in connection with the most frequently reproduced portrait, which presents a rather wooden face decorated with a set of not very becoming chin whiskers. But that daguerreotype was not taken until 1856, about the time when his health began to decline, and he was, during most of his life, clean shaved. Though of only average height, or even somewhat less, he gave an impression of abounding health, and both Emerson and Ellery

Channing testify to something striking about his whole bearing as well as about the keen resoluteness of his expression. The gray-blue eyes were deep set, the nose was prominent and aquiline (like one of the portraits of Caesar, Channing called it), the mouth was prominent with full, often pursed, lips. His complexion was fair, his hair light-brown and abundant. But it was the poised readiness of his body which must have been the most striking feature of his appearance. "His whole figure," says Channing, "had an active earnestness, as if he had no moment to waste. The clenched hand betokened purpose. In walking, he made a short cut if he could, and when sitting in the shade or by a wall side, seemed merely the clearer to look forward into the next piece of activity. Even in the boat he had a wary, transitory air, his eyes on the outlook—perhaps there might be ducks, or the Blanding turtle, or an otter or sparrow." More surprising to those who tend to think of him as earnest and solemn is the fact that he was full of humorous high spirits. He danced, not only vigorously but well. He sang popular songs. And no one, said Channing, laughed more or better.

Reading and writing, the most solitary of the intellectual pursuits, were naturally those which Thoreau found most congenial. The year before he went to live with Emerson he had written Sister Helen a letter in which he declared somewhat sportively that "an honest book's the noblest work of Man" and suggested that she also should write something. "If you cannot compose a volume, then try a tract. . . . You will not lack readers— here am I, for one." He himself was keeping on with the *Journal* which was to cover many hundreds of pages before he left the Emerson house and which, though it was intended in part as a storehouse for material later to be worked up for a public, no doubt did not please him the less for the fact that in the form then being set down it was addressed primarily to himself.

He had no intention of becoming so committed to authorship as to discover too late that it also was a profession. He had, so he admits in 1842, sometimes "felt mean enough" when asked by some earnest seeker "what errand I had to mankind"; but that was merely because he could not explain what the errand was, not at all because he did not think that he had as much of one as he, at least, needed to have.

> At evening walked to see an old schoolmate who is going to help make the Welland Canal navigable for ships round Niagara. He cannot see any such motives and modes of living as I; professes not to look beyond the securing of certain "creature comforts." And so we go silently different

ways, with all serenity, I in the still moonlight through the village this fair evening to write these thoughts in my journal, and he, forsooth, to mature his schemes to ends as good, maybe, but quite different. So are we two made, while the same stars shine quietly over us. If I or he be wrong, Nature yet consents placidly. She bites her lip and smiles to see how her children will agree. So does the Welland Canal get built, and other conveniences, while I live.

Meanwhile he was, so at least he professed to believe, serenely and indescribably happy. A few days before he met his industrious friend he had written for his own benefit: "I am startled that God can make me so rich even with my own cheap stores. It needs but a few wisps of straw in the sun, or some small word dropped, or that has long lain silent in some book." "My life at this moment," as he had somewhat earlier confessed to himself, "is like a summer morning when birds are singing," and about the same time he was assuring a correspondent: "I love my fate to the very core and rind, and could swallow it without paring it, I think."

In the household it was clearly to Lidian Emerson, his patron's second wife, that he was most drawn. She was fifteen years his senior, shy, melancholy, witty, and religious in a relatively conventional way; not much given to the new thoughts effervescing around her. Certainly the relations between her and her husband, though of course on a very high plane, were not warm and the philosopher lived with her what he himself called a "bachelor existence." But Thoreau, who had a tendency to hope that any shy reserved person was that ideal friend to whom friendship need not be revealed and with whom one could communicate without saying anything, seems, after Ellen Sewall's cool letter, to have made Lidian his "sister."

Unlike most young men, he feared most not that he would never be more than he was, but only that he might come to be less; that getting ahead or even merely making a living might become his chief business. Already at twenty-three, before he had gone to live with Emerson and thirteen years before he was to proclaim the same thought to a large public in his only much-read book, he was entering in the *Journal* a warning: "Most who enter on any profession are doomed men. The world might as well sing a dirge over them forthwith." "The farmer's muscles," he added, "are rigid," and so, he might have gone on, are those of the professional writer or even prophet. "I am," he confessed in a letter to Mrs. Emerson's sister, "as unfit for any practical purpose—I mean for the furtherance of the world's ends—as gossamer for shiptimber; and I, who am going to be a pencilmaker tomorrow, can sympathize with God Apollo, who served King Admetus for a while on this earth." Apollo, he admits, found this to his advantage at last and so perhaps will he, "though I shall hold the nobler part at least out of the service."

Emerson, who complained about his young protégé's indulgence in a spirit of contradiction, seems to have complained also about his tendency to say nothing at all, for Emerson was probably the "friend" who "thinks I *keep* silence, who am only choked with letting it out so fast" and to whom Thoreau replies in the *Journal*: "I have been breaking silence these twenty-three years and have hardly made a rent in it. Silence has no end; speech is but the beginning of it."

Curiously enough, Thoreau, on his side, does not, during all this time, mention Emerson's name in his *Journal* where it does not occur before an undated passage belonging apparently to the Walden period. Here he wrote of him: "There is no such general critic of men and things, no such trustworthy and faithful man. More of the divine [is] realized in him than in any." Yet even this entry is elsewhere not without its qualifications and the qualifications became more and more important. Later, at least, Thoreau thought there was an alloy of patronage in Emerson's praise and that Emerson was one of those who "flatter you, but themselves more."

It has already been admitted that the reading of *Nature* probably first encouraged Thoreau to trust in his own originality. Certainly he later learned much from Emerson even though some of what he learned had to be unlearned again. But we can only guess just how completely he had ever regarded himself as a disciple and just how soon he became aware of a restiveness which certainly began presently to affect him whenever he felt that he was yielding too much to any man's influence. And in any case it is easy to see what some of the fundamental differences between the two men were. In the sage of Concord Thoreau soon began to suspect that there was too much of the merely genteel, too little of the genuine wildness which he valued so much in himself and which he cultivated by direct association with physical nature.

Being a man who felt impelled to lead a life of outward as well as of inward nonconformity, he was suspicious of those whose inner life was compatible with a decorous, genteel position in a community like Concord, and he may have been mentally including Emerson in his condemnation when he came, in the first chapter of *Walden,* to complain: "The success of great scholars and thinkers is commonly a courtier-like success, not kingly, not manly. They make shift to live merely by conformity, practically as their fathers did. . . . The philosopher is in advance of his age even in the outward form of his life. He is not fed, sheltered, clothed, warmed, like his contemporaries. How can a man be a philosopher and not maintain his vital heat by better methods than other men?"

Looking back he liked to believe that he had always been less a member of any group than an individual going about his own business, and that to describe "how I have desired to spend my life in years past" would some-what surprise even those of his readers who were, like Emerson, ac-quainted with his actual history. "In any weather, at any hour of the day or night, I have," he goes on, "been anxious to improve the nick of time, and notch it on my stick too; to stand on the meeting of two eternities, the past and the future, which is precisely the present moment; to toe that line. . . . To anticipate, not the sunrise and the dawn merely, but, if possible, Nature herself!"

It must be remembered that Thoreau, though he wrote only one book now, or ever, very widely read, has managed to acquire three different reputations, and that of the three only one—his reputation as a member of the Transcendentalist group—obviously owes very much to Emerson's influence. Moreover, that reputation is now not much more than a fact of literary history since New England Transcendentalism, considered as a theory of knowledge and a special technique for attaining Truth, hardly interests very many today outside the group whose concern is chiefly with the historical study of a literary movement. His other two reputations, the two in which Emerson's influence is far less important, are, on the other hand, both very much alive since he is today both hailed as a prophet of social reform and cherished as the chosen spokesman of thousands who have resolved to turn their backs upon society and to seek, as he once did, salvation for the individual soul through solitary communion with all that part of nature which is not human.

The fact that the *Journal* begins after he had already made contact with Emerson, at least through the printed page, and only shortly before he felt Emerson's personal influence, tends to obscure the question of what native impulses first emerged and leads easily to the assumption that he was, chronologically, first of all a moralist of Transcendental leanings. Thus there is no doubt that the earlier portions of the *Journal* reveal a struggle after Emersonian profundities or that the young writer was trying to find expression for himself in a style of writing and of thinking which the mere physical propinquity of a great writer made it almost inevitable he should imitate. Even his first published work, *A Week on the Concord and Merrimack Rivers,* which ostensibly describes a journey made in the autumn of 1839, is a curious narrative frequently interrupted by long passages of sometimes rather callow mysticism. But the fact that he went not to the study but to the river for communion with the Oversoul is itself significant. It suggests the possibility that the philosophy is chiefly an attempt to justify an expedition which would earlier have been made without any such justification and that the boatman was antecedent to the philosopher—perhaps even that the first appeal of Transcendentalism was the fact that it seemed to invest with high moral purpose activities which to family and fellow townsmen seemed irresponsible when indulged in by a grown man without a profession.

What, then, if we may try to reconstruct the pre-Emersonian Thoreau, was the first thing he wanted, and what was the first eccentricity he was compelled to develop in order not to deprive himself of it?

He had, it must be remembered, been raised in genteel poverty. Recently the pencil business had prospered, and as it became more and more the manufacture of graphite for electrotypers rather than for pencils, it was to prosper still more. But his father had been long an unsuccessful man and his mother, among other things, took in boarders. The very first choice he had to make was, then, the choice between living and making a living, between sacrificing himself to the so-called necessities, and learning how to do well enough without them. The choice that he made was not the usual one and it testifies to a native originality of mind as well as of temperament. But a proper understanding of his thoughts and his life must begin with the realization that this particular choice had to be made.

It is true that he ultimately developed a moral philosophy in which doing without superfluities became a virtue in itself and he certainly implied that the richest and the most secure would do well to adopt what he called "voluntary poverty." But his own poverty was not, in the first instance, voluntary. His choice was not a choice among many possibilities but only between two narrowly defined alternatives—between doing without and paying the enormous price which must be paid for middle-class decencies by those who have neither inherited wealth nor an obvious talent for any well-paid activity.

To say this is not to say that his declared preference for living close to the bone was mere rationalization or that his wisdom is invalidated by the fact that he acquired it through a struggle with a personal problem. But he did make virtue of necessity, or rather of what had become necessity once he had resolved not to pay for the superficialities what he would have had to pay, and that fact helps us to understand at least the more extravagant of his self-denying ordinances.

When, for instance, he despises foreign travel or ridicules the man who thinks theaters or concerts necessary to cultivate the soul, it is well to remember that he was discounting what he could not have rather than what he could, and that, as a matter of fact, he traveled as much as he was able conveniently to travel—namely, to Cape Cod, Canada, and the Maine woods. In his own mind he probably did not always keep clear the distinction between what was not worth having and what was merely not worth the price which he would have had to pay for it, but the distinction is nevertheless a valid one. "It has not," he was to say later, "been my design to live cheaply, but only to live as I could, not devoting much time to getting a living."

Indeed when he came to write the first chapter of *Walden* he was to be perfectly explicit: "Finding that my fellow-citizens were not likely to offer me any room in the court house, or any curacy or living anywhere else, but I must shift for myself, I turned my face more exclusively than ever to the woods, where I was better known. . . . My purpose in going to Walden Pond was not to live cheaply nor to live dearly there, but to transact some private business with the fewest obstacles." By the time *Walden* was written he was ready to proclaim further (at least in a sort of parenthesis) that the art of doing without which he had discovered in the search for a possible means of living his own life might be equally useful even to those who had quite other lives to lead. He pointed out for instance that it required in his day about fifteen years for the average workman to earn the money to pay for the kind of house in which he usually lived, and he was sure that this was too large a portion of anyone's life to be expended merely to provide shelter, no matter what marginal activity seemed to the laborer most worth indulging. But in the beginning his scheme of life was developed merely to solve an individual problem.

If we can accept as accurate the memories he was later to set down, the life which was not to be sacrificed to making a living had been, up to the time he went to college, mostly an instinctive one, and when the time came for him to supply a sketch for the Class Book at the end of his college career, he wrote: "I shall ever pride myself on the place of my birth. . . . If I forget thee, O Concord, let my right hand forget her cunning. . . . To whatever quarter of the world I may wander, I shall deem it good fortune that I hail from Concord North Bridge." It may be that simple homesickness contributed more to produce that outburst of local patriotism than the composer of it cared to admit or was even conscious of, and when on other occasions he expatiated upon the delights of the region where it had been his good fortune to be born, it was not upon domesticity but upon wilderness that he always dwelt. "I can easily walk ten, fifteen, twenty, any number of miles, commencing at my own door, without going by any house, without crossing a road except where the fox and the mink do. . . . There are square miles in my vicinity which have no inhabitant." Again: "Those resorts which I most love and frequent, numerous and vast as they are, are as it were given up to me, as much as if I were an autocrat or owner of the world, and by my edicts excluded men from my territories. . . . I find such ample space and verge, even miles of walking every day in which I do not meet nor see a human being, and often not very recent traces of them."

On occasion he can remember that he walks "as one possessing the advantages of human culture, fresh from society of men, but turned loose into the woods, the only man in nature, walking and meditating to a great extent as if man and his customs were not." More often, however, he resents or thinks that he resents the intrusion of civilization or of human society and congratulates himself that, though he can see civilization and the abodes of men from afar, "these farmers and their works are scarcely more obvious than woodchucks." More typical Americans might be looking forward to the day when the still spacious country would be teeming with an industrious population; Thoreau looked back to the very recent past when the wilderness, of which he felt he was catching the last glimpse, was undisturbed. In his latest and soberest years, after he had reluctantly consented, on occasion, to think socially, he became, to some extent, that very tame and civilized thing, a "conservationist," and he even made a plea for the establishment of national parks. But in youth and young manhood he was fiercely individualistic. "I am convinced," he wrote in *A Week on the Concord and Merrimack Rivers,* "that my genius dates from an older era than the agricultural. . . . There is in my nature, methinks, a singular yearning towards all wildness. . . . Gardening is civil and social, but it wants the vigor and freedom of the forest and the outlaw. . . . There are other, savager and more primeval aspects of nature than our poets have sung. It is only white man's poetry."

Even the farmers of Concord were too domestic for him. "The same thing which keeps the hen-hawk in the woods, away from the cities, keeps me here. That bird settles with confidence on a white pine top and not upon your weathercock. That bird will not be poultry of yours, lays no eggs for you, forever hides its nest." The plain living of New England was not plain enough, at least for his imagination, and its economy was too complicated as well as too utilitarian. It infuriated him to think that huckleberries should be *sold*. He argued with his father about the *use* of making maple sugar when he could have bought it cheaper at the store. "He said it took me from my studies. I said I made it my study; I felt as if I had been to a university." Neighbors who would not hesitate to shoot the last pair of hen hawks in the town to save a few of their chicks disgusted him by this "narrow and groveling economy." "I would rather never taste chickens' meat nor hens' eggs than never to see a hawk sailing through the upper air again. This sight is worth incomparably more than a chicken soup or a boiled egg." Even the wildness of the woods, as he now found them, was too tame for him. "When I consider that the nobler animals have been exterminated here—the cougar, the panther, lynx, wolverine, wolf, bear, moose, deer, the beaver, the turkey, etc., etc.—I cannot but feel as if I lived in a tamed, and, as it were, emasculated country. . . . Is it not a maimed and imperfect nature that I am conversant with? As if I were to study a tribe of Indians that had lost all its warriors. . . . I take infinite pains to know all the phenomena of the spring, for instance, thinking that I have here the entire poem, and then, to my chagrin, I hear that it is but an imperfect copy that I possess and have read, that my ancestors have torn out many of the first leaves and grandest passages, and mutilated it in many places. I should not like to think that some demigod had come before me and picked out some of the best of the stars. I wish to know an entire heaven and an entire earth."

Few of the poets and philosophers who have made nature their theme or have sought in her their God ever had, or ever desired to have, Thoreau's kind of experience with nature's least humanized aspects. In tastes as well as in feelings he was at least as much akin to the Audubons and the Muirs as he was to the Wordsworths or the Emersons, and he considered himself indescribably fortunate to have been born not quite too late to catch a glimpse of a country not yet all tamed. An English book which suggests that the Englishman's right to walk through now vanishing woodland paths might be defended by paving them with "asphalt laid upon a good foundation" filled him with mingled consternation and contempt. When a tree is cut down in Concord, he asks, "Does not the village bell sound a knell? . . . I see no procession of mourners in the streets, or the woodland aisles. The squirrel has leaped to another tree; the hawk has circled further off, and has settled now upon a new eyrie, but the woodman is preparing to lay his axe at the root of that also." And it was in part at least this sense that increasing gentility as well as increasing tameness was cutting off even the new philosophers from the very nature they professed to be turning to, that is responsible for his soon-to-develop sense of alienation from Emerson. It was not that he was unwilling to make, with Emerson, the assumption that association with nature would communicate to man the profoundest truths; but he doubted if men like Emerson, busy only with their thoughts in quiet studies, actually had much contact with anything except these same thoughts, or that their occasional careful interviews with an emasculated nature could possibly give them more than an emasculated vision of the truths they sought.

In his friend and first master, Thoreau was later to discover something which he described as almost "cockney," and Emerson, in unconscious retaliation for an insult he had never heard, spoke with good-natured mockery of Henry's "edible religion"—for Thoreau, expecting no very favorable answer, nevertheless liked to put to nature the question how far she alone would support him and to put it practically, by eating in the woods whatever seemed even possibly edible. Refusing to stop, like other country boys, with such things as huckleberries and maple sugar, he once indeed went so far as to make an unsuccessful experiment with the seeds of skunk cabbage. Acorns he professed to find quite palatable, though better raw than cooked, and "From my experience with wild apples I can understand that there may be a reason for a savage preferring many kinds of food which the civilized man rejects." "It takes," he added, "a savage or wild taste to appreciate a wild apple."

No doubt he congratulated himself in being, unlike the cockney Emerson, close enough to the savage to retain some lingering kinship with the savage palate, just as he was getting some last glimpse of the savage's physical world. Farmers were lesser men than hunters, and Emerson was so little of a farmer, even, that Thoreau doubted if he would be willing to "trundle a wheelbarrow through the streets, because it would be out of character." "To get the value of the storm we must be out a long time and travel far in it. . . . Some men speak of having been wetted to the skin once as a memorable event in their lives, which, notwithstanding the croakers, they survived." Had most of the nature philosophers ever been, metaphorically, wet to the skin with her rain even once?

Thoreau was no Rousseauist. His noble savage, insofar as he *was* noble, was not so because he was assumed to have in perfection the finest qualities of the civilized man but rather because he possessed qualities quite different, and if the instinctive sympathy with wild nature was probably Thoreau's first distinguishing characteristic, it is also the one that persisted with least modification through life, so that in his latest writings it plays an even larger part than it had in the first, and *The Maine Woods* —far less transcendental than *A Week on the Concord and Merrimack*

*Rivers*—becomes a sort of despairing protest against the final destruction of the one world in which he felt thoroughly at home. An Indian guide, pointing to a belt of dead trees near a lake, explained that all the caribou had left because "no likum stump, when he sees that he scared." So, in the same way, was Thoreau himself scared.

Sometimes he was exalted to think how much was left, as he was, for instance, when he reflected that much of America was still unsettled and unexplored: "Like the English in New Holland, we live only on the shores of a continent even yet. . . . The very timber and boards and shingles of which our houses are made grew but yesterday in a wilderness where the Indian still hunts and the moose runs wild. New York has her wilderness within her own borders; and though the sailors of Europe are familiar with the soundings of her Hudson, and Fulton long since invented the steamboat on its waters, an Indian is still necessary to guide her scientific men to its headwaters in the Adirondack country." More often, however, it was the inevitable and rapid destruction of wild nature which horrified him, and his realization that this necessarily went hand in hand with what his fellow citizens regarded as progress is probably the original source of his rationalized conviction that the so-called "development" of America was, in truth, its destruction, morally as well as physically.

"The Anglo-American," he wrote, "can indeed cut down, and grub up all this waving forest, and make a stump speech, and vote for Buchanan on its ruins, but he cannot converse with the spirit of the tree he fells, he cannot read the poetry and mythology which retire as he advances." "The very willow-rows lopped every three years for fuel or powder, and every sizable pine and oak, or other forest tree, cut down within the memory of man! As if individual spectators were to be allowed to export the clouds out of the sky, or the stars out of the firmament, one by one. We shall be reduced to gnaw the very crust of the earth for nutriment."

Most of those who long, or think that they long, for the simple life do so because they have turned with disgust from the spectacle of competitive society, and in desperation they are driven to the assumption that nature will comfort them. But from such passages as the above it is not difficult to conclude that the evolution of Thoreau's convictions follows the path in an opposite direction—not, that is to say, from hatred of human society to the supposition that nature will be lovable, but from a love of nature to the assumption that human society is hateful. He did not love trees because he despised stump speeches but despised stump speeches because only by cutting down trees could they be made.

In an environment more primitive than that of Concord, at the frontier or even beyond it, such a temperament as Thoreau's might possibly have satisfied its instinctive needs without the concurrent development of a philosophy, and without the consciousness of any necessity for social protest. He might have been hunter, or trapper, or scout, or possibly no more than a merchant or surveyor to whom the recreations of the outdoors were inevitable and unremarked. But Thoreau had grown up in an intellectual environment, he had been to college and developed an intellectual life. In the society of which he was a part, man was assumed to be, first of all, a moral being whose activities required justification. What would have been on the frontier a merely normal, active life would be shiftlessness and animality in Concord.

Fortunately for him, some connection could be made between the new doctrine that man was to seek salvation through the contemplation of nature and what he himself had long delighted to do. Had the intellectual leaders of Concord been the New England theologians of the preceding century, he would no doubt have thrown in his lot with the scamps. Had they been Yankee philosophers of another stamp, preaching the gospel of commercial or industrial enterprise, he would have been a ne'er-do-well. As it was, he threw in his lot with the Transcendentalists, and he set about asking the nature which he knew in his own way the questions which they, from a considerably greater distance, tried to put to her.

Even before he went to live in Emerson's house he had been aware of his contempt for conventional Christian moralizing, for he had noted somewhat smugly that when reading, for instance, a book on agriculture, he made it his practice to "skip the author's moral reflections, and the words 'Providence' and 'He' scattered along the page, to come to the profitable level of what he has to say." Now he wondered if much that he heard from the Transcendental brothers was not the same sort of thing in different words, and if they were not contracting from their so-called nature the very disease he was trying to cure himself of. "I never met a man who cast a free and healthy glance over life, but the best live in a sort of Sabbath light, a Jewish gloom." "What offends me most in my compositions is the moral element in them. The repentant never say a brave word. . . . Strictly speaking, morality is not healthy. Those undeserved joys which come uncalled and make us more pleased than we are grateful are they that sing." "The moral aspect of Nature," he concluded, "is a jaundice reflected from man"; and it is difficult to imagine any thought less Emersonian. Whitman would have enthusiastically agreed. Coleridge may have been more gently implying the same thing when he warned his dear

William that "in our life alone does Nature live." But from the standpoint of New England Transcendentalism it was sheer atheism.

For all his unworldliness, Emerson was in some respects more worldly than Thoreau, more ambitious for him than he was for himself, and disturbed by the fact that Thoreau's light was kept hidden under the bushel of his contented reserve. He evidently felt that life as handy-man-companion was proving all too acceptable, and at the end of two years he expelled Thoreau gently into the world. He suggested, and Henry agreed, that the latter should go to live for a time with Emerson's lawyer brother on Staten Island—ostensibly as a tutor for the brother's young son but actually to make contacts with those who might buy his literary goods.

When on May 1, 1843, Thoreau set off he was almost twenty-six years old and he had, so far, managed to avoid deep entanglement with any profession, even that of literature. What he really thought of his patron's plan to launch him on the world it is difficult to say, and it is at least possible that he was consistent enough to hope, secretly, that it would fail. But he consented, nevertheless, and undertook to peddle his genius in the same market where he had peddled his father's pencils some seven years before.

William Emerson was a sincere and kindly man but completely absorbed in his profession, and the impression produced on Thoreau by the metropolis itself is summed up in the statement: "I walked through New York yesterday—and met no real and living person." The city, he remarked dryly, "is large enough now, and they intend it shall be larger still." To Sister Sophia he wrote of the honeysuckle on Staten Island and how it differed from that of Concord; to his mother about the seven-year locust which was having its year. Obviously he was homesick, though he interrupts a paragraph devoted to thoughts of home with the protestation that he is not.

Armed with a letter from Emerson, he called on the elder Henry James. He explained Transcendentalism to James in a three-hour conversation and came away liking the man very much. "He has naturalized and humanized New York for me," although (in the same letter): "I don't like the city better the more I see it, but worse. I am ashamed of my eyes that behold it. . . . When will the world learn that a million men are of no importance compared with *one* man." Horace Greeley he described as "cheerfully in earnest . . . a hearty New Hampshire boy as one would wish to meet," and Greeley was sufficiently impressed not only to act as a sort of agent for Thoreau in his never very large literary negotiations but also long to remain, next to Emerson, the warmest admirer he had among men of letters.

But despite politeness and sometimes something more from these and from lesser men, there was little indication that Thoreau's talents were salable. The *Democratic Review,* to whose editor Hawthorne had introduced him, bought an insignificant essay on *The Landlord* and also commissioned a review of the book by the German Utopian, Etzler, in whose scheme for a highly mechanized world Thoreau managed to work up the appearance of mild interest—not, as has already been said, because he approved of mechanization, but because Etzler predicted a society in which everybody would live in almost uninterrupted leisure. Many of the magazines paid nothing yet got all the contributions they could print at this price, even though Thoreau thought most of them were worth no more. Those that did pay showed little eagerness to employ Thoreau. He had pretended to Emerson that he hoped for success; to the members of his family he was presently writing in a tone of resignation, with which there was, quite possibly, mingled a good deal of relief. He called on the Harper firm but was told that since it was making fifty thousand a year there seemed no reason to experiment. "My bait will not tempt the rats—they are too well fed. . . . They say there is a 'Ladies' Companion' that pays,—but I could not write anything companionable."

As for the city, it continued to remain unattractive. "Seeing so many people from day to day, one comes to have less respect for flesh and bones, and thinks they must be more loosely joined, of less firm fiber, than the few he had known. It must have a very bad influence on children to see so many human beings at once,—mere herds of men." And so, before the end of November, he was back in Concord, after an absence of less than seven months. He returned, not to Emerson's house, but to pencil-making and the bosom of his own family.

Of the two fiascoes—that in New York and that in the Emerson household—the latter was much the more important. It apparently convinced him that his sympathy with even the most intellectually attractive group he had ever known was far from perfect, and that even to them he was not so closely akin as he had, no doubt, once liked to hope. They were protestant and aloof, so far as most Americans and most of America was concerned, but he was protestant and aloof even from them. For the time being, at least, he had had enough of influences, even of influences as important as he recognized that of Emerson to have been. He must withdraw far enough to sort out his own thoughts and convictions, to separate what was really his or had been made his from all that he had passively taken over from others. He must set into some sort of order the complex of convictions, sensibilities, tastes, and prejudices which would explain him and his way of life even if they were never systematic enough, or possibly even consistent enough, to be called a philosophy. And so the symbolic retirement to the hut near the edge of Walden pond was both inevitable and not far away.

It is possible that his relations with Lidian Emerson had also something to do with the closing of an epoch. She had been the first person outside his own family to whom he had written from Staten Island, and in the first of the three letters he wrote her from there, he is professing to think of her "as some elder sister of mine." Nearly a month later he thanks her rapturously for some communication which he calls "very noble"; but the next letter from him is dated nearly four months later and is in so merely chatty a vein as to suggest the possibility that Lidian may—quite unnecessarily—have shied away from his ardor. His letters to her had not, indeed, been very different from those written shortly before to her sister, Mrs. Lucy Jackson Brown, since to Mrs. Brown also he could say: "We always seem to be living just on the brink of a pure and lofty intercourse," and it does not seem safe to assume that in the case of either he was seeking anything more than someone to whom he could whisper: "Solitude is sweet."

Mr. Canby quotes from a torn manuscript in the Huntington Library part of a suppressed essay, or notes for an essay, called "A Sister" which he believes refers to Mrs. Emerson. Elsewhere in the same manuscript Thoreau wrote: "By turns my purity has inspired and my impurity has cast me down." He then goes on to declare that his most intimate acquaintance with woman has been a sister's relation, "or at most a Catholic's virgin mother relation—not that it has always been free from the suspicion of lower sympathy." But before these admissions are taken to mean too much, it should be remembered that his idea of what constituted "impurity" was, and always remained, more than monkish, and the succeeding fragment continues a self-examination which makes it sufficiently clear that whatever might have been found in the depths of his subconsciousness, he was, both on the conscious level and just below it, resolved to cultivate his aloofness rather than to seek any experience which would overcome it. "Woman is a nature older than I and commanding from me a vast amount of veneration—like Nature. She is my mother at the same time that she is my sister, so that she is at any rate an older sister. . . . I cannot imagine a woman no older than I."

What drove him toward Walden was, then, not what is ordinarily called disappointment in love nor anything much like it. Instead it was primarily the failure of sympathy between him and the only group with

whom sympathy had seemed possible. There was no one except himself
to whom he could turn, and he would go away—not far away because
mere physical distance or mere physical propinquity meant nothing—but
just far enough to symbolize his voluntary withdrawal from community
life; just as far, that is to say, as Walden pond where he would still be
surrounded by those particular manifestations of nature which had first
awakened him to her charms, and yet reassuringly remote from the influence of men whose irrelevancies were all the more distracting because
they just failed to be relevant.

What he found there was not new thoughts, for nearly every leading
idea in the book which grew out of his stay had already been at least
hinted in the *Journal* and sometimes expressed very well indeed. What he
did discover was a new urgency, and that new urgency enabled him both
to find a more personal utterance and to separate what was peculiarly his
from most of what had merely been imbibed as part of the Transcendental atmosphere. As long as he had been only an earnest young man
trying to live up to both himself and his high-minded friends, the effect
of a given hundred pages of his manuscript is diluted with mystical
meanderings which at times are distressingly pretentious. But by the time
he came finally to put everything into the form of an account of his life
in the woods, he had discovered not only that the form provided some
sort of unity but also that the very fact that he was defending his eccentricity against the world, instead of apologizing to himself for not being
exalted or ineffable enough, gave to his utterance a humor, a pungency,
and a certain defiant finality which make it unforgettable.

[From *Henry David Thoreau,* William Sloane Associates, Inc., 1948.]

SOMEWHERE ALONG THE ROAD TOWARDS A RENEWED FAITH IN HUMAN
potentiality I discovered that my ultimate reliance was not on art but
on nature. Most of what I had to say on that subject belongs in a previous
collection *The Best Nature Writing of JWK,* but one essay not included
there will suggest what an ultimate reliance on nature means to me.

## Birds and Airplanes

Charles Lindbergh was recently quoted as saying that if he had to choose,
he would rather have birds than airplanes. This makes a splendid addi-

tion to my list (*The American Scholar,* Spring, 1968) of pioneers in technology who lost enthusiasm for their inventions once they had been exploited: Alexander Graham Bell who wouldn't have a telephone in his
house; Sloan who said he sometimes regretted that the internal combustion engine had ever been invented; and Vladimir Zworykin who, when
asked his favorite TV program, replied comprehensively, "none."

Mr. Lindbergh's is a less sweeping statement. He still flies airplanes,
and for us also the choice is not one we have to make. But it reminds us
that there is a more general choice we do have to make, namely, that
between some regard for the earth as nature made it and the determination to have faster airplanes, more development, reclamation, technology,
and so forth, even though they are creating an environment more and more
restricted to the mechanical and man-made along with the near extinction
of every living thing except man—who flourishes (if that is the word) so
exuberantly that he is on the point of trampling himself to death unless
he starves or poisons himself first. How many of us would, in this sym-
bolical sense, "choose birds"? A growing number certainly. Possibly
enough, though at the present moment they do not seem to be. But at
least there is no doubt that Mr. Lindbergh is among them.

When we were in the midst of our mafficking over the moon landing
he was asked to comment and he chose to end with the following:

> Science and technology inform us that, after millions of years of success-
> ful evolution human life is now deteriorating genetically and environ-
> mentally at an alarming rate ... that is why I have turned my attention
> from technological progress to life, from the civilized to the wild. In
> wildness there is a lens to the past, to the present, and to the future, of-
> fered to us for the looking—a direction, a successful selection, and an
> awareness of values that confronts us with the need for, and the means
> of, our salvation. Let us never forget that wildness has developed life,
> including the human species. By comparison, our own accomplishments
> are trivial.
>
> If we can combine our knowledge of science with the wisdom of wild-
> ness, if we can nurture civilization through roots in the primitive, man's
> potentialities appear to be unbounded. Through his evolving awareness,
> and his awareness of that awareness, he can merge with the miraculous—
> to which we can attach what better name than "God"? [*Life* Magazine,
> July 4, 1969]

Mr. Lindbergh's adjuration "Let us never forget that wildness has developed life, including the human species" together with his warning that "by comparison, our own accomplishments are trivial" reminds me that Thoreau used the word Wildness in this special sense and it led me to wonder if Mr. Lindbergh had chosen it for that reason. Part of the relevant passage in Thoreau is as follows: "The West of which I speak is but another name for the wild, and what I had been preparing to say is, that in wildness is the preservation of the world. Every tree sends its fibers forth in search of the wild. The cities import it at any price. Men plow and sail for it. From the forest and wilderness come the tonics and barks which brace mankind."

What I think Thoreau meant and what it is clear that Mr. Lindbergh means is that we are, after all, the creation of those forces which we know so little about that we are compelled to call them simply "Nature." Whatever else these forces may be they are not human intelligence, human contrivance, or human intentions; yet they have, nevertheless, brought us somehow from a beginning as some humble glob of macromolecular protein to the state where we are ready to believe ourselves superior to that same "Nature," ready to cut ourselves off from her entirely, and to direct evolution according to our own notions of what we should and can make ourselves become. Thoreau, again like Mr. Lindbergh, would believe now more strongly even than he did in his own rather simple society that man obviously does not know what is good for him. The American Academy of Arts and Sciences (to which I have the honor to belong) publishes a quarterly called *Daedalus* which, so I have sometimes thought, might more suggestively be entitled *Icarus*.

It is very important, I think, that the meaning of the word Nature as Thoreau and Mr. Lindbergh used it be distinguished from the more common one which refers simply to the animals, the plants, and the landscape which nature has created. And I think "trust in wildness" is a good substitute for the simple "love of nature" when we mean trust in Nature as both the creator and sustainer of health, happiness and joy. Outdoor recreation, interest in natural history, the desire to observe beauty spots are all worthy, even necessary concomitants to this deepest kind of love of Nature. But they are not in themselves enough to lead us back along the dangerous road we have been following to a more promising future.

Faith in Wildness or in Nature as a creative force has a deeper significance for our future. It is a philosophy, a faith; it is even, if you like, a religion. It puts our ultimate trust not in human intelligence but in whatever it is that created human intelligence and is, in the long run, more likely than we to solve our problems.

This is a modern version of ancient pantheism and therefore not wholly new. But it must not be confused with eighteenth- and nineteenth-century Romanticism which is, sometimes, even its antithesis. We no longer delude ourselves with the romantic notion of an all-wise and all-benevolent Nature upon whose bosom we should, but never have been willing, to rest. "Nature's kindly law" is, like that reaction against it— "Nature, red in tooth and claw," wholly inadequate to characterize that wildness which Thoreau celebrated. It is as often cruel as it is kind. No preexisting all-powerful intelligence could have conceivably planned the chaos of conflicting tendencies, problems and solutions which is the history of living things from the beginning down to the present. It is a history of frequently conflicting experiments, not the working out of any logical preconceived plan. Hence I at least cannot imagine it as directed by any intelligence superior to the outward manifestations of this evolutionary process.

And yet, in spite of the appearance of chaos and the constant conflict generated by what seem to be cross-purposes, Nature has (as even the most mechanical biologist will admit) "tended" although she never did and could not "intend." Something has been working itself out and to some of us, however difficult it may be to understand, Nature has tended towards something less simple than the so-called survival of the fittest— which after all means no more than the survival of those who survive. Reluctant as most biologists are to admit the fact, Nature has tended towards progress in two other directions. No creature met the test of mere survival more triumphantly than the sea squirt, but from the beginning of life onward the tendency has been towards a better and better chance for survival of the individual as opposed to that of the species. The higher you go in the scale, the less and less true it is that "So careful of the type she seems,/So careless of the single life." And no less significant is the fact that Nature has tended if not intended to increase the degree of consciousness in newly evolved forms and to make survival depend more and more upon conscious intelligence. How the strict theory of natural selection could account for either of these facts I do not understand, but that is no reason for refusing to acknowledge a tendency as plain as any of those which natural selection does account for. If a God did not create Nature then perhaps Nature is creating a God.

Another critical difference between the modern love of Nature and that of the Romantic poets has to do with the extent to which their celebration of Nature tends to be aesthetic rather than philosophical. Even Wordsworth's pantheism is fundamentally different from ours when he describes his God as "that being whose dwelling is the light of setting suns" rather than, as a modern pantheist would be inclined to say, "whose dwelling is in the mysterious proteins and even more mysterious genes." But it is Coleridge who is furthest from what I take to be the most characteristic modern view.

> O Lady! we receive but what we give
> And in our life alone does Nature live.

This makes the nature the Romantic poets celebrate a creation of man, not man's creator. A modern poet, Frost, makes the contrast in verses as clear as they are whimsical. The poem is called "Lucretius versus the Lake Poets" and is preceded by Walter Savage Landor's well-known: "Nature I loved; and next to Nature, Art."

> Dean, adult education may seem silly.
> What of it, though? I got some willy-nilly
> The other evening at your college deanery.
> And grateful for it (let's not be facetious!)
> For I thought Epicurus and Lucretius
> By Nature meant the Whole Goddam Machinery.
> But you say that in college nomenclature
> The only meaning possible for Nature
> In Landor's quatrain would be Pretty Scenery.
> Which makes opposing it to Art absurd
> I grant you—if you're sure about the word
> God bless the Dean and make his deanship plenary.*

Not long ago I had the pleasure of accompanying Mr. Lindbergh on a short survey of Baja California, Mexico, in connection with his work for the World Wildlife Fund, to which he now devotes his chief attention. One of the things one could not help being aware of was the fact that he is still, perhaps, the most widely known man in the whole world

---

*From "Lucretius versus the Lake Poets" from *The Poetry of Robert Frost,* edited by Edward Connery Lathem. Copyright 1947, © 1969, by Holt, Rinehart and Winston, Inc. Reprinted by permission of Holt, Rinehart and Winston, Inc.

and that his fame is based, not at all upon his career as a general in the Air Force, but upon his lonely flight across the Atlantic Ocean in 1927.

This pleasant experience of mine was before the landing on the moon, but I doubt that the names of the astronauts are, even at this moment, as well known as Lindbergh's, and I feel quite positive that while the first landing on the moon will no doubt be long remembered the names and personalities of the first men to make such a landing will not.

If I am right in that guess then it raises an interesting question to which I think the answer is rather simple: it was the man who was most important when Lindbergh flew the ocean. And without subtracting anything from the credit due to the extraordinary skill and daring of the three astronauts it can hardly be denied that in their case the relative importance of any single human being or any trio of human beings was far less than that of science and technology. Lindbergh's flight attracted the admiration of the world because it was primarily an exhibition of human skill and of human resource, not something which depended upon advanced technology. He had an airplane but it was an ordinary airplane of the sort to which people were already accustomed. His triumph was the triumph of a man not the triumph of computers, of a large group of nearly anonymous specialists, plus the vast sums of money which had created hundreds of instruments and machines for this special purpose. Hence Lindbergh's flight made an appeal to the imagination which was so lasting that nearly fifty years later he never reveals his identity except when necessary and (as I can testify) is greeted by gasps when he is compelled to do so. Only human beings, not machines, can become heroes. Or at least that was true for my generation. Perhaps the generation now growing up has already developed an opposite reaction. Perhaps its members will admire computers and group technology more than human resource and courage. Perhaps its only hero will be those abstractions, Science and Technology, rather than human enterprise, but I hope not.

[First published in *The American Scholar*, 1970.]

# Joseph Wood Krutch
## 1893–1970

A world in which "environment" has become the word of the day might profit from looking back at the prescient works of Joseph Wood Krutch, who died last week in Arizona. Twenty years ago that cultivated critic and teacher exchanged Manhattan for an adobe home in the Southwest to escape the crowds, to get air he could breathe and to enjoy "the natural beauty of the desert and its wildlife."

It was not on some college campus in 1970 that this wistfully prophetic man, denouncing an economy of waste, wrote that the ultimate good was not a rising standard of living but rather a system of values whose end is man. The idea ran through his writings over a period of four decades, coupled with warnings that the reality revealed by science was not necessarily, or even generally, compatible with the human spirit.

As a philosophical view, his work had a curiously old-fashioned ring —until suddenly the world, largely ignoring him, took up his early contention that "smog, pollution, the horrors of war" could be eliminated by a technological society if only it had the sense of values to put such objectives above its greater desire for "more speed, more power and more wealth." Rejecting the notion of man as the master of Nature, he liked to cite Thoreau's view of a world "more to be admired than it is to be used."

Three years ago, in a deeply pessimistic mood, this fine humanist and naturalist concluded that while most of his fellow-citizens were hopelessly materialistic, most of the intellectual minority had become "nihilist—interested chiefly in destruction and violence." The current wave of concern for the environment, the contempt for materialism voiced by so many youthful Americans, and now perhaps their growing rejection of nihilism as well—these should turn a generation unfamiliar with Joseph Wood Krutch to a reading of his books with delight to themselves and profit to the world.

*A* New York Times *Editorial, May 26, 1970.*
© *1970 by The New York Times Company.*
*Reprinted by permission.*